脱口说英语

作者权威⊙内容全面⊙质量精准
高效实用⊙语音纯正⊙印刷精美

情景口语大全

SPOKEN ENGLISH

主审⊙北京外国语大学 江 涛
主编⊙浩 瀚 陈 燕
审订⊙【美】Eve Bower

附赠 超值12小时MP3光盘一张

朗读
【美】Henry（男）【美】Dana（男）
【美】Laura（女）【美】Molly（女）

石油工業出版社

图书在版编目(CIP)数据

脱口说英语:情景口语大全/浩瀚,陈燕主编.
北京:石油工业出版社,2007.7
ISBN 978-7-5021-6024-1

Ⅰ.脱…
Ⅱ.①浩… ②陈…
Ⅲ.英语-口语
Ⅳ.H319.9

中国版本图书馆 CIP 数据核字(2007)第 047131 号

书名:脱口说英语:情景口语大全
作者:浩瀚,陈燕主编

出版发行:石油工业出版社
(北京安定门外安华里 2 区 1 号 100011)
网　　址:www.petropub.com.cn
编辑电话:(010)64523602　发行部:(010)64523604
经　　销:全国新华书店
印　　刷:石油工业出版社印刷厂

2007 年 7 月第 1 版　2008 年 10 月第 5 次印刷
700×1000 毫米　开本:1/16　印张:23
字数:600 千字

定价:39.80 元(含光盘)
(如出现印装质量问题,我社发行部负责调换)

本书编委会

主　编　浩　瀚　陈　燕

副主编　王建伟　何　冰

编　委　孙　伟　赵修臣　李　红　李江宏　李子强
林　娟　刘梓红　李　硕　王　勇　李洪峰
姚　青　李庆磊　马　兰　刘雷雷　郭美娟
蔡　丹　韩　磊　李明亚　陈伟华　王亚彬
王应铜　尹晓洁　宋美盈　马　迅　李文萍
赵秀丽　李林德　徐光伟　徐继宁　顾　蓓
韩江红　徐　萍　李林海　王克强　张　燕
蔡　翠　李洪伟　黄丽娟

策　划　北京浩瀚英语研究所

English Talk Show In Scenes

脱口说英语——情景口语大全

英语是中国人与世界沟通的有力武器！

英语是带给中国人自信和快乐的美妙语言！

英语是中国人爆发潜能的金钥匙！

我们可以这样开开心心学英语——

学英语，要学最实用、最地道、最流行、最简明的英语。如果你还想在口语上大有突破，那么请跟随我们《脱口说英语——情景口语大全》的节奏去学习、去模仿、去消化、去领悟……

本书分为社交辞令、生活花絮、人在职场、消遣娱乐、四通八达、行者无疆、体育看台、现代教育八部分，几乎涵盖了与我们日常活动息息相关的全部内容，意在把读者带到英语语境中，全新开发大家的语言潜力。从“闪亮词语”到“七彩精句”再到“鲜活会话”，是我们学习词汇、句型到流畅表达的过程。我们把与主题相关的最常用词和经典句子总结到“闪亮词语”与“七彩精句”中，分专题学习。把这些口语要素积累下来，就成了脱口而出的“鲜活会话”了。“身临其境”部分是一个看图说话的过程，现在我们可以在任何语境中和任何人自由交流了。

有了坚持不懈的努力，有了我们全新的英语口语训练理念——《脱口说英语——情景口语大全》，谁说学英语“谈何容易”？谁对英语“谈虎色变”？

CHAPTER 1 Communications 社交辞令

CHAPTER 2 Daily Life 生活花絮

CHAPTER 3 Jobs 人在职场

CHAPTER 4 Entertainment 消遣娱乐

CHAPTER 5 Vehicles 四通八达

CHAPTER 6 Travelling 行者无疆

CHAPTER 7 Sports 体育看台

CHAPTER 8 Modern Education 现代教育

Communications

CHAPTER

1

社交辞令

★招呼问候★ 1 Greeting

Words and Phrases 闪亮词语 点滴积累

new(/recent) friend(/acquaintance) 初交;新朋友
friend in-friend-only 泛泛之交
fellow worker 工友
old(/close) friend 故交,深交
deceased friend 故友
fellow lovers of the cup;drinking buddy 酒友
fast(/steady/unfailing) friend 可靠的朋友
old partner(/workmate) 老搭档
old friend 老交情;老朋友
sworn friends 盟友
bosom friend 密友
boyfriend 男朋友
girlfriend 女朋友
amateur performer (of Beijing Opera,etc.) 票友

Useful Sentences 七彩精句 连点成线

Simple Greetings 简短问候

1. *Hi!* 嗨!
2. *Hello!* 你好!
3. *Hello, everyone!* 大家好!
4. *Howdy!* 你好!
5. *Hello, there!* 你好!
6. *Hey!* 嘿!

Greetings for various times of the day 一天中不同时间的问候

1. *Good morning!* 早上好!
2. *Morning!* 早!
3. *Good afternoon!* 下午好!
4. *Afternoon!* 下午好!
5. *Good evening!* 晚上好!
6. *Evening!* 晚上好!
7. *Good night!* 晚安!

Formal Greetings 在正式场合的问候

1. *Welcome!* 欢迎!
2. *You are very welcome!* 热烈欢迎!
3. *You are very welcome to join us!* 欢迎光临!
4. *A warm welcome!* 热烈欢迎!
5. *Let me express our warm welcome to you!* 请允许我对您表示热烈欢迎!

Greeting a person you haven't seen for a long time 问候一个久未相见的人

1. *I haven't seen you for a long time!* 好久不见!
2. *I haven't seen you for ages!* 我好几年没看到你了!
3. *Hi, long time no see!* 嗨,好久不见了!
4. *It's been quite a while, hasn't it?* 好一阵子没见面了,不是吗?
5. *I am glad to see you again.* 很高兴再见到你。
6. *It's nice to see you again.* 能再次见到你真高兴。
7. *What have you been doing lately?* 最近忙些什么呀?
8. *Where have you been keeping yourself?* 最近去哪里了?

Fashion Conversation 鲜活会话 由线到面

Conversation 1

A:Hi,Jill! How's it going?

A:嗨,吉尔,最近怎么样?

B: Well, I am still alive and kicking.
B: 哎,眼下还凑合吧。
A: Are you leaving for America soon?
A: 你是不是马上要去美国了?
B: I guess so. Perhaps next Monday.
B: 估计是这样,也许下个星期一就走了。

Conversation 2

A: How are you getting along? I haven't seen much of you lately.
A: 你最近过得怎么样? 我最近很少见到你。
B: Keeping busy.
B: 忙死了。
A: Doing what?
A: 忙什么?
B: I am supposed to give my oral defense tomorrow.
B: 明天我就要答辩了。
A: Well, keeping busy before oral defense is all in the day's work.
A: 哦,答辩前夕不忙就怪了。

Conversation 3

A: Look, who is here!
A: 天哪,是你!
B: Jack, fancy meeting you here.
B: 杰克,真想不到在这里见到你。
A: Mr. Li, what a small world!
A: 李先生,这个世界真小啊!
B: Boy, I am glad to see you again!
B: 再次见到你真高兴!
A: Me too. It's been almost 10 years since we last met in Chicago.
A: 我也是。上次在芝加哥见到你是10年前的事了。
B: Yeah, how time flies! How are you these years?
B: 时间过得真快呀! 你怎么样?
A: Couldn't be better. And how about you?
A: 好极了,你呢?
B: Just so-so.
B: 不好也不坏吧。

Conversation 4

A: Good morning, Mr. Smith.
A: 史密斯先生,早上好。
B: Good morning, Jack.
B: 你好,杰克。
A: How are you?
A: 您好吗?
B: Very well, thank you. And how are you?
B: 很好,谢谢你。你怎么样?
A: Fine, thanks. Where are you going?
A: 好,谢谢。您上哪儿去?
B: I'm going shopping. And you?
B: 我去买东西。你呢?
A: I'm going home.
A: 我回家去。
B: Oh, you must come over and see us some time. I'd like you to meet my daughter.
B: 哦,你应找个时间到我家来看看,见见我的女儿。
A: That's very nice of you. I'd be pleased to come.
A: 您太客气了。我十分愿意。
B: Very good. Nice to have met you, Jack. Goodbye.
B: 很好。见到你太好了,杰克。再见。

Conversation 5

A: Hello, Jill.
A: 嗨,吉尔。
B: Hello, Liu Ming, I haven't seen you for a long time. How's everything going?
B: 嗨,刘明,很久未见到你了,你好吗?
A: Just fine, thanks. How about you?
A: 很好,谢谢。你好吗?
B: Also fine, thanks.
B: 我也很好,谢谢。
A: You don't look very well.
A: 你的脸色不太好。

B: I'm not feeling too well. I've caught a cold.	B:我觉得不太舒服,我感冒了。
A: Is it because of the bad weather? It's been really miserable for the past few days.	A:你是因为天气不好病了吗?这几天的天气真让人受不了。
B: Hasn't it! It's been cold and windy recently. Do you like the weather here?	B:可不是嘛!最近很冷,风又大。你喜欢这儿的天气吗?
A: Not really, but I've got used to it now.	A:不太喜欢,但是我已经习惯了。
B: Oh, I'm going to attend a conference in Beijing next autumn. What's the weather like in Beijing?	B:噢,我明年秋天要到北京参加一个会议,那儿的天气怎么样?
A: Not quite good. It's windy and dry. We have got continental climate there. It's dry all the year round. Usually autumn is the best season of the year in Beijing.	A:天气不很好,风多又干燥。那里是大陆性气候,终年干燥。秋天通常是北京一年中最好的季节。
B: Is it cold in autumn there? Should I take any warm clothes with me?	B:那儿的秋天很冷吗?我需要带很多保暖衣服吗?
A: No, it isn't very cold at that time. You'll only need some light wool clothing and some jackets and shirts.	A:不用,那时不会太冷。你只需带些毛衣,加上几件外套和衬衣就行了。

Conversation 6

A: Hello, Rose. Fancy meeting you here. How are things going with you?	A:你好,罗斯。真没想到能在这里见到你。近来过得怎么样?
B: Not too bad, thanks, and you?	B:还不错,谢谢,你呢?
A: Pretty good. How are your parents these days?	A:很好。你父母亲这些日子还好吗?
B: Oh, they are fine. They are enjoying their retirement.	B:他们都很好。他们正在享受退休生活。
A: Oh, good. It's nice to hear that. Well, I'm going to watch a football match. Remember to give my regards to your family.	A:噢,那太好了。这真让人高兴。好了,我要去看足球赛了。代我向你全家问好。

On the Scene 身临其境 面面俱到

主题:杰克与珍妮在图书馆不期而遇,请你看图,根据如下提供的关键词,将他们的对话写出来。

关键词语:exam *n.* 考试　　fed up 厌倦
awful *adj.* 糟糕的　　match *n.* 比赛

参考答案

Jenny: Hello, Jack! Fancy meeting you here! Working again, are you?

Jack: Yes, I've got to, if I want to pass all the exams.

Jenny: How's your life? All right?

Jack: Yes, not too bad, thanks. I'm a bit fed up with revising though. Are you?

Jenny: Pretty good, thanks. I'm going to watch a football match this afternoon. It's terrible weather though, I hope it doesn't rain.

Jack: Yes, awful! How's Jane?

Jenny: Oh, she's all right. But busy as usual. Well, I'd better be going. I suppose the match starts at 4:30.

珍妮：你好，杰克！真没想到在这里见到你。又在用功了，是吗？

杰克：是啊，如果我想通过所有的考试，就不得不这样。

珍妮：生活过得怎么样？不错吧？

杰克：还不错，谢谢。不过我对复习应考有点厌倦了。你呢？

珍妮：相当好，谢谢。今天下午我要去看足球赛，只是天气不大好，我希望不要下雨才好。

杰克：唉，天气确实糟糕。简怎么样？

珍妮：噢，她很好，只是一直很忙。噢，我想我该走了。比赛4:30开始。

★热情介绍★ 2 Friendly Introduction

Words and Phrases 闪亮词语 点滴积累

relatives and friends;kith and kin 亲友
schoolmate 同窗好友
childhood friend 童年朋友
foreign friend 外国朋友
good friends despite difference in age 忘年之交
sworn friend 刎颈之交
alumnus 男校友
alumna 女校友
false friend 虚假的朋友
schoolmate;fellow student 学友
friend and mentor 益友
far-away friend 远方朋友
comrade-in-arms 战友
newcomer 新同学,新同事

Useful Sentences 七彩精句 连点成线

Introduce somebody 介绍他人

1. *Mr. Green, (this is) Mr. Smith.* 格林先生,(这位是)史密斯先生。
2. *May I introduce you to my friend Susan?* 我可以把你介绍我的朋友苏珊吗?
3. *Would you like me to take you around and introduce you?* 让我带你四处转转,并把你介绍给大家好吗?
4. *I'd like to introduce our director Mr. Sidney Carson.* 我愿向诸位介绍我们的主任西德尼·卡森先生。
5. *Do you know Mr. Carl Mond?* 你认识卡尔·蒙德先生吗?
6. *Have you met Mary?* 你见过玛丽吗?
7. *Yes, we've already met actually.* 是的,其实我们已见过面。
8. *No, I haven't had the pleasure.* 不,我还没这份荣幸。
9. *Meet my brother Brown.* 见见我的弟弟布朗吧。
10. *Oh, here's David. David, meet John.* 哦,大卫来了。大卫,来见见约翰。
11. *Look, here's John! John —Tom, Tom —John.* 瞧,约翰来了!约翰,这是汤姆;汤姆,这是约翰。

Introduce oneself 自我介绍

1. *May I introduce myself?I'm Jill.* 我可以作个自我介绍吗?我叫吉尔。
2. *How do you do?My name is Tom.* 你好!我是汤姆。
3. *Hi. I'm Helen.* 你好!我是海伦。
4. *Excuse me. I don't believe we've met. I'm Jack.* 对不起,我相信我们还没有见过面。我是杰克。
5. *Allow me to introduce myself: John Brown, director of the English Department.* 请允许我自我介绍:约翰·布朗,英语系主任。
6. *Hello. This is Li Ping speaking.* 喂,我是李平。

Responding 应答

1. *I'm so glad to meet you.* 认识你很荣幸。
2. *Pleased/Glad/Happy/Nice to meet you.* 见到你真高兴。
3. *It's a pleasure to meet you.* 很高兴和你见面。
4. *Nice meeting you.* 见到你很高兴。
5. *How do you do?* 你好!

Fashion Conversation 鲜活会话 由线到面

Conversation 1

A:Welcome,newcomer! I'm Jones Grey.

A:欢迎你,新同学。我叫琼斯·格雷。

B:I'm Flora Fulton. Nice to meet you. | B:我叫弗洛拉·富尔顿。很高兴认识你。

A:Judging by your accent, I guess you came from the North. | A:听口音,你是从北方来的吧?

B:Yes. Where are you from, then? | B:是的,你的家在哪儿?

A:I'm from Atlanta. | A:我的家在亚特兰大。

B:Really? Atlanta is a very beautiful city. | B:是吗?亚特兰大可是个美丽的城市。

A:Yes, it is. | A:是的。

B:I have been dreaming to visit Atlanta. | B:我一直希望能有机会去亚特兰大玩玩。

A:Welcome. Here comes the school bus, let me help you to carry your luggage. | A:欢迎去玩。校车来了,让我给你提行李吧。

B:Thanks a lot. | B:多谢。

Conversation 2

A:Hi, Kathy. | A:嗨,凯茜。

B:Hi, Lynn. How nice the weather is today! Are you going out for sightseeing? | B:嗨,林恩。今天天气真好,你们是出去游玩吗?

A:Yes, we are. This is my friend Wade. | A:是的,这是我的朋友韦德。

B:How do you do, Wade? | B:你好,韦德。

C:How do you do, Kathy? Would you like to go out together with us? | C:你好,凯茜。和我们一起玩去吧。

B:I would like to go very much, but I'm sorry that I have a drawing class this afternoon. | B:我也很想和你们一起去。不过真遗憾,我今天下午还得去上绘画课。

A:That's a pity, but you may go with us next time. | A:真是遗憾,那下次一定和我们一起去。

C:Look, there comes the bus. | C:瞧,公共汽车来了。

B:See you, then. | B:再见。

A&C:Bye-bye. | A&C:再见。

Conversation 3

A:I believe you're Mr. Thomas, aren't you? | A:我想您是托马斯先生吧?

B:Yes, I am. And may I have your name please? | B:是的,我是。您是哪位?

A:My name is York. I'm very glad to meet you. | A:我是约克,很高兴见到您。

B:I'm very glad to meet you too. | B:见到您我也很高兴。

A: I'm from International Travel Service, Beijing Branch. | A:我在国际旅行社北京分社工作。

B:Oh, really? Mr. Li, the manager, is an old friend of mine. | B:是吗?那里的经理李先生是我的一位老朋友。

A:Thomas, have you met my colleague, Miss Li? | A:托马斯,您见过李莉小姐吗?她是我的同事。

B:No, I don't think I've had the pleasure. Will you introduce me to Miss Li? | B:我想我以前没见过她,您能介绍我和李小姐认识吗?

A:Certainly. It's my pleasure. | A:当然可以。

B:Thanks. | B:多谢。

A:Hello, Miss Li, I'd like you to meet Thomas. Thomas, this is Miss Li. Miss Li, this is Thomas. | A:嗨,李小姐,我想介绍你跟托马斯认识。托马斯,这位是李小姐。李小姐,这位是托马斯。

C:How do you do, Thomas. | C:您好,托马斯。

B:How do you do, Miss Li. | B:李小姐,您好。

C:I've heard a great deal about you, but I didn't ex- | C:久闻大名,想不到今天见到您了。见到您很高

pect to meet you today. I'm very pleased to meet you.

B: Me, too.

兴。

B:我见到您也很高兴。

Conversation 4

A: Good evening, Mr. Wu.

B: Good evening, Mr. Smith.

A: Have you met my wife, Juliet?

B: No, I haven't had the pleasure.

A: Mary, This is Mr. Wu, my Chinese friend.

C: How do you do, Mr. Wu? Welcome.

B: How do you do?

A: Have a glass of wine, Mr. Wu. And let me introduce you to some of my guests.

B: Thank you.

A:吴先生,晚上好!

B:史密斯先生,晚上好!

A:您见过我的太太朱丽叶吗?

B:没有,我还没有这个荣幸。

A:玛丽,这是我的一位中国朋友,吴先生。

C:吴先生,您好,欢迎您。

B:您好。

A:吴先生,喝杯酒吧。现在让我将您介绍给我的一些客人。

B:谢谢。

Conversation 5

A: Mr. Li, may I introduce Mr. Chen? He's my English teacher.

B: How do you do?

C: How do you do?

B: Susi's told us quite a lot about you.

C: Oh, dear — nothing too terrible, I hope?

B: No, not at all. She's very happy about things.

A: Now, everyone, supper is ready. Let's have it.

A:李先生,让我介绍一下陈先生好吗?他是我的英语老师。

B:您好!

C:您好!

B:苏西向我们谈了许多关于您的情况。

C:哎呀——我希望不是些使人不快的事吧?

B:不,一点也不。苏西对一切都很满意。

A:各位,晚饭已准备好了,咱们吃吧。

On the Scene 身临其境 面面俱到

主题:汤姆的好朋友西蒙来到他家做客,汤姆把琳达介绍给他认识,请你看图,根据如下提供的关键词,将他们的对话写出来。

关键词语:pleasure *n.* 高兴　　help yourself 自便
drink *v.* 喝　　coffee *n.* 咖啡

参考答案

Tom:Simon,let me introduce you to Linda. You don't know each other,do you?
Simon:No,I've not had the pleasure of meeting her yet.
Linda:How do you do? I'm pleased to meet you.
Simon:How do you do?
Tom:Please sit down. Help yourself just like at home. What would you like to drink?
Simon:A cup of coffee,please.
汤姆:西蒙,请允许我把你介绍给琳达。你们两位还不认识吧,是不是?
西蒙:没有,我还没有这个荣幸认识她呢。
琳达:您好!很高兴认识您。
西蒙:您好!
汤姆:请坐。请随意,像在家里一样。想喝点什么?
西蒙:请来一杯咖啡。

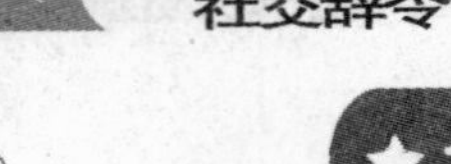

★接听电话★ 3 Telephone Calls

Words and Phrases 闪亮词语

a collect call 向受话人收费的电话(受付电话)
a pay phone 付费电话(投币公用电话)
a local call 地区电话
an international call 国际长途电话
emergency call 紧急电话
a person-to-person call 叫人电话
a station-to-station call 叫号电话(不叫人电话)
area/city/country code 区/城市/国家号
directory assistance 查号台
IDD = International Direct Dialing 国际长途直拨电话
operator 接线员
a telephone directory 电话号码簿
look up the number in the directory 查出号码
dial the number 拨号码
call back 回电话
give somebody a call/make a (telephone) call (for somebody) 打电话
answer/receive the phone/call 接电话

Useful Sentences 七彩精句

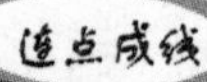

Making a phone call 开始通话

1. *Could I speak to Tom, please?* 我可以请汤姆接电话吗?
2. *Could I talk to Helen?* 我可以找海伦接电话吗?
3. *Hello. I'd like to talk to John.* 喂,我想请约翰接电话。
4. *Hello. Is Tom in?* 喂,汤姆在吗?
5. *Hello. May I speak to Mr. Smith, please?* 喂,我可以和史密斯先生说话吗?
6. *Hello. Peter speaking. I'd like to speak to Betty.* 喂,我是彼得,我想和贝蒂说话。
7. *Is that you, Tom?* 是你吗,汤姆?
8. *Hello, this is Mary speaking. May I have a word with Helen?* 喂,我是玛丽。我可以和海伦说几句话吗?

Receiving a phone call 接电话

1. *Extension six two two six, please.* 请接6226分机。
2. *I'll call back later/again.* 我以后再打。
3. *I'll ring him up again.* 我会再打给他的。
4. *Hello. This is Peter here. Who's (that) speaking/calling?* 喂,我是彼得。请问你是谁?
5. *Oh, Mary. It's nice to hear your voice.* 喂,玛丽。听到你的声音我很高兴。
6. *Yes, speaking.* 是的,是我。
7. *What did you say? I can't catch what you are saying.* 你说什么?我听不懂你说的话。
8. *Hold on a second, please. I'll fetch her up.* 请等一下,我把她找来。
9. *I'll just see if he's in.* 我去看看他在不在。
10. *A moment, please. /Would you wait a minute, please?* 请等一会儿。
11. *Don't hang up, please.* 请不要挂断。
12. *He left the office a moment ago.* 他刚离开办公室。
13. *He's on another phone.* 他在接另一个电话。
14. *I'm afraid that she won't be back till five o'clock.* 恐怕她要5点钟才能回来。
15. *I'm afraid you've dialed the wrong number.* 恐怕你打错了。
16. *Sorry, but he can't come to the phone right now. Can you call back a little later?* 对不起,他现在不能来接电话。你能不能过一会儿再打来?
17. *Sorry. I can't hear you.* 对不起,我听不见你所说的话。
18. *The line is bad/busy.* 电话占线/正忙。
19. *I couldn't get through.* 我无法接通。

Telling somebody he is wanted on the phone 告诉某人有电话找他

1. *A long-distance call for you, Tom.* 汤姆，你有个长途电话。
2. *Are you ready to take the call?* 你愿意接这个电话吗？
3. *John. Telephone.* 约翰，电话！
4. *Somebody is asking for you on the telephone.* 有人来电话找你。
5. *Someone wants you on the phone.* 有人来电话找你。
6. *There's a phone call for you.* 有电话找你。
7. *You're wanted on the phone.* 有你的电话。
8. *Tom, a long-distance call from Beijing.* 汤姆，你有个北京的长途电话。

Asking whether a caller has any message 询问打电话人是否有口信

1. *Could I take a message for you?* 我给你捎个口信好吗？
2. *Do you have any message that I can pass to him?* 你有什么口信让我传给他吗？
3. *Any message for him?* 有口信留给他吗？
4. *Do you want/Would you like to leave a message?* 你想留个口信吗？
5. *Is there any message I can give him?* 有什么话让我转告他吗？
6. *May I take a message?* 留个口信好吗？

Fashion Conversation 鲜活会话 由线到面

Conversation 1

A: Hello. A：喂。
B: Hello, may I speak to Jack, please? B：喂，请杰克接电话好吗？
A: Who shall I say is calling? A：请问你是谁？
B: Black, his friend. B：他的朋友布莱克。
A: Just hold the line a minute, Mr. Black. A：请等一等，布莱克先生。
C: Hello, Black. Jack speaking. C：喂，布莱克，我是杰克。
B: Good morning, Jack. How are you? B：早上好，杰克。你好吗？
C: I'm fine, thank you. And you? C：很好，谢谢，你好吗？
B: I'm all right. What are you up to? B：不错。你在忙什么？
C: Nothing particular. What's on your mind? C：没什么特别的。你有什么事吗？
B: Could you come over to my place this evening? I'd like you to meet some of my friends. B：今晚你能到我这里来吗？想叫你见见我的朋友。
C: OK. C：那好吧。

Conversation 2

A: Hello, this is Black speaking. May I speak to Mr. Smith, please? A：喂，我是布莱克。我找史密斯先生。
B: I'm sorry, he's just out for a meeting. B：对不起，他刚好出去开会了。
A: What time is he expected back? A：估计他什么时候回来？
B: Around one o'clock. May I take a message? B：大约1点钟。要我带口信吗？
A: Well, would you ask him to call me back as soon as possible? A：好吧，请你叫他尽快给我回个电话好吗？
B: Sure. Can I have your name and telephone number? B：当然可以。能告诉我您的名字和电话号码吗？

A: My name is Tom. My number is 1234 – 5678.
B: I will give Mr. Smith your message as soon as he comes back.
A: Thanks.

A：我叫汤姆，电话号码是1234 – 5678。
B：等史密斯先生一回来我就转告他。
A：谢谢。

Conversation 3

A: Operator, can I help you?
B: I'm calling from a pay phone in Highfield Shopping Center. I've been trying to get through to a number for the past fifteen minutes, but I keep getting a funny noise.
A: Are you sure it's the right number, sir?
B: Yes, I've checked in the telephone book. Are the lines overloaded?
A: What kind of sound are you getting?
B: A continuous humming sound.
A: Did you put in enough money?
B: Yes, I put in the correct amount.
A: What number are you calling, sir?
B: 311 – 980 – 6565.
A: I'm sorry, sir. Could you repeat that more slowly, please?
B: 311 – 980 – 6565.
A: Ah, that explains it, then. We've been having a lot of trouble with West Central Heights because of crossed lines. The weather's very bad there. One moment, and I'll try and get the number for you.
I'm just trying to connect you, sir. Your number's ringing now, sir. Put in 75 cents, please.
B: Thanks.

A：我是总机，需要帮忙吗？
B：我正在高地购物中心的付费电话处。我想打个电话，但都15分钟了，还总是听到一种奇怪的噪音而无法接通。
A：你的电话号码正确吗？
B：是的，我已查了电话号码簿。是线路超负荷了吗？
A：你听到了什么声音？
B：连续的"呜呜"声。
A：你付的钱够吗？
B：够，我投进的钱正合适。
A：你在打哪个号码，先生？
B：311 – 980 – 6565。
A：对不起，请你再说慢点。
B：311 – 980 – 6565。
A：噢，是这么回事，在西部中央高地地区，电话经常串线，那里天气很差。请等一会儿，我给你接通。先生，我正设法给你接通。你要的电话响了，请投入7角5分钱。
B：谢谢。

Conversation 4

A: Long Distance. May I help you?
B: Yes, I'd like to place an overseas call to London.
A: All right, sir. Is this a station call or a personal call?
B: A station call, please. The number is 34 – 177 – 8865.
A: May I have your number, please?
B: My number is 1234 – 5678.
A: Will you please hold the line?
(*after a moment*)
A: Hello, your party's line is busy, would you care to wait, sir?

A：这是长途台，需要我帮忙吗？
B：是的，我想打一个通到伦敦的国际电话。
A：好的，先生。是叫号电话还是叫人电话呢？
B：叫号电话。号码是34 – 177 – 8865。
A：请问你的电话号码是多少？
B：我的电话号码是1234 – 5678。
A：请你稍等一会儿。
(*一会儿之后*)
A：喂，先生，对方线路很忙，你介意等一会儿吗？

B: Never mind, then. I'll try again in about an hour. Thank you, operator. | B:那算了吧。我大约一个小时之后再试一次。谢谢你,接线员。

A: You're welcome. Thank you for calling. | A:不客气,多谢来电。

Conversation 5

A: Hello. Overseas operator. May I help you, ma'am? | A:喂,我是国际台接线员。需要我帮忙吗,女士?

B: Yes. I'm going to call Los Angeles some time next week, and I'd like to find out the time difference and the charges. | B:是的,我想在下周给洛杉矶打个电话,我想了解一下时差及费用。

A: The time difference between Los Angeles and Beijing is 16 hours. For example, if you place a call at 2 p.m. on Tuesday in Beijing, it is 10 p.m. Monday in Los Angeles. | A:洛杉矶和北京的时差是16个小时。举例来说,如果你在北京星期二下午2点打电话,洛杉矶是星期一晚上10点。

B: I see. How about the charges? | B:我知道了,费用呢?

A: The charges vary according to the types of call you make. The cheapest is a station-to-station call, then a person-to-person call. The mini charge will apply for the first three minutes, then each additional minute will be charged. | A:费用根据您打电话的种类不同而有差别。最便宜的是叫号电话,然后是叫人电话,最低费用适用于前3分钟,其后每多一分钟再追加一分钟的费用。

B: Will you quote the charges? | B:你会告诉我费用吗?

A: Yes, if you notify the operator when you place a call. | A:如果你打电话时通知接线员的话,我会的。

Conversation 6

A: Hello, Sue. It's Tom. | A:喂,苏,我是汤姆。

B: Hi, Tom. | B:你好,汤姆。

A: I've been trying to get hold of you forever. | A:我找你找了好久了。

B: Really? I've been staying at home all day long. | B:真的吗?我一直都待在家里。

A: But your line is always busy. | A:不过你的线路总是很忙。

B: Oh. Maybe the receiver is off the hook. | B:啊,可能是听筒没放好。

A: I see. I'm calling to invite you to dinner tonight. | A:我知道了。我打电话是想邀请你今天晚上来吃饭的。

B: What? I can barely hear what you are saying. | B:什么?我几乎听不到你在说什么?

A: I'm calling to invite you to dinner tonight. | A:我打电话邀请你今晚来吃饭。

B: The connection is too bad. We must have gotten our lines crossed. | B:通话情况太糟了,我们的线路一定和别人的串线了。

A: Why don't we hang up and try again? | A:我们何不挂断重打?

B: Good idea. | B:好主意。

On the Scene 身临其境 面面俱到

主题:约翰给鲍勃打电话商量同学聚会的事宜。请你看图,根据如下提供的关键词,将他们的对话写出来。

关键词语:speak to 与……通话　　gathering *n.* 聚会

classmate *n.* 同学　　miss *v.* 思念
Friday *n.* 星期五

参考答案

John:Hello, may I speak to Bob?
Bob:Speaking.
John:Oh, Bob. How are you? This is John.
Bob:Hi, John. I'm fine, and how about you?
John:I'm fine, too. I have rung up several times, but the line was always busy.
Bob:You did? You must have some good news for me, right?
John:Yes. Lisa suggested that we have a gathering with the old classmates this weekend. Would you like to join us?
Bob:Why not? I miss everyone. Now tell me the time and place.
John:We haven't decided yet. I'll call again and tell you this Friday.
Bob:Good. Thank you for calling me.
约翰:你好。我能和鲍勃通话吗?
鲍勃:我就是。
约翰:嗨,鲍勃。我是约翰。你好吗?
鲍勃:嗨,约翰。我很好。你呢?
约翰:我也很好。我给你打了几次电话,总是占线。
鲍勃:是吗? 你一定有什么好消息告诉我,对吧?
约翰:是的。丽莎建议我们这个周末和老同学聚一聚。你也来参加吗?
鲍勃:为什么不去? 我很想念大家。告诉我时间和地点吧。
约翰:还没有定呢。这个周五我再打电话告诉你。
鲍勃:好的。谢谢你给我打电话。

★问路指路★ 4 Asking and Directing the Way

Words and Phrases 闪亮词语 点滴积累

straight ahead 正前方
at the corner 在街角
traffic light 红绿灯
go straight 朝前走
turn left 向左拐
turn around 向回转
traffic police 交通警察
at the cross roads 在十字路口
at the T-cross 在丁字路口
at the end of the road 在这条路的尽头
on your right 在你的右侧
at the corner of the road 在这条路的路口上
on the opposite of the road 在路的对面
safety belt 安全地带
railway crossing 铁路与公路交叉点
street-crossing/pedestrain crossing 人行横道
road signs 路标

Useful Sentences 七彩精句 连点成线

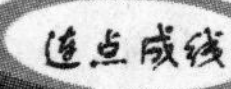

Asking the way 问路

1. *Excuse me. Could you tell me the way to the cinema?* 对不起,请问到电影院去怎么走?
2. *Excuse me. Could you tell me where the nearest bank is?* 对不起,请问最近的银行在哪儿?
3. *Excuse me. How can I get to the post office?* 对不起,请问去邮局怎么走?
4. *Excuse me. Which bus goes to World Park?* 对不起,请问哪一班公共汽车到世界公园?
5. *Excuse me. Where's the washroom?* 对不起,请问厕所在什么地方?
6. *Excuse me. Which is way to the station, please?* 对不起,请问去车站的路怎么走?
7. *Could you tell me the way to the station, please?* 您能告诉我去车站的路怎么走吗?
8. *How can I get to No. 4 Middle School?* 我怎样才能到四中?

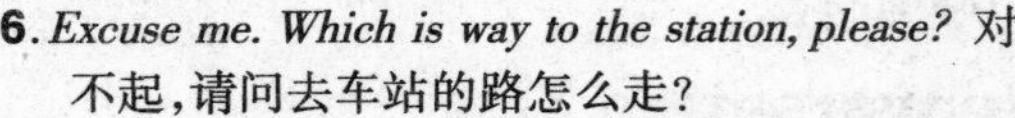

Directing the way 指路

1. *Go down the street and turn right at the first crossing.* 沿着这条街往前走,在第一个十字路口往右拐弯。
2. *Follow this road until you come to a bookstore.* 顺着这条路一直走到书店。
3. *Go straight on, then take the first turning on the right.* 一直走,到第一条横马路再往右拐。
4. *Go this way about ten minutes. When you see a post office, turn left.* 往这边走约10分钟。当你看到邮局时,往左转。
5. *I think it's opposite the post office.* 我想它就在邮局对面。
6. *I'm afraid you're going in the opposite direction.* 你恐怕方向走反了。
7. *I'm going there myself. Let me lead you the way.* 我自己也要去那儿,我给你带路吧。
8. *I'm sorry, I'm from out of town myself.* 对不起,我自己也是从镇外来的。
9. *I'm sorry, but I'm new around here, too.* 对不起,这儿我也不熟悉。
10. *It'll take you about fifteen minutes to get there.* 到那儿大约要15分钟。
11. *It's about two miles away.* 大约两英里远。
12. *It's about two traffic lights from here.* 从这儿走大约两个红绿灯的路程。
13. *It's about five minutes' walk.* 步行约5分钟。

Fashion Conversation 鲜活会话 由线到面

Conversation 1

A: Excuse me, sir. Is there a barber's near here?	A:先生,劳驾。这附近有理发店吗?
B: Yes, the nearest one is at the third cross of this road.	B:有。最近的理发店在这条路的第3个十字路口处。
A: I'm a stranger here. How can I get there, please?	A:我对这儿很陌生。请问我怎么去那儿?
B: Just walk down the road for a few minutes, and you'll find it on your right.	B:沿着这条路只走几分钟,你会在你的右侧看到理发店。
A: Thank you very much.	A:非常感谢你。

Conversation 2

A: Excuse me, please. Could you tell me how to get to the No. 18 Middle School?	A:劳驾,请问去十八中怎么走?
B: Walk down this road, take the fourth turn to the right. Then you'll see it.	B:沿着这条路走下去。在第4个路口向右拐,你就会看到。
A: Is it far from here to there?	A:从这儿到那里很远吗?
B: No. It's only about five minutes' walk.	B:不远。只需要5分钟的路程。
A: Many thanks!	A:多谢!
B: Not at all.	B:不客气。

Conversation 3

A: Excuse me, sir, could you please tell me the way to the Xidan Bookstore?	A:先生,劳驾,您能告诉我到西单书店怎么走吗?
B: Yes, of course. Would you like to walk there or take a bus?	B:当然可以。您要走着去还是乘车去?
A: Er... Is it far from here?	A:呃……离这儿远吗?
B: It's just about ten minutes' walk. Go along this street, on the third cross you'll find it on your left.	B:只要10分钟就走到了。沿着这条街走,在第3个十字路口,你会看到书店在你的左侧。
A: Then I'll walk. Many thanks.	A:那么我就走着去。多谢了!
B: Not at all.	B:不用谢。

Conversation 4

A: Excuse me, sir. Is this the road to the Peace Store?	A:先生,劳驾。这条路通向和平商场吗?
B: You could get there this way, but it'd be faster to go along the Wort Street.	B:从这儿走你可以到那儿,不过从沃特街走更近一些。
A: Where's Wort Street, please?	A:请问沃特街在哪儿?
B: Turn right at the third intersection, you'll see the street and then walk along the street to the south.	B:在第3个路口向右拐,你会看到沃特街的,然后沿着那条街向南走。
A: How far is it from the Wort Street?	A:从沃特街到那儿还有多远?
B: Just walk for a few minutes, you'll find it.	B:只走几分钟,你就可以找到了。

A: Thank you very much.

A: 非常感谢您。

Conversation 5

A: Where on earth are we?

B: Judging by all the traffic, I'd say we're near the outskirts of the city.

A: What did I do wrong? Did I take a wrong turn?

B: I'm not sure, but I think you turned right when you should have turned left on the flyover bridge.

A: Well, now we should turn back a few kilometres.

B: It seems that the traffic sign is much more important than the map.

A: 我们究竟到哪儿了?

B: 从整个交通情况来看,我想我们快到这个城市的郊区了。

A: 我怎么搞错了? 我拐错了弯吗?

B: 我说不上,可我想在立交桥上应该向左拐,而你却向右拐了。

A: 唔,现在我们得往回走几公里啦。

B: 看来交通标志比地图重要得多。

Conversation 6

A: Excuse me. I wonder if you can help me.

B: I'll try my best.

A: I'm completely lost. I'm trying to find the way to my daughter's home.

B: Please tell me where your daughter's home is.

A: Her home is between the China hotel and Li Sheng Theater.

B: Turn right at the second traffic lights and you will see it on your left.

A: I'm grateful to you.

B: It's a pleasure.

A: 劳驾,不知道你是否能帮个忙?

B: 我会尽力帮助你。

A: 我完全迷路了。我正在找去我女儿家的路。

B: 请告诉我你女儿家在哪儿?

A: 她家在中国饭店和黎声戏院之间。

B: 在第二个红绿灯右转,你就可以在左边看到了。

A: 真是太感谢你了。

B: 愿意为你效劳。

On the Scene 身临其境 面面俱到

主题:一位从悉尼来的友人,由于第一次来美国,想打听帝国大厦怎么走。请你看图,根据如下提供的关键词,将他们的对话写出来。

关键词语: Empire State Building 帝国大厦
recognize *v.* 认得出
crossroad *n.* 十字路
stranger *n.* 陌生人,外地人
direction *n.* 方向

参考答案

Stranger: Excuse me, Sir. Could you tell me how to get to the Empire State Building?

Native: Yes. You must be a stranger. Where do you come from? I can't recognize your accent.

Stranger: I'm from Sydney, Australia. This is my first visit to the States and I want to see as many sights as I can.

Native: Well, turn to the right at the traffic lights.

Stranger: Will it take me long to get there?

Native: No, it's no distance at all. In fact I'm going in the same direction. Come and I'll show you the way when we get to the crossroads.

Stranger: That's very kind of you.

Native: Not at all.

外地人:劳驾,先生。请问帝国大厦怎么走?

本地人:噢,你一定是外地人。你从哪里来?我听不出你的口音。

外地人:我来自澳大利亚的悉尼。这是我第一次到美国来,我想尽可能多地看到一些风景。

本地人:好,在红绿灯的地方向右拐。

外地人:到那儿需要很长时间吗?

本地人:不,不远。其实我要去同一方向。到十字路口时,我会给你指路。

外地人:你真太好了。

本地人:不客气。

★找人商量★ 5 Discuss with Others

Words and Phrases 闪亮词语 点滴积累

viewpoint; standpoint; point of view 观点
sense; idea; concept 观念
old-fashioned idea 过时的思想
rationalization proposal 合理化建议
just(/reasonable) opinion 合理意见
absurd idea 荒唐念头
economic view 经济眼光
way of looking at a thing; view 看法
admirable(/ingenious) idea; wonderful idea 精彩的观点
sensible opinion 明智见解
thought; idea; intention 念头
slave ideology 奴化思想
biased/prejudiced idea/view; prejudice 偏见
bright(/clear) idea 巧主意
authoritative opinion 权威性意见
confirmatory opinion 确定的意见
mass opinion 群众的意见
Confucian ideas 儒家思想
commercial view 商业眼光

Useful Sentences 七彩精句 连点成线

Asking for advice 问人意见

1. *Can you give me some advice on how to learn English?* 请你给我就如何学习英语提些建议好吗？
2. *Do you think I should tell him the secret?* 你认为我该告诉他这个秘密吗？
3. *How do you think I should make up the lost lesson?* 你认为我该如何弥补少上的课？
4. *How would you advise me to prepare for the coming exam?* 你说我该怎样准备即将到来的考试？
5. *I'd like your advice about my plan.* 我想请你对我的计划提些建议。
6. *What do you think I can do to help him?* 你认为我能做什么来帮助他？
7. *What do you think I should do?* 你看我该怎么办？
8. *What would you do in my position?* 你处在我的地位会怎么办？
9. *Where do you think you advise me to choose?* 你认为我该去哪里？

Advising someone to do something 劝告某人做某事

1. *Don't you think it might be a good idea to wait another 10 minutes?* 你认不认为我该再等10分钟？
2. *I advise you to go and ask your teacher.* 我建议你去问你的老师。
3. *I think it might be a good idea to see a doctor.* 我认为去看医生是个好主意。
4. *Have you tried doing it in another way?* 你试过用另一种方法去做吗？
5. *Perhaps you should practise reading English every morning.* 也许你应该每天早晨练习读英语。

Advising someone not to do something 建议某人不要做某事

1. *I advise you not to look down upon him.* 我劝你不要小看他。
2. *I don't think it'll do you any good to smoke.* 我认为吸烟对你不会有什么好处的。
3. *I don't think it's a good idea to tell him the news.* 我认为你告诉他这消息不好。
4. *I don't think you should keep silent.* 我认为你不应该保持沉默。
5. *I wouldn't suggest putting off the meeting.* 我建议不要推迟会议。
6. *I would advise against buying the machine.* 我建议不要买这台机器。

Responding to advice 对建议的回答

1. *Yes, that's a good idea. Thank you very much for being so understanding.* 是的，这是个好主意。谢谢你这么理解我。
2. *Well, I could do that, I think.* 嗯，我想我会那样做的。
3. *No, I don't need to see the doctor. But you're right, I may need more rest.* 不，我不需要去看医生。但你是对的，我也许需要多休息。
4. *Well, I don't really like moving. But thank you all the same.* 嗯，其实我不想搬走。但是还是要谢谢你的好意。

Fashion Conversation 鲜活会话

Conversation 1

A: Peter, why don't you go outside and play basketball with your friends?	A: 彼得，为何不到室外去和你的朋友一起打篮球呢？
B: No, Mum. I'd rather stay inside.	B: 不，妈妈，我宁愿待在家里。
A: I just can't understand why you want to stay at home. It is such a wonderful day today.	A: 我只是不懂你为何想待在家里。今天天气真好。
B: I prefer staying at home and watching TV.	B: 我更喜欢待在家里看电视。
A: Didn't you just finish watching a basketball game on TV?	A: 你不是刚刚看完一场电视篮球比赛吗？
B: Yes, but a football game is next.	B: 是的，但足球赛马上就到了。
A: Oh, Peter. You really should go and play ball yourself rather than watching games.	A: 哦，彼得，你真应该去自己打打球了，而不是看比赛。
B: I just enjoy watching games.	B: 我就是喜欢看比赛。
A: You really shouldn't watch so much television.	A: 你真不应该看这么多电视。

Conversation 2

A: What's the problem? You don't look happy.	A: 出什么事啦？你看上去不高兴。
B: I failed my oral test.	B: 我口语考试没通过。
A: Why don't you go to the English corner to talk to your classmates in English often?	A: 为何不常去英语角和你的同班同学谈谈呢？
B: When I talk to Chinese, I always want to speak Chinese.	B: 当我和中国人讲话时，我总是想说汉语。
A: You should always keep in mind: the more you practice, the better English you can speak.	A: 你应牢记：你练得越多，英语说得就越好。

Conversation 3

A: You're going to Beijing tomorrow?	A: 你明天打算去北京？
B: That's right. Do you think it'll be cold?	B: 对。你认为天气会冷吗？
A: It might be. You'd better take a heavy sweater with you. The nights are usually quite cold at this time of year.	A: 可能会的。你最好带一件厚毛衣。每年的这个时候夜晚总是很冷。
B: Do you think I'll need a cotton coat?	B: 你认为我需要带件棉上衣吗？
A: Not for now, I think. But I believe there'll be rain, so take your raincoat with you.	A: 我认为现在没有必要。但是我认为会下雨，因此带上你的雨衣。

Conversation 4

A: What would you like to be in the future?

B: A teacher.

A: But if I were you, I would be a singer. You've got such a beautiful voice.

B: I wouldn't like to be a singer, but I'd like to become a music teacher to teach children to sing. The dream developed in my mind when I was a child.

A: Are you sure about that?

B: I'm quite sure. I always love working with children.

A:你将来想干什么？

B:教师。

A:但是如果我是你的话,我会当一名歌手的。你嗓子这么好。

B:我不想成为歌手,但是我想当一名音乐教师,去教儿童唱歌,这是我从小勾勒出来的梦想。

A:你确定吗？

B:我很确定。我总是喜欢和儿童在一起。

Conversation 5

A: What's the matter, Mr. Smith? You look a bit pale.

B: I feel terrible. I have hardly slept a wink for several nights.

A: You can not sleep, can't you?

B: Right.

A: Well, it might do you good to quit smoking or at least cut down on it. Watch you diet and...

B: And exercise more, right? Quite some people have told me the same thing, but somehow I just couldn't force myself to do that.

A: You'll only make things worse for yourself, if you go on this way.

A:史密斯先生,你怎么了？你看起来有点苍白。

B:我感觉难受。我好几个晚上睡不着。

A:你失眠了,是吗？

B:是的。

A:那么,戒烟可能对你有好处,或者至少少吸一点。注意你的饮食,还有……

B:多锻炼,对吗？有很多人曾经告诉过我同样的事情,但是不知怎么的,我就是做不到。

A:如果你继续这样下去,只会让情况变得更糟。

Conversation 6

A: It's a little hard for me to learn English. Why is it so easy for you?

B: Maybe because I have learned earlier than you. But also, I really work hard at it.

A: Well, I always do my work and go to class. But I just make little progress. What else do you think would help?

B: Well, you might try reading some English newspapers. And always talk to foreigners when you get a chance, though sometimes it's hard. You won't learn if you don't open your mouth. If I were you, I'd like to talk to the English teacher. He might have some good ideas.

A: Thank you very much.

A:学英语对我来说有一点难,为什么对你来说这么容易？

B:也许是因为我学得时间比你早。但是,我也真的努力学了。

A:哎,我总是做作业并去听课,但我就是没多大进步。你认为还有什么可以帮助学习的吗？

B:有,你可以试着读一些英语报纸。如果有机会,就同外国人交谈,尽管有时感觉有点吃力。如果你不张开嘴说的话,你是学不会的。如果我是你,我会和英语老师谈谈。他也许有些好主意。

A:非常感谢。

On the Scene 身临其境 面面俱到

主题:贝蒂的同学请她帮忙研究一下自己刚刚写的申请信。请你看图,根据如下提供的关键词,将他们的对话写出来。

关键词语:application *n.* 请求,申请
be interested in 对……感兴趣
judge *vt.* 判断
appreciate *vt.* 赏识,感激
opinion *n.* 意见,看法
education *n.* 教育
ability *n.* 能力,才干

参考答案

Jill:Betty, would you please read this letter of application I've just written? I'd like to have your opinion.

Betty:I'd be glad to tell you what I think.

Jill:Good! I'm interested in your advice.

Betty:If I were you, I would change the beginning. You should write about your education first because we like to judge a man by his abilities.

Jill:I agree. I appreciate your helping me.

吉尔:贝蒂,帮我看看我刚写好的申请信,提点儿意见。

贝蒂:很高兴能告诉你我的想法。

吉尔:太好了,我想知道你的建议。

贝蒂:如果我是你,我就会把开头改一下。你应该把教育背景放在前面,我们总是以能力来判断一个人。

吉尔:我同意,谢谢你的帮忙。

★约会安排★ 6 Appointment

Words and Phrases 闪亮词语 点滴积累

visiting one's friends 访友
informal invitation 非正式邀请
farewell 告别
farewell call 告别拜会
farewell party 告别会
personal contact 个人接触
honoured(/distinguished) guest(/visitor) 贵宾
state guest 国宾
visitors from abroad 国外来客
passing visitor 过客
exchange visit 互访
costume party; masquerade(/fancy dress) ball 化装舞会
happy get-together(/reunion) 欢聚
welcome 欢迎
meeting visitors(/guests) 会客
arrange 安排

Useful Sentences 七彩精句 连点成线

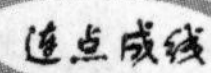

Requesting an appointment 主动相约

1. *Do you happen to be free this evening?* 今晚你有空吗?
2. *Do you have any plans for this weekend?* 这个周末你有什么打算吗?
3. *Let's make a date to go camping.* 我们约一个时间去野营。
4. *I wonder if the manager could spare me an hour tomorrow.* 不知经理明天能否给我一小时的时间。
5. *I'd like to make an appointment for this Saturday.* 我想在这个星期六约个时间见面。
6. *May I have an appointment with you this afternoon?* 今天下午我可以和您约个时间见面吗?
7. *Would you make an appointment for me?* 您可以约定一个时间跟我见面吗?
8. *I'd like to make an appointment with Mr. Smith.* 我想约一个时间跟史密斯先生见面。

Asking about when and where to meet 询问何时何地见面

1. *What time/When do you think would be suitable for us to meet?* 你认为我们什么时间见面合适?
2. *When will you come to see me?* 你什么时候来看我?
3. *When shall I come?* 我什么时候来?
4. *When/Where shall we meet?* 我们什么时候/在哪儿见面?
5. *What time would you like me to come?* 你要我什么时候来?
6. *At what time can I see you?* 什么时候我能见你?
7. *What's the best time/place to meet?* 什么时间/地点见面最好?
8. *Can you make it this afternoon?* 今天下午行吗?

Telling when and where to meet 说明何时何地见面

1. *Any time will suit me.* 什么时间都行。
2. *I'll be coming over here at 4 o'clock.* 我4点钟过来。
3. *I'll be free at 5 this afternoon.* 今天下午5点钟我有空。
4. *Any day next week will do.* 下周任何一天都行。
5. *Any day this week except Saturday is OK.* 除周六外什么时间都行。
6. *Please come whenever it is to your convenience.* 您何时方便就何时来。

Say when and where is not convenient to meet 表示何时何地见面不方便

1. *I won't be free until next Friday.* 下星期五之前我没空。
2. *I'm afraid I can't make it this weekend.* 本周末恐怕我不能应约。
3. *I'm sorry, I'm expecting visitors this evening.* 对不起,今晚我有客人来。
4. *I'm afraid I can't manage it.* 不行,恐怕我安排不了。

Fashion Conversation 鲜活会话 由线到面

Conversation 1

A: Hello. This is Philip Industries. A:喂,这里是菲利普工业公司。
B: Hello. I'd like to speak to Mr. Weeks. B:喂,我要找威克斯先生。
A: What name can I give? A:你是哪一位?
B: Victor of Johnson Autos. B:约翰逊汽车公司的维克多。
A: Wait a minute! I'll get him. (***A few seconds later***) A:请稍等,我去叫他。(*几秒钟后*)
C: Good afternoon, Mr. Victor. Weeks speaking. How are you? C:下午好,维克多先生。我是威克斯。你好吗?
B: I'm fine. Thank you. And you? B:我很好。谢谢。你怎么样?
C: I'm quite all right. C:我非常好。
B: Mr. Weeks, I'm calling to confirm an appointment with you. Your secretary, Miss Zhang made it with me the day after tomorrow. B:威克斯先生,我打电话来确认一下我们会面的时间与地点,你的秘书张小姐把时间定在后天。
C: OK. Is it at 9:30 next Monday morning at my office? C:好的。是下周一上午9:30在我的办公室吗?
B: That's right. B:是的。
C: I will be expecting you. C:我会等你的,请放心。
B: So see you then. B:那我们到时候见。
C: Thank you for calling. Have a nice weekend. C:谢谢你打电话来。周末愉快。
B: Thank you. You, too. Good-bye. B:谢谢,也祝你周末愉快。再见。
C: Good-bye. C:再见。

Conversation 2

A: What do you plan to do on Sunday morning? A:星期日上午你准备做什么?
B: Nothing special. B:没什么事情。
A: How about going to English Corner with me? A:和我一起去英语角怎么样?
B: Oh, I'd rather not. B:我不想去。
A: Why not? A:为什么不去?
B: You know, I am poor at English, especially at spoken English. I feel too nervous to speak even in English class, not to speak of in English Corner, when facing more people. B:你知道我的英语很糟糕,尤其是口语。在英语课上我都紧张得说不出话来,更不用说在英语角了,还要面对那么多人。
A: That's why you should go there. If you don't dare to speak English owing to the fact you are afraid of making mistakes, you simply will never learn A:所以你才应该去那里。如果你因为怕说错而不敢说英语,你将永远也学不会。去英语角就是给你一个开口说英语的好机会。英语角里的人

English. To go to the Corner is to give you a good chance to open your mouth to speak. People there are from factories, institutes, colleges, middle schools or even primary schools. Some of them have only learned English for a couple of years.

来自工厂、学院、大学、中学、甚至小学，他们中的一些人只学过一两年英语。

Conversation 3

A: Hello, International Trade Corporation.
B: Hello! May I talk to Mr. George Adam, please?
A: Hold on, please.
C: Hello, Adam speaking. Who is calling?
B: Good morning, Mr. Adam. This is Eric.
C: Eric?
B: Yes. We met at Mr. Green office two months ago. Do you remember?
C: Oh, yes, I remember now. So what can I do for you?
B: Well, Mr. Adam, I'd like to make some trading arrangements with your corporation. So I was wondering if I could come and meet you at 10:00 a.m. tomorrow.
C: I'm afraid I have another appointment at ten.
B: Then, how about 3:00 p.m. tomorrow?
C: I don't think so. Why don't I call you back?
B: OK. Let me tell you my telephone number.
C: Oh, it is not necessary. I can consult telephone directory.
B: When can I expect your call?
C: Maybe in a week or so.
B: I look forward to your call.
C: I have an urgent meeting to attend right now. Thank you for calling. Good-bye.
B: Thank you for your time. Good-bye.

A：喂，国际贸易公司。
B：喂。请给我找一下乔治·亚当先生可以吗？
A：请稍等。
C：喂，我是亚当，您是哪位？
B：早上好，亚当先生。我是艾瑞克。
C：艾瑞克？
B：是的。我们两个月前在格林先生的办公室见过面。您还记得吗？
C：喔，是的，我想起来了。你找我有什么事？
B：喔，亚当先生，我想同你们公司确定一些贸易上的安排。不知道我是否能在明天上午10点前来同您会一次面。
C：恐怕10点钟我另有约会。
B：那么明天下午3点如何？
C：我想也不行。还是等我给你回电话好吗？
B：好吧。让我告诉您我的电话号码。
C：喔，不必了。我可以查电话号码本。
B：那我什么时候等着您的回电？
C：大概一周左右吧。
B：我盼望您的回电。
C：我现在要去开一个紧急会议。谢谢你打电话来，再见。
B：谢谢您为我花费了宝贵时间。再见。

Conversation 4

A: Hello. I wish to speak to Mr. Li.
B: This is he speaking.
A: Oh, how do you do, Mr. Li? This is Eric Dyce speaking.
B: Hello, Mr. Dyce. I have a present for you from Mr. Rowley of Beijing.
A: Oh, thank you. Mr. Rowley had told me that you were coming to Shanghai. May I call on you at your hotel tomorrow?
B: Yes, it's all right. Shall we say three in the after-

A：喂，我想跟李先生讲话。
B：我就是。
A：你好，李先生。我是埃里克·戴斯。
B：你好，戴斯先生，北京的罗利先生让我带件礼物给你。
A：噢，谢谢你。罗利先生告诉我说，你要到上海来，我明天可以到你住的旅馆拜访你吗？
B：可以，就在下午3点钟怎么样？

noon?　

A: Great. Then I'll be at your hotel at three. | A: 很好,3 点我就到你住的旅馆来。

B: All right. | B: 好的。

A: How could I get there? | A: 我该如何才能到您那儿?

B: The hotel is near to People's Square. Its name is Bai Ju Hotel. | B: 我的宾馆在人民广场附近,叫百菊宾馆。

A: What's your room number? | A: 你的房间号是多少?

B: It's Room 310 on the third floor. But I'll be waiting for you in the lobby. If you can't find me, please call me. | B: 我的房间是 3 楼 310 号,我在大厅等你。如果你找不到我,请给我打电话。

A: I'll do that, Mr. Li. See you tomorrow. | A: 好,就这样,李先生,明天见。

B: See you! | B: 再见。

Conversation 5

A: I want to meet you. Are you free this evening? | A: 我想见你。今晚你有空儿吗?

B: Well, actually, I'm not free today. | B: 哦,今天我确实没空儿。

A: The pity of it! | A: 真遗憾!

B: Do you have anything urgent? | B: 你有急事吗?

A: No, I just want to meet you. | A: 没有,我只是想见你。

B: How about tomorrow instead? | B: 明天怎么样?

A: Hmm, that's all right. Shall we meet at the bar near the beach? | A: 嗯,那好吧。我们在海滩附近的酒吧见面好吗?

B: All right. See you then. Bye. | B: 好的,明天见。

A: Bye. | A: 再见。

On the Scene 身临其境 面面俱到

主题:汤姆给玛丽打电话,想约她 8 点钟到奥迪安戏院看电影。请你看图,根据如下提供的关键词,将他们的对话写出来。

关键词语:Odeon cinema 奥迪安戏院　　The Lost Soul 逝去的灵魂
start *v.* 开始　　pick... up 开车接……

参考答案

Tom: Hello, this is Tom Johnson. May I speak to Mary, please?
Mary: Oh, hello, Tom. It's Mary here. How are you?
Tom: Fine, thanks. And you?
Mary: Very well, thank you.
Tom: Listen, Mary, I'm calling to ask if you are busy tonight.
Mary: Let me see. No, I don't think I've got anything planned. Why?
Tom: Well, I thought we might have dinner together and go to the movies.
Mary: Oh, that sounds like fun. What are we going to see?
Tom: There's a really good film on at the Odeon cinema tonight. It's called ***The Lost Soul***.
Mary: Great! What time does it start?
Tom: At eight o'clock. We'll have dinner first.
Mary: Then let's have it at Ruby Restaurant at 6:00 p. m.
Tom: That's all right. I'll pick you up at your office at 5:30.
Mary: Thank you for calling. Bye-bye, Tom.
Tom: Bye, Mary.
汤姆:喂,我是汤姆·约翰逊。可以让玛丽接电话吗?
玛丽:喂,汤姆,我是玛丽。你好吗?
汤姆:很好,谢谢。你呢?
玛丽:很好,谢谢你。
汤姆:听着,玛丽,我打电话来是想问今晚你忙不忙?
玛丽:让我想想。我想我还没有计划要做什么。你有事吗?
汤姆:唔,我想我们可以共进晚餐,然后一起看电影。
玛丽:听起来不错,看什么电影?
汤姆:今晚奥迪安戏院上映一部非常好的片子,片名叫《逝去的灵魂》。
玛丽:好极了!什么时间开始放映?
汤姆:八点钟。我们可以先吃晚餐。
玛丽:那么我们下午六点在红宝石饭店见。
汤姆:那好。我五点半到你办公室接你。
玛丽:谢谢你。再见。
汤姆:再见。

分手告别 7 Farewell

Words and Phrases 闪亮词语 点滴积累

see off 送行
airport 机场
mind how you go 走好
parting 分手，离别
pull in 进站；靠岸
miss 思念
call on 拜访，访问
all the best 祝一切都好
stay 逗留
regard 问候
keep in touch 保持联系
be off 离开

Useful Sentences 七彩精句 连点成线

Simple good-byes 简短道别

1. *Good-bye!* 再见！
2. *Bye-bye!* 再见！
3. *See you!* 再见！
4. *See you then!* 到时候见！
5. *So long!* 再见！
6. *See you later!* 等会儿见！
7. *See you around!* 回头见！
8. *See you in a little while!* 一会儿见！
9. *See you tomorrow!* 明天见！
10. *See you again soon!* 不久以后再见！
11. *Catch you later!* 回见！
12. *Farewell!* 后会有期！
13. *Let's get together soon!* 让我们很快再相聚！
14. *Say hi to Jill.* 代我问候吉尔。
15. *Please say hello to your parents for me!* 代我问候你父母！
16. *My father asks me to say hello to you.* 我父亲让我向您问好。

Saying goodbye to hosts 客人向主人道别

1. *I'm sorry, but we have to go now.* 真遗憾，我们得回家了。
2. *I'm afraid it's time to say goodbye.* 抱歉，我们得说再见了。
3. *Sorry, it's about time we leave.* 真遗憾，我们该离开了。
4. *Mrs. Green, thank you very much for your wonderful dinner.* 格林太太，非常感谢您丰富的晚餐。
5. *It's really late, I must be on my way now.* 噢，都这么晚了，我该必须得走了。
6. *Mr. Li, I'd like to say goodbye to you.* 李先生，我该向您道别了。
7. *I really appreciate your hospitality!* 感谢你们的盛情款待！
8. *I had a very good time at your party. Thank you, Mr. Brown.* 谢谢您，布朗先生。我在这个宴会上玩得很高兴。
9. *Thank you for a very enjoyable evening.* 谢谢您，这真是一个愉快的夜晚。
10. *Thank you for inviting us.* 谢谢您邀请了我们。

Saying good-bye to guests 主人向客人道别

1. *So good to see you.* 见到你们真好。
2. *Thanks for coming!* 谢谢你们来！
3. *Thanks for dropping in!* 谢谢你们顺道拜访！
4. *Do you have everything?* 东西都拿了吗？
5. *It's been our pleasure!* 这是我们的荣幸！
6. *Glad you could come.* 很高兴你们能来。
7. *How nice of you to come!* 你们能来真是太好了！
8. *Why don't you stay a little longer?* 为什么不再待一会儿呢？
9. *Can't you stay for a while?* 你能再待一会儿吗？
10. *It's been a delightful visit.* 您到敝处，令我深感荣幸。
11. *Come back soon!* 再来啊！
12. *Come back anytime!* 随时再来！

13. *Do come back soon!* 一定要再来！

14. *Please say hello to your parents for me!* 代我向你的父母问好！

15. *Please give my best wishes to your family!* 代我向你的家人表示最美好的祝愿！

Leaving a place 离开某地

1. *Go!* 走！

2. *Let's go!* 咱们走吧！

3. *Are we going?* 该走了？

4. *We have to go.* 咱们得上路了。

5. *It's high time we left.* 到点了，该走了。

6. *Let's head out!* 咱们赶快上路吧。

7. *Are we ready to leave?* 我们能走了吗？

8. *Are you about finished?* 你的事快完成了吗？

9. *Ready to go?* 可以走了吗？

10. *Let's get out of here!* 咱们快撤吧！

11. *Let's split!* 咱们快溜吧！

12. *Let's make like the wind and blow.* 咱们快走吧。

Fashion Conversation 鲜活会话 由线到面

Conversation 1

A: Hello, Mr. Green. I've come to say good-bye.
B: You're leaving so soon? When are you off?
A: Early tomorrow morning.
B: We'll miss you. Hope to see you again someday.
A: I hope so, too. Thank you, Mr. Green, for everything you have done for me during my stay here.
B: You're welcome.
A: Don't forget to give me a call if you're ever in Beijing. Take care of yourself. Bye!
B: Take care. Have a good journey, and all the best.

A：你好，格林先生。我是来向你道别的。
B：你这么快就要走？你什么时候离开？
A：明天清早。
B：我们会很想念你的。希望以后能再见到你。
A：我也希望如此，谢谢你。格林先生，谢谢你对我在这儿时为我所做的一切。
B：不用客气。
A：如果你到了北京的话，不要忘了给我打电话。保重！再见！
B：保重。祝你旅途愉快，万事如意。

Conversation 2

A: Miss Yang, I'm calling to say good-bye.
B: No, not so soon. I feel you have just come.
A: I have the same feeling. But all good things must come to an end, as they say.
B: We're sorry that you couldn't stay longer.
A: I wish I could stay a little longer, but lots to do back home.
B: Have you had your ticket confirmed already?
A: Yes, I did it at the reception desk. But can you do me a favor? I want to stay in Nanjing for one night. And can you book a single room there?
B: No problem. I'll take care of that. What's the time of the flight?
A: At 3 p. m..
B: Then we must arrive at the airport one hour before departure time. Will you please check out by 12? We'll pick you up and head straight to the

A：杨小姐，我给你打电话是和你告辞的。
B：不，时间太短了。我感觉你好像刚来。
A：我有同样的感觉。但是正如他们所说，天下没有不散的筵席。
B：对你不能再多待些时候，我们感到真难过。
A：我希望我能再多呆一段时间，但家里有许多事等着干。
B：你订好票了吗？
A：对，我到订票处订了。但是，你能帮我个忙吗？我想在南京住一晚上，你能为我在那儿订一个单人间吗？
B：没问题。这事由我包了。飞机什么时候起飞？
A：下午3点。
B：那么我们必须在起飞一小时前到机场。在12点之前你能结好账吗？我们将去接你，并直接把你送往机场。我们将在附近的餐馆吃午餐。

airport. We shall have lunch at a nearby restaurant.	
A: OK. Thank you very much.	A:好。非常感谢你。

Conversation 3

A: It's very kind of you to come to see me off, Mr. Li.	A:李先生,你来为我送行简直太好了。
B: Not at all. It's the least (little) we could do.	B:不用客气,这是举手之劳。
A: Thank you.	A:谢谢。
B: Give my best regards to your parents.	B:请代我向你父母致以最亲切的问候。
A: I'll do that. Thank you, Mr. Li, for everything you have done for me during my stay here.	A:我会的。谢谢你的惦念,李先生,谢谢你在我住这儿期间为我所做的一切。
B: You are welcome. I hope you can come again to Shanghai.	B:不用客气。我希望你下次还能来上海。
A: I hope so, too. Good-bye.	A:我也希望如此,再见。
B: Good-bye. I wish you a very pleasant journey home.	B:再见。祝你回家旅途愉快。

Conversation 4

A: Mr. White. I'm calling to say goodbye. I'll be leaving tomorrow. But before I leave, I want to thank you for what you've done for me during my visit here.	A:怀特先生,我打电话是向你告别的。明天我就要走了。但在我离开之前,我想向你道谢,谢谢你在我参观期间为我所做的一切。
B: It's very kind of you to say that, Tom. We are glad to have you. Now I'm sure you're excited to be back home soon.	B:汤姆,你这么说真是太客气了。我们非常高兴能和你在一起。但你现在一定在非常兴奋地想不久后将回到家中。
A: Oh, yes.	A:对,是那样。
B: When will you leave?	B:你什么时间离开?
A: The plane will leave at 10:00.	A:飞机将在10:00起飞。
B: I'll come to see you off at the airport, won't I?	B:我去机场为你送行。行吗?
A: No, sir, thank you.	A:不用了,先生,谢谢你。
B: OK. Please give our best regards to your wife and children.	B:好。请代我们向你的太太和孩子致以最亲切的问候。
A: Thanks a lot. And if you ever visit my country, be sure to come and stay with us a few days.	A:太感谢了。如果你去我们国家观光旅游的话,请一定要到我家,并在我家住上几天。
B: I'll do that. Pleasant journey!	B:我会的。祝你旅途愉快。
A: Thank you. Goodbye.	A:谢谢你,再见。
B: Goodbye.	B:再见。

Conversation 5

A: How time flies! You've been in this country for over three years. I didn't realise your departure was imminent.	A:光阴似箭。你来这个国家已经呆了3年多了。我还不知道你很快就要离开了。
B: It's time for me to go home, you know. Before I leave, I want to thank you again for all that you've done for me. Without your help, I would	B:到我回家的时候了。走之前,我想再次感谢你为我所做的一切。没有你的帮助,我绝不可能有那么多的收获。

never have achieved so much.

A:I've really done nothing. It is your own efforts that have made your stay so fruitful.

B:It's been a really unforgettable experience. I'll miss you. Henry. I hope we'll meet again some day in my country.

A:I hope so too. We'll keep in touch.

A:我其实没做什么。是你自己的努力才使你的访问获得了这么多的成果。

B:这确实是一段难忘的经历。亨利,我会想念你的。我希望我们以后能在我的国家见面。

A:我也希望如此。我们将保持联系。

On the Scene 身临其境 面面俱到

主题:杰克到罗斯家做客,现在杰克要告辞,罗斯想留他吃饭。请你看图,根据如下提供的关键词,将他们的对话写出来。

关键词语:late *adj.* 晚的,迟到的　　dinner party 晚宴
United States 美国

参考答案

Jack:Well,I'm afraid I must be going now. I had no idea it was so late.
Rose:Stay for dinner with us.
Jack:I'm afraid I can't.
Rose:Are you sure you can't stay for dinner?
Jack:No,really I can't. I have a dinner party to go to tonight. You see,I am going to the United States the day after tomorrow.
Rose:I won't keep you then. It was very nice of you to come to see me.
Jack:It has been a pleasure. Good-bye.
Rose:Good-bye. Thank you again for coming.

杰克:呃,我想我该走了。没想到已经这么晚了。
罗斯:留下来和我们吃饭吧!
杰克:恐怕不行喔!
罗斯:你真的不能留下来吃晚饭?
杰克:真的不行。我今晚要赴晚宴。你知道,我后天要到美国去了。
罗斯:那我就不留你了。你来看我真是太好了。
杰克:我很高兴,再见。
罗斯:再见。再次感谢你的光临。

表达谢意 8 Thanks

Words and Phrases 闪亮词语

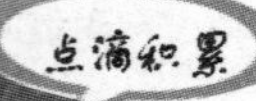

thank 感谢
grateful 感谢的；愉快的
pleasure 愉快
help 帮助
thanks 多谢
kindness 好意；仁慈
do sb. a favour 给某人帮忙
appreciate 感激；欣赏
be obliged to someone 感谢某人
come to one's aid 帮助某人
gratitude 谢意
appreciation 感激
thankful 感谢的，感激的
assist 援助；帮助
credit 赞许
thank-you speech 谢词

Useful Sentences 七彩精句

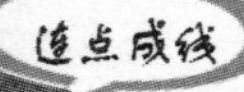

Saying "thank you"— formal 道谢——正式用语

1. *Thank you.* 谢谢你！
2. *Thank you very much.* 非常感谢！
3. *You have my thanks.* 非常感谢！
4. *You have my gratitude.* 非常感谢！
5. *Thanks ever so much.* 非常感谢！
6. *Thank you so much.* 非常感谢！
7. *Thank you for your help.* 谢谢你的帮忙！
8. *Thank you for all you've done.* 谢谢你为我们所做的一切。
9. *Thank you for everything.* 谢谢你所做的一切。
10. *I'm deeply grateful.* 我内心十分感激。
11. *I'm in your debt.* 我欠你一份人情。
12. *I'm indebted to you.* 我很感激你。
13. *Thanks very much.* 太感谢你了！
14. *I can't thank you enough (for...)* （对于……）我真是对你感激不尽。
15. *I really appreciate your timely help.* 我非常感谢你及时的帮助。

Saying "thank you" — informal 道谢——非正式用语

1. *Thanks.* 谢谢！
2. *Thanks much.* 非常感谢！
3. *Thanks for everything.* 非常感谢！
4. *Thanks so much.* 非常感谢！
5. *Thanks a lot.* 十分感谢。
6. *Thanks a million.* 千恩万谢。
7. *Thanks heaps.* 非常感谢。
8. *I owe you one.* 我得谢谢你。
9. *I owe you big.* 我得好好感谢你。

Acknowledging someone's thanks— formal 对他人的致谢作出回应——正式用语

1. *You're welcome.* 别客气。
2. *You're most welcome.* 不用谢。
3. *You're entirely welcome.* 哪儿的话。
4. *My pleasure.* 别客气。
5. *It was my pleasure.* 不要客气。
6. *The pleasure was mine.* 能为你服务我非常高兴。
7. *The pleasure was all mine.* 能为你服务我非常高兴。
8. *The pleasure was entirely mine.* 能为你服务我非常高兴。

Acknowledging someone's thanks— informal 对他人的致谢作出回应——非正式用语

1. *It was nothing.* 没什么。
2. *Don't mention it.* 不用客气。

3. *No problem.* 没关系。
4. *No sweat.* 小事一桩。
5. *Any time.* 不用谢。
6. *No trouble.* 这没什么麻烦的。
7. *No skin off my nose.* 这没费多大的事。
8. *No skin off my teeth.* 仅举手之劳而已。

Fashion Conversation 鲜活会话

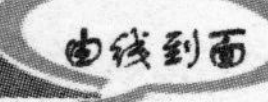

Conversation 1

A: Chen, I really don't know how to thank you.
B: I'm glad I was able to help.
A: It's most kind of you.
B: Don't mention it, Jack. It was the least I could do.
A: If there's ever anything I can do for you, don't hesitate to let me know.
B: Thank you.
A: I'm most grateful.
B: It was a pleasure.

A:小陈,我真不知道该怎么感谢你。
B:能够帮助你,我很高兴。
A:你太好了。
B:不用提了,杰克。这是我应该做的。
A:如果有什么需要我帮忙的话,请不要客气地告诉我。
B:谢谢。
A:我很感激你。
B:不用谢。

Conversation 2

A: Hello. May I speak to Mr. Green?
B: Yes, speaking.
A: How do you do, Mr. Green? This is Kathy. I'm calling to thank you for the wonderful dinner we had yesterday. I enjoyed it very much.
B: You're welcome. I'd like you to join us for dinner again sometime.
A: Thank you, Mr. Green. I'm returning to China today.
B: Today?
A: Yes. I appreciate all help and in particular, all the time that you've spent on my account during my stay here.
B: Don't mention it. I was very pleased to help you.
A: If there's anything that I can help you with in the future, please let me know.
B: I'll do that. Thank you. Have a safe trip home.

A:你好。请找格林先生接电话,好吗?
B:我就是,请讲。
A:格林先生,你好。我是凯茜。我打电话向你致谢,谢谢昨天晚上你为我提供的丰盛的晚餐。我非常喜欢。
B:不用客气。我希望有时间你能再同我们共进晚餐。
A:谢谢你,格林先生。今天我要返回中国了。
B:今天?
A:对。我感谢你给我提供的所有的帮助,特别是在我留在这儿期间你为我所花费的一切。
B:不用客气。我很高兴能对你有所帮助。
A:如果将来有什么能帮得上忙的,请告诉我一声。
B:我会的。谢谢你。祝你一路平安。

Conversation 3

A: I got the job you recommended me for last week.
B: That's great! Congratulations.
A: I really don't know how I can thank you enough.
B: Oh, it's my pleasure. After all, you are very qualified for the position.
A: Thank you very much indeed. You helped me rebuild my self-confidence.
B: Don't mention it. You've always been good. What

A:你上周推荐我去应聘的工作,我得到了。
B:太棒了!恭喜你。
A:我真不知道该如何感谢你。
B:噢,没关系。毕竟你十分有资格做这份工作。
A:真的十分感谢。你帮我重新建立了自信。
B:别客气,你一直都很出色。我们出去庆祝一下

do you say we go out to celebrate? 怎么样?

A: That would be great. A:那太好了。

Conversation 4

A: I'm very grateful for what you have done to our son, doctor.
A:大夫,非常感谢你为我儿子做的一切。

B: That's all right, Mr. Green. That's my job. I'm very glad he recovered so soon.
B:别客气,格林先生。这是我的工作。我很高兴他这么快就恢复了。

A: I know he has brought great trouble to you. A million thanks.
A:我知道他给你添了很多麻烦。万分感谢。

B: No trouble at all. He's very cute and brave. By the way, do remember to keep him away from sea food for at least two weeks.
B:一点都不麻烦。他很可爱,很勇敢。另外,一定要记住至少两个礼拜不要让他吃海鲜。

A: I will. It's most thoughtful of you.
A:我会记住的。你想得真周到。

Conversation 5

A: Hello, Mary.
A:嗨,玛丽。

B: Jack, you're back, come in please. How are you?
B:杰克,你回来了,请进。还好吧?

A: Fine, only a little tired.
A:不错,就是有点儿累。

B: Have a good sleep, you will be recovered soon.
B:好好睡一觉,你很快就会恢复的。

A: Thank you very much for looking after my house in my absence.
A:多谢你在我不在时替我照看房子。

B: That's all right. Would you have a cup of coffee?
B:没关系,喝杯咖啡吗?

A: Yes, please. It's very kind of you.
A:好呀,你真是太好了。

B: Don't mention it.
B:不值一提。

A: The rooms are very tidy and the flowers grew very well. You are very helpful. I want to thank you for everything you've done for me.
A:房间很干净,花也长得很好。你太热心了。我要感谢你为我做的每一件事。

B: It's my pleasure.
B:很乐意效劳。

A: I bought you some books on literature, I don't know if you like them.
A:我买了一些文学方面的书给你,不知你是否喜欢。

B: Thank you. Thank you for the trouble you've taken.
B:谢谢你。谢谢你如此费心。

A: Not at all.
A:你太客气了。

On the Scene 身临其境 面面俱到

主题:吉姆借给玛丽一盘磁带,她和她的同学都非常喜欢听,现在她想续借。请你看图,根据如下提供的关键词,将他们的对话写出来。

关键词语:lend *v.* 借给　　everyone *pron.* 每个人
no problem 没问题

参考答案

Mary: I really like the tape you lent me the other day.
Jim: I'm glad you like it.
Mary: And thank you very much for letting me keep it so long.
Jim: Not at all.
Mary: Everyone in our class enjoyed it.
Jim: I'm glad to hear you say so.
Mary: Would you mind my keeping it for another week?
Jim: No problem.
Mary: It's very kind of you. I really don't know how I can thank you enough.
玛丽: 你前些日子借给我的磁带我真的很喜欢。
吉姆: 我很高兴你喜欢它。
玛丽: 谢谢你让我借了这么长时间。
吉姆: 没关系。
玛丽: 我们全班同学都很喜欢它。
吉姆: 我很高兴听你这么说。
玛丽: 能让我再借一个星期吗?
吉姆: 没问题。
玛丽: 你太好了。我真不知怎样感谢你才好。

★道歉用语★ 9 Apologies

Words and Phrases 闪亮词语 点滴积累

apologize to sb. for sth. 为……向……道歉
feel really bad about... 对……感到非常抱歉
offer/make/accept on apology 道歉/致歉/接受道歉
apologize 道歉;辩解
pardon 原谅,饶恕
sorry 对不起的;抱歉的
forgive 原谅,宽恕
miss 错过,失去
excuse me 对不起
interrupt 中断,打扰
trouble (使)忧虑,麻烦
excuse... for 因……而道歉
regret 抱歉,后悔
explain 解释
apologetic 表示歉意的
express one's regret 表达歉意
ask for pardon 请求原谅
pardonable 可原谅的
forgiving 宽容的,体谅的
fault 过错
carelessness 粗心
offend 冒犯

Useful Sentences 七彩精句 连点成线

To apologize after having bumped into someone
在撞到某人时,表示歉意

1. *Excuse me.* 对不起。
2. *Oh, pardon me!* 非常抱歉!
3. *How clumsy of me to step on your foot.* 我真笨,踩了你的脚。
4. *I am really so sorry to bump into you.* 撞着你了真是非常抱歉。
5. *I'm sorry.* 对不起。
6. *Please forgive me.* 请原谅我。

To apologize after having unintentionally bothered someone in some other way, or for failing to keep a promise, etc.
因某种方式无意打扰了别人,或未能恪守诺言等,表示歉意

1. *I'm sorry. I'm late.* 对不起,我来迟了。
2. *I'm sorry to have kept you waiting.* 对不起,我让你久等了。
3. *I'm sorry, I met the traffic jam.* 对不起,我遇到了交通堵塞。
4. *I'm sorry, I didn't care about that.* 对不起,我没在意。
5. *I'm so sorry that I couldn't keep my word.* 对不起,我不能守约。
6. *Oh, I'm sorry. I thought you were through with it and put it away.* 噢,对不起。我以为你用过了。我把它放起来了。
7. *I'm sorry I didn't call you up last night, but it was very late when I got home.* 对不起,昨晚我没打电话给你,因为回家时已经很晚了。
8. *I'm sorry, it's very urgent.* 对不起,那事很急。
9. *I'm extremely sorry to say the room you reserved isn't available.* 实在抱歉,你预定的房间还没有落实。
10. *Sorry for not phoning you.* 对不起,没给你打电话。
11. *I'm sorry, but I couldn't get tickets for the concert tonight.* 对不起,我没弄到今晚音乐会的票。

To express regret about not being able to do something 因不能做某事，表示歉意

1. *I'm sorry, but I have a meeting at half past two.* 对不起，我2点半要开会。
2. *I'm afraid I can't. I have a meeting at half past two.* 恐怕不行。我2点半要开会。
3. *I'm sorry, my bike is broken.* 对不起，我自行车坏了。
4. *I'm sorry, but I have promised it to Tom. You can have it when he's through.* 对不起，我已答应借给汤姆了。等他看完你可以看。

To apologize when you think you have inconvenienced someone 在你认为给别人带来不便时，表示歉意

1. *I'm afraid I have given you a lot of trouble.* 恐怕给你增添许多麻烦了。
2. *I'm afraid I have taken up too much of your time.* 恐怕占用你太多时间了。
3. *May I offer my sincerest apologies for the trouble I have given you?* 给你添了这些麻烦，谨向你表示最真诚的歉意。
4. *I've got to apologize for troubling you so much.* 给你添了这么多麻烦，我得向你道歉。

To apologize when interrupting people who are talking or working 打断别人谈话或工作时，表示歉意

1. *Excuse me, Mr. Green, many I trouble you a second?* 对不起，格林先生，我可以耽误你一会儿吗？
2. *Excuse me, Mr. Smith, you are wanted on the telephone.* 对不起，史密斯先，你有电话。
3. *Excuse me, May I speak to you for a minute?* 对不起，我可以跟你说一会儿话吗？

To apologize when you have to leave for a moment 不得不告退片刻时，表示歉意

1. *Excuse me, I'll be back right away.* 对不起。我马上就回来。
2. *Will you excuse me for a few minutes? I have to see the teacher.* 对不起。我可以出去几分钟吗？我得见下这位老师。
3. *May I be excused, Mr. Green?* 对不起，格林先生。
4. *I'll be right back.* 我去去就回。
5. *Will you excuse me for a minute? I want to make a telephone call.* 对不起，我一会儿就回来，可以吗？我想打个电话。
6. *Excuse me. I have something urgent.* 对不起。我有点儿急事。
7. *Excuse me. I shan't be a moment.* 对不起，我一会儿就回来。

Other Apologies 其他道歉

1. *Please let me apologize.* 请让我致歉。
2. *I'm terribly sorry. /I'm awfully sorry.* 非常抱歉。
3. *Please forgive me. /Pardon me.* 请原谅我。
4. *Sorry to trouble you.* 对不起，麻烦你了。
5. *I can't tell you how sorry I am.* 我不知如何道歉才好。
6. *I beseech your forgiveness.* 我恳请你原谅。
7. *Can you ever forgive me?* 你真的原谅我吗？
8. *I am sorry that I interrupt you.* 对不起，打扰你了。
9. *Excuse me for my smoking here.* 请原谅我在这儿抽烟了。
10. *I'm sorry, it was all my fault.* 对不起，都是我的过错。

Responding to Apologies 对别人道歉的答语

1. *Not at all.* 一点也不。
2. *That's all right.* 没有关系。
3. *That's all right. I quite understand.* 没关系，我理解。
4. *That's OK, you owe me one!* 没有关系，你欠我份人情！

5. *Never mind.* 没关系。
6. *Never mind about that. /No, not in the least.* 不，一点关系也没有。
7. *Not at all. I'm always glad to help you.* 一点也不。我很高兴能帮助你。
8. *Not at all. I'm always glad to be of service to you.* 一点也不。我很高兴能为你效劳。
9. *Never mind. It doesn't really matter.* 没关系。实在没有什么要紧的。
10. *No harm.* 不碍事的。
11. *Please don't feel bad about it. /Please don't take it too hard.* 请别为此不快。
12. *Please don't be.* 请不要这样。
13. *Please don't worry.* 请别担心。
14. *Please think nothing of it. /Don't think any more about it.* 请别想它了。
15. *It's nothing.* 没什么。
16. *There's no reason to apologize.* 没有理由道歉。
17. *There's no reason to apologize for such a trifle thing.* 没有理由为如此小事道歉。
18. *Please don't blame yourself.* 请不要自责。
19. *That's perfectly all right.* 完全没有关系。
20. *Don't let it worry you. /Don't let that distress you.* 不要为此烦恼。

Fashion Conversation 鲜活会话 由线到面

Conversation 1

A: Tom! You've really done it this time?
B: What? What happened?
A: I told you to get this consignment out last week. We can't very well run a light bulb conference without any light bulbs, can we? What am I going to do with you?
B: Please, give me one more chance. I'll never let it happen again. I'm very sorry.
A: Well, I guess I could give you one more chance, but this is the last time. I hear that Ronald who normally does night shift is taking three weeks vacation. Can you think of anyone who would be willing to work nights while he is gone?
B: Um, me?
A: Bingo!

A：汤姆！这次你真的把事情做了吗？
B：什么？究竟发生了什么事？
A：上个礼拜我已告诉你去把货发了，我们总不能开一个没有电灯泡的电灯泡会议吧，对不对？你想要我拿你怎么办呢？
B：求求你再给我一次机会吧，我不会再让那种事情发生的。真的非常抱歉。
A：好，我想我还能多给你一次机会，但这是最后一次。我听说上夜班的罗纳德会有三个礼拜的假期，你认为谁愿意在他离开的期间上夜班呢？
B：我吗？
A：对！就是你！

Conversation 2

A: Hello, this is 3472296.
B: Hello, Bobby. It seems that I can't arrive at your home by 12 o'clock.
A: What happened? We're all expecting you, Hans, Dick, Archie...
B: I'm so sorry. I've been held up by the damn traffic jam for half an hour. I'd have arrived but for that.
A: I see. Where are you now, Tang?
B: Thirty meters ahead is the Waterloo Bridge.
A: It's not far away from here. It's — let me see — about 20 minutes' walk. Can you walk here?

A：你好。这里是3472296。
B：你好，波比。我似乎不能在12点以前赶到你家了。
A：怎么啦？我们都在等你呀，汉斯、迪克、阿尔奇……
B：实在对不起，这该死的交通堵塞已耽误我半个小时了。否则的话，我早该到了。
A：明白了，小唐，你现在在哪里？
B：前面30米处就是滑铁卢桥。
A：离这儿不远，大概——让我想想——步行到这儿只需20分钟，能步行过来吗？

B:I've thought of that, but what can I do with my car? If only I took a taxi!
B:我早想过了,但车怎么办?我要是搭车来的就好了。

A:That's too bad. But don't worry. We'll put off dinner till one o'clock.
A:太遗憾了,但别担心,我们把吃饭时间推迟到1点就是了。

B:I'm so terribly sorry to keep you waiting.
B:让你们久等,实在过意不去。

A:It doesn't matter. Bye.
A:没关系。再见。

B:Bye.
B:再见。

Conversation 3

A:Hello!
A:你好。

B:Hi, Adele. Hi, Ted. I hate to bring this up, but that new stereo system you got...
B:你们好,阿黛尔、特德。我本不想提的,只是你新买的音响……

A:Yeah?
A:怎么啦?

B:You were playing it very late last night.
B:昨晚你一直放到很晚。

A:Yeah?
A:是吗?

B:It kept me awake.
B:吵得我睡不着。

A:Oh, I'm sorry.
A:呵,对不起。

C:It kept me awake a couple of hours too.
C:吵得我也几个小时都没睡着。

A:I'm sorry, I... I didn't realize it was that loud.
A:对不起。我……我没意识到声音竟有那么大。

B:It was that loud, and it was pretty late, and check with Mary if you don't believe me.
B:真有那么大呢,又很晚了。你不信的话,可以问问玛丽。

C:It's true. It was a bit loud.
C:是的,声音是稍微大了点。

A:I'm very sorry. I didn't realize it. I promise I'll keep it down in the future.
A:很对不起。我确实没意识到会有那么大。我保证以后把声音开小些。

B:Oh, it's no problem. It's OK. You know, it only happened once.
B:噢,没什么,没什么大不了的,才这一次嘛。

C:I am glad we've straightened everything out.
C:我很高兴,大家把事情说清楚了。

Conversation 4

A:You shouldn't have told her the truth. What can we do now?
A:你不应该把真相告诉她。我们现在该怎么办?

B:I'm sorry. It's all my fault.
B:对不起。都是我的错。

A:You are always like this. I've told you many times not to tell her.
A:你总是这样。我告诉过你很多次不要告诉她。

B:Sorry, I had no intention.
B:对不起,我不是故意的。

A:It's too late to say sorry now. Oh, what am I going to do?
A:现在说对不起太晚了。唉,我现在该怎么办?

B:I know I was an idiot. But if there is anything I can do to make up, please do tell me.
B:我知道我是个白痴。但是要是我能做什么事补救的话,请一定告诉我。

Conversation 5

A:Why, Tom? It's five to six already and you are still writing here.
A:汤姆,怎么回事?已经差5分6点了,你还在这儿写。

B:So what? Are we going anywhere?
B:那又怎么样?我们要去哪吗?

A:Yes, have you forgotten? We have arranged to go to May's to watch some videos tonight.
A:是啊,你忘了吗?我们说好了今晚去梅那里看录像。

B: Oh, I'm sorry I forgot all about it. Well, can I take a rain check?
B：噢，对不起，我一点都不记得了。唉，我不能去了，下次吧。

A: What's the matter with you? You are the one who persuaded all of us to go there.
A：你怎么了？是你说服我们所有人去那儿的。

B: I'm terribly sorry, Jack. But I have to finish this paper by tomorrow or Professor Martin will kill me.
B：非常对不起，杰克。但是这篇论文明天之前一定要完成，否则马丁教授会杀了我的。

Conversation 6

A: Have another cup of milk?
A：再来一杯牛奶？

B: Thanks. Oh, I'm sorry the milk is spilled out.
B：谢谢。噢，对不起，牛奶溢出来了。

A: Did it spill on your suit?
A：它洒到你的西服上了吗？

B: No. But I spilled it on the tablecloth. I'm terribly sorry.
B：没有，但是我把它洒到桌布上了。

A: Don't worry.
A：没关系。

B: I'm afraid it's too hard to wash off the stain.
B：恐怕这痕迹很难洗掉。

A: It's nothing to get upset about.
A：不必感到不安。

B: I have to apologize for my carelessness. Is there anything I can do?
B：我必须为我的粗心道歉。我能做点什么吗？

A: Just forget about it.
A：不要记挂在心上了。

B: I really feel great shame. Let me buy a new one for you.
B：我真的感到很惭愧，让我给你买块新的吧！

A: Don't be silly. It's out of the question.
A：不要傻了，什么事也没有。

B: But...
B：但是…

A: Let's enjoy ourselves.
A：让我们愉快地玩吧。

On the Scene 身临其境 面面俱到

主题：梅斯在她的论文答辩上迟到了。请你看图，根据如下提供的关键词，将他们的对话写出来。

关键词语：article *n.* 文章　knock sb. out 使某人筋疲力竭的
speak up 大声地说

参考答案

Professor Robinson: We can't wait any longer...

Mase: (rushing in) I'm terribly sorry to be so late. I had an article...

Professor Robinson: You'll knock yourself out the way you're working, Mase. Why don't you slow down?

Mase: I can't afford to.

Professor Robinson: All right. Now that everybody's here. Shall we be getting started? Miss Mase, are you ready?

Mase: Yes, thanks, Professor Robinson. Before I start, I'd like to thank Professor Robinson for all his help in giving me unlimited access to his research materials. These materials proved invaluable, especially as my own papers have not yet arrived from China.

Professor Robinson: Excuse me, Miss Mase. Would you mind speaking up, please? I can't hear you very well.

Mase: Sorry. I'll try to speak louder. The topic of my paper is ***The Structure of the Crust and Upper Mantle in Northern China and Their Relation to Cenozoic Tectonism.*** Fortunately I did bring some slides with me, which I hope will make things clearer. Over the last 3 years I have spent a total of 9 months in northern China with a team of 10 other geologists.

Professor Robinson: What area of northern China exactly?

Mase: Jinlin province.

鲁滨逊教授:我们不能再等了……

梅斯:(奔入)非常抱歉,来得太晚了,我有一篇文章……

鲁滨逊教授:梅斯,你这样工作下去,一定会筋疲力竭的。为什么要这样紧张呢?

梅斯:我也是事出无奈。

鲁滨逊教授:不要说了。既然大家都来了,我们现在开始好吗?梅斯小姐,你准备好了没有?

梅斯:准备好了,谢谢,鲁滨逊教授。在我开始宣读论文之前,我首先要感谢鲁滨逊教授的帮助,他让我充分地利用了他的科研资料。事实证明,这些资料是非常宝贵的,尤其是在我自己的资料尚未从中国寄来的时候。

鲁滨逊教授:对不起,梅斯小姐。请你说话的声音大一点。我听不太清楚。

梅斯:很抱歉。我将尽量高声一些。我论文的题目是《中国北部地区的地壳和上地幔结构及其与新生代构造的关系》。幸亏我带来一些幻灯片,我希望这样能把问题解释得更清楚。我和其他10位地质学者组成一个队在过去3年内总共花了9个月的时间在中国北部地区工作。

鲁滨逊教授:确切地说在中国北部的什么地区?

梅斯:吉林省。

★有事相求★ 10 Requests

Words and Phrases 闪亮词语 点滴积累

appreciate 感激
aid 援助,帮助
each other 相互
consult 请教
offer 提供
confidential 推心置腹的
disinterested 无私的
expedient 有益的
honorable 高尚的
intimate 亲密的
loving 充满友爱的
patronizing 居高临下的
platonic 纯精神的
precious 珍贵的

Useful Sentences 七彩精句 连点成线

Words of request 请求用语

1. *Would you do me a good turn?* 请为我做件事行吗?
2. *Any chance of using your bike?* 能借自行车一用吗?
3. *May I have the honour of attending your lecture?* 我能否有幸听你的讲座?
4. *Do you think it would be possible to give me a pay-raise?* 你认为可以给我加薪吗?
5. *May I use your dictionary?* 我能用一下你的词典吗?
6. *Could you possibly clean the room?* 请把房间打扫干净可以吗?
7. *May I ask a favour?* 帮个忙行吗?
8. *Could you lend me your pen?* 可以借用一下你的钢笔吗?
9. *Would you please open the window?* 请打开窗子好吗?
10. *Would you mind turning off the radio?* 请你关掉收音机好吗?
11. *May I trouble you to move your bicycle a bit?* 麻烦你把自行车挪一挪行吗?
12. *Don't make any noise, will you?* 别吵闹,行吗?
13. *I was wondering whether you could post the letter for me?* 不知你能否帮我寄这封信?
14. *You couldn't get me a ticket, could you?* 你能不能帮我弄一张票?
15. *If you don't mind, I'd like to have a look at the picture.* 如果你不介意,我想看看这张照片。

Words of answering request 回答请求用语

1. *I'd be delighted to have your attending.* 我很乐意你来参加。
2. *I'd like to say yes, but that's just impossible.* 我倒是想答应的,不过那却不可能。
3. *I'm sorry, but I'm using it right now.* 对不起,我现在正在使用。
4. *It'll be no bother to me.* 这对我一点儿也不费事。
5. *That's no trouble at all.* 一点儿也不麻烦。
6. *Well, if I can.* 好吧,如果我能的话。

Refuse to help 拒绝帮助用语

1. *I'm sorry, but…* 我很抱歉,但是……
2. *Well, I'd like to, but…* 我很愿意,只是……
3. *I'm afraid you may not…* 恐怕您不可以……
4. *I'm sorry. You'd better not…* 对不起,您最好别……
5. *Sorry, but…* 对不起,只是……
6. *No, I'm afraid I can't help you.* 不,恐怕我帮不了忙。

Fashion Conversation 鲜活会话 由线到面

Conversation 1

A: Er... Do you mind if I smoke?	A:呃,我抽烟,你介意吗?
B: Just go ahead.	B:抽吧。
A: Oh, I forgot where I put my cigarette.	A:哦,我忘记把烟放在哪儿了。
B: Shall I get you some?	B:我给你拿一包来,行吗?
A: Er... no, no. Look, I've got another packet here.	A:呃,不,不用。瞧,我这儿还有一包呢。
B: Let me get you an ashtray.	B:我给你找个烟灰缸来。
A: Thanks.	A:谢谢。

Conversation 2

A: Would you lend me your typewriter?	A:能借你的打字机用一下吗?
B: I'm sorry, it is out of order. It could not be used right now.	B:对不起,它出故障了。它现在不能用。
A: It doesn't matter. I'll ask Jim if he has one.	A:没关系。我去问问吉姆看他是否有一台。
B: He surely has, even a new one.	B:他肯定有,甚至还是新的呢。
A: (*He goes to Jim*) May I use your typewriter, Jim?	A:(*他向吉姆走去*)吉姆,我可以用你的打字机吗?
C: Of course. Here you are.	C:当然了。给你。
A: Thank you. I just want to type something.	A:谢谢。我只想打印一些东西。
C: There is no hurry. I'm not using it now anyway.	C:不用急。反正我现在也不用。
A: (*After using it*) I've just finished typing. Thank you.	A:(*用完后*)我打印完了。谢谢你。
C: You are welcome.	C:不用客气。

Conversation 3

A: Can I help you with those packages?	A:要我帮你搬运这些行李吗?
B: Huh? Why, yes. I could use some help. It is very kind of you.	B:啊? 什么,可以。我正需要帮助。你太好了。
A: No trouble at all. Are you parked nearby?	A:一点也不麻烦。你的车停在附近吗?
B: Right over there. The blue great truck.	B:就在那儿。那辆蓝色大卡车。
A: Where do you want me to put these?	A:你想让我把它们放在哪儿?
B: In the front will be fine. Just let me open the door of it.	B:放在前面即可。我来给你开车门。
A: It looks as if you're having new year early at your house.	A:看起来好像你在家提前过新年似的。
B: No, it's my twin brothers' birthday, so I had to buy presents for two!	B:不,因为我的双胞胎弟弟要过生日,所以我不得不为他俩买些礼物。

Conversation 4

A: 331-2739. Marlene is speaking.	A:这里是3312739,我是马琳。
B: How've you been, Marlene? I haven't seen you around for some time.	B:马琳,你近来怎样? 我已经有一段时间没见到你了。
A: Well, I haven't been too well lately.	A:哦,我近来身体有点不大好。

B: Oh, I'm sorry to hear that. I hope it isn't anything serious.	B:呵,听你这么说,我很不安,希望没什么严重的吧?
A: No, not too serious, but the doctor says I've got to stay in bed.	A:是的,没什么严重的,但医生说我得卧床休息。
B: How long did the doctor say you'd have to stay in bed?	B:医生说要卧床休息多久?
A: At least a month.	A:至少一个月。
B: My goodness, for a whole month. Well, I'll talk to the neighbors and we'll see about having your meals brought in.	B:天啦,一个月!喔,我跟邻居说说,商量一下给你送饭。
A: That's very nice of you but it won't be necessary. I'm going to go to my sister's.	A:你真太好了,但不必了,我到妹妹家去住。
B: Oh, I see. How long will you stay at your sister's?	B:哦,是这样。准备在你妹妹家住多久?
A: I probably won't be back until spring.	A:可能开春才回来。
B: Not until spring! My, you'll be gone a long time.	B:开春!哎呀!你要走那么长时间!
A: I was wondering if you'd mind watching my house for me while I have gone.	A:我走了后,你帮我照看一下房子,可以吗?
B: Why, sure. I'll be glad to keep an eye on things.	B:噢,当然可以,我还很乐意呢。
A: I've got an extra key. I'd like you to have in case you need it.	A:我还有把钥匙想给你,万一需要呢。
B: That's good idea. If I've got a key I can go in and check on things.	B:那好。我有钥匙的话,就可以进屋来查看一下。
A: I really appreciate this, Lily. Hope it won't be too much trouble.	A:真是太感谢你了,丽丽。希望这不会给你添太多的麻烦。
B: No trouble at all, Marlene. Just hope you get well quickly. Goodbye.	B:一点也不麻烦,马琳。希望你快好起来。再见。
A: Goodbye, and thanks.	A:再见。谢谢。

On the Scene 身临其境 面面俱到

主题:罗斯给她的朋友汤姆打电话问他是否收到自己的金婚请柬,并要他提前一天到达,好帮助自己安排庆典事宜。请你看图,根据如下提供的关键词,将他们的对话写出来。

关键词语: invitation card 邀请卡　wedding anniversary 结婚纪念日
be counting on 期盼　preparation *n.* 准备
occasion *n.* 场合

参考答案

Tom: Hello, Rose. How are you getting along these days?

Rose: Pretty fine, Tom. I'm wondering if you have received the invitation card.

Tom: Yes. Thank you. And I've posted a card to say that I will attend your 50th wedding anniversary. Oh, I posted last Sunday.

Rose: I haven't received it. It may have got lost. I am really glad that you'll come.

Tom: I'm counting on the day of your anniversary.

Rose: Would you come a day earlier? Frankly, I want your ideas and help with the preparation. You are an expert on such occasion.

Tom: You're lucky, Rose. I'm free for the two days before your anniversary. I'll be with you on July 2, that is, a day earlier than your anniversary.

Rose: That's my friend.

Tom: How many guests have you invited? 20?

Rose: Double that. That's why I want your help.

汤姆:你好,罗斯,最近过得怎样?

罗斯:相当不错,汤姆。我正想问一下你收到请柬没有?

汤姆:收到了,谢谢。我回了你一张卡告诉你,我要参加你的金婚庆典。嗯,我是上周星期天寄的卡。

罗斯:我还没收到,可能寄丢了吧。你能来,我真的很高兴。

汤姆:我在盼着那天早日到来呢。

罗斯:你提前一天来,好吗?坦率地说吧,我需要你给我出主意,帮我筹备。你在这方面可谓是行家了。

汤姆:算你走运吧,罗斯,你金婚纪念日前的两天我正好有空。我7月2日,也就是提前一天来。

罗斯:够朋友!

汤姆:你邀请了多少客人?20位?

罗斯:20的两倍,这正是我要你帮忙的原因。

Daily Life

CHAPTER

2

生活花絮

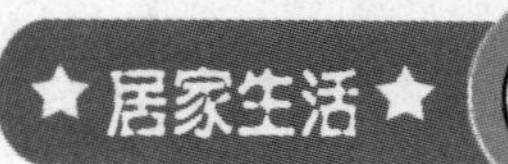

★居家生活★ 1 At Home

Words and Phrases 闪亮词语 点滴积累

everyday life 日常生活
get up 起床
breakfast 早饭
lunch 午饭
supper 晚饭
wash face 洗脸
brush teeth 刷牙
take out the garbage 倒垃圾
clean up the room 打扫房间
reading 阅读
watching TV 看电视
surfing the internet 上网

Useful Sentences 七彩精句 连点成线

Get up 起床

1. *It's time to wake up!* 该起床了!
2. *I don't want to get up.* 我真不想起。
3. *Get up soon!* 快点儿起床!
4. *I don't want to.* 我真不想起。
5. *Would you turn off the alarm clock?* 能帮我关掉闹钟吗?
6. *You finally got up.* 你终于起来了。
7. *I'm still sleepy.* 我还困着呢。
8. *Did you stay up late last night?* 昨晚你熬夜了?
9. *Let's fold up the futon.* 把被子叠好。
10. *Was I sawing logs last night?* 昨天晚上我打呼噜了吗?
11. *Did I keep you up?* 影响你睡觉了吗?
12. *I had a nightmare.* 我做了个可怕的梦。
13. *You left the light on.* 你一直没关灯啊。
14. *Oh, I was so tired.* 哦,我当时太累了。

Dress on and have breakfast 穿衣吃饭

1. *What dress should I wear?* 我应该穿什么衣服?
2. *The red one!* 穿红的吧!
3. *Hurry up and get dressed.* 快换衣服。
4. *Put those pajamas away!* 把睡衣收好!
5. *Oh, I'm going to wash those.* 啊,我正要洗呢。
6. *What time do you have breakfast?* 你几点吃早饭?
7. *I have breakfast at seven o'clock.* 我在七点吃早饭。

Prepare to work 准备上班

1. *When do you leave home for work?* 你什么时间离家去上班?
2. *I usually leave home at 7:30.* 我通常7:30离开家。
3. *How do you go to work?* 你怎么去上班?
4. *I usually go to work by bicycle, but when it gets really cold in winter, I take the bus.* 我通常骑自行车上班,但冬天很冷的时候,我就坐公共汽车。

Fashion Conversation 鲜活会话 曲线到面

Conversation 1

A:Tom, wake up! It's almost seven o'clock.
B:Oh, morning, Mom. Did the alarm clock ring?
A:Yes, it did.
B:But I didn't hear it at all.
A:What time did you set it last night?

A:汤姆,醒醒!都快7点了。
B:早上好,妈妈。闹钟响了吗?
A:响过了。
B:可我一点都没听到。
A:你昨晚定在几点钟了?

B: Six o'clock.

B:6 点啊。

A: Hurry up, or you'll be late for school. Are you feeling ill?

A:快点吧,否则你上学就要迟到了。你不舒服吗?

B: No. I'm only sleepy because I stayed awake the whole night.

B:没有,只是困而已,因为昨晚一夜没合眼。

A: Breakfast is ready. Get dressed and get out of bed. Don't forget to wash your face and brush your teeth before you eat breakfast.

A:早饭准备好了。穿好衣服下床。别忘了吃早饭前洗脸刷牙。

B: OK, I'm coming.

B:好的,我就来。

Conversation 2

A: Mary, your room is a disaster! Look at those dirty clothes and socks! They're everywhere.

A:玛丽,你的房间一团糟!看看那些脏衣服,脏袜子,到处都是。

B: I'm sorry, mom.

B:对不起,妈妈。

A: Try to keep your room neat, OK? Now take those dirty clothes away and clean up your room.

A:要尽量保持房间的整洁。现在拿走那些脏衣服,打扫打扫你的房间。

B: Sure, Mom. I'll be finished in a minute.

B:好的,妈妈。我一会儿就干好。

Conversation 3

A: Did you hear the weather forecast today, darling?

A:亲爱的,你听了今天的天气预报了吗?

B: Yes, the radio says it's going to rain.

B:听了。广播说,天要下雨。

A: Oh, well, I guess there's no point of hanging this out, then.

A:噢,好,我想那就不能把这晾晒出去了。

B: Why aren't you using the dryer?

B:为什么你不用烘干机?

A: I don't want the electric company to get rich.

A:我不想让供电公司赚更多的钱。

B: Then why did you buy the dryer, if you don't feel like that?

B:如果你不喜欢烘干机的话,你为什么要买它?

A: Because everyone of my friends and neighbours has one and I don't want to look poor.

A:因为我的朋友们和邻居们都有,所以我不想让我自己显得太穷。

Conversation 4

A: Mary, how have things been?

A:玛丽,事情怎么样了?

B: Oh, much the same. My husband and I still seem to have rows all the time.

B:噢,和往常一样。我丈夫和我仍旧每日争吵不休。

A: What do you quarrel about?

A:你们吵什么?

B: Oh, everything. For example, when he gets home, he expects me to run around and get his tea. He never does anything at home.

B:噢,什么事都吵。比如,当他回家时,他希望我围着他转,给他沏茶,他在家从来什么都不做。

A: Oh.

A:噢。

B: And yesterday! He even invited four of his friends to come round for a drink and didn't tell me before.

B:并且昨天,他事先没通知我就邀请了他的 4 个朋友来家大喝一顿。

A: I see.

A:我知道了。

B: And he is so untidy. He's worse than the kids. He always throws his clothes on the floor. After all,

B:他太邋遢。甚至比小孩子都差。他总是把衣服扔到地板上,毕竟,我不是他的仆人。太烦人了。

I'm not his servant. You see, that's the trouble.

Conversation 5

A: Do you have dry toast or buttered toast for breakfast?	A:你早饭吃干烤面包还是黄油烤面包?
B: Some days I have dry toast, and some days I have buttered toast.	B:有时我吃干烤面包,有时我吃黄油烤面包。
A: Do you have orange juice or pineapple juice for breakfast?	A:早饭喝橘子汁,还是喝菠萝汁?
B: Sometimes I have orange juice and sometimes I have pineapple.	B:有时我喝橘子汁,有时喝菠萝汁。
A: Do you have tea or coffee for breakfast?	A:早饭喝茶还是喝咖啡?
B: Once in a while I have tea. Usually, I have coffee.	B:我偶尔喝茶,通常喝咖啡。
A: Do you have a big breakfast or a light breakfast?	A:你是吃丰盛的早餐呢,还是少量的早餐?
B: Usually, I have a light breakfast. Once in a while I have a big breakfast.	B:通常,我吃少量的早餐,偶尔吃丰盛的早餐。
A: Do you leave the house at eight o'clock or nine o'clock?	A:你在8点还是在9点离开家?
B: Some days I leave the house at 8:00 and some days at 9:00.	B:有时我在8点离开家,有时9点。
A: Do you get to work at nine o'clock or ten o'clock?	A:你在9点还是10点开始工作?
B: Sometimes I get to work at 9:00 and sometimes at 10:00.	B:有时我在9点工作,有时在10点。
A: What do you do after dinner each evening?	A:晚上你吃完晚饭后都干什么?
B: Usually, after dinner I listen to the radio for a while.	B:通常,晚饭后我听一会儿收音机。

On the Scene 身临其境 面面俱到

主题:吃完早餐后,丈夫对妻子做简短道别。请你看图,根据如下提供的关键词,将他们的对话写出来。

关键词语:what would you like... 你想要……
be late 迟到
have an appointment 有个约会
lock the door 锁门
gonna 将要
take care 保重

参考答案

(*After having breakfast*)

Wife:What time will you be home? Are you gonna be late today?

Husband:Well,I have an appointment today. I won't have supper at home.

Wife:How do you go to work?

Husband:I'd like to take the bus. Do you stay at home today?

Wife:No. I wanna visit a friend,Mary.

Husband:OK. Don't forget to take out the garbage. Be sure to lock the door when you leave. I'm leaving now. Bye.

Wife:Take care. Bye.

(吃过早饭后)

妻子:你什么时候回来?今天会晚些回来吗?

丈夫:我今天有个约会,不回家吃晚饭了。

妻子:你怎么去上班?

丈夫:我想坐公车去。你今天待在家里吗?

妻子:不,我想去拜访我的一个朋友玛丽。

丈夫:好的,别忘了倒垃圾。出门前记得锁门。我走了。再见。

妻子:当心点,再见。

★梦的解说★ 2 Dream

Words and Phrases 闪亮词语 点滴积累

nightmare 恶梦
dream 梦,梦想
dreamer 梦想家
hope to be 希望
desire 渴望
unrealistic dream 不切实际的梦想
unreal dream 不现实的梦想
sweet dream 祝你好梦
dream of/about 梦想
dream boat 梦中情人,梦寐以求的(东西)
dream on 别做梦了
have a dream 做梦
day dreaming 白日梦
pipe dream 白日梦
dream up 空想出

Useful Sentences 七彩精句 连点成线

Talk about dream 谈梦

1. *I keep a dream diary.* 我写关于梦的日记。
2. *I wonder what my dream means.* 我想知道我的梦有什么意义。
3. *I can't remember what I dreamed last night.* 我不记得昨晚做过什么梦了。
4. *I dream in color.* 我的梦是彩色的。
5. *I dream in black and white.* 我的梦是黑白的。
6. *Yellow represents peace and intellect.* 黄色代表和平与智慧。
7. *Brown represents commitment and may mean you should be more down to earth.* 咖啡色代表承诺,也可能表示你应该更脚踏实地一点儿。
8. *I dreamed that I was falling.* 我梦见我坠落了。
9. *I dreamed that I was flying.* 我梦见我在飞。
10. *I dreamed that... died.* 我梦见(某人)死了。
11. *I dreamed that I was in the desert.* 我梦见我在沙漠里。
12. *I need a good night's sleep.* 我需要好好睡一觉。
13. *I slept well last night./I didn't sleep well last night.* 我昨晚睡得很好。/我昨晚睡得不好。
14. *Did you sleep well?* 你睡得好吗?
15. *He is in a deep sleep.* 他睡得很熟。
16. *He fell into a deep sleep.* 他进入了梦乡。
17. *I recently dreamed of her often.* 我最近老是梦见她。
18. *What did you dream?* 你梦见什么了?
19. *What you dream at night is what you were thinking in the daytime.* 日有所思,夜有所梦。
20. *You are day-dreaming.* 你真是做白日梦。

Fashion Conversation 鲜活会话 由线到面

Conversation 1

A:I really had a bad dream last night...
B:A nightmare? About what?
A:About... you.
B:Are you mad at me? What happened?
A:No, but I don't want to scare you...
B:Tell me!

A:我昨夜做了一个很不好的梦……
B:噩梦吗?关于什么的?
A:关于……你。
B:你在生我的气吗?怎么了?
A:没这回事,但我不想吓你……
B:快告诉我!

Conversation 2

A: Mary, I dreamed about you again...
B: Oh! Was it good or bad?
A: Good. You met a man in a blue suit and you were talking with him secretly.
B: I'm married! I wouldn't do that!
A: Listen. My book about dreams says it means victory or opportunity.
B: Well, you were right once... But I love Jack and Jack alone!
(*after a while*)
A: Mary, the man in my dream may just be a symbol.
B: I hope so. How do you remember all these dreams?
A: I keep a dream diary. I write them down every morning.
B: That helps you remember?
A: It helps to think about dreaming before you sleep.
B: It sounds too easy.
A: After having a good night's sleep, you may write down what you are thinking when you wake up. It takes practice.

A：玛丽，我又梦到你了……
B：哦！是好梦还是噩梦？
A：是好梦。你跟一个穿着蓝色套装的男人在一起，还偷偷摸摸地在谈事情。
B：我已经结婚了！我才不会那样呢！
A：听着。我的关于梦的书上说这代表着胜利或机会。
B：嗯，算你对……但我爱杰克，而且只爱他一人！
（*过了一会儿*）
A：玛丽，梦里的那个男人或许只是个象征。
B：但愿如此。你怎么能记住这么多梦呢？
A：我一直在记梦的日记。我每天早上都把它们记录下来。
B：这样能帮你记住吗？
A：在睡前想想要做梦，有助于你记住所做的梦。
B：听起来太容易了。
A：睡一夜好觉后，当你醒过来的时候，就可以写下你正在想的事。这得多多练习。

Conversation 3

A: Oh, Alice, I have news for you!
B: I have to tell you my dream first.
A: Go ahead.
B: I was in a dark green forest, all alone, smelling the trees...
A: Hmmm... maybe you need to go camping...
B: Funny. The book says that green means self-awareness and forest symbolizes tranquility.
A: I think you are realizing your destiny.

A：哦，艾丽斯，我有消息告诉你！
B：我得先告诉你我的梦。
A：说吧。
B：我在一个阴暗的绿色森林里，只有我一个人，闻着树木的味道……
A：喔……你可能需要去露营了……
B：真好笑。书上说绿色代表自省，而森林象征宁静。
A：我想你开始了解自己的命运了。

Conversation 4

A: What?
B: You have a talent for knowing things before they happen. You should become a psychic.
A: I was right only one time.
B: No, two times. Remember the man in the blue suit dream?
A: Yes... victory or opportunity...
B: I just found out that I beat 300 applicants for the job that I wanted!

A：怎么了？
B：你有预知的天份，你应该做个通灵人。
A：我只说中过一次。
B：不，是两次。还记得穿蓝套装的男人那个梦吗？
A：记得……代表胜利或机会……
B：我刚刚得知我击败了300个竞聘者，得到了我想要的工作！

A:Congratulations!
B:Thank you!
A:Not at all.

A:恭喜你!
B:谢谢!
A:不客气。

Conversation 5

A:Wade, how are you doing?
B:Not good. I guess I think too much of my wife.
A:Oh, but your wife has been in heaven for seven year.
B:Yes, but I recently dreamed of her often.
A:What did you dream?
B:Last night I dreamt I was walking down an unfamiliar road when I reached a dark and miserable house. Grey clouds covered the sky, and so I went inside the house where I found a poor, pathetic person, wearing clothes similar to those my wife wore. I didn't recognize her and felt sorry for her.
A:Anything else in the dream?
B:No, nothing else. When I woke this morning, I felt the misery and unhappiness of it all day.
A:I think you burden a lot from the job. You'd better have a good rest.

A:韦德,还好吗?
B:不太好。我想我太思念我妻子了。
A:哦,但你妻子已经去世七年了。
B:是的,但我最近老是梦见她。
A:你梦见什么了?
B:昨晚我梦见我在一条不熟悉的街道走,这时我来到了一座黑暗、阴惨惨的房子前。天空乌云密布,所以我走进房子里,在那儿我看见一个可怜、悲惨的人,穿的衣服跟我妻子穿得很像。我没有认出她来,感到非常抱歉。
A:在梦里还有其他的吗?
B:没有,没有其他的了。当我今早醒来,我整天都能感觉那种悲惨,不幸。
A:我想你可能是工作压力太大了。你最好好好休息一下。

On the Scene 身临其境 面面俱到

主题:阿黛尔在与洛伊丝谈论自己的梦。请你看图,根据如下提供的关键词,将她们的对话写出来。

关键词语:come on 得了吧 superstition *n.* 迷信
colleagues *n.* 同事 whisper *n.* 耳语
sequence *n.* 次序,顺序 wake up 醒来

参考答案

Adele: Do you know a saying "What you dream at night is what you were thinking in the daytime"?

Lois: Come on, that's superstition, do you believe that?

Adele: Yeah, one day I was sitting in my office, listening to a group of colleagues whispering and talking about me. I couldn't hear what they were saying but it worried me.

Lois: Then what happened?

Adele: That night I dreamt exactly the same sequence again, except that in my dream I saw something I'd missed during the day. While they were whispering they were all looking down at something.

Lois: What were they looking at?

Adele: I didn't see it in my dream, but the next morning when I woke up I realized exactly why they'd been whispering and talking about me. That day was my birthday.

Lois: Wasn't it possible that they'd been looking down at a birthday card?

Adele: Yeah, my dream was right. I did get a card from my colleagues, whom I'd suspected of talking about me.

阿黛尔:你听过"日有所思,夜有所梦"这句话吗?

洛伊丝:行了,那是迷信,你相信吗?

阿黛尔:是的。一天我坐在办公室里,听见一群同事在那儿嘀嘀咕咕谈论我。我听不清他们在说什么,这让我很不安。

洛伊丝:那后来呢?

阿黛尔:那天晚上我居然又梦到了同样的场景,只不过在梦里我看见了白天错过的东西。当他们嘀嘀咕咕的同时,还在低头看着什么东西。

洛伊丝:在看什么呢?

阿黛尔:在梦里没看见是什么东西,但第二天早上当我醒来我清楚地知道他们在嘀咕、谈论我什么。那天是我的生日。

洛伊丝:他们低头看的不会是生日卡吧?

阿黛尔:是的,我的梦是对的。我确实从我的同事,就是我怀疑谈论我的那些同事那里收到了一张卡。

★烹饪技术★ 3 Cooking Skill

Words and Phrases 闪亮词语 点滴积累

cooking utensils 烹饪用具
stainless kitchen utensils 不锈钢厨具
range;stove 炉灶
coal stove 煤炉
(egg-shaped) briquet stove 煤球炉
briquet stove 煤饼炉
honeycomb briquet stove 蜂窝炉
charwood stove 炭炉
firewood stove 柴炉
gas range 煤气炉
kerosene stove 煤油炉
electric stove 电炉
roaster 烤炉
tongs 火钳
poker 拨火棍
pot 锅;壶;罐
jar 坛;罐;广口瓶
steamer 蒸笼
stew pot with strainer;casserole;tureen 蒸锅
pan 平锅
aluminium pan 钢精锅;铝锅
enamel pan 搪瓷锅
round roaster 圆形烧锅
meat tureen 菜锅
soup tureen 汤锅
bellied stew pan 砂锅
dixie;dixy 大铁锅(行军用)
Chinese frying pan 炒菜锅
stir-fried 扒,炒
fried... with vinegar 醋熘
fried 干烧,炸
steamed 蒸
fried dried 油爆
quick-fried 熘
boiled 煮

Useful Sentences 七彩精句 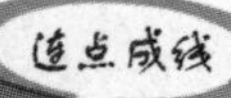 连点成线

Talk about cuisines 谈论菜系

1. *French cuisine is famous throughout the world.* 法国菜在全世界都很闻名。
2. *Italian cooking is very popular in the United States.* 意大利式烹调在美国很受欢迎。
3. *Guangdong, Sichuan, Shandong and Jiangsu cuisines are the four most famous Chinese cuisines.* 粤菜、川菜、鲁菜和苏菜是中国的四大菜系。
4. *Sichuan cooking is noted for its hot flavors.* 川菜以辣味而闻名。
5. *Cantonese cuisine is famous for raw and lightly-cooked foods and their original flavors.* 粤菜以生淡和独特风味而著称。
6. *Shandong cuisine is characterized by its seafood dishes.* 鲁菜以海鲜为特征。
7. *The Jiangsu cooking style is known for its wide variety of ingredients and sweetish flavors.* 江苏菜的烹调风格以用料广泛、味道微甜而著名。
8. *Generally speaking, besides flavors, the Chinese cuisine gives special attention to the food's nutrition, colors and textures.* 一般来说,除了味道以外,中国烹调特别注重食物的营养、色调和质感。

Cooking skills 烹饪技巧

1. *First braise the onions.* 先炖洋葱。
2. *Saute the potatoes.* 炸马铃薯。
3. *Stir-fried green peppers are delicious.* 青椒快炒很好吃。
4. *Brown the meat first and then add vegetables.* 先把肉煎成褐色,再加青菜。
5. *Have you ever tried using a pressure cooker?* 你曾试过用压力锅吗?
6. *Use the cleaver to cut the chicken.* 用切肉刀切鸡。

7. *Garlic and ginger are essential for Chinese cooking.* 大蒜和姜是中式烹调不可缺少的。
8. *Add some minced onions to the soup.* 加些洋葱屑于汤中。
9. *Marinate the pork chops before frying them.* 炸猪排前先用卤汁浸一下。
10. *Did you add the MSG?* 你加了味精吗?
11. *Is the sauce ready?* 调味酱好了吗?
12. *Let the beans ferment for two weeks.* 让豆子发酵两个礼拜。
13. *Wait until the oil is hot.* 等到油热。

 How to cook 烹饪方法

1. *Let's cut the meat into two-inch pieces.* 把肉切成两英寸的片(丝)。
2. *Chop the onion and divide it into six parts.* 把洋葱切碎,分成6份。
3. *Cut the fish in half.* 把鱼切成两半。
4. *Put a cherry on top of the ice-cream and serve.* 在冰淇淋上边放一颗樱桃,然后端出。
5. *Serve the hot pot while it's boiling, with the lamb slices, vegetables, and sauces on separate plates.* 在火锅煮开时,把它和单放的羊肉片、蔬菜、佐料一起端上桌。
6. *Mix the flour, eggs, sugar and salt in a bowl, slowly add two cups of milk and then a half cup of water, mixing constantly.* 在碗里搅拌面粉、鸡蛋、糖和盐,慢慢加入两杯牛奶,再加入半杯水,持续搅拌。

Fashion Conversation 鲜活会话 迎面到面

Conversation 1

A: Hi, Mom. What are you cooking?	A: 妈,您在做什么饭?
B: Fish.	B: 鱼。
A: Can I help you?	A: 我能帮你吗?
B: I don't think so.	B: 我想你帮不上。
A: It's fun to cook.	A: 烹饪很有意思。
B: really? I think it's fun to eat.	B: 真的吗? 我想吃起来更有意思。
A: Let's make a sandwich.	A: 我们做三明治吧。
B: No.	B: 不行。
A: What about a cake, Mom?	A: 那么蛋糕呢,妈妈?
B: OK. Are you ready?	B: 好吧。准备好了吗?
A: Yes.	A: 是的。
B: Take some milk, some flour, add some sugar.	B: 放点牛奶,放点面粉,再加点糖。
A: Yeah. But how much?	A: 是的。但是放多少呢?
B: Check, There is a book, If you are not sure of the quantities to use, look them up.	B: 核对一下。那儿有书。如果你不确定该用多少,就查一下。
A: Yes.	A: 是。
B: Add some eggs, then mix everything together. Cook it. It's a cake.	B: 加鸡蛋,然后搅拌。烤一下,蛋糕就做好了。
A: I'm hungry. (***Bill puts the bowl on the edge of the table***)	A: 我饿了。(*比尔把碗放在了桌子边沿*)
B: Don't put that bowl there, Someone might knock it over.	B: 别把碗放在那儿,那样容易被碰翻的。

Conversation 2

A: Mmm... smells great! What's cooking, good-	A: 嗯……好香! 做什么呀,帅哥?

looking?

B: Microwave pizza, homemade French fries and garlic bread!

B:微波炉比萨,自制薯条以及大蒜面包!

A: Leave it up to you to nuke up a lunch.

A:午餐交给你的结果就是用微波炉做午餐。

B: You'd be surprised at how good microwave pizza is. And it heats up really fast.

B:等会你就会知道微波炉比萨有多好吃了,而且加热又快。

A: Great. How fresh. And you don't know how to make fries!

A:太好了,还是刚做好的呢。那你应该不会做薯条吧!

B: Sure I do. I cut potatoes into strips and put them in the deep fryer.

B:当然会。马铃薯切成长条放进油锅里炸。

A: And the bread?

A:那面包呢?

B: Come on! What are toasters for? Spread on some garlic butter and toast!

B:拜托!烤面包机是干嘛的?抹上一些蒜味奶油,放进去烤就好了!

A: It seems that I've underestimated you. Everything sounds great.

A:我好像低估你了。听起来不错。

B: Wait until you taste it!

B:等你尝过就知道了!

Conversation 3

A: When I was in China, I was often treated to dumplings in my friends' homes or at restaurants. I loved dumplings, but it's a shame I never got to learn how to make them. You're an expert dumpling maker. Give me a lesson and I'll pay you with all the dumplings you can eat.

A:我在中国的时候,在朋友家或在饭馆,他们经常用饺子招待我。我非常喜欢吃饺子,可遗憾的是我一直没学会包饺子。你是包饺子的专家。你给我上一课,我请您吃饺子,能吃多少就吃多少。

B: OK, it's a deal. Have you got the necessary ingredients?

B:好,一言为定。需要的配料你都有吗?

A: I think I have. I've got the wrappers from Chinatown, the minced pork, Chinese cabbage, green onion, and garlic. What else do we need?

A:我想都有吧。我有唐人街买来的饺子皮、猪肉末、白菜、大葱、大蒜。还需要别的吗?

B: That's about all. If you like shrimp, we could put some in the stuffing to give it a better taste.

B:差不多了。如果你喜欢虾,我们可以在馅里放一些,好让味道更好。

A: Sounds good. I'll get some.

A:好主意。我去拿点虾来。

B: Now the first thing is to chop the cabbage, green onion, garlic, and shrimp. Your food processor makes the job easy. ... Not let's place the minced pork and the chopped ingredients in a large mixing bowl. Add three tablespoons of soy sauce, a half spoon of sugar, a little salt, and a bit of pepper. Blend them thoroughly. By the way, do you use MSG?

B:第一件事就是要把白菜、葱、蒜和虾切碎。你的食品处理机令这个工作方便多了。……现在把肉末和菜放在大搅拌盆里,加上三汤匙酱油、半匙糖、一点盐、一点胡椒。搅拌均匀。顺便问一句,你用味精吗?

A: No, I don't. I'm afraid I don't have any at home. Is that an important spice?

A:我不用的。恐怕我家里没有味精。这是很重要的调料吗?

B: No, it's not. But back in China, we used it a lot. It seems to me that you Americans are afraid of MSG, so forget it. Now, let's do the real thing.

B:不重要。不过在中国的时候,我们用很多味精。我觉得你们美国人很怕味精,那就算了。现在,我们来真正地包饺子吧。

A: Are we going to put the stuffing onto the wrappers and wrap them up?

A：是不是要把馅放在饺子皮上，然后包起来？

B: Exactly. Please watch how I do it. Fold the wrapper and press the edges against each other. Now make several small folds along the edges to ensure that the stuffing won't come out. That's it.

B：没错。请注意我怎么做。把饺皮叠起来，沿边缘挤压。再沿着边打几个小折，确保馅儿不漏出来。这就行了。

A: Wonderful. Let me have a try... How does it look?

A：真棒！我来试一试…… 这个饺子怎么样？

B: Perfect. I'll give you an A minus. The minus is for your speed, and speed will come with practice. In a few weeks you'll be able to make fifteen to twenty dumplings per minute.

B：好极了。我给你打优减。减主要是因为你的速度慢。速度随着熟练程度会加快。过不了几个星期，你就能一分钟包到15到20个饺子了。

A: Oh, the cooking schools will compete with one another to hire me as an instructor then. But what do we do next?

A：嚯，要是那样，那些烹饪学校就要抢着雇我作教员了。可是，下一步怎么做呀？

B: Let's bring the water to a boil. Put the dumplings in. As soon as the water returns to boiling, add a cup of cold water. Do this twice to that the stuffing will be adequately cooked while the dumplings will stay in shape.

B：我们把水烧开，把饺子放下去。水再一次烧开时，立刻加一杯凉水进去。这样烧开两遍，馅就能充分煮熟，而饺子仍然能保持形状。

A: A cup of cold water at a time for two times.

A：一次加一杯凉水，加两次。

B: Use a strainer to remove the dumplings from the pot when the water boils for the third time. Place them on dinner plates and you're ready to serve. One more thing, besides cooking them in water, you can also steam them or fry them in oil. But that'll be another lesson.

B：水第三次烧开后用漏勺把饺子从锅里捞出来，把饺子放在大餐盘上就可以上桌了。还有，饺子除了用水煮，也可以蒸或者用油煎。不过那就是下一节课的内容了。

On the Scene 身临其境 面面俱到

主题：在家庭自助餐会上，大家吃得非常开心。请你看图，根据如下提供的关键词，将他们的对话写出来。

关键词语：Mexican tacos 墨西哥玉米饼　　Italian pasta 意大利面
Greek pitas 希腊口袋饼　　Beijing duck 北京烤鸭

参考答案

Holly: Your dumplings are the hit of the party.
Yijun: This is my first potluck, but I think I could get used to this idea.
Holly: Yeah, everyone really pitched in. We have enough food to feed a small army.
Yijun: Mexican tacos, Italian pasta, Greek pitas, Beijing duck... what a weird mix!
Holly: That's potluck for you. You get to try a little sample of what each person likes.
Yijun: Speaking of people, where's Taylor? We're running low in the dessert department.
荷莉:你的水饺是餐会上的抢手货。
怡君:这是我第一次办自助餐会,但我还挺喜欢这个点子的。
荷莉:对呀,大家真的很尽心尽力。我们的食物多到可以给一支小型军队吃了。
怡君:墨西哥玉米饼,意大处面,希腊口袋饼,北京烤鸭……好怪的组合!
荷莉:自助餐会就是这样啊。每个人喜欢的食物你都有机会吃一点试试。
怡君:说到人,泰勒呢?我们的甜点快要吃光了。

★享用中餐★ 4 Chinese Food

Words and Phrases 闪亮词语 点滴积累

crisp fried bamboo shoots & salted vegetable 干烧冬笋
fried bean curd with sliced pork & pepper 家常豆腐
sour & hot soup 酸辣汤
saute pork shreds with leek sprouts 肉丝炒韭菜
saute maws shred with green pepper 肚丝炒青椒
saute pork shreds & French beans 肉丝炒刀豆
saute cabbage & pepper in sweet & sour sauce 醋熘白菜
saute veal shreds with celery 牛肉丝炒芹菜
saute shredded dried bean curd with scallion 香干炒大葱
dry saute French beans 干烧刀豆
saute eggplants with fish flavour 鱼香茄子
stuffed cucumbers 酿黄瓜
stewed bean curd with minced pork in pepper sauce 麻婆豆腐
ham & vegetable melon soup 火腿冬瓜汤
squids with rice crusts 鱿鱼锅巴
saute shrimps with green peas 青豆虾仁
assorted meats in earthen pot 什锦砂锅
saute mushroom & leaf mustard with chicken fat 蘑菇芥菜
thick pancake 锅饼
slightly fried 锅贴
steamed twisted roll 花卷
stewed rice 烩饭
wonton 馄饨
home-style 家常饼
millet pancake 煎饼
boiled dumpling 饺子
amuse-bouche 可口小吃
hand-pulled 拉面
unleavened 烙饼
cold noodles with sauce 凉拌面
steamed bread 馒头
rice 米饭
rice-flour noodles 米粉条
steamed rice cake 米糕

Useful Sentences 七彩精句 连点成线

The taste 谈论味道

1. *Delicious.* 非常可口。
2. *That tastes great.* 味道好极了。
3. *Tastes great.* 味道太好了。
4. *That's as sweet as honey.* 这像蜜一样甜。
5. *That's as sweet as sugar.* 这像糖一样甜。
6. *That tastes terrible.* 这味道太可怕了。
7. *That tastes like chicken.* 这吃起来像鸡肉的味道。
8. *That turns my stomach.* 这使我反胃。
9. *That's unfit for human consumption.* 这东西不宜供人食用。

Eatery 在餐馆

1. *Could we see the menu, please?* 请给我们看看菜单好吗?
2. *Waiter, we'd like a menu, please.* 服务员,我们要一份菜单。
3. *Anything cold?* 有凉菜吗?
4. *What Chinese food have you got?* 你们有些什么中餐?
5. *What kind of seafood do you have?* 你们有哪些海味?
6. *What's the specialty of the house?* 你们餐馆有什么特色菜?
7. *What's the soup of the day?* 这一天供应什么汤?
8. *What's really good?* 有什么真正好吃的?
9. *All right, I'll order the same.* 行,我也点同样的。
10. *Order anything you like. I'm not particular about food.* 点你喜欢吃的东西吧,我对吃并不讲究。

11. *A clear soup for me, please.* 请给我一份清汤。

Eat and drink more 劝菜,劝酒

1. *Please try the first dish.* 请尝尝第一道菜吧。
2. *Can I offer you another helping of roast beef?* 我再给你一份烤牛肉好吗?
3. *Do have some fried meat pie, it's delicious.* 吃点馅饼吧,味道好极了。
4. *Don't you want to have any more?* 不想再吃点儿吗?
5. *Help yourself to some roast duck.* 请吃点儿烤鸭吧。
6. *May I offer you some fruit juice?* 给你来点儿果汁好吗?
7. *Would you like some chicken?* 来点儿鸡肉吧?
8. *You haven't tried any steamed dumplings yet. Do have some.* 你还没尝过蒸饺吧,来点儿吧。
9. *Please eat some chicken.* 吃点鸡肉吧。
10. *Help yourself.* 请随便吃。
11. *Here, take some more.* 来,再吃一点儿。
12. *Try some of this, please.* 请尝尝这个吧。
13. *Why aren't you having any soup?* 怎么不喝点汤?

Answering 被劝菜后的应答

1. *I don't think I could eat another piece.* 我觉得我一块都吃不下了。
2. *I've eaten too much, I'm afraid.* 恐怕我吃得太多了。
3. *It's very tasty, but I couldn't manage another bite.* 味道真好,可是我再也吃不下了。
4. *I'm afraid I can't eat any more.* 恐怕我一点儿都吃不下了。
5. *I've had more than enough.* 我已经吃得太多了。
6. *I'm really full.* 我真的吃饱了。
7. *Maybe I could manage just a very small piece.* 也许我能勉强再吃一小块。
8. *You know, I've always been a light eater.* 你知道的,我一向吃得很少。

Fashion Conversation 鲜活会话 由线到面

Conversation 1

A: Sir, here is a plate of dumpling for you and your wife.	A:先生,这盘饺子是你和你太太的。
B: But I didn't order it.	B:可我没点这道菜呀。
A: It's on the house.	A:是免费赠送的。
B: It's very kind of you.	B:谢谢。

Conversation 2

A: Can you manage chopsticks?	A:你能用筷子吗?
B: Why not? See. (***He shows off his skill***)	B:为什么不能?看。(*他展示了一下他的技术*)
A: Good mastery. How do you like our Chinese food?	A:好功夫。你觉得我们中国食物怎么样?
B: Oh, great! It's delicious. You see, I'm already putting on weight. There is one thing I don't like however, MSG.	B:太好了,真好吃。你看,我都发福了,就是有一样,不太喜欢味精。
A: What's wrong with MSG? It helps to bring out the taste of the food.	A:味精怎么了?它可以使人吃起菜来津津有味。
B: According to some studies it may cause cancer.	B:一些研究表明,它可能引起癌症。
A: Oh, don't let that worry you. If that were true, China would't have such a large population.	A:噢,不要担心。如果那是真的,中国就不会有这么多人了。
B: I just happen to have a question for you guys.	B:我正有一个问题要问你们,为什么中国人都把

Why do the Chinese cook the vegetables? You see what I mean, most vitamins are destroyed when heated.

蔬菜炒熟啊？我是说，当加热的时候，很多营养都被破坏了。

A: I don't know exactly. It's a tradition. Maybe it's for sanitary reasons.

A:我不太知道。这是一个传统，或许是由于卫生的原因吧。

Conversation 3

A: A table for how many, sir?
B: Four. We'd like a table by the air-conditioner.
A: This way, please.
(*After they are seated*)
A: Would you like to order now?
B: Just a minute. Let me take a look at the menu first. (*He reads*) What's your specialty today?
A: Fish and pickle soup.
B: Is it spicy?
A: A little bit. There is black pepper in it.
B: That's okay, as long as there is no chili in it.
C: Why, you don't like chili? Without chili nothing has much taste.
B: Come on. Not everyone is from Sichuan. Let's have that fish soup. What about eggplant and pork in soy sauce?
C: Okay.
B: And fresh-water shrimp?
C: Okay.
A: How would you like the shrimp? Cooked in tomato sauce or scalded in clear water?
B: Scalded. That's the best way to preserve their freshness, and we can dip them in soy sauce and vinegar.
C: Okay. (*To waitress*) Could you recommend one more dish for us?
A: Why don't you have a chafing dish? It's just in for the season. You have a choice of mutton or beef.
C: That's a good suggestion. Mutton, then.

A:先生，您几位？
B:4位，我们想要一个靠近空调的桌子。
A:请这边来。
(*坐下之后*)
A:你们现在点菜吗？
B:稍等一下，让我先看一下菜单。(*他看了一会儿*)今天特价菜是什么？
A:榨菜鱼汤。
B:辣吗？
A:有一点儿。里面放了些黑胡椒。
B:好吧。只要里面没有辣椒。
C:哇，你不喜欢吃辣椒？没有辣椒菜不会很香的。
B:打住，并不是人人都来自四川，要一份鱼汤，茄子和猪肉酱怎么样？
C:好的。
B:淡水虾？
C:好。
A:你们喜欢怎么做虾，是清水煮还是用番茄酱做的？
B:清水煮。这是保鲜的最好方法，我们可以蘸酱油和醋。
C:好的。(*对侍者*)你可以给我们推荐一个菜吗？
A:为什么不来一个火锅呢？现在正是时候，你可以选羊肉或牛肉的。
C:好主意，羊肉火锅。

Conversation 4

A: What shall we order?
B: This is my first time in a Chinese restaurant. Your order, please. Would you tell me how to have Chinese food in a restaurant?
A: All right.
C: Good evening, sir. Here is the menu. Would you like to order now or later?

A:我们点什么菜呢？
B:这是我第一次来中国餐馆。这次你来点菜吧，你可以先介绍一下怎么在中餐馆用餐吗？
A:好的。
C:晚上好，先生。这是菜单。你们是现在点菜还是过一会儿再点？

A: Wait a moment, please. But would you give me a glass of Coca-Cola or something to drink? I'm really thirsty.

A:请等一下。但是请你给我一杯可口可乐或其他一些喝的好吗？我真的很渴。

C: OK. I'll come back in a few minutes.

C:好的，我过几分钟再来。

B: Following the Chinese way, what should we have first?

B:按中国人的习惯，我们应该先点什么呢？

A: You know, in a Chinese restaurant, people always have cold dishes and drinks first, then hot dishes and rice. We make soup or tea the last course.

A:在中国餐馆里吃饭，人们常先边喝酒边吃凉菜，然后是热菜和米饭，最后是汤或茶。

B: Oh. That's really different from ours. We have tea or soup first. It's called an appetizer. Then we'll order the entree. Excuse me, shall we call the waiter now? You know, good food in a restaurant always makes my mouth water.

B:噢，这和我们国家的习惯还真不同。我们先喝茶或汤，这叫开胃汤，然后才点主菜。对不起，我们现在可以叫服务员了吗？每当在饭馆里看到美味，我都有点流口水。

A: Ah, I'm also feeling hungry. Let's talk about it more when the food comes.

A:啊，我也饿了。饭来了后让我们再谈吧。

B: That's a good idea.

B:好主意。

Conversation 5

A: All the food smells tasty today and makes my mouth water.

A:今天所有的食物闻起来都很香，使我都流口水了。

B: Let' s line up here. This line seems a little shorter.

B:我们在这儿排队吧。这一队看起来短些。

A: What's on the menu today?

A:今天的菜单上有什么？

B: Fish, beef, pork, chicken, vegetables and beancurd. For staple food we have rice, steamed bread, stuffed buns and noodles.

B:有鱼、牛肉、猪肉、鸡肉、青菜和豆腐。主食有米饭、馒头、包子和面条。

A: Oh, we 're lucky today, aren't we?

A:噢，今天我们很幸运，是吗？

B: I' d rather take stewed cabbage with beef.

B:我想吃牛肉炖白菜。

A: I think I' ll take fried fish, because fish is one of my favorites.

A:我想吃油炸鱼，因为鱼是我最喜欢的。

B: That' s good, we can share what we have. Here we are. You go ahead. (*They get everything ready*)

B:那太好了，我们可以分享我们的菜。到我们了，你先买。(*他们买好了午饭*)

A: Here is a free table. Let's sit down . Help yourself to some fish please. Isn' t it delicious and appetizing?

A:这里有一张空桌子。我们坐下吧，请吃鱼。难道不美味可口吗？

B: I' m sorry. I don't like it. It's a little too salty.

B:很抱歉我不喜欢。有点咸。

A: I see you people from south prefer sweet, don' t you?

A:我知道你们南方人喜欢吃甜，是吗？

B: Yes, I like the fish cooked in sweet and sour sauce best. Try some beef, please.

B:对，我喜欢吃糖醋鱼。请吃点牛肉吧。

A: Thank you. I' m through with one steamed bread and I'd like a second helping.

A:谢谢你。我已吃完一个馒头了，而且我还想吃一个。

B: Your appetite is good.

B:你的胃口不错。

A:I' m always feeling hungry. | A:我总感到饿。

On the Scene 身临其境 面面俱到

主题:朱迪第一次来中国,饭店服务员向她隆重推荐中国各色菜肴。请你看图,根据如下提供的关键词,将他们的对话写出来。

关键词语:cuisine *n.* 烹饪风格　　menu *n.* 菜单
be pleased to 很高兴　　salty *adj.* 咸的
spicy *adj.* 有风味的　　flavour *n.* 滋味,香味
pungent *adj.* 刺激性的

参考答案

Judy:This is my first visit to China. Could you tell me what different kinds of Chinese cuisine you serve here?

Waiter:As you can see from the menu, we serve Shanghai, Guangdong, Sichuan and Beijing cuisine.

Judy:Could you please tell me about their different features?

Waiter:I would be pleased to. Generally speaking, Guangdong food is a bit light, Sichuan food has a strong and hot taste, Shanghai food is rather oily, and Beijing food is salty and spicy.

Judy:Very interesting. I'd like to know something more about these Chinese cuisines.

Waiter:Well, Sichuan cooking is famous for its rich, hot flavour. It is particular about the use of seasonings. So no two dishes ever taste alike. Some of the famous dishes are pork shreds with fish seasoning, chicken cubes with chili pepper, and spicy braised crucian carp.

Judy:There are so many kinds of dishes of different flavours and they are all so delicious and nutritious. It's hard to decide which to take. But I think I'll have Sichuan food this time as I like hot food, you know. Will you recommend me some dishes?

Waiter:Certainly. But how much would you like to spend, Madam?

Judy:I don't care about the money. I'd like to have some good dishes typically Sichuan.

Waiter:Would you like pork shreds with fish seasoning, chicken cubes with chili peppers and sour pungent soup?

Judy:Very nice. Let me try them.

朱迪:这是我第一次来中国参观。能告诉我你们提供的不同种类的中国菜吗?

侍者:正如您在菜单上看到的。我们供应上海菜、广东菜、四川菜和北京菜。

朱迪:你能告诉我它们各自的特点吗?

侍者:我很乐意。通常来说,广东菜有点儿淡,四川菜有很浓烈的辣味,上海菜相当油腻,北京菜咸而香料味重。

朱迪:很有意思。我想了解更多关于中国菜的情况。

侍者:嗯,四川菜以它的油腻辣味而著称。用调料很特别,因此没有任何两道菜味道相同。一些菜很有名如鱼香肉丝、辣子鸡丁和干烧鲫鱼。

朱迪:有这么多不同风味的菜,它们都很美味,富含营养,很难决定去吃哪一种。但我想这次我要吃四川菜,我喜欢辣菜。你能给我推荐一些菜吗?

侍者:当然可以。但你想花多少钱,女士?

朱迪:我不介意花多少钱,我想吃典型川菜。

侍者:你喜欢鱼香肉丝、辣子鸡和酸辣汤吗?

朱迪:很好,我要尝一下。

★品味西餐★ 5 Western Food

Words and Phrases 闪亮词语 点滴积累

fruit salad 水果色拉
chicken shredded salad 鸡丝色拉
egg salad 蛋色拉
tomato salad 番茄色拉
cucumber salad 黄瓜色拉
chicken & ham salad 火腿鸡肉色拉
crack sausage 克拉香肠
cold roast beef 冷烧小牛肉
cold ham 冷火腿
boulogne sausage 大红肠
cucumber 黄瓜生菜
onion soup 洋葱汤
cream of chicken 奶油鸡丝汤
cream of asparagus; cream asparagus soup 奶油芦笋汤
beef tea 牛肉茶
chicken tea 鸡肉茶
ox tail soup 法式牛尾汤
cream of spinach 奶油菠菜汤
consomme turtle 甲鱼清汤
consomme vegetable 素菜清汤
chicken & ham soup 火腿鸡丁汤
creamed Napoleon soup 拿破仑奶油汤
beef soup with vegetables 牛肉蔬菜汤
beef balls soup 牛肉丸子汤
thick soup 浓汤
light soup 清汤
consommé with cheese fingers 清汤奶酪条
consommé with poached eggs 清汤卧果
broth 肉汤
mixed meat soup 肉杂汤
pureed vegetable soup 蔬菜泥子汤
sour cabbage soup 酸菜汤
soup with macaroni 通心粉汤
mashed pea soup 豌豆泥汤
calf's head soup 小牛头汤
sturgeon soup 鲟鱼汤
minestrone 意大利菠菜汤

Useful Sentences 七彩精句 连点成线

Pizza 比萨饼店

1. *I'll have a small pizza.* 我想要一份小号的比萨饼。
2. *I'd like a medium pizza, please.* 我要一份中号的比萨饼。
3. *I'd like a large, please.* 我要一份大号的。
4. *I'd like thin crust, please.* 我要皮薄的。
5. *I'd like a vegetarian pizza.* 我想要一份蔬菜比萨饼。
6. *I'd like pepperoni and mushrooms.* 我想要份意大利辣香肠蘑菇。
7. *I'd like one medium cheese pizza, please.* 请给我来份中号的干酪比萨饼。
8. *I'd like a small thin crust, sausage and onion.* 我想要份小号的薄片比萨饼,加香肠和洋葱。
9. *I'd like half cheese, half sausage.* 我想要一半干酪,一半香肠的。
10. *I'd like just cheese.* 我要干酪的就行了。
11. *I'd like a pizza with the works.* 我想要份浇头齐全的比萨饼。
12. *I'd like the works.* 我想要份浇头齐全的。
13. *I'd like everything but onions.* 除了洋葱外我全要。
14. *What do you have to drink?* 你那里有什么喝的?
15. *Do you have any specials?* 你们那里有什么特色?
16. *When will that be ready?* 什么时候做好?
17. *I have a coupon.* 我有一张礼券。
18. *How much will it be?* 多少钱?

Cafes 咖啡店里

1. *I'd like a burger and fries.* 我想要一份汉堡包和炸薯条。
2. *I'll have a burger with everything.* 我要一个汉堡包和所有的配料。
3. *I'll have a cheeseburger and fries.* 我想要一个干酪汉堡包和炸薯条。
4. *I'll have an order of fries.* 我想点一份炸薯条。
5. *I'll have a cheeseburger, large fries, and a milk shake.* 我想要一份干酪汉堡包、一大份炸薯条和一份奶昔。
6. *I'll have the roast beef special.* 我要一份烤牛排特色菜。
7. *What about a small sandwich?* 小长条三明治怎么样?
8. *A large bowl of chili, please.* 请来一大份辣椒。
9. *Do you have any vegetable soup?* 你们这儿有蔬菜汤吗?
10. *What about liver and onions?* 洋葱炒猪肝有没有?

Western Food Restaurant 西餐厅

1. *How would you like that prepared?* 你想怎么样烧这道菜?
2. *How would you like your steak prepared?* 你想这牛排怎么烧?
3. *How would you like your steak?* 牛排你要几成熟?
4. *How would you like that done?* 你想怎样烧这道菜?
5. *How would you like that?* 你想怎样烧这菜?
6. *What kind of potatoes would you like?* 你想要哪种土豆?
7. *Mashed, boiled, hashbrowns, or french fries?* 土豆泥,煮土豆,土豆煎饼,还是法式炸薯条?
8. *Would you like a baked potato, fries, or rice?* 你要烤土豆,炸薯条还是米饭?
9. *That comes with a salad.* 这菜配上色拉。
10. *Would you like soup or salad with that?* 你是要配汤还是色拉?
11. *Soup or salad?* 要汤还是色拉?
12. *The soup of the day is split pea or chicken noodle.* 今天的例汤有豌瓣汤或鸡肉面条汤。
13. *Our dressings are Ranch, Italian, Thousand Island, Greek, and house.* 我们这里的调料有大牧场,意大利,千岛,希腊以及本店自己配制的。
14. *Would you like some fresh ground pepper?* 你想要点新鲜的胡椒粉吗?
15. *Say when.* 若够了就关照一声。

Fashion Conversation 鲜活会话 由线到面

Conversation 1

A: I'd like two fish burgers and one large ice tea with plenty of ice, please.	A:我要两份鱼堡,一杯多加冰的冰茶。
B: For here or to go?	B:在这儿吃还是带走?
A: to go, please.	A:带走。
B: Anything else? What about some French fries?	B:再来点别的东西?来点炸土豆条怎样?
A: Thanks. I think that's enough for me.	A:谢谢。我想已经够了。

Conversation 2

A: I'll have the roast beef, please.	A:请给我来盘烤牛肉。
B: Rare, medium or well?	B:是烤生一些,中等还是熟一些?
A: Medium.	A:中等。
B: And what's yours, folk?	B:您呢,先生?
C: I'll have the liver and onion.	C:我要洋葱炒猪肝。
B: O.K. Soup or juice?	B:好的。要汤还是要饮料?
A: What kind of soup do you have?	A:你们有些什么汤?

B: Chicken, tomato, clam chowder,...
A: I like clam chowder.
B: What kind of dressing on your salad?
A: Oil and vinegar.
B: Something to drink?
A: No, we'll split the beer.
B: Anything else?
A: Not me. I have quite enough.
C: Me too.
B: Just a moment, please.

B:有鸡汤、西红柿汤和杂烩汤……
A:我喜欢杂烩汤。
B:色拉上面淋什么调味品?
A:油和醋。
B:来点饮料吗?
A:不了,我们一起喝啤酒。
B:还要点儿别的吗?
A:不要了,我足够了。
C:我也一样。
B:请稍候。

Conversation 3

A: What's the best thing that you ate in the US?
B: I would say the pizza, definitely! They're crazy about it! But, it's really different from Chinese pizza.
A: Why? What's the difference? What' toppings do they have?
B: Well... There are so many different kinds. Let's see... They have all the usual combinations like Hawaiian and Seafood. Of course, Vegetarian is very popular, as well. Plus, there're a lot that I think are really disgusting because they like to put so much cheese on everything!
A: What else is different?
B: They use traditional Italian Pizza ovens, so the crusts are different. One example is the crispy crust, which they bake at a really high temperature so that it comes out really thin and crispy. The dough recipes are different, too. There's whole wheat, sourdough, corn meal and so on.
A: Anything really strange or special?
B: The strangest one that I ever ate was in Chicago. They make something called a Chicago deep-dish pizza. It's made in a special pizza pan with really thick, spongy crust, and twice the number of toppings that you find on other pizzas.

A:在美国你吃到的最好吃的东西是什么?
B:当然是比萨饼了!那些美国人对比萨饼简直痴狂!但是,美国的比萨和我们在中国吃到的可大不相同。
A:为什么这么说?有什么不同?那他们都有什么样的比萨馅料?
B:嗯……在美国比萨饼的种类很多。他们有所有各种口味的组合,像夏威夷风味的和海鲜风味的,当然还有非常流行的素馅比萨。不过,那儿有很多比萨让我觉得倒胃口,因为美国人无论吃什么都喜欢加很多的奶酪。
A:那还有什么别的不同吗?
B:他们使用一种传统的意大利比萨烤炉,所以烤出的比萨的饼底也是千差万别的。举例来说,有一种香脆的饼底,就是一定要在高温下烘烤才能烤出真正又薄又脆的这种比萨来。面粉的成分也是不同的,有全麦的、发面的、玉米面的等等。
A:还有什么奇特的吗?
B:最奇特的就是我在芝加哥吃过的一种比萨。他们创造出这种名为"芝加哥深碟比萨"。它是在一种特殊的比萨盘里制作而成的,它的面饼又厚又软,而且它的馅料是一般比萨饼的两倍呢!

Conversation 4

A: Would you like to order now, sir?
B: Yes, I think so. Xiao Li?
C: Yes, I'll have the salmon teriyaki, please.
A: And what kind of potatoes would you like to go with that?

A:你现在点菜吗,先生?
B:是的。小丽,你来。
C:好的,我要一份红烧马哈鱼。
A:配什么样的土豆?

C: Baked, please. For the vegetable, I'd like broccoli. C: 烧土豆吧。菜嘛，我要花椰菜。

A: And would you care for soup or salad to start with? A: 先来点儿汤还是沙拉？

C: I think I'll have a salad, please. C: 我想我就要沙拉吧。

A: All right. With what kind of dressing? A: 好的。放什么调料？

C: I'd like blue cheese. C: 青丝奶酪。

A: Yes. And you, sir? What will you have? A: 好的。您呢，先生？你要点什么？

B: Those lobster tails on this menu sound pretty good. B: 这儿的去头龙虾听起来不错。

C: Oh, I'm very sorry, sir. We don't have any lobster now. A: 很抱歉，先生，今天我们没有龙虾。

B: No lobster? OK... I guess I'll take the steak then. Rare. B: 没有龙虾？那我就要牛排吧。要嫩的。

A: Yes. What about potatoes? Mashed, boiled or baked? A: 好的。土豆呢？是土豆泥，煮土豆还是烧土豆？

B: Mashed potatoes. For vegetable, I'd like asparagus. B: 土豆泥。蔬菜我要芦笋。

A: And, soup or salad? A: 要汤还是沙拉呢？

B: Oh, I'll try the cream of cauliflower. B: 我想尝一尝奶油菜花汤。

A: Good. Anything to drink while you wait? A: 好。等菜时要点儿喝的吗？

C: An iced water, please. C: 冰水。

B: Make that two. B: 来两杯吧。

Conversation 5

A: May I take your order now? A: 你们可以点菜了吗？

B: We're thinking of having your regular dinner. Can you tell us what courses there are, please? B: 我们想吃你们这儿的套餐。能告诉我们说都有哪几道菜吗？

A: Of course. Our regular diner includes appetizer, soup, salad, choice of the main course, dessert and coffee. A: 当然可以。我们的套餐包括开胃食品、汤、色拉，主菜可选一种，还有点心和咖啡。

B: All right, we'll have it. B: 好的，我们就要套餐吧。

A: Today's mutton chop is very good, would you like to have it as the main course? A: 今天的羊肉不错，主菜就点它吗？

B: That's a good idea. And as for dessert, we'll have apple pie. We'd like to have some coffee afterwards. B: 好主意。至于甜点心，我们要苹果派。饭后给我们来点咖啡。

A: Good, here're your appetizer. Your dinner will be ready in five minutes. A: 好，这是你们的开胃小吃。过五分钟你们的饭菜就好。

Conversation 6

A: Good morning, Mr. Black! A: 您早，布莱克先生！

B: Good morning, Miss Zhang! You are on the dot ('on time). B: 您好，张小姐，你很准时。

A: It took me a lot of trouble to come here. A: 来这里相当麻烦。

B: Yes?
A: The buses were too crowded. I couldn't get on. So, I had to take a taxi.
C: (*waiter*): What can I serve with this morning, sir?
B: Please, my friend first.
C: (*waiter*): Yes, What would you like for breakfast, madame?
A: What do you have for an English breakfast?
C: (*waiter*): Here they are on the menu. You can have toast and butter, two fried eggs, two pieces of bacon, orange or tomato juice, and tea or coffee.
A: I like orange juice, tea, and the others, together with some cheese.
B: I want two soft boiled eggs, two pieces of toast and a cup of coffee. That is all. Don't boil the eggs for more than two minutes.

B:怎么了?
A:公共汽车太挤了,我上不去,所以,我只好坐出租车来。
C:(*侍应生*)先生,今天早上吃点什么?
B:请先问我的朋友。
C:(*侍应生*)是。早餐你喜欢吃什么,女士?
A:英国式的早餐有什么东西呀?
C:(*侍应生*)它们都写在菜单上。你可以要牛油土司、两个煎蛋、两块熏(猪)肉、橙汁或者番茄汁,再来咖啡或茶。
A:我喜欢橙汁、茶和其他连同一些奶酪的东西。
B:我要两个溏心蛋、两片土司和一杯咖啡,这就够了。煮蛋时不要超过两分钟。

On the Scene 身临其境 面面俱到

主题:罗斯和孙小姐来西餐快餐店吃工作午餐。请你看图,根据如下提供的关键词,将他们的对话写出来。

关键词语:Italian noodles with ham 意大利火腿粉
a bowl of gruel 一碗麦片粥
four pieces of sandwiches 四块三明治
a cup of coffee 一杯咖啡
sandwich *n.* 三明治

参考答案

Rose: What would you like for lunch Miss Sun?
Miss Sun: I would like Italian noodles with ham.
Rose: I don't wish for much food now.

Miss Sun: Why? You don't feel hungry?
Rose: Yes. I had quite a breakfast this morning.
Miss Sun: What did you eat?
Rose: I ate a bowl of gruel, four pieces of sandwiches, and a cup of coffee.
Miss Sun: That was a lot, four pieces of sandwiches.
Rose: I was hungry this morning.
Miss Sun: Two pieces of sandwiches would be more than enough.
Rose: Now, let's not talk about breakfast, but lunch.
Miss Sun: As I have said, a bowl of Italian noodles.

罗斯:孙小姐,午餐你喜欢吃什么?
孙小姐:我喜欢吃意大利火腿粉。
罗斯:我现在不想吃很多。
孙小姐:为什么?你不感觉饿吗?
罗斯:是的。早餐我吃得太饱了。
孙小姐:你吃了什么?
罗斯:我吃了一碗麦片粥、四块三明治和一杯咖啡。
孙小姐:四块三明治那是太多了。
罗斯:因为今天早上我很饿。
孙小姐:两块三明治已经够多的了。
罗斯:现在不要谈早餐,还是谈午餐吧。
孙小姐:我已经说过,我要一碗意大利(火腿)粉。

★饮品甜点★ 6 Drink and Pudding

Words and Phrases 闪亮词语 点滴积累

bread 面包
white bread 白面包
black bread 黑面包
cream bun 奶油面包
roll 面包卷;小圆面包
toast 土司;烤面包片
crumb 面包屑
jam 果酱
chicken sandwich 鸡蛋三明治
chicken & ham sandwich 鸡蛋火腿三明治
egg sandwich 鸡蛋三明治
hamburg sandwich 汉堡三明治
cake 蛋糕
cupcake 小蛋糕
birthday cake 生日蛋糕
Christmas cake 圣诞蛋糕
chocolate cake 巧克力蛋糕
pudding 布丁
bread pudding 面包布丁
butter pudding 白脱布丁
Italian cassata 意大利冰糕
lotus flower short cake 荷花酥
orange & almond cream 牛奶蛋冻
strawberry with cream 奶油草莓
hot dog 热狗
pizza 意大利馅饼

Useful Sentences 七彩精句 连点成线

Ask for drinks 要饮料

1. *I want my coffee served now.* 我希望现在上咖啡。
2. *May I have another black coffee, please?* 请再给我一杯黑咖啡,好吗?
3. *Do you like your coffee strong or weak?* 您喜欢咖啡还是淡茶?
4. *I'd like (some) coffee.* 我想要杯咖啡。
5. *I'd like coffee with cream.* 我想要杯奶油咖啡。
6. *I'd like coffee with cream and sugar.* 我想要杯加奶油和糖的咖啡。
7. *I'd like a Coke.* 我想要杯可口可乐。
8. *I'd like some Coke.* 我想要点可口可乐。
9. *I'd like a diet cola.* 我想要杯健怡可乐。
10. *I'd like a mineral water.* 我想要杯矿泉水。

Refreshments 要茶点

1. *Five to four, it's our tea time.* 4点差5分了,是我们的茶点了。
2. *It's tea time now.* 那是茶点时间了。
3. *Would you like Chinese or Indian tea?* 你爱喝中国茶还是印度茶?
4. *Rather weak, please.* 宁愿淡一点。
5. *The tea is excellent, but I find it rather strong. Give me a little more warm water.* 这茶很好,不过对我太浓了,给我一点温开水吧。
6. *Put in some more hot water, but I'm afraid it'll be too weak then.* 那么再放点开水吧。这样一来会不会太淡了呢。
7. *Your tea isn't sweetened yet; here's the sugar-basin; Please help yourself to suit your own taste.* 你的茶还没有加糖;糖缸在这儿,请你按自己的口味放吧。
8. *Here are cakes, will you help yourself to some?* 这是点心,吃一点好吗?
9. *Please take some sandwiches.* 请用点三明治。
10. *I'd like a cream-filled pastry, please.* 请给我来一个奶油馅甜面包。
11. *I'd like a raspberry danish.* 我想要个紫莓丹麦式大白面包。
12. *I'd like a long bread.* 我想要一个条形面包。
13. *I'd like a chocolate donut and a cup of coffee.* 我想要一个巧克力炸面圈和一杯咖啡。
14. *I'd like a big box of donut holes.* 我想要一大盒炸面团。

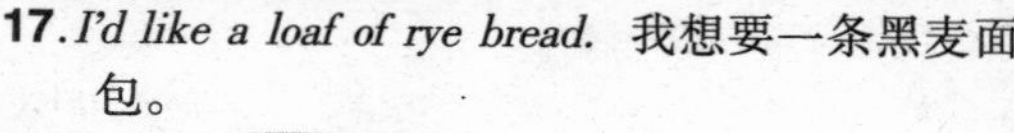

15. *I'd like to order a cake.* 我想订一块蛋糕。
16. *I'd like a dozen cookies.* 我想要一打曲奇。
17. *I'd like a loaf of rye bread.* 我想要一条黑麦面包。

Fashion Conversation 鲜活会话 由线到面

Conversation 1

A: Man, I'm beat! Let's go get some coffee. I know a great cafe where they have a real Italian espresso machine.	A:哥们儿,我累坏了。我们去喝杯咖啡吧!我知道一家很不错的咖啡厅,那儿有货真价实的意大利浓咖啡机。
B: But, I can't drink strong coffee. The taste is just too bitter.	B:但是,我不能喝很浓的咖啡,太苦了。
A: There are lots of different kinds of coffee, so you don't have to drink espresso. You could try a cappuccino. The milk gives it a smoother taste.	A:那里有好多种不同的咖啡呢,所以你不一定非得喝意大利浓咖啡。你可以试试卡布其诺,里面的牛奶使咖啡的味道更加醇美。
B: Actually, I'm kind of hot and I could use a cold drink, if you know what I mean.	B:实际上,我觉得有点儿热,就想喝点冷饮,你明白我的意思吧?
A: Well, you could get an iced coffee or a frappuccion.	A:那好,你可以来一杯冰咖啡或者"星冰乐"。
B: I don't know. I guess a normal black coffee would be OK. How do you know so much about coffee culture?	B:我没听说过。我想我来杯普通的黑咖啡就行了。关于咖啡文化你怎么了解那么多?
A: I used to work at Starbucks!	A:我曾经在"星巴克"工作过!

Conversation 2

A: Would you like to see the menu?	A:您要看菜单吗?
B: No, that's okay. I'll just have ice cream.	B:不用了。我只要点冰淇淋。
A: Oh. Do you want a cone or a cup?	A:噢,您要甜筒装还是杯装?
B: A cup.	B:杯装。
A: How many scoops?	A:几勺呢?
B: Three scoops, but I'll have different flavors.	B:三勺。我要三种不同的口味。
A: Okay. Our flavors are vanilla, chocolate, strawberry, butter pecan, coffee, blue moon and cherry.	A:好的。我们有香草、巧克力、草莓、奶油核桃、咖啡、蓝色月亮,还有樱桃。
B: Hmm... I'll have one scoop of chocolate, one of blue moon, and one of butter.	B:嗯……我要一勺巧克力、一勺蓝色月亮、一勺奶油核桃。
A: Chocolate, blue moon, and butter pecan,... Really?	A:巧克力,蓝色月亮,奶油核桃,是吗?
B: Yes. Why not?	B:是的。怎么了?
A: It is very strange to have blue moon and butter pecan in the same cup.	A:蓝色月亮和奶油核桃放在一起比较奇怪。
B: But that's what I want.	B:但我点的就是这些。
A: Are you sure?	A:你肯定吗?
B: Yes. Do you serve?	B:我肯定,你这样卖吗?
A: Sure. I'll get it for you.	A:好的。我装给你。

Conversation 3

A: Can you tell me how to make tea with dried tealeaves in a teapot, please?	A:你能告诉我如何用茶壶把茶叶沏成茶吗?
B: Yes, with pleasure. First get the boiling water ready. Before you put some dried tealeaves in a teapot, warm the pot with hot water and empty it out. Put tealeaves into the pot, add fresh boiling water and then leave them to steep for three minutes before serving.	B:非常乐意。首先准备好沸腾的开水。把茶叶放入茶壶之前,先用热水把茶壶涮一下,然后将水倒掉。放入茶叶,倒入沸水,泡3分钟后即可饮用。
A: Could I add flavors to it by putting some chrysanthemum flowers or ginseng?	A:我可不可以放些菊花或人参以改善其口感呢?
B: Sure. You can also add milk or squeeze lemon into it. Some people even serve tea with sugar. I, however, prefer to have pure clear tea.	B:当然可以。也可以加牛奶或柠檬汁。有些人喝茶时还喜欢加糖。可我喜欢喝清茶。
A: But I like it mixed with milk. It is both nutritious and refreshing.	A:我喜欢喝茶时加牛奶,既营养又提神。
B: You said it. Each person has his own preference.	B:你说得对。每人都有其个人的偏好。
A: Do you drink tea very often?	A:你经常喝茶吗?
B: Sure. I drink several cups of tea a day and I enjoy the mild soothing aroma rising from the tea cup to my nostrils.	B:当然了,我每天喝好几杯茶,我喜欢闻从茶杯中飘出的淡淡的沁人肺腑的清香。

Conversation 4

A: Did you know that eating chocolate gives you the same feeling as being in love?	A:知道吗,吃巧克力可以带给你恋爱般的感觉啊。
B: I guess that's why we give chocolate on Valentine's Day.	B:我想这大概就是我们在情人节送巧克力的原因吧。
A: That makes sense. What kind of chocolate bars do you like to eat? Do you like milk chocolate, white chocolate or dark chocolate?	A:有道理。你喜欢吃什么样的巧克力?牛奶巧克力,白巧克力还是黑巧克力?
B: White chocolate is too sweet, but when they put lots of almonds in it, it's OK. Dark chocolate is too bitter, but it's good for making chocolate chip cookies. I guess my favorite is good, old-fashioned milk chocolate. It's the best!	B:白巧克力太甜了,不过要是里面有很多杏仁的话,就好多了。黑巧克力又太苦了,但是做成巧克力夹心曲奇就好吃多了。我看我最喜欢的还是传统的牛奶巧克力。这才是最好的!
A: I like chocolate everything! I like chocolate milk, chocolate ice cream, chocolate mousse and chocolate covered nuts and raisins.	A:只要是巧克力我就喜欢!我喜欢喝巧克力奶,吃巧克力冰淇淋,巧克力奶油甜点,还有带坚果和葡萄干的巧克力。
B: You know, chocolate is made from cocoa beans. The Mexican Indians invented cocoa powder. They used it to make hot chocolate. The Spanish brought it to Europe and from there it went everywhere. Now everybody's crazy about chocolate.	B:你知道,巧克力是由可可豆制成的。墨西哥的印第安人发明了可可粉。他们用可可粉制作热巧克力。西班牙人把它带到欧洲,然后再从那里传遍世界各地。现在每个人都为巧克力而疯狂。
A: Me too! I'm really addicted. I guess I'm a choco-	A:我也是!我真的是吃上瘾了。我想我是个巧克

holic! | 力狂!

Conversation 5

A: Would you like anything to drink? | A:你喜欢喝点什么吗?
B: A cup of lemon tea. | B:是的,一杯柠檬茶。
A: What about some beer? | A:来点啤酒怎么样?
B: No, thanks. I don't drink beer at noon. | B:不,谢谢你,中午我不喝啤酒。
A: Why? | A:为什么?
B: Because my face turns red. | B:因为我的脸会红。
A: What's wrong with that? | A:那样不好吗?
B: It's just not good. | B:实在是不好。
A: Do you feel dizzy? | A:你觉得头晕吗?
B: A little bit, not much. | B:有一点,不太厉害。
A: That's why you consider it not good. | A:所以你便认为这样不好。

Conversation 6

A: What will you order for lunch? | A:午餐你要些什么呢?
B: I'll just have a piece of cake and a cup of tea. | B:我只要一块糕和一杯茶。
A: What kind of cake will you take? | A:你要什么蛋糕?
B: I want a piece of sponge cake with raisins. | B:我要一块葡提蛋糕。
A: This shop always serves good cakes. | A:这家店供应的糕饼不错。
B: Waiter, a cup of lemon tea, a piece of sponge cake with raisins, and a cup of tea. | B:侍应生,一杯柠檬茶、一块葡提子蛋糕和一杯茶。
A: Thank you, Mr. Johnson. You're always very kind to me by inviting me out for lunches. | A:谢谢你,约翰逊先生,你经常请我吃午饭,你太好了。
B: Oh, it's nothing. I enjoy inviting you to lunches. | B:哦,没有什么,我喜欢邀请你吃饭。

On the Scene 身临其境 面面俱到

主题:天气很热,汤姆和玛丽来到冰淇淋屋吃冰淇淋。请你看图,根据如下提供的关键词,将他们的对话写出来。

关键词语:parlor *n.* 小摊　　special *n.* 专车
strawberry *n.* 草莓　　yogurt *n.* 酸奶酪
absolutely *adv.* 完全地　　traditional *adj.* 传统的

参考答案

Tom: Wow! It's hot today! Do you want to get an ice cream cone?

Mary: No. Let's go to an ice cream parlor! They have way more flavors to choose from there. I feel like having something special like Neapolitan ice cream.

Tom: What's that?

Mary: It's three different flavors mixed together. Chocolate, strawberry and something green with candied fruit.

Tom: Do they have ice cream bars, frozen yogurt or frozen chocolate mousse?

Mary: Absolutely! They also have real Italian gelati and French sorbets. They do a great baked Alaska.

Tom: Maybe vanilla ice cream milkshake would be good. What's your favorite flavor?

Mary: Well... I like the traditional flavors like rum raisin, butter pecan, maple walnut, strawberry, chocolate and vanilla. But now there are some new flavors from Asia like green tea and durian.

Tom: God! Even talking about it makes me feel like I'm gaining weight!

Mary: That's OK. We can go jogging after we eat!

汤姆:天呀,今天可真热!想吃圆筒冰淇淋吗?

玛丽:别呀,我们还是去冰淇淋屋吧!那里有更多的口味可供选择。我想吃点特别口味的,比如"那不勒斯"冰淇淋。

汤姆:那是什么?

玛丽:它是把三种口味混合在一起。有巧克力,草莓和一些绿色的果脯。

汤姆:他们有雪糕、冰冻的酸奶或者冰冻的巧克力奶油冻吗?

玛丽:当然有了!他们还有纯正的意大利胶凝冰糕和法国的果汁冰糕。他们最拿手的是"火焰雪山"冰淇淋。

汤姆:还是香草冰淇淋奶昔好些。你最喜欢什么口味的奶昔?

玛丽:嗯……我还是喜欢比较传统的口味,比如朗姆酒葡萄干、奶油山核桃、枫糖核桃、草莓、巧克力和香草口味,但是现在有几种来自亚洲的新口味,像绿茶口味和榴莲口味。

汤姆:天呀!光是说说这些就让我觉得发胖了!

玛丽:没关系,吃完我们可以去慢跑。

★酒品小尝★ 7 Alcoholic Drinks

Words and Phrases 闪亮词语 点滴积累

small beer 淡啤酒
barley broth 烈性啤酒
draught beer 生啤酒
short; dark beer 黑啤酒
fruit wine 果子酒
verjuice 酸果汤
collins 冰镇果子酒
wine made of sorghum; kaoliang wine 高粱酒
Wujiapi liquor 五加皮
cider; applejack 苹果酒
tiger-bone liquor 虎骨酒
Shaoxing wine 绍兴酒
red (grapes) wine; ruby; port wine 红葡萄酒
sherry 雪利酒
gin; geneva; jacky 杜松子酒
cocktail 鸡尾酒
champagne 大香槟；香槟酒
vodka 伏特加酒
rum 朗姆酒
whisky 威士忌酒
brandy 白兰地
brandy of French 法国白兰地

Useful Sentences 七彩精句 连点成线

Asking for order 寻问

1. *What's yours?* 你想要点什么？
2. *What'll you have?* 你想要点什么？
3. *What'll it be, friend?* 要点什么，朋友？
4. *What do you have on tap?* 你们桶里有什么样的啤酒？
5. *What kind of beer do you have?* 你们这里有什么样的啤酒？
6. *What beers you got?* 你们有什么啤酒？
7. *What kinds of wine do you have?* 你们有什么样的酒？
8. *Do you have any imported beer?* 你们这里有进口啤酒吗？

Order 点酒

1. *I'll have a beer.* 我想来杯啤酒。
2. *I'll have a Bud.* 我想要杯百威啤酒。
3. *I'll have a draft.* 我要一杯生啤。
4. *Make it a cold one.* 给我来瓶冰冻啤酒。
5. *Pour me a beer.* 给我倒杯啤酒。
6. *I'd like a glass of beer.* 我想要杯啤酒。
7. *I'd like a stein of beer.* 我想要杯啤酒。
8. *I'd like a pitcher of beer.* 我想要杯低度啤酒。
9. *I'd like a dark beer.* 我想要杯度数高的啤酒。
10. *I'd like a domestic beer.* 我想要一杯国产啤酒。
11. *I'd like a draft beer.* 我想要一杯生啤酒。
12. *I'd like an ale.* 我想要杯麦芽酒。
13. *I'd like a lager.* 我想要杯贮藏啤酒。
14. *I'd like a glass of wine.* 我想要杯葡萄酒。
15. *I'd like some champagne.* 我想要点香槟。
16. *I'd like a scotch.* 我想要杯苏格兰威士忌酒。
17. *I'd like a scotch on the rocks.* 我想要杯加冰块的苏格兰威士忌酒。
18. *I'd like a whiskey with soda.* 我想要杯加汽水的威士忌酒。
19. *I'd like a gin and tonic.* 我想要杯杜松子药酒。
20. *I'd like a gin and tonic with a twist.* 我想要杯加片柠檬的杜松子酒。
21. *I prefer a dry Martini or a dry wine.* 要干马提尼酒。
22. *Give me another.* 再给我来一杯。
23. *I'd like it on the rocks.* 我喜欢酒里放冰块。

Fashion Conversation 鲜活会话 由线到面

Conversation 1

A: Thank God, it's Friday! Time for a drink! Let's hit the bars!	A:谢天谢地,今天是星期五!是该去喝几杯的时候了!我们去酒吧吧!
B: OK. I don't mind going bar hopping with an expert like you.	B:好的,我可不介意和你这样一个专家一个酒吧接着一个酒吧地去喝。
A: Should we start with beer or wine or go straight to the hard liquor?	A:我们是先喝啤酒或葡萄酒,还是直接喝烈性酒呢?
B: I think I'll have a glass of wine. Let's see... they have red wine, white wine and port. They even have sangria! It's the happy hour special.	B:我想我会要一杯葡萄酒。让我想想……他们那儿有红葡萄酒,白葡萄酒和波尔多红葡萄酒,他们连桑格利亚汽酒都有!现在正是特价时间。
A: Port's too sweet. It's a dessert wine. A dry red French wine would be nice with meat. A glass of chilled white German wine would be good with fish. But, we're not eating and it's hot out, so I think I'll have a tall glass of sangria with ice.	A:波尔多红葡萄酒太甜了,属于餐后酒。那种微酸的法国红葡萄酒要在吃肉的时候喝,一杯冰镇的德国白葡萄酒要在吃鱼的时候喝。但是,现在外面太热了,我们又没在进餐,我还是来一杯加冰的桑格利亚汽酒吧。
B: Good choice! But, what's your favorite kind of hard liquor?	B:不错!你最喜欢哪种烈性酒?
A: I like to stick to the clean stuff, like vodka, gin, white rum and other clear spirits. They don't give me a bad hangover the next day.	A:我喜欢喝白酒,像伏特加、琴酒、白朗姆酒等,它们不会让我宿醉到第二天早上。

Conversation 2

A: Good evening, Mr. Frank. Bourbon on the rocks?	A:弗兰克先生,晚上好!波旁威士忌加小冰块?
B: No, this time I'll try Chinese alcohol.	B:不,这次我要尝尝中国酒。
A: What about Mao Tai, one of the most famous liquors in China. It's good indeed; it never goes to the head.	A:茅台怎么样?它是中国知名白酒。这酒真的不错,不上头。
B: Do people here drink a lot of liquors?	B:这儿的人喝很多白酒吗?
A: Some do, and some don't. Many people in the north are fond of liquors. I think it has something to do with the climate.	A:有的人喝很多,有的人不喝。很多北方人喜欢白酒。我想这与气候有关。
B: Yes, it has. Have you ever heard "Tequila Santa"?	B:确实有关。你听说过龙舌兰酒吗?
A: Yes, it's a very well-known kind of spirits in Mexico. People drink it with salt and lemon.	A:听说过。它是墨西哥名酒。人们喝这种酒时加盐和柠檬。
B: Right. It's very strong. Just like alcohol. (***Frank sips Mao Tai***) Oh, it's good. Are there any other famous Chinese liquors?	B:是的。这种酒劲儿很大,就像是烈酒。(*弗兰克啜了一小口茅台*)噢,不错。还有什么其他的中国酒吗?
A: Yes, besides Mao Tai, we have Wu Liang Ye, Fen Jiu, Xi Feng and so on.	A:有,除了茅台,白酒类我们还有五粮液、汾酒、西凤酒等等。
B: They say that Shao Xing wine tastes quite good. What's it?	B:听说绍兴酒味道不错,它是什么酒?

A: It's rice wine, a kind of still wine, somewhat like Japanese Sark.
B: I see. Thank you for telling me so much. I'll try them next time.
A: I'm always at your service.

A：米酒，是一种没有气体的酒。有点儿像日本的萨克酒。
B：我明白了。谢谢你给我介绍了这么多，下次再品尝那些酒吧。
A：愿意为您效劳。

Conversation 3

A: Tonight is party night! What drinks will we need?
B: Well, not everyone will want to drink beer. Make sure there's some soft drinks.
A: I don't think we need to much soft drink. Two bottles of cola will do. What about wine?
B: Just buy cask wine. Now, have you gotten ice yet?
A: No, once I've filled the tub with beer cans, then I'll get ice. If the cans are buried under the ice they'll be colder, and the colder beer is, the better.
B: I think a bottle of champagne would be a good idea.
A: Yuk! Well, if you say so. Personally I'd rather die of thirst than drink champagne.

A：今晚是个派对之夜。我们喝什么样的饮料？
B：不是每个人都想喝啤酒的。记得准备些饮料。
A：我想，我们并不需要太多的饮料。买两瓶可乐就行了。买什么酒呢？
B：就买桶装酒吧！你们这有冰吗？
A：没有。我要先把桶装满啤酒罐，然后才去弄冰块。如果酒罐埋在冰块下，很快就能变凉的，啤酒越凉越好。
B：我觉得买瓶香槟也不错。
A：哈哈，如果你们说要买就买吧。我个人是宁可渴死也不喝香槟的。

Conversation 4

A: Neva, this is a nice bar!
B: Yes, we made a wise decision.
A: Where would you like to sit, Neva?
B: I'd like to sit not too near the piano so that I can watch the musicians from a distance.
A: Great. That's just after my thought.
C: Good evening. Would you like something to drink?
A: Yes, but give us a few minutes first.
C: Certainly, Ma'am. Please take your time.
A: Let's see... Cocktail, Brandies, Wines, Scotch..., I'll have beer, Budwiser. What about you, Neva?
B: I'll have coconut juice. Do they have that?
A: I think so. Let's see. Hello, Bartender, one tin of coconut juice for him and a bottle of Budwiser for me.
C: Yes, sir. Just a moment.
C: Here are your beer and juice. And the bill.
A: Yes, thank you.
C: You're welcome!

A：内瓦，这是个很好的酒吧。
B：是的。我们做了个聪明的决定。
A：内瓦，你想坐哪儿？
B：我想坐在离钢琴不太近的地方，这样我们可以从远处观看乐队。
A：太好了。和我想的一样。
C：晚上好。来点什么喝的吗？
A：是的，不过我们先看看菜单。
C：当然。请慢慢看吧。
A：我看看，……鸡尾酒、白兰地、葡萄酒、苏格兰威士忌……我要啤酒，百威。你呢，内瓦？
B：我要椰子汁。他们有吗？
A：我想有。喂，服务生，一听椰子汁给他，我要一瓶百威啤酒。
C：好的，请稍等。
C：你们的啤酒和椰子汁，还有账单。
A：好的，谢谢。
C：不客气。

Conversation 5

A: What happened to this place? Everything's glowing green.

B: They remodeled. Their new theme is outer space. It's awesome, isn't it?

A: It's frightening how such bad taste is becoming popular...

B: But the drinks taste great! I think I'll have a Bloody Mary.

A: I'm going to have my usual.

B: A non-alcoholic beer? Come on, drink a beer and kill a few brain cells. You've got plenty.

A: OK, I'll have a Heineken on draft. But stop me before I have too many.

A:这地方怎么了?每个东西都泛着绿光。

B:他们重新装潢过了。他们的新主题是外层空间。美呆了,不是吗?

A:这种烂品味还能流行得起来,实在是挺吓人的……

B:但是饮料的口味挺棒的!我想我要点一杯血腥玛丽。

A:我还是喝老样子。

B:不含酒精的啤酒吗?拜托,来杯啤酒杀一些脑细胞吧,你有的是。

A:好吧,我要来一扎喜力啤酒。但别让我喝太多了。

On the Scene 身临其境 面面俱到

主题:贝雷先生来到宾馆内设的酒吧来品尝中国酒,侍者给他调配了上海鸡尾酒。请你看图,根据如下提供的关键词,将他们的对话写出来。

关键词语:cocktail *n.* 鸡尾酒　mixture *n.* 混合物

bartender *n.* 酒吧服务员　excellent *adj.* 卓越的

参考答案

Bartender: Good evening, sir.

Mr. Bellow: Good evening.

Bartender: Ah, yes, sir. Are you staying at our hotel?

Mr. Bellow: Yes, I'm in Room 908.

Bartender: Thank you, Mr. Bellow. Have you anything in mind as to what to drink or may I make a few suggestions?

Mr. Bellow: I have had enough Gin Fizz and Bloody Marys. But I have no idea about Chinese cocktails.

Bartender: Would you prefer our cocktail —— Shanghai cocktail? It's a mixture of real Chinese ingredients.

Mr. Bellow: That's good.

(***The bartender makes the cocktail for Mr. Bellow and hands it to him***)

Bartender: Here is your Shanghai cocktail, sir.

Mr. Bellow: Thank you. Oh, it tastes excellent.
Bartender: It's a new cocktail of our hotel.
Mr. Bellow: How do you mix it? I'd love to try it myself when I am back home.
Bartender: (*He tells Bellow how to make Shanghai cocktail*)...
Mr. Bellow: I hope I can mix it myself. By the way, do you take credit cards here or shall I pay in cash?
Bartender: Since you are staying at our hotel you may sign the bill. The hotel will charge you when you leave.
Mr. Bellow: Thank you.
Bartender: You are most welcome, sir. Goodbye.
Mr. Bellow: Bye-bye.
侍者:晚上好,先生。
贝雷先生:晚上好。
侍者:哎,先生,你现在住在我们的宾馆吗?
贝雷先生:是的,在908号房。
侍者:谢谢你的光临,贝雷先生。你需要什么,喝点什么,我向你推荐。
贝雷先生:我对金酒菲士和血腥玛利非常熟悉了,但对中国的鸡尾酒一点不知道。
侍者:那要不要品尝一下我们的鸡尾酒——上海鸡尾酒,中国独特配方的酒。
贝雷先生:好的。
(*侍者调好酒,递送给贝雷先生*)
侍者:这就是我们上海的鸡尾酒,先生。
贝雷先生:谢谢,噢,尝起来不错。
侍者:它是我们宾馆最新潮的酒。
贝雷先生:你们怎样做的,我想回家自己尝试一下。
侍者:(*他告诉贝雷先生鸡尾酒怎么做的*)……
贝雷先生:我希望能做成。顺便问一下,这里是信用卡签付还是现金支付?
侍者:既然你现住在宾馆,只要签个单子就行了。到你退房时,宾馆直接跟你结账。
贝雷先生:谢谢。
侍者:欢迎光临,再见。
贝雷先生:再见。

★时尚发型★ 8 Fashionable Hairstyles

Words and Phrases 闪亮词语 点滴积累

shampoo cream 洗发膏
hair darkening cream 染发膏
hair styling cream 定型发膏
ultrarapid hair conditioner 生发露
limb depilatory 脱毛露
hair oil/tonic 发油;头油
brilliantine;(hair) vaseline 发蜡
vitamin hair oil 维生素发油
hair styling mousse 定型摩丝
nourishing hair conditioner 营养护发素
lemon cream rinse 柠檬护发素
hair lotion 美发水
rinse 洗发液
shampoo 洗液;洗剂
cream shampoo;shampoo liquid 洗发精;洗发水
hair shampoo 头发香波
amino cream shampoo 氨基酸型波
hair dye 染发药水
curls 卷发
wave set 卷发器
shaving cream 剃须水
hair remover 脱毛剂

Useful Sentences 七彩精句 连点成线

Styles 发型

1. *What kind of hairstyle do you prefer?* 您喜欢哪种发型?
2. *My hair is very thick, so what kind of hairstyle will be easiest to maintain?* 我的头发很厚,哪种发型比较容易整理?
3. *This shoulder-length featherish style will make your face look slimmer.* 齐肩的羽毛剪发型可使你的脸型看起来修长些。
4. *Just a little trim around the sides.* 只要在两侧附近,稍微修剪一下。
5. *I'd like an Afro-hairstyle.* 我想要非洲式的发型。
6. *What hairstyle do you feel will look best on me?* 你觉得什么样的发型看起来最适合我?
7. *I'm afraid I dislike this style.* 恐怕我不喜欢这个发型。
8. *Show me some pictures of different styles.* 给我看一些不同发型的照片。
9. *Can you do my hair in this style?* 你能帮我做这种发型吗?
10. *How would you like set, madam?* 夫人,您想做什么样的发型?
11. *Would you like to look up the computer to see which one fits you best?* 您要不要看电脑,看一看哪一种发型对您最合适?
12. *Here are the photos of the latest hair styles, ma'am.* 夫人,给您最新发式照片。
13. *You'll look very smart with this hair-do, ma'am.* 夫人,您理这个发式会显得很时髦。
14. *How would you like your hairstyle today?* 您今天想要做个什么发型?

Shampoos 洗发

1. *I want to have a shampoo and blowdry.* 我要洗发,然后吹干。
2. *What time do you prefer?* 你想约几点?
3. *What kind of shampoo do you prefer?* 您喜欢用哪种洗发精?
4. *I brought my own shampoo and conditioner. Here you go.* 我自己带了洗发精和润丝精,在这里。
5. *Let's rinse your hair now.* 我们现在去冲水。
6. *The water is too hot/cold.* 水太烫/冷了。
7. *If you wash and style your hair too often, it will make your hair look dull.* 你若经常洗发、做造型,那会使你的头发看起来没光泽。
8. *I'd like to have my hair washed and set.* 我想洗头,并且做头发。
9. *I'd like a shampoo.* 我想洗头。
10. *No hair oil, please.* 不要发油,谢谢。

11. *What kind of shampoo would you like, Madam?* 太太，您喜欢哪种洗发香波？
12. *I'm using a dandruff shampoo.* 我正在用去头屑洗发精。
13. *Would you just hold this towel over your eyes while I give you a rinse?* 请您用这块毛巾遮住眼睛，我要给您冲洗一下。

Haircut 剪发

1. *I'd like to get a haircut.* 我想要剪头发。
2. *Could you recommend a stylist for me?* 你可以帮我推荐一位设计师吗？
3. *We close at 9: 30, so the latest appointment for cutting is 7 o'clock.* 我们 9:30 打烊，剪发的预约最晚到 7 点。
4. *I'd like my hair cut to shoulder-length.* 我想把头发剪到肩膀的长度。
5. *My hair has lost it's shape. I need to get a haircut.* 我的头发都没型了，得修剪一下。
6. *I want my hair cut very short, so in the morning I can just get up and go.* 我想把头发剪得很短，这样早上我可以一起床就走。
7. *I'd like you to use clippers (scissors, razor).* 我希望你用推子(剪刀、剃刀)。
8. *Don't cut it too short.* 别剪太短。
9. *Take some more off the side.* 旁边多剪些。
10. *Go easy with the electric clipper, I just want a trim.* 电剪拿轻一点，我只是要修剪一下。
11. *I'd like a crew cut.* 我要剪平头。
12. *Can you do something about my split-ends?* 你能不能处理我头发的分叉？

Perms 烫发

1. *What is the latest time that I can make an appointment?* 最晚可以预约到几点？
2. *Do you have a particular stylist in mind?* 您要特定的造型师吗？
3. *If you want to make an appointment to have a perm, it should be no later than 4 o'clock.* 如果你要预约烫头发的话，最晚不能超过 4 点。
4. *What kind of services would you like to have that day?* 您那天想做些什么样的服务呢？
5. *Do you offer sleeked perms?* 你们有离子烫吗？
6. *I want to perm my hair very curly like corkscrew curls.* 我想要烫得卷，像有许多螺旋般。
7. *I'd like to get a perm, but I don't want my hair to look too curly.* 我想烫头发，但我不要烫得太卷。
8. *My hair looks deadly flat. I'd like to have a perm today.* 我的头发看起来好塌，我今天想烫头发。
9. *How curly do you want your perm?* 您想要多卷？
10. *Your hair is a little flat, so you might get a body perm to add a little volume.* 你的发型有点平，你可以做个弹性烫，使发量看来多些。
11. *Your hair is not in good condition right now, so you had better come back to do the perm next month.* 你的头发现在不太健康，最好下个月再来烫头发。
12. *Do you want a cold wave, madam?* 女士，您想冷烫头发吗？
13. *What will you have a perm or a set?* 您要电烫还是用发卷做头发？
14. *Do you want a permanent wave or a cold wave?* 您想电烫还是冷烫？
15. *We have many kinds of permanent: regular, cold perm, straight perm and foam.* 我们有很多种烫法：普通烫、冷烫、直发烫和泡沫烫。

Highlights 染发

1. *I dislike this color.* 我不喜欢这种颜色。
2. *I'd like to dye my hair brown.* 我想把头发染成棕色。
3. *My mother want to have a highlights.* 我妈妈想染发。
4. *I want some highlights today.* 我今天想做染发。
5. *What kind of colors do you suggest that I dye my hair?* 你建议我把头发染成什么色？
6. *Do I need to dye my hair?* 我需要染发吗？
7. *What color do you want for your highlights?* 你想挑染成什么色？
8. *If you want to dye your hair blond, I'll have to bleach it first.* 如果您要染成金色的话，我必须先帮你的头发做漂白。
9. *Intricate highlighting is very popular now.* 挑染现在很流行。
10. *If you don't want the highlights to look too loud, you should choose only one or two shades lighter*

than your natural color. 如果你不想挑染得看起来太抢眼的话,你应该选择比你的自然发色只淡一点点的颜色。

Hair treatment 护发

1. *Do you need a steam treatment?* 要做一下护发吗?
2. *I just want a trim and the steam treatment.* 我只要修一下,再做护发。
3. *I'd like to have a steam treatment.* 我想做一下护发。
4. *My hair splits very badly, what should I do?* 我头发分叉很严重,我该怎么办?
5. *Would you like to have the steam treatment today?* 您今天想做一下护发保养吗?
6. *Your hair is very dry. You might consider a steam treatment.* 你的头发很干,可以考虑做一下保养。
7. *You can try this leave-in conditioner. It will keep your hair from tangling.* 你可试用这种不用冲水的护发乳,它可预防你的头发打结。
8. *I want to have a steam treatment today.* 我今天想做一下护发。
9. *To protect your hair, you should coat it with a protective spray.* 为了保护头发,你应该在头发上喷一层护发露。
10. *Your hair is naturally wavy, so it gets fuzzy easily.* 你是自然卷,所以你的头发容易起毛毛的。

Fashion Conversation 鲜活会话 由线到面

Conversation 1

A: All right, sir. It's your turn. Sorry to have kept you waiting.
B: That's OK.
A: How do you like your hair cut?
B: Cut it short in the back, and part it in the middle.
A: How's that, sir?
B: Please part it a little farther to the left.
A: How about that?
B: Very good.
A: Will you please tilt your head to the right?
B: Certainly. I'm afraid both sides aren't even.
A: Then I'll snip off a little more. How's that?
B: Fine. How much do I owe you?
A: That's $4.
B: Here's five dollars. Keep the change.
A: Thanks.

A:好了,先生,现在该你了。真对不起让你等那么久。
B:没关系。
A:你想要个什么发式?
B:把后面剪短一点,并留个中分式。
A:先生,怎么分?
B:请把它分得稍靠左一点。
A:这么样行吗?
B:非常好。
A:请你把头向左边倾斜一下好吗?
B:当然可以。我恐怕两边头发不一样齐。
A:接着我将稍剪短一点。这回怎么样?
B:好。理发费是多少?
A:4 美元。
B:这是 5 美元,剩余的为小费。
A:谢谢。

Conversation 2

A: Good morning, sir. Please take a seat here.
B: Thank you. Just a haircut, please.
A: Certainly, sir. Would you like some shampoo?
B: Yes. Do you have any dandruff shampoo?
A: Yes. I'll use it. Will you step down and bend over the basin?
B: Sure. Will you please put some more hair tonic on?

A:早上好,先生。请坐这个位子。
B:谢谢。我只理发。
A:好的,先生。您要洗头吗?
B:是的,你们有去头皮屑的洗发精吗?
A:有。我会用的。请您到水槽边弯下好吗?
B:当然可以。请帮我多抹点护发素好吗?

A:Certainly. Your part is on the right,isn't it?
A:好的。您的头发向右分,对不对?

B:That's right.
B:对。

A:How does that look,sir?
A:看起来怎么样,先生?

B:Splendid.
B:棒极了。

A:Now you're through,sir.
A:现在全好了,先生。

B:Thanks. How much?
B:谢谢。多少钱?

A:Ten yuan.
A:10 块钱。

B:Sorry. I have no change, only a one hundred yuan note with me.
B:对不起,没有零钱,只有一张 100 的。

A:It doesn't matter. Just a moment, please. I'll go and get the change for you. Here's your change, sir.
A:没关系。请稍等。我去取找钱给您。给您找钱,先生。

B:Thank you.
B:谢谢。

Conversation 3

A:What can I do for you,sir?
A:我能为您效劳吗,先生?

B:I'd like a haircut and a shave,please.
B:请给我理理发,修修面。

A:Well,how would you like your hair-cut,sir?
A:好的,先生,您想把头发理成什么样的?

B:Just a trim,please.
B:只修剪一下就行。

A:OK. . . Is it OK?
A:好的……这样行吗?

B:Please cut the sides shorter,but not so much at the back.
B:两边再剪短些,但后面不要剪得太多。

A:It's such a hot season, isn't it? May I suggest thinning out the top?
A:天气太热了,不是吗?把头顶的头发剪得薄些吗?

B:That's a good idea. But only a little,and leave the front as it is now.
B:好主意。但稍微剪薄点就行,前面的头发保持原样。

A:Now,is it OK?
A:瞧,行吗?

B:I still prefer a little more off the temple.
B:鬓角应再剪短些。

A:OK. . . Is it satisfactory?
A:好的……这样您满意吗?

B:Very satisfactory. And now for the shave? My beard is rough.
B:非常满意。现在该修面了吧?我的胡须很硬。

A:Don't worry,sir. I've never cut a customer. . . Shall I trim your moustache?
A:先生,您不用担心,我从未刮伤过任何顾客……要我给您修一下胡须吗?

B:Yes,please.
B:好的。

A:Now it's done. How does it look?
A:现在好啦,看起来如何?

Conversation 4

A:Very sorry to have kept you waiting so long. What do you want,madam?
A:很抱歉让您等了这么久。您的头发怎么做,夫人?

B:I want to have a haircut and a permanent.
B:先剪一下然后再烫。

A:How do you like your haircut today?
A:今天头发怎么剪?

B:Would you cut it a little?
B:能稍微剪一些吗?

A:Then, do you want a tight, medium or natural curly permanent?
A:要大花,中花,还是自然卷?

B:I'd like to have it medium.
B:我喜欢中花。

A:How about your hair-style?
A:发型呢?

B: Can you name some choices? B:你能提些建议吗?

A: We have various kinds of patterns such as hair bobbed, chaplet hair style, hair done in a bun. A:我们有各种发型,如:剪短发,烫花,盘头。

B: I want a chaplet one. B:我想烫花。

A: Which wave do you prefer? A:要多大的花呢?

B: I like to have it in big waves. B:要大波浪。

A: It looks wonderful. A:看上去很漂亮。

B: Turn the chair so that I can see myself in the mirror. B:转一下椅子让我自己看看。

A: What do you think of it? A:您觉得怎么样?

B: Beautifully done. Many thanks. B:做得不错,谢谢。

Conversation 5

A: Good morning, sir. A:早上好,先生。

B: Good morning. I'd like to have some highlights. B:早上好。我想染发。

A: I'm sorry, but would you mind waiting? We're awfully busy right now. A:对不起,您介意等一下吗?我们现在正忙着。

B: No, of course not. Do you have today's newspaper or latest magazine? B:不,当然不介意。你们有今天的报纸或者近期的杂志吗?

A: No. But you can watch TV, there's a good performance on it. A:没有。但您可以看看电视,有好节目呢。

B: OK. That will do. B:好的,那样也行。

A: All right, sir. It's your turn now. I'm so sorry to have kept you waiting. Thank you for your patience. A:好了,先生。现在轮到您了。真抱歉让您等了那么久,谢谢您的耐心。

B: It's nothing. B:没什么。

A: What color do you like? A:您喜欢什么颜色?

B: Natural color. Please. B:自然色。

A: Ok. How about some hair tonic? A:好的,要不要用一些护发剂?

B: No, thanks. B:不,谢谢。

Conversation 6

A: OK, next! A:好啦,下一位是谁?

B: I am. I want a hair-cut. B:是我。请理发。

A: I'm sorry to keep you waiting. We are busy today. A:对不起,让您久等了。今天我们特别忙。

B: It doesn't matter. Today is Sunday, we go to work at week days and have no time. B:没关系,今天是星期天。平日上班,大家抽不出空来。

A: How do you want your hair cut? Any particular way? A:您要怎样理?要什么特别的式样?

B: Trim it a little on the sides. B:边上修剪一下。

A: Shall I take some off the top? A:顶上要不要剪掉一些呢?

B: Oh, just a little, please. A little, there isn't too much left up there, you see. B:唷,就一点点,一点点吧!你看,顶上的头发已经不多了。

A: You are a young man to be losing your hair that way. A:您年纪轻轻的,就这样脱发。

B: What's worse, it's getting thinner and thinner on the top. It seems to be something that runs in my family. My father was bald when still in his twenties. And my uncle was as bald as a bat.

B: 更糟糕的是，顶上的头发越来越少。看来这是我家的遗传。我父亲刚刚20出头就秃头。我叔叔的头光得如蝙蝠。

A: Have you ever done anything for it?

A: 您采取过什么办法没有?

B: Yes. I've used as much hair-tonics as possible, yet it keeps right on falling.

B: 当然。我尽量多用生发水，但头发还是不断地脱。

A: Don't feel badly. Anyhow, your hair is black.

A: 不要难过。不管怎样，您的头发还是黑的。

B: People say those whose hair is grey won't lose their hair, while those whose hair likes to lose will always have black hair.

B: 人们说，头发白的人不会脱发，而脱发的人总是黑发。

A: Perhaps.

A: 也许吧。

On the Scene 身临其境 面面俱到

主题：米勒夫人来到玛丽的发廊烫发。请你看图，根据如下提供的关键词，将她们的对话写出来。

关键词语：perm *n.* 电烫　　bob 剪短发
shampoo and set 洗头及做波浪发型
Golden Texture 金太克丝乔
roller *n.* 发卷

参考答案

Mary: How would you like your hair done today? Do you want a perm like you had last time?

Mrs. Miller: No, nothing all that fancy today. With summer coming on, my hair's a bit too long now, so I'd better have it bobbed. Could you give it a good trimming all the way round? Then I'll have a shampoo and set.

Mary: Right you are, bob, shampoo and set. What shampoo do you prefer?

Mrs. Miller: Golden Texture, please.

Mary: It's always been one of the most popular brands. Now, would you just hold this towel over your eyes while

I give you a rinse? That's it... Now for a good rubbing. Ready for the set now? I'll start putting the rollers, clips and pins in. Now, would you come over here under the dryer, please? Here are some magazines for you to look through while you sit there.

玛丽:今天你想要什么发型?像上次一样的电烫吗?

米勒夫人:不,今天不做那种发型。夏天快来了,我的头发现在有点儿长,所以我最好把头发剪短。您能把我的头发好好修剪一下吗?然后我洗洗头,把头发做成波浪形。

玛丽:好啦,剪短发,洗头及做波浪发型。您喜欢用哪种洗发水?

米勒夫人:用金太克丝乔。

玛丽:这种洗发水是最受欢迎的牌子之一。我给您洗头时,请用毛巾捂住双眼好吗?对,就这样。现在好好地擦一擦头发。准备好做发型了吗?我现在开始上发卷,得用夹子和头夹。现在请坐到烘干器罩下面来。这儿有一些杂志可供您翻看。

★美容扮俏★ 9 Beauty Parlor

Words and Phrases 闪亮词语 点滴积累

series of cosmetic 系列化妆品
beauty box 化妆盒
vanishing cream 美容霜
lemon cream 柠檬霜
foundation cream 粉底霜
nourishing cream 营养霜
cold cream 冷霜;油底霜
pearl cream 珍珠霜
beauty cream 润肤霜
cleaning cream 清洁霜
day cream 日霜
night cream 晚霜
slimming cream 减肥霜
sun cream;sunscreen cream 防晒霜
cream 乳剂;膏状物
snow cream 雪花膏
acne cream 暗疮粉刺膏
face friends;face cream 面友
face powder 香粉
dusting powder 扑粉
talcum/toilet powder 爽身粉
prickly heat powder 痱子粉
pearl powder 珍珠粉

Useful Sentences 七彩精句 连点成线

Getting facials 脸部护理

1. *Do you want a face massage?* 您要做一下面部按摩吗?
2. *I need to have a facial to relax a little bit.* 我需要去做个脸部护理,放松一下。
3. *Do you offer facials?* 你们有做脸部护理的服务吗?
4. *My skin looks so dull, what kind of facial treatments will improve it?* 我的肤色看起来好暗淡,我应该做哪一种疗程来改善?
5. *My face has started breaking out. Can I still have a facial?* 我脸上长痘痘,还可以做脸部护理吗?
6. *My lips are peeling. Do you have a special treatment for the lips?* 我的嘴唇在脱皮,有没有针对嘴唇的特殊疗程?
7. *Must I clean my face before doing the steam?* 蒸脸前我一定得做脸部清洁吗?
8. *Is "lavender facial steam" good for acne-prone skin?* "薰衣草的蒸脸"对长痘痘的肌肤很有效吗?
9. *You should use this facial masque often.* 你应该常使用这种滋养面膜。
10. *I'm sure the facial massage will relax your tired skin and flesh.* 我想面部按摩一定会消除您肌肤的疲劳。
11. *Would you try a special mask to get rid of the filth and grease?* 您要不要用面膜来去除您皮肤中的油污?
12. *Now, shall we use the youth cream?* 现在,我给您用青春营养霜好吗?
13. *It's time to smooth your beautiful face with sun protection cream.* 现在该在您漂亮的脸上擦防晒霜了。

Getting manicures 指甲护理

1. *I want to have a manicure and a pedicure.* 我想做一下手部和脚部指甲的修护。
2. *May I also have a French pedicure?* 我也可以做脚部的法式指甲修护吗?
3. *Can you rub in some cuticle cream first and just gently push them back?* 你可以先帮我擦一些指甲周围表皮专用的柔肤霜,再轻轻将它们往后推吗?
4. *Could you just cut those overgrown cuticles on the sides?* 你可不可以只修剪两侧多长出来的表皮?
5. *Ouch, it hurts. Could you be a little gentler?* 哎唷,

好痛。可以稍微轻一点吗？

6. *I have a meeting in an hour. Can you put on the quick dry as the topcoat?* 我一小时后有一个会议，你可以给我在最上层擦快干油吗？

7. *I'd like to do the tip.* 我要贴假指甲。

8. *How much is it for a designed manicure?* 造型式的手部指甲修护要多少钱？

9. *Do you offer a special treatment for dry and cracked nails?* 你们有针对干裂指甲的特别疗程吗？

10. *This raspberry color looks too rich.* 这个小红莓的颜色看起来太浓了。

11. *There are a couple of colors that I'd like to try.* 有几种颜色我想试擦看看。

12. *Which polish color are you interested in?* 您想擦哪种颜色的指甲油？

13. *Would you like to have a French manicure?* 您想做法式的指甲修护吗？

14. *Would you like your nails filed square or round?* 您想将指甲修成方形还是圆形？

15. *Are you planning to get a manicure later?* 您打算以后修指甲？

Cosmetics 化妆品

1. *I want to buy a new lipstick. Do you know any good brands?* 我想买一支新的唇膏，你知道哪个牌子比较好用吗？

2. *How much for this black mascara?* 这支黑色的睫毛膏要多少钱？

3. *What is included in your gift package?* 你们的赠品包括了什么？

4. *With this coupon, you'll give me a 15% discount for purchasing night cream, right?* 有这张折价券，我买晚霜会是八五折的优惠，对吗？

5. *Excuse me, how can I get the extra free handbag?* 对不起，我要怎样才可以得到那个额外的免费手提袋？

6. *I'm sorry. The gift package is exclusive for customers who purchase our new foundation.* 很抱歉，这项礼品只赠送给购买我们新上市粉底霜的客人。

7. *There are two different sets of eye shadows in our gift package, which one would you like to have?* 我们的赠品中有两种不同组合的眼影组，您想选择哪一组？

8. *I'm not sure if this color matches my skin tone, can I try it first?* 我不确定这个颜色是否适合我的肤色，我可以试用看看吗？

9. *My skin is very sensitive. Do you have trial samples that I can try first?* 我的皮肤很敏感，有试用品可以让我先试用一下吗？

10. *If my skin is allergic to the product, can I bring it back for a refund?* 如果我的皮肤对那个产品过敏，我可以拿回来退吗？

11. *I'm sorry, if you have any allergic reactions, we can only promise an exchange.* 很抱歉，如果您有任何过敏的反应，我们只能接受换货的服务。

12. *Excuse me, could you show me how to put on this eye shadow?* 对不起，你可以示范给我看怎么用这些眼影吗？

13. *If I don't like the lipstick's color that is in your gift package, is it possible to replace it with a different color?* 如果我不喜欢赠品中的口红的颜色，我可以换一个不同颜色的吗？

14. *I'm sorry. You can not change any item from the gift package.* 对不起，赠品中的产品是不可以替换的。

15. *What color do you usually wear for the eye shadow?* 您通常使用什么颜色的眼影？

Skin care products 保养品

1. *Do you carry alcohol-free toners?* 你们有没有不含酒精成分的化妆水？

2. *I've started getting wrinkles. Do you have any anti-wrinkle products?* 我开始有皱纹，你们有卖防皱的产品吗？

3. *My skin is very sensitive. I can't use a moisturizer that contains fragrances.* 我的肌肤很敏感，没办法用含香味的保湿霜。

4. *Do you carry anything that can improve dry and cracked lips?* 你们有没有可以修复干裂嘴唇的产品？

5. *The eye cream I bought last time was too greasy, do you have a lighter one?* 我上次买的眼霜太油腻了，有比较清淡的吗？

6. *I heard that you antiaging gel works really well. I'm interested in buying one bottle.* 我听说你们

的抗老化精华露非常棒,我想买一瓶。

7. *Do you sell moisturizer that is especially made for the neck?* 你们有颈部专用的保湿霜吗?

8. *I have oily skin, so I want something that is light but can still keep enough moisture for the winter.* 我是油性皮肤,所以我需要那种比较清爽但在冬季又足以保湿的产品。

9. *My skin looks dull. What would you recommend that I use?* 我的皮肤看起来很暗淡,你会建议我用些什么产品?

10. *I feel my pores enlarging. Is there anything I can use to shrink them?* 我觉得我的毛细孔变大了,有没有什么产品可以修复?

11. *Do you have products to ease breakouts?* 你们有治痘痘的产品吗?

12. *You can try to use this honey and almond enriched facial scrub. It will exfoliate the dead skin.* 你可以试用这种富含蜂蜜及杏仁成分的磨砂洁面霜,它可以去除老化的皮肤。

13. *The skin under your eyes is very sensitive. You shouldn't apply regular moisturizer there.* 眼睛下围的肌肤很敏感,你不应该在那儿擦一般的保湿霜。

14. *If your skin is sensitive, you'd better do a "patch-test" before you apply the products on your face.* 如果你的皮肤很敏感,你最好在脸部使用产品前先做一下"过敏反应测试"。

15. *This is a sample of our "antiwrinkle eye cream" Would you like to take it home and try it?* 这是我们的"防皱眼霜"试用品,你想带回家试用吗?

Perfume 香水

1. *The perfume is particularly elegant in smell.* 这种香水香味特别高雅。

2. *That's a nice perfume.* 那是不错的香水。

3. *Where's my cologne?* 我的古龙香水呢?

4. *Can I recommend this Qingfei perfume?* 我能为您推荐清妃香水吗?

5. *It's advertised everywhere, very popular.* 这种东西的广告随处可见,很受欢迎。

6. *It's the thing that would take a lady's fancy.* 这正是女士中意之物。

7. *I want to buy some perfume for my girlfriend.* 我想买香水给我女朋友。

8. *Thank you for your advice.* 谢谢你的建议。

9. *I'd like to buy some perfume.* 我想买一瓶香水。

10. *I like Qingfei perfume better.* 我比较喜欢清妃香水。

11. *Do you need perfume?* 需要香水吗?

12. *I'm much obliged to you for your patient explanations and introduction.* 非常感谢你耐心的解释和介绍。

Fashion Conversation 鲜活会话 由线到面

Conversation 1

A: Let's start with the cleaning masque.
B: What are the ingredients in your cleaning masque?
A: It's a combination of oatmeal, yogurt and honey.
B: What are they good for?
A: Oatmeal is a very gentle exfoliator that can remove dead skin from your face.
B: Uh-huh. What about yogurt and honey?
A: Yogurt can soften the skin, and honey is one of the best natural humectants.
B: I see. Will you do the "rose petal facial steam" for me?
A: No. I plan to do the "peppermint and rosemary facial steam" because the combination of these

A:我们从清洁面膜开始。
B:你们清洁面膜的成分是哪些东西?
A:是由燕麦、优酪乳及蜂蜜混合而成的。
B:它们有哪些好处?
A:燕麦是很温和的去角质剂,它可以去除你脸部老化的角质。
B:喔,那优酪乳和蜂蜜呢?
A:优酪乳可以柔软肌肤,而蜂蜜则是最好的天然润湿剂。
B:了解了。你今天会帮我做"玫瑰花瓣蒸脸"吗?
A:不,我打算帮你做"薄荷和迷迭香蒸脸",因为这两种植物混合可使疲劳的肌肉放松。

two plants will soothe tired muscles.

B: Great.
B: 好极了。

A: Now, no more talking and relax for a while. I'll massage your scalp.
A: 现在,不要再说话,放松休息一下。我帮你做头皮按摩。

B: OK. This is the part of facials that I like best. I'll enjoy it!
B: 好的,这是做脸部护理过程中我最喜欢的一部分,我会好好享受的!

Conversation 2

A: Usually, it's $60 for a manicure and $80 for a pedicure, but with this special discount, the total is only $120.
A: 通常修手部的指甲是60美元,修足的是80美元,但在这个特惠折扣后,总共只要120美元。

B: That's nice! I'd like to give it a try.
B: 很棒啊! 那我试试看。

A: All right. Do you want your cuticles cut, too?
A: 好的。您要剪修指甲周围的表皮吗?

B: No.
B: 不要。

A: Would you like the shape square or round?
A: 您喜欢修成方形还是圆形?

B: Square, but with rounded edges, please.
B: 方形,请将两边稍微磨圆一些。

A: All right, it's done. Please follow me to the drying section.
A: 好的。请随我到烘干区。

B: How long will it take to get them dry?
B: 烘干要多久啊?

A: About fifteen minutes, you'll be all set.
A: 大约15分钟就好了。

B: I see. Thank you.
B: 我知道了,谢谢你。

Conversation 3

A: Welcome, miss. May I help you?
A: 欢迎光临,小姐。要买东西吗?

B: I hope so. I want a lipstick.
B: 是的,我想买口红。

A: Do you have any particular brand in mind?
A: 你喜欢什么牌子的?

B: I like Lifei very much.
B: 我很喜欢丽妃。

A: We have different shades of Lifei lipstick. May I know what color you usually wear?
A: 我们有各种不同颜色的丽妃口红,请问你平常都用什么颜色的?

B: Pink. But today, I'm thinking of buying one in a dark shade. You know I will be a teacher next month. I wish to look more serious.
B: 粉红色的。但是,今天我想买深色的。你知道,下个月我就要当老师了,我希望看上去严肃些。

A: Yes, I see. How do you like this one?
A: 我明白了。你觉得这种怎么样?

B: Not too bad. May I have a try?
B: 还不错,我可以试试吗?

A: Certainly, miss.
A: 当然可以。

B: Mmm... It's still too bright. Any darker shades?
B: 嗯,还是太浅了,再深一点的有吗?

A: Not from the Lifei group, I'm afraid.
A: 恐怕丽妃系列中没有。

B: Well, any brand will do, so long as I can get the right color.
B: 哪一种都可以,只要颜色合适就行。

A: How about this one, then? It's with much transparent touch.
A: 那么这种怎么样? 它富有透明感。

B: Oh, that's the very thing I need.
B: 噢,正是我想要的。

Conversation 4

A: Could I try some on my hand?
A: 我可以在手上试一下吗?

B: Of course. See, it can be absorbed quickly.
B: 可以呀,你看,它很快就被吸收了。

A: Hmm, I don't feel greasy at all, and my skin seems to instantly become smoother.

A:嗯,一点也不会觉得油,而且我的皮肤好像马上就变得光滑了。

B: Amazing, right? Do you need anything else?

B:很神奇,对吧?你还需要别的什么吗?

A: Yeah. I always get rough skin in winter. Why?

A:是的,我总觉得皮肤在冬天变得好粗糙,为什么呢?

B: Well, since the weather becomes cool and dry, your skin gets dehydrated easily.

B:嗯,因为天气变得冷而且干,所以皮肤很容易丧失水分。

A: So how can I keep it soft and supple?

A:那我要如何才能让它们保持柔嫩细致呢?

B: You can use a gentler, creambased facial cleanser, and always remember to follow that with a thick moisturizer.

B:你可以用比较柔和、霜状的洗面乳,而且永远记得洗完脸后要擦上滋润型的保湿霜。

A: Do you sell them?

A:你们有那样的洗面乳吗?

B: Yes, we do. This is our "ultra moisturizing cleansing cream".

B:有的。这是我们的"超效保湿清洁洗面乳"。

A: Ha, just suits my needs.

A:哈,正好符合我的需求。

Conversation 5

A: This is a bottle of Parisian perfume. It is very fragrant and will keep indefinitely, and has the reputation for quality that is unequalled.

A:这是一瓶巴黎香水,它味香持久,其质量信誉无与伦比。

B: Yes, I do agree.

B:是的。我赞成。

A: Do you want a bigger bottle?

A:您要大瓶的吗?

B: No, this will do for now. I'd like to test this one first, if you don't mind.

B:不,这个就行了。如果你不介意的话,我想试试这个。

A: Not at all. Try this one, Madam. The scent is really soft and alluring.

A:没关系(别客气)。夫人,试试这个。这香味真是柔和诱人。

B: Hmm. It smells wonderful. But I am looking for something I can wear every day. Can you recommend anything?

B:嗯。闻起来真不错。但我要一种可以每天都擦的。你能推荐别的吗?

A: Then we have the perfume you want. It's also from France. Look, here it is.

A:我们有您要的那种香水,也是法国产的。看,这就是。

B: This fragrance is also good. OK. I just take this bottle.

B:这种香味也挺不错的。行,我就买这瓶了。

A: Here you are.

A:给您。

Conversation 6

A: I'm looking for some blush. Do you still have some in "Peach Rose"?

A:我在找腮红。你们还有桃红色的腮红吗?

B: Oh yes. That is a beautiful color. It has been a very popular blush this season. I have two left.

B:噢,有。那种颜色很漂亮。这一季那种颜色一直很受欢迎。我还剩下两盒。

A: Great. I'll take one.

A:很好。我要买一盒。

B: Have you heard about our special promotion this month? If you purchase at least $18 in any Elizabeth Arden product, you will receive this black tote with a sample of lipstick, mascara and two shades of eye shadow.

B:你有没有听过我们这个月的特别促销?如果你买伊丽莎白雅顿的产品超过18美元,你可以得到这个黑色袋子里的赠品,里面有一支样品口红、睫毛膏和两个颜色的眼影。

A: Wow. That sounds like a bargain. I'm running

A:哇。那听起来很划算。我的面霜和化妆水都快

low on facial moisturizer and toner. Could you ring those up for me too along with the blush?
用完了。请你把那两样跟腮红一起算。

B: I'd be glad to. Do you need anything else?
B: 好的。你还需要别的吗?

A: I almost forgot. It's mom's birthday Saturday. I need to get her some more Channel. Could you get me the 17 oz bottle of Channel perfume?
A: 我差一点儿忘记。星期六是家母的生日。我要买一些香奈儿的产品给她。请你给我一瓶17盎司的香奈儿香水。

B: That will be my pleasure. I'll wrap the perfume up in a gift box for you, too.
B: 好的。我也会帮你把香水用礼盒包起来。

Conversation 7

A: Hi, I would like to know more about your moisturizers, could you tell me more about them?
A: 嗨,我喜欢你们的保湿产品,你可以帮我介绍一下吗?

B: Sure. Do you know your skin type?
B: 好的。你知道你是属于哪一类的肌肤吗?

A: I'm not sure. My T-zone gets oily easily, but my cheeks are dry in the winter.
A: 我不太确定。我的T字部位容易出油,但我的两颊在冬天时却很干。

B: I see. This "Crème do Olives" is our best seller for combination skin.
B: 我知道了。这个"橄榄滋润霜"是我们混合性肌肤卖得最热门的产品。

A: What is good about it?
A: 它好在什么地方?

B: It contains a very powerful antioxidant potion made of olive-leaf extracts and Mediterranean herbs.
B: 它含有一种高效能的抗氧化成分,是由橄榄叶萃炼精华和地中海植物混合而成的。

A: Won't it be too oily for my T-zone?
A: 它对我的T字部位不会太油吗?

B: Not at all. It's rich, but not heavy.
B: 一点也不会。它很滋润,但并不油腻。

On the Scene 身临其境 面面俱到

主题:杨小姐工作很累了,她来到吉尔的美容店来做美容按摩。请你看图,根据如下提供的关键词,将她们的对话写出来。

关键词语:
- exhausted *adj.* 耗尽的,疲惫的
- treatment *n.* 治疗
- specially *adv.* 特别地
- release *n.* 释放
- tense *adj.* 紧张的
- muscle *n.* 肌肉
- facial *adj.* 面部的
- session *n.* 会议,开庭

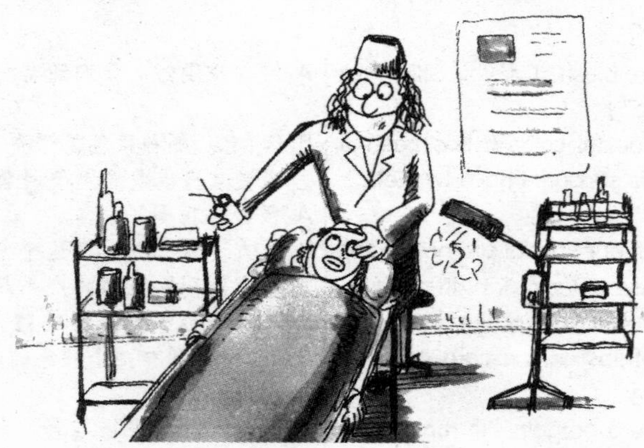

参考答案

Jill: Miss Yang, you look exhausted. Would you like to try our "restorative treatment"?
Miss Yang: What kind of treatment is that?
Jill: It's a specially designed treatment to release tense muscles, and it includes a hydrating facial and a hair and scalp massage.
Miss Yang: How long does it take?
Jill: About 100 minutes.
Miss Yang: How much is it for that?
Jill: $200. But, trust me, it's worth trying. After you finish the session, you'll feel terrific!
Miss Yang: All right, if you say so.
吉尔:杨小姐,您看起来好累,要不要试试我们的"提神补元疗程"?
杨小姐:那是个什么样的疗程?
吉尔:它是一个特别为放松紧绷肌肉而设计的疗程,包含一个补充水分的脸部疗程和头部的按摩。
杨小姐:整个疗程要多久?
吉尔:大约100分钟。
杨小姐:多少钱呢?
吉尔:200美元。不过,相信我,很值得的。当你做完整个疗程后,你会觉得全身舒畅极了。
杨小姐:好吧,既然你这样说。

★天气情况★ 10 Weather

Words and Phrases 闪亮词语 点滴积累

drizzle 小雨
storm 暴风
shower 阵雨
typhoon 台风
downpour 倾盆大雨
whirlwind 旋风
hurricane 暴风雨
temperature 温度
thunderstorm 雷雨
humidity 湿度
thunder 雷
snowstorm 暴风雪
lightening 闪电
the cold wave 寒流
breeze 微风
catastrophe(calamity)天灾
gale 强风
flood 洪水

Useful Sentences 七彩精句 连点成线

Asking about the Weather 询问天气

1. *Isn't it a nice day today?* 今天天气好极了,是吗?
2. *Beautiful weather, isn't it?* 天气很好,不是吗?
3. *Cold today, isn't it?* 今天天冷,不是吗?
4. *What do you think of the weather?* 你们认为天气怎样?
5. *Do you think it will rain?* 要下雨吗?
6. *It looks like it.* 看起来要下雨了。
7. *What's the weather like out?* 外面天气怎样?

Terms about Wind 有关风的用语

1. *The wind's rising.* 起风了。
2. *The wind is coming up.* 风刮起来了。
3. *The wind is starting to blow.* 开始刮风了。
4. *Apparently the wind's getting stronger.* 显然风越刮越大。
5. *The wind's getting up.* 风越刮越大。
6. *The wind's going down.* 风势在减弱。
7. *The wind has stopped.* 风停了。
8. *It's rather windy today.* 今天风很大。
9. *There's much wind today.* 今天风很大。
10. *It looks as if a storm is coming up.* 看起来要有大风暴了。

Terms about Rain 有关雨的用语

1. *It looks like rain.* 看上去像要下雨了。
2. *It looks as if it is going to rain.* 看来要下雨了。
3. *The rain's setting in.* 雨开始下起来了。
4. *It's beginning to spot.* 开始下小雨了。
5. *It's beginning to sprinkle.* 开始落雨点了。
6. *It will be pouring in a minute.* 马上要下大雨了。
7. *I think this will only be a shower.* 我想这是阵雨。
8. *See how big the rain-drops are!* 瞧,多大的雨点!
9. *It was only a shower. In a few minutes the sun was out again.* 刚才是阵雨,几分钟后太阳又出来了。
10. *The rain's beginning to let up.* 雨开始下小了。
11. *The rain's letting up a little.* 雨下得小一点儿了。
12. *It's not raining so hard now. It has stopped raining.* 现在雨下得不大了。雨已停了。

Terms about Snow 有关雪的用语

1. *It's snowing.* 正在下雪。
2. *It's snowing hard/heavily.* 正在下大雪。
3. *See how big the snow-flakes are!* 瞧,雪花有多大!

4. *I think there'll be a snow.* 我想要下雪了。
5. *Do you think it will snow?* 你认为会下雪吗?
6. *It's thawing.* 雪在溶化。
7. *Is it snowing?* 在下雪吗?
8. *We had a snow yesterday.* 昨天下了一场雪。

Terms about a lovely day 有关晴天的用语

1. *It's a lovely day.* 真是个好天气。
2. *It's a beautiful day.* 天气很好。
3. *It's a sunny day.* 真是个艳阳天。
4. *It's fine today.* 今天天气很好。
5. *The sky is clear.* 晴空万里。

Terms about bad weather 有关阴天的用语

1. *It's so cold today.* 今天真冷啊。
2. *The rain doesn't seem to be any sign of its stopping.* 看来雨不会停。
3. *It's very hot and stuffy.* 天气真是闷热呀。
4. *I'm fed up with the gloomy weather.* 我受够了这阴沉沉的天气。
5. *The weather is horrible!* 鬼天气,真讨厌!
6. *It is boiling today.* 真是热得要命。

Fashion Conversation 鲜活会话 由线到面

Conversation 1

A:My, what a downpour! And there doesn't seem to be any sign of its stopping.
B:I think it will let up in a little while. A downpour like this never lasts long here at this time of year.
A:I hope so.
B:Shall we have a chat in the sitting room over tea for a while?
A:Well, thank you.

A:哎呀,好大的雨呀!没有一点要停的样子。
B:我想马上就会停的。这里每年这个时间像这样的大雨是不会下很久的。
A:但愿如此。
B:我们在客厅待一会儿,喝茶聊天好吗?
A:好,谢谢。

Conversation 2

A:Oh, it's an oven out there, Rose.
B:Well, I'm glad you finally came in. I was scared you'd fry.
A:Oh, I thought I was gonna pass out. Look at me! I'm dripping.
B:Well, here's some cool lemonade.
A:Aah! Just what I want to drink.

A:罗斯!外面就像个大烤箱。
B:我真高兴你终于进来了。我怕你会被烤焦。
A:我还以为我要昏倒了。看看我!冒了一身的汗。
B:这里有一杯冰凉的柠檬汁。
A:喔!正合我意。

Conversation 3

A:What is the weather like today?
B:It has stopped snowing, but there's a bitter cold wind.
A:Look at the icicles there hanging from the eaves!
B:And the streets are covered with ice.
A:Do you happen to know what the temperature is today?
B:I missed today's weather forecast over the radio.

A:今天天气怎么样?
B:雪已经停了,但是仍刮着寒风。
A:看屋檐上挂着的垂冰。
B:还有被冰覆盖着的街道。
A:你恰巧知道今天的气温吗?
B:我错过了今天收音机上的天气预报。

A:It feels like 15 degrees below zero at least. I don't mind the cold weather, but I do hate it when it gets slippery.
A:好像至少得零下15度。我并不介意这冷天,但是当地面变滑时,我就特别恨它。

B:The ice will soon be thick enough for skating. I'm so fond of winter sports!
B:很快这冰就厚得可以滑冰了。我太喜欢冬天的运动了。

A:That's fine. Let's go skating together tomorrow.
A:那确实不错。明天我们一块去滑冰吧!

Conversation 4

A:I wonder when this wet weather will clear up?
A:我在想,什么时候才会雨停放晴。

B:Not for a while, cause we're in the middle of the monsoon season.
B:暂时还不会,我们正处于雨季。

A:I'm sick and tired of this hot, muggy weather.
A:我受够了这闷热的天气。

B:But it beats frigid weather of winter, doesn't it?
B:但它总比干冷的冬天要好点吧。

Conversation 5

A:It is boiling today, isn't it?
A:今天的天气热得要命,是不是?

B:Yes, it's very hot and stuffy.
B:是的,今天天气很闷热。

A:It's been looking like rain for several days. But it hasn't rained yet.
A:好几天总是要下雨的样子。但还是没下。

B:There are thick black clouds in the sky now. It looks as if a thunder storm is coming in.
B:现在天空乌云密布,看起来,一场雷雨即将来临。

A:The wind is rising.
A:刮风了。

B:It's a bit windy. But I like the breeze.
B:是有点风,但我喜欢微风。

A:It's beginning to sprinkle.
A:开始下小雨了。

B:The weatherman says some showers are expected this afternoon.
B:天气预报说今天下午将有阵雨。

A:It's turning warmer, isn't it?
A:天气在转暖,是不是?

B: Yes, the temperature is going up today. The temperature has climbed to 36℃.
B:是的,今天气温在上升,已上升到36摄氏度了。

A:After a heavy rain, the temperature should drop a lot.
A:大雨过后,今天气温会降很多。

B:Yes, there will be a cool day tomorrow.
B:是的,明天会是个凉爽的日子。

Conversation 6

A:How miserable a day it is!
A:多么糟糕的天气!

B:Yes, the weather is horrible!
B:是的,这鬼天气,讨厌极了!

A:Is the weather always like this?
A:天气总是这样吗?

B:No. I think the weather will be fine.
B:不是,我认为天气会好的。

A:I hope you are right. We don't want to be stuck here all morning.
A:我希望你说得是对的,我们不想整个上午都被困在这儿。

B:Too true.
B:千真万确。

A:What is the weather forecast for today?
A:今天的天气预报怎么说?

B:Rainy in the morning, overcast in the afternoon.
B:上午有雨,下午阴天。

A:It's been miserable for the past few weeks.
A:前几周尽是些讨厌的天气。

B:I think weather like this never lasts long.
B:我认为这样的天气不会持续很久的。

A:Do you think the weather will be fine tomorrow?
A:你认为明天天气会好吗?

B: I wonder whether it will be fine tomorrow. But the weatherman says it will clear up tomorrow.
A: I hope so.

B:我不知道明天是否会是个晴天,但是天气预报说明天会转晴。
A:希望如此。

On the Scene 身临其境 面面俱到

主题:姐妹俩人在屋中谈论窗外的大风,莉莉鼓励露茜要坚持自己做的事情,不要害怕寒冷。请你看图,根据如下提供的关键词,将他们的对话写出来。

关键词语:howl *v.* 咆哮　　numb *adj.* 失去知觉的
partly cloudy 有时多云　　five below zero 气温零下5度
encouragement *n.* 鼓励

参考答案

Lucy: It's freezing cold today, and how the wind howls! My hands are numb.
Lily: It always gets cold after a snowfall.
Lucy: I missed the weather forecast this morning. Did you hear it?
Lily: Yes. It said partly cloudy today, with a strong wind from the northwest. The highest temperature during the day will be five below zero.
Lucy: What about tonight?
Lily: Still colder. The temperature will drop to eighteen below.
Lucy: Looks as if we're in for a cold spell right when we're starting to have our winter vacation.
Lily: You'll have more time staying indoors, reading novels, watching TV, and even eating your meals on the bed. The cold weather never troubles me in vacation.
Lucy: That's true. But you'll miss the outdoor fresh air and the beautiful snow scenery. I want to take some photos of this.
Lily: Do you have spirit then? A cold weather like this is nothing when you're really interested in doing something. You'll be lost in your work and forget totally the coldness.
Lucy: I'm going to try my best. Thank you for your encouragements.

露茜:今天天气真冷,而且风吼得多大啊!我的双手已经麻木了。
莉莉:下雪后天气总是变冷的。
露茜:我今天早晨没有听天气预报。你听了吗?
莉莉:是的。天气预报说今天有时多云,西北风很大。白天最高气温零下5度。

露茜:今天晚上怎么样?

莉莉:更冷。气温将降到零下18度。

露茜:寒假快要开始的时候,似乎我们已经处于寒冷时期。

莉莉:你将有更多的时间待在室内,看小说、看电视,甚至在床上吃饭。假期中寒冷的天气从来没有使我感到过麻烦。

露茜:对。但是你会错过户外新鲜空气和美丽的雪景。我想拍些这方面的照片。

莉莉:你真的很想吗?当你真正对做某事感兴趣时,像这样的寒冷又算什么呢?你会沉迷于工作之中,完全忘记寒冷的。

露茜:我将尽最大努力。谢谢你的鼓励。

★婚姻大事★ 11 Marriage

Words and Phrases 闪亮词语 点滴积累

forced(/coercive) marriage 逼婚
bigamy 重婚
first marriage 初婚
polyandrist 重婚女人
polygamist 多偶制
unlawful(/illegal) marriage 非法婚姻
remarrying the original spouse 复婚
marrying above 高攀
trial marriage 婚前同居
marriage system 婚姻系统
freedom of marriage 婚姻自由
marriage portion; dowry 嫁妆
consanguineous (/near-kin/close relative) marriage 近亲结婚
May-December marriage 老少配
customary marriage 旧式婚姻
marriage by capture 抢婚
happy(/successful) marriage 美满婚姻
be well-matched in social and economic status 门当户对
marrying low 门户不当
uxorilocal marriage 入赘婚
hypergamy 上攀婚
well-assorted marriage 十分相配的婚姻
running away from wedding 逃婚

Useful Sentences 七彩精句 连点成线

Proposal 求婚

1. *I need you so much.* 我真的很需要你。
2. *I can't live without you.* 没有你我真不知怎么活。
3. *I want you to be my wife.* 我想让你做我的妻子。
4. *Will you marry me?* 你会娶/嫁给我吗?
5. *I want to live together with you.* 我想和你一起生活。
6. *Let's get married.* 我们结婚吧。
7. *I'd like to register our marriage.* 我想登记结婚。
8. *Please be my man/woman forever.* 请当我永远的爱人吧。
9. *Please marry me.* 请嫁给我吧。
10. *Let's get engaged.* 让我们订婚吧。
11. *I never want to leave you, will you marry me?* 我永远不离开你,你嫁给我吧!
12. *I think you and I would have beautiful children together.* 我想,我们将会生下许多漂亮的孩子。
13. *I want to spend eternity with you. Let's get married.* 我要一辈子和你在一起,让我们结婚吧。
14. *We'll live a happy life.* 我们会幸福的。
15. *I want to make an ideal home with you.* 我想要和你一起建立理想的家庭。
16. *Let's start a new life together.* 让我们一起展开新生活吧。
17. *Please be mine forever and marry me.* 我要你永远属于我,因此请嫁给我吧。
18. *I am afraid I already have a girl/boy friend.* 我很抱歉,我已经有女朋友/男朋友。

Marriage 婚礼

1. *What worries you most, Father?* 你最担心的是什么,父亲?
2. *Congratulations on your good marriage.* 祝贺你们喜结良缘!
3. *Where are you going on your honeymoon?* 你们会去哪里度蜜月?
4. *Hong Kong is a good place for the newly weds.* 对新婚夫妇来说,香港是个好地方。
5. *Jack, do you take Mary to be your lawfully wedded wife?* 杰克,你愿意玛丽做你的合法的妻子吗?
6. *Mary, do you take Jack to be your lawfully wedded husband?* 玛丽,你愿意杰克做你的合法的丈夫

吗?

7. *What about our marriage?* 那我们的婚事怎么办?

8. *How do you think about Jennifer?* 你认为珍妮芙怎么样?

9. *What is there to say? You seemed to have decided everything completely, are you not?* 还有什么好说的呢?你好像把每件事都决定下来了,不是吗?

10. *I'm very happy about this marriage.* 我对你们的婚姻非常满意。

11. *I fail to see how marrying a beautiful, brilliant girl constitutes rebellion.* 我看不出娶一位漂亮、聪明的女孩算得上反叛。

12. *I've no excuse except a mother's for wanting an impossible ideal for her son.* 我除了做母亲的想给儿子找个十全十美的妻子外,没有别的理由。

13. *I can't marry Roy.* 我不能跟罗伊结婚。

14. *How did you meet your wife? Was it a blind date?* 你怎么认识你老婆的?相亲吗?

15. *Not exactly. She was the girl who jumped out of the cake at my friend's bachelor party.* 不是。她是在我朋友的告别单身派对上,从蛋糕里跳出来的那个女孩。

16. *We're invited to a February wedding in Texas!* 二月份有人邀请我们参加在德州的婚礼!

Live together 婚姻生活

1. *You're such a wonderful husband!* 你真是个好老公!

2. *Right. Because I let you take care of the money.* 对啊。因为我让你管钱。

3. *But I don't like thinking that I'll never have that spark again.* 可是我不想觉得我无法再有那样的火花了。

4. *I know. But once you say "I do", it's a one-way street from there on.* 我知道。只要一旦说"我愿意",从此就是一条不归路了。

5. *Why not? We could get back with a taste of their own medicine...* 为什么不行?我们能够以其人之道还治其人之身地讨回来啊……

6. *We decide to start from nothing.* 我们下定决心从一无所有开始。

7. *I am in another phase of my life.* 我展开了人生另一个全新的阶段。

8. *I want to pamper his/her every whim.* 我希望了解他/她所有的情绪。

9. *I am on to the next step of my life.* 我将开始全新的生活。

10. *I want to cater to his/her every need.* 我希望满足他/她所有的需要。

11. *I find joy in everything we do.* 无论我们做什么事我都觉得很快乐。

12. *Everything looks rosy.* 任何事情看起来都是好的。

13. *I have all the responsibility.* 我在任何事情上都有责任感。

14. *We decide to build our relationship on love.* 我们决心在我们的爱情上建立良好的关系。

15. *I want to make him/her happy.* 我希望他/她幸福快乐。

16. *Even with no money there is love.* 我们虽然贫穷却拥有真爱。

17. *We will be in another phase of my life.* 我们将开始一个全新的阶段。

18. *She wears the pants in the house.* 她当家掌权。

19. *He never cheats on his wife.* 他从没有背着老婆乱来。

Fashion Conversation 鲜活会话 曲线到面

Conversation 1

A: Nice of you to come to see me.
B: It's my pleasure!
A: You didn't go?
B: No, I couldn't.
A: Isn't that wonderful.
B: I thought about you all that night.
A: So did I.

A:你能来看我真是太好了。
B:别客气!
A:你没走?
B:是的,没走。
A:太好了。
B:我昨晚想了你一整夜。
A:我也是。

B: What are we going to do?
A: Well, I. . . .
B: No, you have no time for that.
A: For what?
B: For hesitating. No more hesitating.
A: And I. . .
B: Going to get married.
A: Pardon?
B: Going to get married. I know, this is a marvelous sensation.
A: Do be sensible.
B: Why?
A: Because you don't understand me.
B: Then I'll learn to, and spend the rest of my life doing it.
A: Why don't you think of other women?
B: No, only it's you.
A: But how can you tell that?
B: Now listen, darling. None of your quibbling. None of your questioning. None of your doubts. This is positive, you see? This is affirmative, you see? This is final, you see? You're going to marry me, you see?
A: Yeah!

B:我们今天怎么办?
A:我……
B:不,你没有时间了。
A:为什么?
B:犹豫,你不能再犹豫了。
A:那我应该……
B:准备结婚。
A:什么?
B:准备结婚,我知道这是一种奇妙的感觉。
A:请理智一点。
B:那为什么呢?
A:因为你不了解我。
B:那我就用我的一生去了解你。
A:为什么你不考虑别的女人?
B:不,只能是你。
A:何以见得?
B:亲爱的,听着。不能含糊,不能疑问,不许怀疑。这是明确的,懂吗?这是肯定的,懂吗?这就定了,懂吗?要嫁给我,懂吗?
A:我懂。

Conversation 2

A: Have you ever thought of getting married, Mike?
B: Well, once or twice. Why?
A: I'd like to live with you forever.
B: So, would you like to marry me?
A: Yes.

A:迈克,你想过结婚的事吗?
B:想过一两次,你为什么问这个问题?
A:我想一辈子和你在一起。
B:那么,你想嫁给我吗?
A:是的。

Conversation 3

A: Rose, how long have we known each other?
B: Why do you ask so?
A: Don't you think we have to discuss something important?
B: What do you mean?
A: Have you ever been thinking of living with an American?
B: You mean your proposing to me now?
A: Do you want to think of my suggestion?
B: En. . .
A: I am serious, Rose.
B: . . .
A: Don't refuse me so soon; just think about it,

A:罗斯,我们认识多久了?
B:你为什么这么问?
A:你不认为我们应该讨论点重要的事情吗?
B:你是什么意思?
A:你想过跟一个美国人一起生活吗?
B:你是在向我求婚吗?
A:你愿意考虑我的提议吗?
B:嗯……
A:我是认真的,罗斯。
B:……
A:不要这么快拒绝我,请好好想想。

please.

B: Where do you think is the proper place to live?

B: 你觉得什么地方生活比较好呢?

A: Wooo... you mean you accept it? Is that true?

A: 喔……你的意思是说你接受了吗? 是真的吗?

B: I can't find a good excuse to turn down a marriage proposal given by a man like you.

B: 我真的找不到一个好的理由来拒绝你这样的男人的求婚啊。

A: It depends on where you like to live.

A: 你喜欢住哪就住哪好了。

Conversation 4

A: Do not fear that if ever I am lucky enough to win Linda for my wife, there will be any question of my putting any separation between you and her. That is not my intention now, nor will it ever be.

A: 不要担心,倘若我幸运的娶了琳达作了我的妻子,不存在把您和她分开的任何问题。这不是我现在的打算,也将永远不会有这样的打算。

B: You speak manfully and nobly, and I thank you. I will speak freely with you. Have you any reason to believe that Linda returns your love?

B: 你说得很果敢、很豪爽,我很感激你,我可以和你坦诚地谈谈,你有理由相信琳达会答应你的求婚吗?

A: None, as yet, none.

A: 没有,到现在还没有。

B: Do you desire my permission to speak to her?

B: 你希望我允许你和她说?

A: No, sir, not yet.

A: 不,先生,我还没这样想呢。

B: Then what do you want from me?

B: 那么你想从我这儿得到什么呢?

A: I want a promise that if Linda ever confesses to you that she loves me, you will not say anything against me, but that you will tell her what I have I know that she would never accept me if she thought that it would make any difference to your happiness.

A: 我想要一个许诺,假如琳达向您表白也爱我,您不要说对我不利的话,但您要告诉她我所说的,我知道假如她想到这将会对您的幸福产生任何变化她都不会接受我。

B: I promise, if at any time she declares that you are necessary to her happiness, I will give her to you. Nothing shall prevent it.

B: 我允诺,无论何时她说她的幸福需要你,我都会把她给你。什么也不会阻碍。

A: Thank you. Your confidence in me ought to be returned with fall confidence on my part.

A: 谢谢,您对我的信任应得到我全身心的报答。

B: Tell me when I ask you, not now, if you should be successful, if Linda should love you, you may tell me on your marriage morning. Do you promise?

B: 倘若你的婚事办成功,倘若琳达爱你,那么在你结婚的早晨告诉我吧,你答应吗?

A: Willingly.

A: 非常愿意。

B: Give me your hand. She will be home presently. It is better that she should not see us together tonight. Go! God bless you!

B: 握个手吧,她马上就要回来,最好不要让她看见我们今晚待在一起,去吧! 上帝保佑你!

Conversation 5

A: Darling, I've bought you a diamond wedding ring. What do you say?

A: 亲爱的,我给你买了个结婚钻戒。你看怎么样?

B: God gracious! It's the very thing I've been dreaming of.

B: 老天! 这正是我梦寐以求的东西。

A: How do you like the design?

A: 你觉得这个样式怎么样?

B: Perfect. You've made a good choice. | B:好极了。你的眼力不错。

On the Scene 身临其境 面面俱到

主题:婚礼上,牧师正在宣布玛丽与杰克成为正式夫妻。请你看图,根据如下提供的关键词,将他们的对话写出来。

关键词语:lawfully *adv.* 守法地,合法地
husband *n.* 丈夫
pronounce *v.* 宣告
wife *n.* 妻子
sickness *n.* 疾病

参考答案

Priest: Jack, do you take Mary to be your lawfully wedded wife?
Jack: I do.
Priest: Mary, do you take Jack to be your lawfully wedded husband?
Mary: I do.
Jack&Mary: For better, for worse, for richer, for poorer, in sickness and in health, till death do we part.
Priest: The rings, please... I now pronounce you a couple.

牧师:杰克,你愿意玛丽做你的合法结婚的妻子吗?
杰克:我愿意。
牧师:玛丽,你愿意杰克做你的合法结婚的丈夫吗?
玛丽:我愿意。
杰克 & 玛丽:无论生活好与坏,无论富裕与贫穷,无论患病与健康,我们至死不分离。
牧师:请戴戒指…… 我现在宣布你们结为夫妻。

★怀孕生子★ 12 Pregnant

Words and Phrases 闪亮词语 点滴积累

delivery room 产房
puerpera; parturient 产妇
induced labor 催生术
oxytocin; pitocinase 催生药
multiparous woman 多产妇
prepared childbirth 分娩准备
pregnancy 怀孕
midwife 接生婆
siamese twins 连体孪生
successive pregnancy 连续怀孕
child about-to-be-born 临产胎儿
secret pregnancy 秘密怀孕
difficult delivery; dystocia 难产
embryo 胚胎
rupture of membranes 破水
Caesarian(section); C-section 剖腹产
zygote 受精卵
twins 双胞胎
antenatal training 胎教
lanugo 胎毛
fetal heart tones 胎音
painless childbirth 无痛分娩
emesis 呕吐
fertility drug 助孕药
confinement in childbirth; laying-in 坐月子

Useful Sentences 七彩精句 连点成线

About pregnant 有关怀孕

1. *Dave! I just took a home pregnancy test.* 达夫！我刚刚用了验孕剂。
2. *It's blue! We're going to be parents!* 是蓝色！我们要做爸爸妈妈了！
3. *How was your gynecologist appointment?* 你去妇产科看得如何？
4. *They did an ultrasound to make sure my baby is healthy.* 他们给我做B超以确定宝宝的健康。
5. *Did they tell you when your due date is?* 他们告诉你预产期了吗？
6. *They said it should be around October 24th.* 他们说应该在10月24日左右。
7. *How should I take care of my health while I'm pregnant?* 怀孕期间，我的健康方面有什么需要注意？
8. *You shouldn't smoke or drink.* 绝对不要抽烟或喝酒。
9. *Well, eating fish will ensure your baby's brain develops normally.* 嗯，吃鱼能确保婴儿脑部正常发育。
10. *Why fish?* 为什么要吃鱼？
11. *Because fish has an important kind of fatty acid called DHA.* 因为鱼具有一种重要的脂肪酸DHA。
12. *The American Dietetic Association commends two servings a week.* 美国营养膳食协会建议一周吃两份。

Fashion Conversation 鲜活会话 由线到面

Conversation 1

A: Hey, Ann, how are you feeling?
B: Much better today.
A: Oh, look at the baby. It's so beautiful. Is it a boy or a girl?

A：唏，安，感觉如何？
B：今天好多了。
A：噢，这孩子真漂亮。是男还是女？

B:It's a girl.
B:是女孩。

A:Can I hold it for a moment?
A:我可以抱一抱吗?

B:Sure.
B:好哇。

A:Oh,how adorable! She's got your eyes.
A:噢,多可爱!她的眼睛很像你。

B:So they say.
B:大家都这样说。

A:When are you returning home?
A:你什么时候出院?

B:Well,the doctor said I have to remain here for at least two more days because I'm rather weak after labour.
B:医生嘱咐我多住院至少两天,因为分娩后我还很虚弱。

A:You can use some time off. You've been working too hard anyway.
A:你可趁机休息一下,你已经很操劳了。

Conversation 2

A:How long are you going to take off work after you have your baby?
A:你产后打算请假多久?

B:I'm only planning on taking three weeks.
B:我只打算请3个星期。

A:Three weeks?! You should really take at least two months,I think.
A:3个星期?我觉得你至少得请2个月。

B:I'd like to,but I'm afraid my boss will replace me while I'm gone.
B:我想啊,但我怕离开之后老板会把我换掉。

A:He can't! Your rights are protected under the Family and Medical Leave Act. You're allowed up to twelve weeks!
A:他不会的!你的权益受"家庭及医疗特别假法案"的保障。你可以请12星期的假!

B:Really?
B:真的吗?

A:It's true. I can give you a copy of the law if you want to see it.
A:千真万确。假如你想看,我可以印一份给你。

Conversation 3

A:Good news! I found out my company has a really liberal maternity policy.
A:好消息!我发现公司对于产假的规定很大方。

B:Do you get time off?
B:你有假放吗?

A:Well,I get three weeks paid vacation while I recover,and even after that I can do some of my work at home.
A:呃,我产后恢复期间有3个星期的带薪假,而之后有些工作我甚至还能在家里做。

B:You mean you'll work as a freelancer?
B:你是说就像是自由职业者一样?

A:Sort of. Most of the work I do is computer programming,so it doesn't really matter if I do it at home or at the office. I'll just E-mail the work to my boss.
A:有点像。我的工作多半是计算机程序设计,我在家里做或是公司做没啥差别。我只要用电子邮件把工作寄给我老板就行。

B:What about the hospital expenses?
B:那医疗费用呢?

A:My company's insurance policy will pay for everything!
A:我公司的保险会负担一切!

B:You sound like you work for a dream company!
B:你听来像是在一个梦幻公司工作!

A:Well, the economy is so good right now that companies who don't have good benefits packages can't hold their workers.
A:现在的经济形势很好,若是公司没有好的福利,就留不住员工。

B: Yes.

B: 是的。

Conversation 4

A: Mrs. Schmidt! What's happening?

A: 史太太！怎么了？

B: You'll never guess what happened today! I went to the doctor after work and the doctor told me...

B: 你绝对猜不出来今天发生了什么事？我下班后去看医生，他跟我说……

A: And the doctor told you to start listening to Bach?

A: 医生要你开始听巴赫？

B: No... He told me I'm pregnant!

B: 不是！他说我怀孕了！

A: Congratulations!

A: 恭喜！

B: And so I bought all these books on having kids and...

B: 所以我才买了这么些育婴书……

A: And they said you should play classical music?

A: 这些书说你应该听古典音乐？

B: How did you know? They say listening to classical music can make your baby smarter!

B: 你怎么知道？书上说听古典音乐会让宝宝更聪明！

Conversation 5

A: You've already had two babies, right? What did it feel like when you were pregnant for the first time? Can you still remember?

A: 你已经有两个小孩，对不对？你第一次怀孕的时候是什么感觉？你还记得吗？

B: Oh, can I ever! After about a month, I started getting morning sickness. I could hardly eat anything without feeling sick to my stomach!

B: 噢，我哪忘得掉！怀孕一个月后我就开始害喜，几乎吃什么东西都会反胃！

A: Oh! That sounds terrible!

A: 哦，听起来好惨！

B: That's not all! After I gave birth, I rubbed vitamin E oil on my skin for two years trying to get rid of my stretch marks!

B: 还不只是那样！生产后我为了想摆脱妊娠纹，足足在肚子上抹了两年维他命E油！

A: Did you have a natural birth?

A: 你是自然生产的吗？

B: The first time I did, but there were complications during my second pregnancy, and so they had to perform a Caesarean.

B: 第一次是，不过我在第二次怀孕时有并发症，所以他们得帮我剖腹产。

A: Were you in labor for a long time?

A: 你生产的时间很久吗？

B: Almost 14 hours!

B: 几乎花了十四个小时！

A: Ahh! Having a baby sounds exhausting!

A: 啊！生小孩听起来好累人！

B: It is, but you forget about it when you see your baby's adorable face. It's all worth it in the end.

B: 是很累人，不过你一看到宝宝惹人怜爱的小脸，你就都忘了。到头来这一切都值得。

On the Scene 身临其境 面面俱到

主题：琳达在街上遇到了待产的小王，她想把女儿菲菲留下来的婴儿服和玩具改日给小王送去。请你看图，根据如下提供的关键词，将她们的对话写出来。

关键词语：look close 看起来快要生了　　due *v.* 生(孩子)

add *v.* 增加　　addition *n.* 加起来

appreciate *vt.* 感激　　check *v.* 查，检查

give sb. a name 给某人取名　think... over 考虑

参考答案

Linda: Oh, Wang. You look close!
Wang: I am! I'm due next week!
Linda: I have some baby clothes and toys left over from when Rose was a baby. I can give them to you!
Wang: Really?! That would be great!
Linda: I'll drop by tomorrow afternoon! Congratulations on your family will add a new addition.
Wang: Thank you, I'm sure you can appreciate how I feel.
Linda: It's nice of you to say that. Have you given it a name.
Wang: Not yet.
Linda: You can check one.
Wang: Maybe you can give it a good name.
Linda: OK, I'll think it over.
琳达:哦。小王!你看起来快生了!
小王:是啊!下周是预产期!
琳达:我有菲菲留下来的婴儿服和玩具。我可以拿给你!
小王:真的?!太好了!
琳达:我明天下午顺道送去!恭喜你们家将要添新成员。
小王:谢谢你,我确信你能体会我的感受。
琳达:谢谢你这么说,你给孩子取名字了吗?
小王:还没。
琳达:你可以查一个。
小王:或许你可以帮忙起个名。
琳达:好,让我想想。

★家庭琐事★ 13 Family Affairs

Words and Phrases 闪亮词语

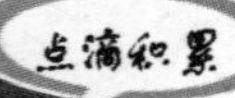

noisy children 爱吵闹的孩子
peaceful child 安静的孩子
unworthy child 不肖之子
legitimate child 嫡子
only daughter(/child) 独生女
only son(/child)独生子
chit of a girl 黄毛丫头
parlous boy 机灵鬼
plump little child 胖娃娃
young but steady;old head on young shoulders 少年老成
boyhood;childhood 少年期
moving(house) 搬家
registering(/applying) for residence 报户口
running one's home;keeping house 持家
family heirloom;cherished tradition(/heritage) 传家宝
family tragedy 家庭悲剧
family background 家庭背景
family member 家庭成员
family circle 家庭圈子
home(/family) life 家庭生活
family income 家庭收入

Useful Sentences 七彩精句

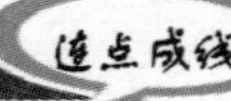

About the family 谈家庭

1. *How many people are there in your family?* 你家有几口人?
2. *Do you have any brothers and sisters?* 你有兄弟姐妹吗?
3. *I'm the only child.* 我是独生子。
4. *I'm still single.* 我现在还是单身。
5. *I'm married, but no child.* 我结婚了,但没孩子。
6. *I don't want to start a family yet.* 我还不想要孩子。
7. *I'm looking for a babysitter.* 我想找个看孩子的保姆。
8. *Do you live alone?* 你自己一个人住吗?
9. *You do have a happy family!* 你有个多么幸福的家庭啊。
10. *You are a proud father.* 你这个当爸爸的很自豪啊。
11. *It's not easy to raise a child these days.* 现如今养个孩子可不容易啊。
12. *You shouldn't spoil your child.* 你可不该惯孩子。
13. *His family is an ordinary family with three generations living together under one roof.* 他的家庭是一个普通家庭,三代同住在一个屋檐下。
14. *China is implementing a family planning policy.* 中国在实施计划生育政策。
15. *Mid-autumn Festival is a traditional festival for family unification.* 中秋节是家人团聚的传统节日。
16. *Compared with the Western, people in the East place much importance on family.* 与西方相比,东方人的家庭观念更浓重。
17. *A young couple started a family.* 一对年轻的夫妇组成了一个家庭。
18. *We have four people in the family, my parents, my elder brother and I.* 我家有4个人,我的父母亲,我的哥哥和我。
19. *The whole family decided to spend their holiday in Hawaii.* 全家决定到夏威夷度假。
20. *He is an orphan, so he is not sure which family name he should have.* 他是个孤儿,因而不知道他自己姓什么。
21. *Many new marriages end in divorce.* 许多现代的婚姻以离婚收场。

Housework 家务劳动

1. *Don't forget to take out the garbage.* 别忘了扔垃圾呀。
2. *I won't!* 忘不了!
3. *It's your turn to take out the garbage.* 今天该你倒垃圾了。
4. *Sorry, I forgot.* 对不起,我忘了。
5. *I'm tired!* 真累啊!
6. *Would you help me set the table?* 你能帮我准备餐具吗?
7. *Would you run to the store?* 你能不能赶紧去趟商店?
8. *Would you change the channel?* 能不能帮我换个台?
9. *Sorry about that.* 对不起,我忘了。
10. *Don't leave your stuff here.* 别把你的东西都堆在这儿。
11. *Will you feed the dog?* 你能去喂喂狗吗?
12. *Please water the plants.* 请帮我给花浇浇水。
13. *What do you want me to do?* 要我帮你做什么呢?
14. *Clean up your room.* 把你的屋子收拾收拾。
15. *We're out of dish detergent.* 洗涤灵用完了。
16. *I'll go get more.* 那我去买一瓶。
17. *Will you help me fold up the clothes?* 你能帮我把衣服叠起来吗?
18. *Please scrub the sink.* 把厨房的池子洗干净。
19. *I have to vacuum my room.* 我得用吸尘器吸吸我的房间了。
20. *Please dust the shelves.* 掸掸柜子上的土。
21. *Will you iron the shirt?* 你能把那件衬衫熨熨吗?

Fashion Conversation 鲜活会话 由线到面

Conversation 1

A: I know you have a son. How old is he?
B: He's going on six.
A: Who's looking after him?
B: My mother-in-law. She retired last year.
A: You really are lucky!
B: Yeah, I know.

A:我知道你有个儿子,他多大了?
B:他快6岁了。
A:谁在照看他?
B:我的岳母。她去年退休了。
A:你可真有福气啊!
B:是啊,我知道。

Conversation 2

A: Mom, look at the puppy we found. Can we keep him?
B: Hmmm, there's no tag on his collar. We'll have to have a family meeting to decide.
A: Is dad coming to the meeting?
B: Of course he is, what a stupid question!
A: But he hates dogs.
C: OK, I'm home. How is everybody?
A: Dad, look! Can we keep him?
C: Absolutely not.
A: But he's so cute and cuddly.
B: Dad said no and I tend to agree with him.
C: I'll not take that dog, please.
A: But dad, I...
C: I said no. Give me the animal.

A:妈妈,看看我找到的这只小狗,我能把它留下来吗?
B:它脖子上没有任何的标签,我们最好开个家庭会议来决定。
A:父亲来参与会议吗?
B:他当然来,多愚蠢的问题啊!
A:但他十分讨厌狗。
C:我回来了,大家好吗?
A:看,爸爸,我们能收留它吗?
C:当然不能。
A:但它十分惹人喜欢。
B:爸爸说不同意,我倾向他的意见。
C:我是不会收留这只小狗的。
A:可是,爸爸……
C:我说不行,把小狗给我。

A: I can't stand this, you never even discussed it with us. | A:我再也不能忍受了,你从不会和我们商量任何东西的。

C: It's not our dog. It's... | C:它不是我们的狗,它……

A: I hate family meetings, no one listens to me! | A:我讨厌家庭会议,没人听我讲。

C: But the dog ... | C:但这只小狗……

B: Don't talk back to your father. | B:不要跟你爸爸顶嘴。

C: If I could just say... | C:我想的是……

A: All I wanted was a dog... | A:我所要的只是小狗……

C: I might just add that... | C:我想加一句的是……

B: Well, dad has his reasons. | B:是的,父亲有他的理由。

C: Right! I... | C:对,我……

A: It's such a cute dog. | A:这只狗多么可爱啊。

C: QUIET! I'm trying to tell you, its not our dog, it's our neighbor's dog. They're out on the street looking for it now, so of course you can't keep it. Next time listen to me. | C:安静!我想告诉你的是,它不是我们的狗,它是邻居的狗,他们正在街上找它呢,所以你不能留下它,下回先听我说。

A: Sorry, dad. | A:对不起,爸爸。

Conversation 3

A: Does your wife work? | A:你太太工作吗?

B: Yes, she does. She works at home. | B:是的,她工作。她在家里工作。

A: Oh, I understand. She cooks and cleans, takes care of the children. She does the housework, is that right? | A:噢,我懂了。她烧饭、清洗、照顾孩子。她专干家务,对吗?

B: No, that's not right. Most of the time I do those things. | B:不对。那些事多数时候是我来做的。

A: Then you're a model husband. | A:那你是个模范丈夫了。

B: Yes. My wife is a writer. She writes on her computer. She has published ten novels already. Her next book will come out later this month. The name of the book is ***The Death of a housewife.*** | B:是的。我的太太是个作家。她在计算机上写作。她已经发表了十部长篇小说。她的下一本书这个月晚些时候出版。书名是《家庭主妇之死》。

A: Unbelievable. I've got to read her new book as soon as it comes out. | A:真了不起。她的新书一出版我就得读一读。

Conversation 4

A: Do you have a big family? | A:你有个大家庭吗?

B: No, I don't. | B:不是。

A: How many people are there in your family? | A:你家有几口人呢?

B: Three. My father, mother and me. How about yours? | B:三口。父亲,母亲和我。你家呢?

A: Five. My parents, my brother, my sister-in-law and me. | A:五口。我父母,我兄弟和他妻子,加上我。

B: Is your brother older or younger than you? | B:你兄弟比你大还是小?

A: He is five years older than me. He got married last Sunday. My brother and my sister-in-law are the same age. | A:他比我大五岁。他上星期日结的婚。我哥和我嫂是同岁的。

B：What is your home like? Do you live in a house or an apartment?
A：We live in an apartment.

B：你的家庭是什么样的？住的是一座宅院还是一套公寓房？
A：我们住在公寓房里。

Conversation 5

A：My parents told me my uncle and aunt are planning a big family reunion in Tokyo this fall.
B：Are you going to the reunion?
A：You bet. All my uncles and aunts will take their children along, too. So I'll meet many cousins there.
B：How nice! But why Tokyo?
A：Because two of my aunts are Japanese. They met and got married to my uncles in Japan. Some of their relatives are still living there.
B：Have you been to Japan before?
A：No. As a matter of fact, I've never traveled outside this country. I'm very excited about it. I can't wait.
B：My parents are going to take me on a trip to Hawaii next month but I've been there twice already.

A：我爸爸妈妈告诉我，我伯伯、伯母正计划今年秋天在东京举行一次大家庭团聚。
B：你去参加团聚吗？
A：那当然。我所有的伯伯、伯母要带他们的孩子去。所以我会见到许多堂兄弟姐妹。
B：真棒！但为什么去东京呢？
A：因为我有两位伯母是日本人。她们是在日本与我伯伯相识并结婚的。她们的一些亲戚还住在那儿。
B：你以前去过日本吗？
A：没有。实际上，我从来没有出国旅行过。这次去团聚我真高兴。我都等不及了。
B：我爸爸妈妈下个月带我去夏威夷旅行。可是那儿我已经去过两次了。

Conversation 6

A：That's a big family. How old is your sister?
B：Fourteen.
A：What about your brother?
B：He's not quite twenty.
A：Do you miss your family?
B：Yes.
A：Do you often go home?
B：No. But I often write to them.
A：How often do you write to them?
B：Once a month.

A：你们家确实是个大家庭，你妹妹多大了？
B：14 了。
A：你哥哥呢？
B：他不满 20 岁。
A：你想念你的家人吗？
B：想。
A：你经常回家吗？
B：不，但我经常给他们写信。
A：你多长时间给他们写一次信？
B：每月一次。

On the Scene 身临其境 面面俱到

主题：特罗伊正与艾丽斯探讨近年来家庭的变化。请你看图，根据如下提供的关键词，将她们的对话写出来。

关键词语：compose of 包括　　nuclear family 核心家庭
traditional family 传统家庭　　include *vt.* 包括，包含
dining room 饭厅

参考答案

Troy: The world changes, the family changes, too.
Alice: What does it mean?
Troy: People like a small family, composed of two parents and one child.
Alice: They say it is a nuclear family.
Troy: I don't prefer it.
Alice: What type of family do you like?
Troy: I like a family composed of many people.
Alice: It is a traditional family.
Troy: It includes grandparents, parents, uncles and aunts, and children...
Alice: Oh, it is too large to live.
Troy: But we can live well.
Alice: How many people do you have in such a family?
Troy: About twenty.
Alice: How do you have your breakfast?
Troy: We have our breakfast together.
Alice: You must have a large dining room.
Troy: Of course!
Alice: You must have three or four cooks, one of them is head.
Troy: Yes.
Alice: Do you like your family?
Troy: Of course, I like it very much.

特罗伊:世界变了,家庭也变了。
艾丽斯:这话是什么意思?
特罗伊:人们喜欢由父母及一个孩子组成的小家庭。
艾丽斯:大家说这是核心家庭。
特罗伊:我不喜欢这种家庭。
艾丽斯:你喜欢什么类型的家庭?
特罗伊:我喜欢由很多人组成的家庭。
艾丽斯:这是传统的家庭。
特罗伊:这个家庭有祖父母、父母、叔伯阿姨以及孩子们……

艾丽斯:噢,这大得无法生活了。
特罗伊:但我们能生活得很好。
艾丽斯:这样一个家庭有多少口人呢?
特罗伊:有20人左右。
艾丽斯:你们怎样吃早餐呢?
特罗伊:我们一起吃早饭。
艾丽斯:你必须有一个大餐厅。
特罗伊:当然!
艾丽斯:你得有三四个厨师,其中有一个是主厨。
特罗伊:是的。
艾丽斯:你喜欢你的家庭吗?
特罗伊:当然,我非常喜欢。

★瘦身减肥★ 14 On a Diet

Words and Phrases 闪亮词语 点滴积累

fitness center 健身中心
gym 健身房
yoga 瑜伽
be(/go) on a diet 节食
trim 匀称漂亮的
slim 苗条的
skinny 骨瘦如柴的
fat 胖的
chubby 圆胖的
take off 去掉
weight 体重
flabby 松软的
thunder thigh 大粗腿
love handle 腰间赘肉
beer belly 啤酒肚
keep fit 保持健康
jog 慢跑
acupressure 穴道按摩
apple diet 苹果减肥餐
lose weight 减肥
gain weight 增重
stretch and contract 伸展收缩
shape one's body 塑身
spot reduction 局部瘦身
get rid of/reduce the fat 消除脂肪
low-fat diet 低脂饮食
work out 健身
curve 曲线
fit 体态刚刚好的

Useful Sentences 七彩精句 连点成线

About the figure 评判身材

1. *Look at my flabby arms.* 看看我这松松垮垮的胳膊。
2. *Don't take that chair. It's for those who are slim and trim.* 别坐那张椅子。那是给苗条的人坐的。
3. *I've lost one kilo already.* 我已经减掉一公斤了。
4. *Look at those girls on TV. They're so thin!* 看看电视上那些女明星。每个都那么瘦!
5. *I've gained extra weight.* 我体重增加了。
6. *I've gained about... kilograms.* 我体重增加了……公斤。
7. *I'm too fat.* 我太胖。

Be careful about food 注意饮食

1. *Is the ice cream dessert out of the question?* 吃冰淇淋甜点更是不可能喽?
2. *How do you keep so thin and beautiful?* 你是怎样保持得如此苗条美丽的?
3. *I don't eat junk food. Like they say: you are what you eat.* 我不吃垃圾食物。就像有人说的:吃什么像什么。
4. *I just love mangos.* 我只喜欢吃芒果。
5. *Think about the calories in the dressing!* 想想那些调料中的热量吧!
6. *I'll let you in on my little secret. I drink eight cups of water a day.* 我来告诉你我的秘诀,我每天都喝8杯水。
7. *It's not right, not eating anything all day.* 成天不吃饭是不行的。
8. *Eating those things is bad for your health.* 你那样乱吃东西会吃坏身体的。
9. *Don't try extreme dieting to lose weight fast.* 切忌极端节食以求快速减肥。
10. *Don't eat snacks in your free time.* 休闲时间别吃零食。
11. *Don't eat late-night snacks.* 不要吃夜宵。

Exercise 运动减肥

1. *Jogging gives me such a high!* 慢跑让我觉得很过瘾!
2. *If we do this every day, we'll be lean and mean in just several weeks.* 假如我们天天这样跑,只要几个星期就会变得又结实又好看了。
3. *Walk more; don't drive so much. Force yourself to take the stairs.* 多走路;少开车。尽量爬楼梯。
4. *To succeed at losing weight, you have to keep working hard to meet your goal.* 要减肥成功,必须持之以恒。
5. *Hey, Mike. What have you done this time?* 嘿,麦克。你这回又搞了什么?
6. *Which means you need to exercise more than I do.* 这表示你比我更需要运动。
7. *It's never too late to change. Just start exercising right away.* 亡羊补牢,为时不晚。只要立刻开始运动就行。

Fashion Conversation 鲜活会话 由线到面

Conversation 1

A: Do you have any good suggestions on how to keep fit? I feel I have put on several pounds recently.
A: 关于保持一个良好的体型你有什么好的建议?我感觉我最近好像体重又增加了好几磅。

B: How much do you weight now?
B: 你现在体重是多少?

A: About 160 pounds. Can you believe it?
A: 大约 160 磅,你敢相信吗?

B: The weight looks good on you. Certainly you don't have to go on a diet, do you?
B: 你的体重还可以。当然你不至于节食减肥吧?

A: You see, I'm getting a thick waist, aren't I? So I need to find a quick fix to it.
A: 你看,我的腰是越来越粗了。所以我必须得找到一个迅速减肥的方法。

B: Maybe jogging can keep your weight down.
B: 或许慢跑是减轻体重的好办法。

A: Yeah, but it takes time. Are there any shortcuts?
A: 是啊,但是费时间。有没有捷径啊?

B: Dieting pills can help you lose weight, but they may have side effects and do harm to your body.
B: 减肥药能够帮你减肥,但是药物有副作用,会对你身体造成伤害。

Conversation 2

A: I'm getting so paunchy that I'm afraid I have to buy a new belt tomorrow. And I think I must go on a diet.
A: 我腹部越来越圆。恐怕我明天就得买新腰带了。我想我必须节食减肥了。

B: You are just a little bit chubby, not paunchy.
B: 只是稍微胖了些,不太胖。

A: You know, I'm a compulsive overeater. I got to watch what I eat.
A: 我总是无法控制自己摄入过多的饮食。我必须得注意自己的饮食了。

B: More physical exercises may help to keep your weight down.
B: 多做一些锻炼可能使你的体重减轻。

A: You said it.
A: 你说得对。

Conversation 3

A: Jerry, you look so fat.
A: 杰瑞,你看起来太胖了。

B: Not only fat, but also tired.
B: 不只是胖,而且我也很累。

A: What's your weight?
A: 你多重?

B: 150 pounds.
B: 150 磅。

A: Do put yourself on a diet, otherwise you'll be too fat.
A: 你必须得合理饮食,否则你就会更胖了。

B: I can't bear eating less. | B: 少吃东西我受不了。
A: That doesn't mean to eat less necessarily. | A: 合理饮食不一定就非得少吃。
B: So what do you mean by diet? | B: 那你是什么意思呢?
A: That means you should eat foods containing less fat. | A: 我是说你要吃含低脂肪的食物。
B: I just can't bear that. | B: 我可受不了。
A: So you must work out regularly. | A: 那你要经常锻炼锻炼。
B: What exercise may I take part in? | B: 我能参加什么运动呢?
A: At the beginning, you may jog. Jogging is an easy fat-consuming exercise. | A: 一开始,你可以参加慢跑。慢跑是一项很容易消耗脂肪的运动。
B: How long should I jog? | B: 我应跑多远呢?
A: You may jog two miles first, and then run longer and longer. | A: 开始你可以跑两英里,然后逐渐增加距离。
B: Do you jog? | B: 你也跑步吗?
A: Yes, I find jogging does good to me, so I keep on doing it. | A: 是的,我发现慢跑对我很有好处,所以我一直跑。
B: May I jog with you? | B: 我可以和你一起跑吗?
A: Certainly. See you tomorrow morning. | A: 当然可以。明天早晨见。

Conversation 4

A: I'm so hungry! I haven't eaten all day! | A: 我好饿! 我一天都没吃东西!
B: Take your mind off it. Look, Rose. This magazine is on China's top ten beauties! | B: 别想了。你看,罗斯。这杂志的内容是中国十大顶尖美女!
A: They're all so thin! Her cheekbones are great. | A: 她们都那么瘦! 她的颧骨很美。
B: She doesn't have an ounce of fat on her face. | B: 她脸上连一盎司肉都没有。
A: Hey, I lost a kilo in a week with my all-fruit diet. If I keep going, I can wear that dress next month. | A: 嘿,我的水果减肥餐让我一星期瘦了一公斤。如果我坚持下去的话,我下个月就穿得下那件衣服了。
B: So why are you dieting this time anyway? Another guy? | B: 那你这次又是为了什么节食? 另一个男人?
A: Dieting. It's the price we pay to make men notice us. | A: 节食,是我们吸引男人所要付的代价。
B: The girls in this magazine are so slender. | B: 这本杂志里的女孩都那么苗条。
A: They're also more younger than us. | A: 她们也都比我们年轻得多。
B: True. You know, I first started dieting when I was ten. | B: 没错。你知道吗? 我10岁时第一次节食。
A: You never worked out? | A: 你从不运动?
B: Oh, no. Too much work. I hate to sweat. | B: 喔,不。太费力。我讨厌流汗。

Conversation 5

A: My stomach's growling again! I'm hungry again. | A: 我的肚子又在叫了! 我又饿了。
B: You'll never lose weight if you listen to your stomach. | B: 如果听胃的话,你永远也别想减肥。
A: Just a little steak, uh... snack? A bowl of clam chowder? | A: 只要一小块牛排,嗯……零食? 一碗蛤蚌汤?

B: You want to be beautiful, don't you? Think about the butter and flour in...
A: You're right. But if I get too thin, my mom will make me go to the hospital again.
B: Most models only eat once a day. If they can do it, so can we.
A: I agree with you, but I think people are pretty bad, too.
B: You lost me.
A: People are always gossiping about one another.
B: Yeah, but that's human nature.
A: We can be so critical of one another.
B: Let's change the stomach, I mean, the subject. How about some food?

B:你想身材漂亮,不是吗?想想里面的黄油和面粉……
A:你说得对。但是我如果太瘦,我妈又会送我去医院。
B:多数模特一天只吃一餐,如果她们可以,我们也行。
A:我同意你的观点,但我想人也很坏。
B:我不懂。
A:人们总是相互说肥道瘦的。
B:对,但这是人类的天性。
A:我们彼此实在是太吹毛求疵了。
B:我们换个胃吧,我是说换个话题。来点吃的如何?

On the Scene 身临其境 面面俱到

主题:伊芙和南希来到快餐店,看着美味却又想着减肥。请你看图,根据如下提供的关键词,将她们俩的对话写出来。

关键词语:fried chicken 炸鸡　　splurge *v.* 消费
fat-free 无脂肪的　　salmon *n.* 鲑鱼
steak *n.* 肉片　　whale *n.* 鲸

参考答案

Eve: Wow! The fried chicken looks great!
Nancy: Where's your willpower? No food enters your mouth unless you say so.
Eve: But I just want to splurge a little bit.
Nancy: Your fruit diet works. Eh, Eve? (*To the waitress*) A fruit plate, please.
Eve: OK, you win. (*to the waitress*) Salad, fat-free dressing on the side, no croutons.

Nancy: Hey, look. Isn't that Inez? Look at what she's eating!

Eve: No wonder her hips look like that.

Nancy: I can't remember my last salmon steak. I bet it's covered in butter.

Eve: She's putting sugar in her coffee. Oh, my god! She's getting dessert, too!

Nancy: Mmh, cheesecake. I'd have to starve myself for a week after eating that.

Eve: It's a wonder she hasn't blown up like a whale.

伊芙: 喔！炸鸡看起来不错！

南希: 你的意志力去哪儿了？除非你自己想要,不然没有食物可以进你的嘴。

伊芙: 但是我只是想稍微要一些。

南希: 你的水果减肥餐有效。是吧,伊芙？(*对着侍者*)请来份水果盘。

伊芙: 好,你赢了。(*对着侍者*)来份沙拉,另外放无脂的沙拉酱,不要炸面包丁。

南希: 嘿,你看。那不是伊内兹吗？你看看她吃的！

伊芙: 难怪她屁股看起来那样。

南希: 我不记得上次吃鲑鱼排是什么时候。我敢说它一定裹着一层黄油。

伊芙: 她正往咖啡里加糖。我的天！她还点了甜点！

南希: 嗯,起司蛋糕。吃了那片蛋糕我得饿一个星期才行。

伊芙: 她没肿成跟鲸鱼一样真是个奇迹。

★突发事件★ 15 Emergency

Words and Phrases 闪亮词语 点滴积累

traffic(/road)accident 车祸
disastrous fire 大火灾
deluge 大水灾
earthquake 地震
bodies of the starved 饿殍
radioactive pollution 放射性污染
air disaster;plane crash 飞机失事
windstorm-caused disaster 风灾
industrial pollution 工业污染
submarine earthquake 海底地震
sea(/marine)disaster 海难
seismic sea wave;tsunami 海啸
drought 旱灾
railway accident 火车事故
disaster from fire 火灾
domestic(/family)misfortune 家庭不幸
tornado 龙卷风
coal-mine disaster 煤矿事故
distress area 贫困地区
strong earthquake 强震
weak earthquake 弱震
landslide;landslip 山崩(滑坡)
casualty 伤亡者
having things stolen;suffering loss 失窃
unemployment 失业

Useful Sentences 七彩精句 连点成线

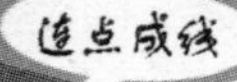

First aid 急救

1. *Is he breathing?* 他还有呼吸吗?
2. *Get some blankets.* 拿些毛毯来。
3. *Get a first-aid kit.* 把急救箱拿过来。
4. *We need some bandages.* 我们需要一些绷带。
5. *Stop the flow of blood.* 把血止住。
6. *Apply pressure to stem the flow of blood.* 用力向下压,把血止住。
7. *Elevate his legs.* 把他的双腿抬高。
8. *Raise his legs.* 把他的双腿抬高。
9. *Elevate the arm.* 把手臂抬高。
10. *Keep him quiet.* 让他别乱动。
11. *Don't move him.* 不要移动他。
12. *Don't move.* 不要动。
13. *Stay right there.* 就在那儿躺着。
14. *Stay put.* 躺着别动。

Requests for help from a police officer 向警官求救

1. *Help!* 救命!
2. *Please help me!* 请救救我!
3. *This is an emergency!* 情况万分紧急!
4. *Please come quick. Someone is hurt!* 请快点来,有人受伤了。
5. *Excuse me, officer, can you help me?* 对不起,警官,能帮我一下吗?
6. *I seem to be lost.* 看来我是迷路了。
7. *I've locked my keys in my car.* 我把钥匙锁在车里了。
8. *Can you help me get the keys out of my car?* 你能帮我从车里把钥匙取出来吗?
9. *My car is missing.* 我的车不见了。
10. *My car has been stolen.* 我的车被人偷了。
11. *I've been robbed.* 我被抢了。
12. *I've been mugged.* 我遭暴力抢劫了。
13. *I've been raped.* 我被人强奸了。
14. *He has a gun.* 他有一支枪。
16. *We're trapped in here.* 我们被困在这里。
17. *There's someone trying to get into my house.* 有人试图闯入我的房子。

A police officer confronting a criminal 警察面对罪犯时

1. *Freeze! Police!* 别动！警察！
2. *Hands up!* 举起手来！
3. *Put your hands up!* 举起手来！
4. *Put your hands on your head.* 把手放在头上。
5. *Take your hands out of your pockets slowly.* 把你的双手慢慢地从口袋里抽出来。
6. *Turn around slowly.* 慢慢地转过身来。
7. *Step out of the car slowly.* 慢慢地从车里出来。
8. *Break it up, you guys.* 你们这些人,不许再扭打(或争吵)!
9. *You're under arrest.* 你被捕了。
10. *I'm taking you in.* 你被捕了。
11. *You have the right to remain silent.* 你有权利保持沉默。
12. *Tell it to a lawyer!* 你可以请律师!
13. *Tell it to the judge!* 你可以向法官申诉!
14. *I don't care who you are!* 我不在乎你是谁!

Self-defense 自卫策略

1. *Girls should not go outside at night by themselves.* 女孩子尽量不要在夜间单独外出。
2. *If there were something wrong, go away at once.* 情况不妙,马上离开。
3. *Calm is the most important thing when you are in danger.* 遇到危险,首先要冷静。
4. *Call the police if you could.* 有机会马上拨打求助电话。
5. *Cry to ask for help if there were some passerby.* 现场若有其他路人,要大声求救。
6. *Remember: Life is the most important.* 要记住:活着是最重要的。

Fashion Conversation 鲜活会话 由线到面

Conversation 1

A: Help! Help!
B: What's the trouble?
A: I was taking a walk when a young man came at me from nowhere and snatched the bag off my hands and ran away.
B: What did the young man look like?
A: Well, he's young, tall and thin.
B: To which direction did he run?
A: Let me see... my right arm... oh, to the south.

A:救命！救命！
B:出什么事了?
A:我正在散步,一个年轻人不知从哪儿向我袭来,抢了我的包,然后逃走了。
B:那个年轻人长得什么样子?
A:唔,他很年轻,又高又瘦。
B:他往哪个方向跑了?
A:让我想想……我的右边……哦,往南跑了。

Conversation 2

A: Do you have a first aid kit in your house?
B: Yes, I do. I put it inside the bathroom cabinet.
A: What do you keep inside the kit?
B: There are bandages, gauze, adhesive tape, cotton and scissors. There are also medicines such as Aspirin, Vicks and Dristan, etc.
A: No doubt that the first aid kit is very useful and helpful in your lives.
B: Of course. But there is one thing you must remember: children must be prevented at all times from getting close to the first aid kit.
A: Is it so serious?
B: Yes. Any misuse of medicine could be fatal. So

A:你家里有急救箱吗?
B:有啊,就在我家卫生间的壁柜里。
A:你那急救箱里都放些什么?
B:里面有绷带、纱布、胶布、棉花和剪刀,还有许多药品,比如阿司匹林、去痛片、头痛药等等。
A:这种急救箱无疑在你们的生活中会非常有用。
B:那当然。不过有一点你必须记住:任何时候都要防止小孩接近急救箱。
A:有那么严重吗?
B:是的。因为任何一种药物误用都可能导致生命

the kit should always be placed at the top of the cabinet where the children can't reach it.

危险。所以急救箱应该始终放在壁柜的顶部，让小孩子们够不着。

A: And it should remain locked all the time.

A: 而且箱子应该一直上锁。

B: That's right.

B: 对！

Conversation 3

A: Listen! A Gas Leak Caused Two Lives! Have you read today's paper?

A: 听着！煤气泄露造成两人死亡！你看了今天的报纸了吗？

B: Yes, I have. Gas leak is the most dangerous situation in our daily life, I think.

B: 看了。漏煤气是日常生活中最危险的情况。

A: You are quite right. But what can you do if it happens to you?

A: 你说得对。不过如果这事儿发生在你身上你该怎么办？

B: If there is a strong smell of gas in the house, go to the kitchen at once and check the stove and the gas hose.

B: 如果闻到屋里有一股强烈的煤气味，赶快到厨房去检查炉子和煤气管道。

A: What if you hear a hissing sound?

A: 要是听到有咝咝的漏气声该怎么办？

B: If so, turn off the stove and open all the windows immediately.

B: 如果是这样，立即关上煤气炉，打开所有窗户。

A: Shall I call the Gas Station for help?

A: 我可以打电话向煤气站求助吗？

B: Oh no. Remember: never make a phone call or touch any electric switch in the house because a spark might cause an explosion.

B: 哦，不行！记住：千万别打电话或接触任何电器开关！因为一丁点儿火花就可能会引起爆炸。

A: Then I just sit there doing nothing?

A: 那我就在那儿傻坐着？

B: You just open all the windows, and take your family members out of the house and inform the Gas Station.

B: 你只能打开所有的窗户，然后带着家人离开住所，并通知煤气公司。

Conversation 4

A: When I find strangers lingering around my house, what shall I do?

A: 假如我发现有生人在门外徘徊，该怎么办呢？

B: Call 110 Station at once, of course.

B: 那还用问吗？马上向110报警呗！

A: How shall I tell them?

A: 我怎么说呢？

B: You just tell them what happens and give them your address and telephone number. The police would be sent here very quickly.

B: 你就告诉他们发生了什么事情，以及你的地址和电话号码。警察很快就会赶到的。

A: And what shall I do if I hear shouting for help or see a robbery taking place?

A: 还有，假如我听到有人求助或者我亲眼看见一场劫案该怎么办？

B: You should again call 110 Station first. Besides, you should try to get some special features about the criminals which would be great help to the police.

B: 你还是应该先向110报警。此外，你应该尽力记住罪犯的一些特征，这对警察的侦破工作会很有用的。

A: OK. Thank you very much for your kindness.

A: 好的。谢谢你的好心指点。

B: Anyway, I do hope we will never have the need to call 110 Station.

B: 不管怎么说，我还是希望我们不要有找110的必要。

A: I hope so, too.

A: 我也是。

Conversation 5

A: How do you think about the social security nowadays?

B: It's not very well, I'm afraid.

A: Yes. I read of a robbery which took place just under the nose of the police and in day time!

B: How horrible! Was the robber caught yet?

A: No. He is still at large about the town.

B: Then we all have to be very careful these days.

A: That's absolutely true. Now, look here, if your door bell rings, you should first peep through the peephole. If it is a stranger, you must ask who it is and what he wants.

B: What if they are just repairmen, or delivery men or postmen?

A: Then they should have identity cards with a picture to prove the company or organization they represent.

B: If they do have the ID, what shall I do?

A: You should check the picture on it and ask him a few questions about the intention of the visit.

B: OK. I'll remember your words.

A：你觉得如今的社会治安状况怎么样？

B：我看不是太好。

A：是不太好。我刚读了一宗抢劫案，就在警察的眼皮底下干的，而且还是大白天！

B：真可怕！抢劫犯抓到了没有？

A：没有。他仍然在逃，四处周游呢。

B：这么说，这些日子我们都得小心喽。

A：一点儿不错。你可听好了：当你们家的门铃响起时，你得先从猫眼里看一看，如果是生人，你就要问他是谁以及来干什么。

B：如果他们是修理工、送货员或者邮递员呢？

A：那他们全都会有带照片的证件，以证明他们所属的公司或机构。

B：如果他们真的有身份证，我该怎么办？

A：你应该核实一下他与照片是否相符。再问清楚他此次到访的意图。

B：好的。我会记住你的话的。

On the Scene 身临其境 面面俱到

主题：威尔的车被人撞了，肇事车辆却已经逃逸，他打电话向吉尔求助。请你看图，根据如下提供的关键词，将他们的对话写出来。

关键词语：run into 撞上　　calm down 冷静下来
wreck *v.* 破坏　　crush *v.* 压垮
hit-and-run 肇事逃逸

参考答案

Will: Jill, help me! Someone ran into my car!

Jill: Calm down, Will. Don't panic. Are you OK?

Will: I wasn't in the car! I'm fine! but my poor car is wrecked!

Jill: Where were you when it happened?

Will: In the library. When I came out, the left side of my car was crushed!

Jill: Oh, man, a hit-and-run! Poor Will!

威尔：吉尔，救救我！有人撞了我的车！

吉尔：威尔，冷静点。别慌，你没事吧？

威尔：我人不在车上！我很好！我那可怜的车可成了废铁！

吉尔：出事的时候你在哪里？

威尔：在图书馆。可是我出来的时候，我车子的左边被撞坏了！

吉尔：老天，肇事逃逸！可怜的威尔！

★商场购物★ 16 Emporium

Words and Phrases 闪亮词语 点滴积累

emerald 翡翠
necklace 项链
sapphire 蓝宝石
bracelet 手镯
earring 耳环
cameo 刻有浮雕之宝石
amber 琥珀
pearl 珍珠
crystal 水晶
ivory 象牙
diamond 钻石
topaz 黄玉
platinum 白金
agate 玛瑙
ruby 红宝石
antique 古董
perfume 香水
lipstick 口红
nail polish 指甲油
quartz watch 石英钟
sunglasses 太阳眼镜
rimless glasses 无边的眼镜
stereo set 立体音响
television set 电视机
tap recorder 录音机
calendar watch 日历表

Useful Sentences 七彩精句 连点成线

Jewellery 珠宝首饰

1. *We have 14K and 18K gold necklaces, bracelets and earrings.* 我们有14K和18K的金项链、手镯和耳环。
2. *Is that a real string of pearls?* 那串珍珠是真的吗?
3. *With diamond, ruby or sapphire?* 是要钻石的、红宝石的还是蓝宝石的?
4. *You have a good eye for pearls.* 你对珍珠很有眼力。
5. *Natural pearls or cultured pearls?* 您要天然珍珠还是养殖珍珠?
6. *You like a jade ring?* 您喜欢玉戒指吗?
7. *I'm afraid you will have to be charged for damages.* 恐怕您得付赔偿费。
8. *You should have been more careful. You know it is very expensive.* 你应该小心一点才是,您知道这很贵的。
9. *If you buy it, we will repair it for you.* 如果您买的话,我们将替您修复。
10. *We charge 50 yuan for the repairing.* 我们收50元的修理费。
11. *You can either buy it or pay 200 yuan for the damage.* 您要么买下,要么付200元赔偿费。
12. *What grade of diamond is this?* 这是哪一等级的钻石?
13. *This bracelet is studded with diamonds.* 这副手镯镶满了钻石。
14. *Can I have this pearl necklace insured?* 我可以为这条珍珠项链投保吗?
15. *I'll have to find a reputable jeweler.* 我得找一个有良好信誉的珠宝商。

Ornament 饰物

1. *We have some wonderful ties just in from Europe.* 我们有一些很好的刚从欧洲运来的领带。
2. *How much does such a smashing tie cost?* 这么新颖的领带多少钱一条?
3. *Tremendous work and effort have gone into every tie.* 每一条领带都是精工细做。
4. *I'll have the blue one with yellow and pink circles.* 我就买那一条蓝色镶有黄色和粉红色圆圈的蓝色领带。
5. *Every tie here is a piece of art.* 这里的每一条领

带都是一件艺术品。

6. *This necktie goes well with your shirt.* 这条领带跟你的上衣很配。

7. *Show me some silk ties, please.* 请给我看些丝绸领带。

8. *Do you prefer necktie or bowtie?* 你喜欢领带还是领结呢?

9. *This tiepin suits my tie very well.* 这个领带针很配我的领带。

10. *I have a brooch to go with the sweater.* 我有一个胸针来配这件毛衣。

11. *I'll take it if it doesn't have any defects.* 如果它没有什么毛病,我就买下了。

12. *This is the last set, so there's no refund and no exchange for it.* 这是最后一套,所以不能退款,不能更换。

13. *We have several kinds of scarves here.* 我们有好几种围巾。

14. *I have been looking for this color and design.* 我一直在寻找这种颜色和式样的围巾。

15. *The color of this scarf can match all of my coats.* 这条围巾的颜色可以和我所有的上衣相配。

Glasses 眼镜

1. *I want to change these lens into stronger ones.* 我要把镜片换成更深的。

2. *Now look at this sight-testing chart, please.* 现在请看这张视力测验表。

3. *Would you tell me the number?* 能告诉我度数吗?

4. *Do you have sun-glasses for ladies?* 你们有女式太阳镜吗?

5. *Your visual acuity is not poor.* 你的视力不差。

6. *You have astigmatism.* 你有散光。

7. *Are they made of unbreakable glass?* 是不会破裂的镜片吗?

8. *My eyes are suffering a lot these days.* 我的眼睛最近很难受。

9. *We have the frames here and we need the lenses.* 我们有眼镜框,需要一对镜片。

10. *I need a new pair of glasses today.* 今天我需要一副新眼镜。

11. *I'm sorry it takes 2 hours to make a new pair.* 很抱歉,配一副新眼镜需要 2 个小时。

12. *Do you have the scratch-proof lenses available?* 你有防刮的镜片吗?

13. *Is this safety lens or glass?* 这是安全镜片还是玻璃镜片?

14. *Do you prescribe contact lenses?* 你可以给我配副隐形眼镜吗?

15. *I need to have the frames of my glasses changed.* 我想换副眼镜架。

Electrical appliance 家用电器

1. *The design of this ventilator is very new.* 这个排风扇的式样很新颖。

2. *I'm looking for an electric rice cooker.* 我想买个电饭锅。

3. *I don't like the color of that dish-washer.* 那个洗碗机的颜色我不喜欢。

4. *I want to see some color TV sets.* 我想看看彩电。

5. *I'd prefer to buy a Japan-made TV set. Do you have Sony?* 我想买台日产电视机。有索尼的吗?

6. *I'd like to buy a TV set. Do you have imported ones?* 我想买台电视机,有进口的吗?

7. *I don't know if you sell black-and-white TV sets here.* 不知你们这儿卖不卖黑白电视机。

8. *Which brand of refrigerator is the best?* 哪种牌子的冰箱最好?

9. *How much does this double door refrigerator cost?* 这台双门冰箱要多少钱?

10. *How long is this icebox guaranteed?* 这台冰箱的保修期是多长?

11. *What's the brand of that refrigerator?* 那台冰箱什么牌的?

12. *I want a fully automatic washing machine.* 我要一台全自动洗衣机。

13. *Could you tell me the advantages of this washer?* 你能说说这台洗衣机的优点吗?

14. *Could you tell me how to operate this washing machine?* 请问怎么操作这台洗衣机?

15. *Are there still any other matters for attention when using the washing machine?* 使用洗衣机时还有什么其他注意事项吗?

Gymnastic appliance 体育用品

1. *That climber seems interesting.* 那个助爬器看起来挺好玩的。
2. *How about this one? It is the latest popular model.* 这个怎么样？这个是最新流行式样。
3. *I want to buy several basketballs.* 我要买几个篮球。
4. *I wonder if you sell football or not.* 不知你们卖不卖足球。
5. *Can you show me some badminton rackets.* 能拿些羽毛球拍给我看看吗？
6. *Show me some good baseball gloves around, please.* 请拿些棒球手套给我看看。
7. *Does this cover come with the racket?* 这球拍套子是和球拍一起的吗？
8. *That sword looks good.* 那把剑看上去不错。
9. *Give me a receipt of the chest expander, please.* 请给我开一张这个扩胸器的发票。
10. *Do you have any basketballs made of genuine leather?* 你们有真皮做的篮球吗？
11. *I bought a climber here two weeks ago, but it hasn't been delivered up to now. What's the reason?* 两周前我在这里买了一个助爬器，但是直到现在还没送到。什么原因？
12. *My son wants to buy a pair of table tennis pats.* 我儿子想买一副乒乓球拍。
13. *Is this bat made of rubber or sponge?* 这个球拍是橡胶做的还是海绵做的？
14. *The pattern is vivid and great and matches your slender figure.* 这种式样活泼端庄，和您苗条的身材正相配。
15. *I prefer besiege chess to chequer chess.* 围棋和跳棋，我更喜欢围棋。

Fashion Conversation 鲜活会话 由线到面

Conversation 1

A: Can I help you, madam?	A：你要点什么，女士？
B: Yes. Half a pound of Swiss cheese, please.	B：我要半磅瑞士硬干酪。
A: Sure. Anything else?	A：好的。还要别的吗？
B: Ah... yes, butter.	B：啊，对了，黄油。
A: Yes. How much?	A：要多少？
B: What's the price?	B：怎么卖？
A: One dollar and ninety cents per pound.	A：每磅1.9美元。
B: Two pounds, please.	B：请来两磅。
A: Here you are. Anything else?	A：给您。还要别的吗？
B: No, thanks.	B：不要了。谢谢。
(***She comes to the check-out counter.***)	(*她来到收银台。*)
C: 8 dollars total, madam.	C：共8美元，女士。
B: Can I pay cash here?	B：我能付现金吗？
C: Sure.	C：当然。
B: Here are ten dollars.	B：这是10美元。
C: Your change, madam.	C：这是找您的钱，女士。
B: Thank you.	B：谢谢。

Conversation 2

A: I like this computer very much. How much does it cost?	A：我非常喜欢这台电脑，请问多少钱？
B: It's the most expensive model in the store. It costs $2000.00.	B：这是店里最贵的型号，它的售价是2000美元。
A: That's too expensive for me. We can't afford all	A：这对我来说太贵了，我负担不起。

that money.

B: This mode's less expensive than that one. It's only $1450.00. But it's not as good as the expensive one.

B:这种型号的比那种要便宜,它只要1450美元,但是它当然没有价钱高的那种好。

A: I don't like this model. The other model's more expensive, but it's worth the money. Can I buy it on installments?

A:我不喜欢这种型号。那种型号是贵点,但它物有所值。我可以分期付款吗?

B: Of course.

B:当然可以。

A: OK, I'll take it.

A:好吧,就买它了。

Conversation 3

A: Hello, Tom, how nice to meet you here!

A:你好,汤姆。真高兴能在这儿见到你!

B: Hello, Li. So you're out shopping, too. What are you going to have today?

B:你好,小李。你也出来买东西。今天打算买些什么?

A: I haven't made up my mind yet. This is such a big store. Perhaps I'll first look at the clothes.

A:到现在还没决定呢。这是家大商店,也许我会先看看衣服。

B: Oh, the clothes counters are over there. You can choose from among a great variety of clothes.

B:噢,卖衣服的柜台在那边。有各种各样的衣服可供选择。

A: The suits look so nice here. How beautiful they are! I think I'd get some beautiful clothes today too.

A:这儿的衣服看起来很好。它们多漂亮呀!我想今天我最好也买几件漂亮的衣服。

B: I want to buy a suit too. By the way, do you know the vegetable counters have a very good delicatessen here? There are a variety of salads and sausages.

B:我也想买衣服,顺便问一下,你知道蔬菜货架那边有家非常好的熟菜店。那儿有各种各样的色拉和香肠。

A: Are they expensive?

A:那些东西贵吗?

B: I don't think you can call the things expensive here. Things are cheaper in a supermarket than in ordinary stores. And it saves time to do one's shopping in a supermarket.

B:我认为你不该说这儿的东西贵。超市里的东西比普通店里的东西便宜多了。并且在超市购物还节省时间。

A: Certainly you're right. Oh, yes, I also need some kitchen things.

A:你是对的。噢,我恰好也需要些厨房用的东西。

B: You can find all the kitchen things you need in the fourth aisle, I think.

B:我想你能在第四长廊里找到你所需要的任何东西。

A: I hope so too. Good-bye.

A:我也希望如此。再见。

Conversation 4

A: It's almost time for us to end our class, Tim. Let's go to the shop.

A:蒂姆,到下课时间了。我们一块去商店吧!

B: But I've nothing in my mind to buy.

B:但我没什么东西要买。

A: Just accompany me there. Then we can go home together.

A:就当陪我到那儿。那样我们就可以一块回家了。

B: OK. Let's go right away.

B:好吧!我们现在立刻去。

C: (an assistant) Hello. What can I do for you?

C:你们好,需要点什么吗?

A: I want to buy a diary book. Would you show me some, please?

A:我想买一本日记本。你能给我几本看吗?

C: Yes. What about this one? This is the most popular kind at present.
C: 当然可以,这一本怎么样? 这是目前最流行的一种。

A: Let me have a look. OK, it has a very beautiful color.
A: 让我看看。好,它的颜色非常漂亮。

C: And it also has an insert of ten pages of colorful pictures.
C: 它还插入了 10 张带彩色图画的纸。

A: Yes. I'll take this one.
A: 是的。我就要这一本了。

C: Anything else?
C: 还需要点别的吗?

A: Oh, yes. I need an envelope and a writing pad.
A: 噢,是的。我需要一个信封和一叠信纸。

C: Here you are.
C: 给你。

A: Thank you very much. How much are they?
A: 非常感谢。多少钱?

C: $5.
C: 5 美元。

A: Here you are.
A: 给你。

C: By the way, do you need an album? We have some new albums now, cheap and beautiful.
C: 顺便问一下,你需要相册吗? 我们现在有一些既便宜又漂亮的新相册。

A: May I have a look at them?
A: 我能看看吗?

C: Of course. Here you are.
C: 当然可以。给你。

A: Yes, beautiful indeed. Mark, come here, please.
A: 是的,真的很漂亮。马克,过来一下。

B: Yes?
B: 来了!

A: What do you think of these albums?
A: 你认为这些相册怎么样?

B: Very beautiful. Yes, I'm just needing one.
B: 非常漂亮。正好我也需要一册。

A: Me, too.
A: 我也是。

C: How about the brown one with the flower design?
C: 这个棕色的带花图案的怎么样?

A: Good. We'll take two.
A: 好的。我们要这两册。

C: That will be $11.00 in all.
C: 一共 11 美元。

A: Here you are. Thank you. Good-bye.
A: 给你。谢谢。再见。

C: Good-bye.
C: 再见。

Conversation 5

A: The design of this furniture is quite special, isn't it?
A: 这些家具的设计很特别吧?

B: Yes, it is. What is it made of?
B: 是挺特别的,这是什么材料做的?

C: It's made of kiln-dried timbers, sir. It's marked by its rose color and fragrant odour.
C: 先生,这是用干燥处理过的木材做的,木色像玫瑰,而且木质有玫瑰花香。

A: Really? Let me smell it. Hm..., there is a light fragrance of rose.
A: 真的? 让我闻闻,嗯……有一股淡淡的玫瑰芳香。

C: Would you like this table, madam? This furniture is colonial style and has multipurpose use, in laid with mother of pearl.
C: 你喜欢这张桌子吗,夫人? 这是殖民地时期的风格,有多种用途,上面镶有珍珠母。

B: Fantastic! I love it.
B: 太好了! 我很喜欢。

A: Is there a chair to go with it?
A: 有没有跟这配套的椅子?

C: Yes, sure. You can choose them from a book of designs. Here you are.
C: 有的,你可以从家具目录中挑选一下。给你目录。

B: Will you ship them to us when finished?
B: 完工后你们会代我们寄运吗?

C: Sure. We'll have it insured, too.
C: 当然会,我们还会购买保险。

B: What does the insurance cover?
B: 包括哪方面的保险?

C: It is a "all-risk" insurance. It includes destroy and lost in transit. We'll arrange it for you.
C: 它是"全保",它包括运送途中的损坏和遗失,我们会安排妥当的。

AB: Thank you very much.
AB: 太谢谢你了。

Conversation 6

A: Good afternoon, young man. What can I do for you?
A: 下午好,小伙子,要帮忙吗?

B: I'm looking for a tennis racket.
B: 我在找网球拍。

A: Would you like this one?
A: 你喜欢这个吗?

B: I don't think that will do. How about the one at your back?
B: 我觉得不好。你后面那个怎么样?

A: This one?
A: 这个吗?

B: No, the other one... yes.
B: 不是,那边那个……对了。

A: This one is especially built for hard, continuous play. And every detail of workmanship and material has been carefully checked to make it a dependable one for tournament use.
A: 这是为长期而剧烈的运动所特制的。各种材料和手工都经过细心考究,使它在比赛时能够成为可靠的拍子。

B: It do look beautiful. Well, I think I'll take it. Now do you have any racket covers?
B: 它的确看起来很美。嗯,我想我买了。有没有网球拍套?

A: This cover comes with the racket.
A: 球拍套是和球拍一起的。

B: How much does it come up to?
B: 总共多少钱?

A: The mark says six hundred yuan, plus tax, it's six hundred and eighty yuan.
A: 标签上是600元。加税一共是680元。

B: Do you accept credit cards?
B: 你们收不收信用卡?

A: Sure. If you'll just wait here, I'll be right with you in a minute.
A: 当然收。如果你愿意在此等待的话,我会马上回来的。

On the Scene 身临其境 面面俱到

主题:艾米来到化妆品柜台,她最终在售货员的推荐下买了一瓶香水和护肤油。请你看图,根据如下提供的关键词,将她们的对话写出来。

关键词语:counter *n.* 柜台　　made in 在……生产
fragrance *n.* 香味　　tonic *n.* 滋补品
pearl *n.* 珍珠　　efficiently *adv.* 有效地

参考答案

Salesgirl: Welcome to our counter. What can I do for you, Miss?
Amy: I'd like a bottle of perfume, the best one, please.
Salesgirl: Ok. This is made in France — one of the best perfumes in the world. It has a European jasmine fragrance.
Amy: Mmm, it's well-known make. I'll have one bottle.
Salesgirl: Anything else?
Amy: Do you have any skin tonic cream?
Salesgirl: Yes. This is a pearl cream made in Japan. It conserves skin efficiently.
Amy: And I'll also have a bottle of it.
售货员:欢迎来到我们柜台来。小姐,需要点什么?
艾米:我想要瓶香水,请拿最好的。
售货员:好,这是法国制造的世界上最好的香水。它有一种欧洲茉莉温馨的气味。
艾米:嗯,它非常有名,我就要一瓶这样的。
售货员:还需要别的吗?
艾米:你这儿还有滋补皮肤用的护肤油吗?
售货员:有。这是产于日本的珍珠护肤油。对保护皮肤非常有效。
艾米:我也要一瓶。

★超市选购★  In the Supermarket

 Words and Phrases 闪亮词语 点滴积累

pear 梨
ananas;pineapple 凤梨
sand pear 沙梨
orange 橙;广柑
citrus 柑橘
pomelo;shaddock 柚子;文旦
lemon 柠檬
banana 香蕉
red bayberry 杨梅
strawberry 草莓
carambola 猕猴桃;杨桃
wild peach 毛桃
watermelon 西瓜
muskmelon 香瓜;甜瓜
"Hami" melon 哈密瓜
papaya (番)木瓜
snake melon 菜瓜
cherry 樱桃
water chestnut 荸荠
pomegranate 石榴
areca 槟榔
toothpaste;dental cream 牙膏
tooth powder 牙粉
toothbrush 牙刷
toilet soap 香皂
soap 肥皂
sandal soap 檀香皂
medicated soap 药皂
towel 毛巾
washing powder 洗衣粉
detergent 洗涤剂
mirror;looking-glass 镜子
cloth brush 衣刷
comb 梳子
toothcomb 篦子
scissors 剪刀
(razor)blade 刀片
nail clippers 指甲刀
nail file 指甲锉
can opener 罐头刀
tooth-pick 牙签

 Useful Sentences 七彩精句 连点成线

Fruits 水果

1. *Are these melons ripe?* 这些西瓜熟了吗?
2. *Could I have two kilos of orange, please.* 请给我两公斤橙子好吗?
3. *Are the strawberries sweet?* 这些草莓甜不甜?
4. *How much are these apples?* 这些苹果多少钱?
5. *Can I sample a litchi?* 我可不可以尝一个荔枝?
6. *Will you give me a discount if I buy in bulk?* 如果我大量购买你会给我折扣吗?
7. *Is the scale accurate?* 秤准吗?
8. *How much do the apples weigh?* 这些苹果有多重?
9. *May I have a look at the strawberries over there?* 我可以看看那边的草莓吗?
10. *How about some guavas, and star fruit?* 买点番石榴和洋桃好吗?
11. *Would you please choose one of them for me?* 请给我挑一个好吗?
12. *The grapes look good.* 这些葡萄看起来不错。
13. *These blueberries look wonderful.* 这些蓝莓看起来很棒。
14. *This cantaloupe is too soft.* 这个香瓜太软了。

Candy 糖果

1. *Are you looking for some sweets?* 你想买些糖果吗？
2. *Will you wrap them up separately?* 帮我分别包起来，好吗？
3. *What's the difference between these two styles of moon cake?* 这两种月饼有什么区别？
4. *Do you want it sliced?* 要切成片吗？
5. *May I pay by credit card?* 我可以用信用卡付款吗？
6. *Do you know where the bread section is?* 您知道哪儿卖面包吗？
7. *Is this birthday cake made today?* 这个生日蛋糕是今天做的吗？
8. *Where is the biscuit made?* 这饼干是哪儿产的？
9. *How much is the coconut candy a kilogram?* 椰子糖一公斤多少钱？
10. *Give me two cream birthday cakes.* 给我两份奶油生日蛋糕。
11. *We have got a fresh stock of all kinds of moon cakes.* 我们刚刚进了一批各种各样的月饼。
12. *I heard sorghum candies is a native product here.* 我听说高粱饴是本地的特产。

Tea 茶叶

1. *I'd like to buy some tea.* 我想买些茶叶。
2. *I've never seen black tea.* 我从没见过红茶。
3. *I'm used to green tea.* 我习惯喝绿茶。
4. *They think jasmine tea more fragrant and pleasant.* 他们认为花茶气味更芬香。
5. *That's why we call it black tea.* 那就是为什么我们叫它红茶的原因。
6. *Chinese tea is world-famous.* 中国的茶叶世界闻名。
7. *They saw Longjing tea is pure and fragrant and has a sweetish and mellow taste.* 听说龙井茶清纯芬芳，口味甘美醇和。
8. *The black tea tastes strong and promotes digestion?* 红茶味浓，而且有助消化。
9. *I like the green tea produced in Hunan.* 我喜欢湖南产的绿茶。
10. *I want to buy some jasmine tea of high quality to bring back home.* 我要买点高级的茉莉花茶带回家。

Wine 酒品

1. *Do you have any French grape wine?* 你们有法国的葡萄酒吗？
2. *What kind of wine is the best in China?* 中国最好的酒是什么？
3. *May I have a look at the liquor produced in Russia?* 能给我看看俄罗斯产的白酒吗？
4. *How much is a bottle of Mao Tai wine?* 茅台酒多少钱一瓶？
5. *I know it's called XO. It's very expensive, isn't it?* 我知道它叫 XO，十分昂贵，对吗？
6. *Is it true that the older a wine gets, the better it is?* 葡萄酒是不是越陈越好呢？
7. *Sir, where can I choose some soft drinks?* 先生，哪儿能找到软饮料？
8. *Any orange juice here?* 这儿有橙汁吗？
9. *Where do I return bottles?* 我在哪里退瓶？
10. *I'll take five tins of beer and a bottle of whisky.* 我要 5 罐啤酒和 1 瓶威士忌。
11. *Show me the best champagne in your counter, please.* 请给我看看你们柜台里最好的香槟酒。
12. *Here is the money for brandy.* 这是买白兰地的钱。

Fashion Conversation 鲜活会话 由线到面

Conversation 1

A: Let's get a shopping cart. First we'll get our vegetables. Here are cucumbers, mushrooms, tomatoes, lettuce and potatoes straight from the farm.

A: 让我们去推一辆小推车。首先我们要买蔬菜。这儿是黄瓜、蘑菇、西红柿、莴苣和土豆。

B: Let's get some lettuce, tomatoes and cucumbers for a salad.
B:我们先挑选一些莴苣,西红柿和黄瓜这些用来做沙拉的蔬菜吧。

A: Let's check out the fruit section. I'd like some watermelons and peaches.
A:我们再逛一下水果区吧,我想买点儿西瓜和桃子。

B: Let's go to the meat section. Want some beef?
B:再让我们去肉类区看看。想要一些牛肉吗?

A: Yes. We can make hamburger with beef.
A:对。我们可以用牛肉来做汉堡。

B: Just as you say.
B:就按你说的办。

A: Here is the fish counter. Look at the lobsters and crabs. Shall we have some?
A:这儿是鱼类柜台。看那些龙虾和蟹子。我们要买点吗?

B: I'm allergic to these things, you know.
B:你知道我对那些东西过敏。

A: Sorry, I forgot. I don't like seafood, either.
A:对不起,我忘了。我也不喜欢海洋食品。

B: Let's go over there and get some milk, a couple dozen eggs and some orange juice.
B:让我们去那边看看,买些牛奶,买二打鸡蛋,再买些橘子汁。

A: Let's get frozen juice. It is really good.
A:我们买点冰冻橘子汁吧,挺好的。

B: We've got enough food to feed a small army. Let's go over to the check-out stand.
B:我们买的食物已经足够了。我们去结账吧。

A: OK. But just let me pick up a bottle of wine and oil as we go by.
A:好。不过我顺路再拿一瓶葡萄酒和油吧!

Conversation 2

A: Excuse me, where is the fruit and vegetable section?
A:请问水果蔬菜区在哪儿?

B: Go all the way to the back and turn right, Aisle 8.
B:往里头走到尽头,右转,在第8走道。

A: Thank you. Here I am. I'd like some oranges.
A:谢谢。到了。我要一些橙子。

B: Yes, and...
B:好的,还要什么?

A: Give me a pound of potatoes and a pound of cabbages.
A:给我一磅土豆和一磅卷心菜。

B: Here you are. Will that be all for you today?
B:在这儿。今天要的都有了吗?

A: Yes, thank you.
A:是的,谢谢。

Conversation 3

A: We have to buy a lot of food and we have to finish fast.
A:我们必须买许多食品并尽快买完。

B: Here's the list. Let's divide it.
B:这是购物单。咱俩分开买。

A: That's a great idea! You get the milk, sausage, beef, fish and eggs. I can get the tomatoes, pea, lettuce, potato chips, bananas and coffee.
A:好主意。你买牛奶、香肠、牛肉、鱼和鸡蛋,我买番茄、豌豆、莴笋、土豆片、香蕉和咖啡。

B: Fine, but where is the beef?
B:好吧。但是牛肉在哪儿?

A: It is over there near the sausage.
A:在那边靠近香肠处。

B: OK.
B:知道了。

A: Well, I have everything. What about you?
A:好了,我买全了,你呢?

B: I can't find the fish.
B:我还没找到鱼。

A: It's over there next to the milk.
A:在那边靠近牛奶的地方。

B: Everything is here. Where to pay it?
B:好了,都在这儿了,去哪里付款?

A: At the cash register in front.
A:在前面收银机处付账。

Conversation 4

A: It's too crowded here. I only need several pairs of socks. Let's go straight to the footwear section.
A: 这太挤了，我就需要几双袜子。我们直接去鞋袜部吧。

B: OK. Look at that lamp. It's on promotion, only ten yuan.
B: 好的。看那个台灯。在搞促销，只要10块钱。

A: I know it's a good bargain but we don't need another lamp.
A: 我知道很便宜但是我们不需要台灯了。

B: Yes, you are right. I just can't resist the temptation every time I go to the supermarket.
B: 是啊，你说得对。我每次一逛超市就抵制不了诱惑。

A: That's how they cheat you into buying things you really don't need.
A: 他们就是这么骗你买一些你不需要的东西的。

Conversation 5

A: I'd like to buy a bottle of wine or liquor for my father. You have so many kinds here that I can't decide which one to buy.
A: 我要买瓶酒给我老爸，种类那么多，我不知道买哪一种好。

B: How about this Scotch whisky? It's distilled from a pure barley malt mash and is aged in cherry casks. Or you may buy this XO cognac brandy. It's 10 years old and contains about 45% alcohol.
B: 这种苏格兰威士忌怎么样？这是麦芽泥蒸馏做的，贮放在樱桃木酒桶内已经长年累月。不然，买这种XO甘邑白兰地。10年老酒，大约含45%的酒精。

A: I see. Would you tell me something about gin, rum and vodka, please?
A: 原来如此。你介绍一下杜松子酒，兰姆酒和伏特加，好吗？

B: Sure. Rums are distilled from the fermented juice of the sugar cane or from fermented molasses. This one is distilled in Jamaica, and bottled in London. Gin is made from a mash of grain and juniper berries and Vodka is distilled from a mash of rye, wheat or potatoes. Vodka mixes easily with fruit juices.
B: 没问题。兰姆酒是用发酵的甘蔗汁或发酵的糖蜜蒸馏而成的。这一瓶在牙买加酿造，在伦敦装瓶。杜松子酒是谷类糊浆和杜松子酱果酿造的，而伏特加则是燕麦、大麦或马铃薯蒸馏而成的，伏特加可以和果汁搭配。

On the Scene 身临其境 面面俱到

主题：韦德在超市里选购衬衫，他想要个大号的，可是没货了。请你看图，根据如下提供的关键词，将他们的对话写出来。

关键词语：on sale 促销　　sell out 卖光了
unlikely *adj.* 未必的　　season *n.* 季节

参考答案

Salesgirl: What about this one? It's on sale.
Wade: It looks nice but what I have in mind is a larger one.
Salesgirl: I'm sorry, larger sizes are sold out.
Wade: Are you getting any more in this week?
Salesgirl: I'm afraid it's unlikely. These are what are left from the last season.
售货员:这个怎么样？在打特价。
韦德:看上去不错,但我想要个大号的。
售货员:对不起,没有大号的。
韦德:这周进货吗?
售货员:恐怕不进了,这是上个季节剩下的。

★服装鞋帽★ 18 Wearing Things

Words and Phrases 闪亮词语 点滴积累

men's wear 男装
women's wear 女装
jacket 夹克,短上衣
slacks 宽松的裤子
jeans 牛仔裤
under wear 内衣裤
children's wear 童装
shoe 鞋
boot 皮靴
rain shoe 雨鞋
sneaker 运动鞋
leather-shoe 皮鞋
tall boot 长靴
slip-on 便鞋
low heel 平跟鞋
clogs 木屐
baseball cap 棒球帽
felt hat 毡帽
safety helmet 安全帽
bonnet 软帽
sombrero 墨西哥宽边帽
beret 贝雷帽
scarf 围巾
sock 短袜
panty-hose 连裤袜
mitten 连指手套
stocking 长袜
glove 手套

Useful Sentences 七彩精句 连点成线

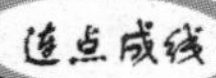

Clothing 服装

1. *Why don't tuck in your shirt?* 你为什么不把衬衫塞进去?
2. *What should I wear?* 我该穿什么呢?
3. *Do you prefer cotton or polyester shirts?* 你喜欢棉的还是涤纶的衬衫?
4. *Are your clothes tailor made?* 你的衣服是定做的吗?
5. *Don't you think that my black tie goes better with that?* 你不觉得我的黑领带更配这个吗?
6. *What do you think about my new dress?* 你觉得我的新衣服怎么样?
7. *What are you planning on wearing to the party?* 你准备穿什么衣服去参加这次宴会?
8. *Don't bother to dress up —come as you are.* 不用穿讲究的衣服——就穿平常的衣服来吧。
9. *I would like my sleeves lengthened.* 我想把袖子加长。
10. *I need my suit altered.* 我要改衣服。
11. *It is too tight. I want to make it loose.* 这太紧了,我想把它加肥。
12. *Can you change the buttons for me?* 帮我把这些扣子换一下,可以吗?
13. *It is too small for me.* 它太小了,不适合我。
14. *Let me try it on.* 让我试试。
15. *This one suits me very well.* 这个非常适合我。
16. *It must be a foreign product.* 它一定是外国货。

Trousers 裤子

1. *The fitting room is over there.* 试衣间在那边。
2. *Would you give me a larger one?* 你能再给我找一条长点的吗?
3. *I like light blue jeans.* 我喜欢浅蓝色的牛仔裤。
4. *I recommend you this jeans.* 我向你推荐这件条裤子。
5. *White coat can match trousers.* 白色上衣好配裤子。
6. *The dark color trousers go well with your jacket.* 这件深色的裤子很配得上你的夹克衫。

Shoes 鞋

1. *It is made of leather.* 是用皮革制成的。
2. *It is too tight.* 鞋挤脚。
3. *The shoes are thin but strong.* 鞋底虽薄但很结实。
4. *The heel is too high.* 鞋后跟太高了。
5. *I like the design.* 我喜欢这个样式。

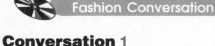

Fashion Conversation 鲜活会话

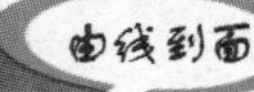

Conversation 1

A: This cap is too small for you. I think a medium size will fit you better.
B: Do you have the medium size?
A: Yes. The blue one is a medium size.
B: Let me try it on.
A: Sure. This one suits you much better.
B: Is it a foreign product?
A: No. It is made in China.
B: Can you guarantee the quality?
A: Absolutely.

A:这顶帽子太小了,你戴不了。我想中号的会更适合你。
B:你这儿有中号的吗?
A:是的。那顶蓝色的帽子就是中号的。
B:让我试试。
A:好的。这顶很适合你。
B:它是外国产品吗?
A:不是,它是中国制造的。
B:你能确保它的质量吗?
A:当然,完全可以。

Conversation 2

A: I see that the leather is not of good quality.
B: That is the best leather.
A: How about the soles?
B: They are thin but strong.
A: I'll try them on.
B: You will wear them easily.
A: The tips are too narrow. I'm afraid I will get corns.
B: Will you please try them on?
A: They are too tight. Can't you get me a pair of larger ones?
B: That doesn't matter, sir. The leather will stretch and your foot will soon accommodate to the shoes.
A: Maybe, but I still want a larger pair.
B: Please try the other pair then.
A: The leather is not good enough.
B: But this is the best calf leather, sir.
A: How much?
B: 100 yuan.
A: It's fair. I'll take it.

A:我看这皮子质量不好。
B:这是最好的皮子了。
A:鞋底怎么样?
B:薄,但很结实。
A:我试试。
B:很好穿的。
A:鞋尖太窄了。恐怕我会长鸡眼的。
B:您愿意试穿一下吗?
A:太紧了,能给我一双大点儿的吗?
B:不要紧的,先生。皮子穿穿就松了。很快就合脚了。
A:或许是吧,但我还是想要一双大点儿的。
B:请试试这双。
A:皮子不够好。
B:这可是最好的小牛皮了,先生。
A:多少钱?
B:100 元。
A:好吧,我就要这双。

Conversation 3

A: What a nice dress, Rose. You look marvelous.
B: You too. Where did you get your new hat?
A: From Friendship Store.

A:罗斯,你的套裙好漂亮。你看起来气度非凡。
B:你也一样。在哪儿买的新帽子?
A:友谊商店。

B: Oh, what a lovely earrings you have. Are they diamond?	B: 多可爱的耳环。是钻石的吗?
A: Yes. It's a birthday present from my husband.	A: 是的。是丈夫送我的生日礼物。
B: Well, you are lucky to have such a considerate husband. Mine hasn't bought me a single rose since we married.	B: 你多幸运有这么体贴的丈夫。结婚后,我丈夫连一枝玫瑰也没有给我买过。
A: Look at that woman with the white chiffon. She looks really marvelous.	A: 看那个穿白色薄纱的女士,她看起来才真正是气度非凡。
B: She is very fashionable, isnt she?	B: 她很时髦,不是吗?
A: Yes. I prefer her dress, and it must be the latest style.	A: 是的。我喜欢她穿的套裙。肯定是最新款的。
B: It makes me feel rather shabby.	B: 它让我感觉很寒酸。
A: Yes. She dressed with an individual flair.	A: 是的。(我也有同感),她穿出了个性。
B: I quite agree with you.	B: 我很同意。
A: But you are quite slim, and have a fabulous figure.	A: 但是你也很苗条,有让人惊叹的身材。
B: Thanks. I am flattered.	B: 谢谢。过奖了。

Conversation 4

A: I love this pair of jeans.	A: 我觉得这条牛仔裤挺不错的。
B: Please try them on if you like. The fitting room is right over there.	B: 喜欢就试试吧。试衣间就在那边。
A: Thank you.	A: 谢谢。
B: Do they fit?	B: 怎么样?
A: No, this size is a little too large for me. Have you got anything smaller?	A: 不太合适。有点长。还有短一点的吗?
B: Yes, I'll show you. Oh, sorry, they are all sold out.	B: 应该有。我给你找一下。哦,很抱歉,小号的都卖光了。
A: When can I get a smaller one?	A: 什么时候还能再进?
B: At least a week later.	B: 最快一周后。
A: That's too long for me. I can not wait for them.	A: 那么晚!我恐怕不能等到那个时候。
B: Maybe you can find some in the next jeans shop?	B: 你可以去隔壁的店看看。
A: Do you think so?	A: 它们能有吗?
B: You can try.	B: 你可以试试呀。
A: Thanks. Bye-bye.	A: 好的,谢谢。再见。

Conversation 5

A: How do I look in this checkered dress?	A: 我穿这件格子衣服看来怎样?
B: Lovely! But it's a bit too flappy at the shoulders.	B: 真美!不过肩部太宽松了些。
A: You're right. And the hemline is too low. Why don't you try it one?	A: 你说得不错!而且裙摆太长了。你何不试穿一下。
B: Oh, no. Pink is definitely not fit for me.	B: 不行。粉红色绝不适合我。
A: Why do you always stick to black and dark brown, Babs? Why not try pink for a change?	A: 你为什么总是只穿黑色和深棕色,芭布斯?为什么不试试粉红色改变一下?
B: Light colors make me look fatter.	B: 浅颜色会使我看起来更胖。

A: You're not fat. Just plump.
B: I can't possibly squeeze into that dress, Linda. My waist is at lest three inches wider than yours.
A: I'm too skinny! I wish I had your bust.
B: Do you also wish to be overweight like me?
A: Who is overweight or not is a matter of opinion.
B: Says who?
A: Says my mother. She is a nutrition expert, mind you.

A:你才不胖。只是丰满。
B:我根本不可能挤进那件衣服里,琳达。我的腰起码比你粗3英寸。
A:我太瘦了!我希望有你那样的胸围。
B:你也希望像我这样体重过重吗?
A:什么人是否过重,是见仁见智的。
B:谁说的?
A:我妈说的。她是营养专家,你可要弄清楚。

On the Scene 身临其境 面面俱到

主题:一对情侣来到服装店买旗袍,售货员向他们推荐了苏州绸缎料子的。请你看图,根据如下提供的关键词,将他们的对话写出来。

关键词语:precious *adj.* 宝贵的　　wow *interj.* 哎唷!天哪!
terrific *adj.* 令人恐怖的　　try sth. on 试穿
excellent *adj.* 卓越的　　figure *n.* 形状

参考答案

Salesgirl: Welcome, sir and madam. Can I help you?
Rose: Yes. I'd like to buy a Qipao for myself. Are there any ready — made ones of my size?
Salesgirl: Yes, there are. You may choose the style you like from this book. I suggest you buy a sleeveless style. It would display your youth.
Rose: Oh, this one. I like this style. Better dark green, with some embroidery on the front.
Salesgirl: Fine. How about this one ? It's made from precious Suzhou silk, and sells pretty well.
Rose: Wow, terrific! Can I try it on?
Rose: Bob, how does it look on me? Do you think the slits are a bit too high?
Bob: No, not at all. You seem to have an excellent figure in it as if the dress was made specially for you.
Rose: Really? That's most kind of you! I'll take it.
售货员:欢迎两位。想买点什么?
罗斯:我想要买旗袍。你们这儿有没有适合我的尺码的现成旗袍?
售货员:有的。您可以从这本书里挑选喜欢的式样。我建议您买无袖的式样,它能体现您的青春活力。

罗斯:啊,这种!我要这种式样的,最好是墨绿的,胸前要有一点儿绣花的。
售货员:好的。这件怎么样?料子是苏州名贵绸缎,也很畅销。
罗斯:噢,真是好看极了。可以试试吗?
售货员:鲍勃,你看还可以吗?开叉是否太高了一点?
鲍勃:一点都都不高。你穿着身材好极了,就像是特意为你定做的。
罗斯:真的?你真太好了!我要了。

★经典住宅★ 19 Classical Housing

Words and Phrases 闪亮词语 点滴积累

residence 住宅
country house 别墅
studio flat 一居室公寓房
house exposed to the west 西晒房屋
west block 西街区
foreign-style house 洋房
new community 新社区
abutting building 毗连房屋
garden house 花园洋房
villa marine 海滨房屋
block of flats 公寓大楼
detached house 独户住宅
roof 屋顶
ridge 屋脊
chimney 烟囱
dormer-window 天窗
balcony 阳台
wall 墙壁
ceiling 天花板
floor 地板;地
staircase;step 楼梯;梯子
corkscrew staircase 回转梯
blinds 百叶窗
balance window 旋转窗
casement 窗叶
window frame 窗框
partition 隔间
foyer 门厅
mainhall 大厅
platform 平台
garret 屋顶层
drying stage 晒台

Useful Sentences  七彩精句 连点成线

New House 新房出售

1. *There are three bedrooms, a large sitting-room, a kitchen and a bathroom.* 有3间卧室,1间大客厅,1间厨房和1间浴室。
2. *We've sold out all the units in the East Tower. Only design B and C remain in the West Tower and those are selling very fast.* 东楼所有单元已售完,西楼的B型和C型也卖得很快。
3. *What's kind of a house do you want to buy?* 你想买什么样的房子?
4. *Could you tell me something about the house?* 你能给我介绍一下房子的情况吗?
5. *But it's too small for me.* 但是对我来说太小了。
6. *But it's too far from my work.* 但是离我的工作地点太远了。
7. *The real estate market is down now. This is a good buy.* 房地产市场正处在低潮,很划得来。
8. *Does C have two balconies?* C型有没有两个阳台?

Second-Hand House 二手房屋

1. *How much is the owner asking for it?* 房主要的价是多少?
2. *What's the asking price?* 要价是多少?
3. *That's quite a big sitting room and a kitchen.* 这房子有个很大的起居室和厨房。
4. *But it's too expensive for me.* 但是对我来说太贵了。
5. *Do you have any information about the second-hand house for sale?* 你有二手房出售的信息吗?
6. *Are there any houses for sale here?* 请问这里有房子要出售吗?
7. *What's the condition of the house?* 房子的状况怎么样?
8. *What happens if the seller doesn't live up to his end of the deal?* 如果卖方不能完全履行合同怎么办?
9. *Would you mind telling me why you want to sell this house?* 您能告诉我您为什么要把房子卖了

吗？

10. *It's a two-bed room one, and renovated building with an eat-in kitchen.* 两居室，全楼经过整修，厨房很大，可以在里面就餐。

Transportation 询问交通问题

1. *Is it close to public transportation?* 这地方靠近公交站吗？
2. *How far from the bus is it?* 房子离公共汽车站有多远？
3. *How close to the subway is it?* 房子离地铁站有多远？
4. *Is it near the train?* 房子附近有没有火车站？

Decoration 装修

1. *The tap is leaking. Can you have a look at it?* 水龙头漏水。你们能来检查修理一下吗？
2. *I want to redecorate my bedroom, David. Can you do me a favor?* 大卫，我想重新装修一下卧室，你能帮我一下吗？
3. *Do you plan to repaint the wall?* 要重新刷墙吗？
4. *I thought we'd just fix up the wood floor, and use some paint for the walls.* 我觉得我们只要整修一下这木头地板就可以了，然后粉刷一下墙面。
5. *How do you want to decorate your house?* 您想怎么装修您的房屋？
6. *What colour do you want?* 您想刷成什么颜色呢？
7. *Are you from the House Repair Service?* 你是房屋维修公司的吗？
8. *Is the bulb OK? Yes, it's a new one.* 灯泡没问题吧？没问题，是个新的。
9. *These two air conditioners are out of order.* 这两个空调坏了。
10. *When will the plumber be available?* 管道工什么时候有空？
11. *What's wrong with it exactly?* 到底是哪里坏了？
12. *How much is it to have the window fixed?* 这扇窗户修一下要多少钱？
13. *It's not worth the trouble to fix it.* 不值得费心去修了。
14. *It's not worth fixing.* 这不值得修。
15. *Will you have it replaced?* 要不要给你换个新的？
16. *Is there anything else we can do for you when we are in this house?* 趁我们的人在这儿，还有别的要修的吗？
17. *How old is this wardrobe?* 这个衣柜的使用年龄大概有多久？
18. *Do you offer delivery?* 你们能送货吗？
19. *What are the costs for delivery?* 运费是多少？
20. *How do I install this door lock?* 我该如何安装这门锁？
21. *Do I need to use a drill to put up these shelves?* 一定要用电钻来钉这些架子吗？
22. *Hello, I would like to order a door.* 你好，我要订做一扇门。
23. *The measurements are 108 by 48 by 3 inches.* 尺寸是高108英寸，宽48英寸，厚3英寸。

Fashion Conversation 鲜活会话 由线到面

Conversation 1

A: I'm thinking about moving out of my place.
B: How come? I thought you liked your house.
A: I do, but with three kids growing up, it's too small.
B: How big is your place?
A: It's about 100 square metre.
B: How many rooms does it have?
A: Just two. I want my kids to have their own rooms.
B: You must have saved up a lot of money.

A：我正打算搬家。
B：为什么？我还以为你喜欢你的房子呢？
A：我喜欢，但3个孩子正在长大，它有点太小了。
B：你家有多大？
A：大约100平方米。
B：有多少间房？
A：只有两间，我希望孩子们有自己的房间。
B：你一定攒了不少钱。

A: Not really. But if I could get a decent price for my house, I could probably afford a detached house with 4 rooms.

A:并不太多,但如果我的房子能卖个不错的价格,我也许可以买得起有4个房间的单元房了。

Conversation 2

A: Hello, Mr. Johnson. I have Mrs. Chen to check out the house.

A:您好,约翰逊先生。这是陈太太,她来看你的房子。

B: Please come in and feel free to take a look around the house.

B:请进来随便参观。

A: Mrs Chen, as you can see, the decoration is in perfect condition. The kitchen is on your left. Look! It is so big that you can fit five people inside. (*They walk to the living room*) The layout of the flat is one dining room, one living room, one master bedroom and two bedrooms. The gross area of this unit is two hundred and thirteen square feet.

A:陈太太,这房子装修挺好的,厨房就在左边,看!厨房可以容纳5个人。(*他们步进客厅*)这间房子的基本设计为三室二厅,包括一个客厅、一个饭厅、一间主人套房连洗手间和两间睡房。建筑面积是213平方英尺。

C: Does this apartment face south?

C:这房子是否向南?

A: The living room faces south and the bedrooms face north. It has a beautiful hill view and quiet environment. Also, it has many amenities such as a grand shopping mall, wonderful playground, and few supermarkets. Also, it is conveniently located for public transportation like the MTR and buses.

A:客厅朝南,卧室朝北,环境幽雅。而且设施齐备:有大型购物商场、儿童游乐场和超市。并且附近有地铁站,交通非常方便。

C: Great!

C:很好。

Conversation 3

A: May I ask if your interest in the unit is for investment or self-use, Mrs Green?

A:格林夫人,你买这套房是投资还是自用呢?

B: The purpose is for investment because I hear from my friend that the rental return for Tai Koo Shing is not bad.

B:我的目的是投资,因为我听说太古城的物业租金回报不错。

A: Sure. Mrs Green, the rent for this unit is around thirty-five thousand Hong Kong dollars. The yield is almost ten percent. There are many Japanese and Westerners who love to live here. It's only because Mr Johnson must go back to England that he has to sell this unit.

A:这是肯定的。格林夫人,这套房子每月租金约3500元,回报率约10%。很多日本人和西方人都喜欢在这里居住。因为约翰逊先生必须返回英国,否则他可不愿意卖这房的。

B: I understand. The flat is under a good condition and I don't have to redecorate it later. But, I've got to discuss it with my husband first. Mr wilson, how about I call you to make an appointment again?

B:我明白。这房子基本情况很好,我不需要重新装修,不过,我要先与我的丈夫商量。威尔逊先生,不如我再给你电话确定另一个约会吧。

A: Sure. Mrs Green, anyway, I should remind you that you must be quick because I have other cli-

A:没有问题。格林夫人,不过,我必须提醒你要快点决定,因为还有其他客户要求看这套房子的。

ents requesting to check this unit later.

B: Okay. I'll call you later.

B:好的,我稍后再给你电话。

Conversation 4

A: Here's your lease. Please sign here and here.	A:这是租约。请在这儿和这儿签字。
B: Just give me a few minutes to read it, all right?	B:请给我几分钟让我看看行吗?
A: Yes, go ahead.	A:好的,请便。
B: The rent is $400 a month. Does that include gas, electricity and heat?	B:租金每月400美元。包括煤气,电和暖气费吗?
A: Yes.	A:包括。
B: How long is the lease?	B:租约的有效期是多长?
A: One year.	A:一年。
B: And I have to deposit one month rent in advance.	B:我还要预付1个月的押金。
A: Yes, it will be refunded to you at the expiration of the lease.	A:是的,租约期满时,押金退回。
B: When can I move in?	B:我什么时候能搬进来?
A: Anytime.	A:什么时候都行。
B: All right. I'll sign it. Here's $800.	B:那好,我签字。给你800美元。
A: Thank you. Here's your copy of the lease and the key.	A:谢谢。这是你的租约副本和房间钥匙。

Conversation 5

A: Hello. I have just seen your advertisement. You haven't rented it yet, have you?	A:你好。我看了您登的广告。您还没有把房租出去吧?
B: No, I haven't. It's still vacant. Come in and have a look.	B:还没有。还空着呢。进来看看吧。
A: Thank you.	A:谢谢。
B: It's just a simple room. My son used to live in it. Now he is grown and gone, and my husband died last year. So I thought maybe I'd take in a roomer.	B:房间很简单。以前是我儿子住,现在他长大了,搬出去住很久了。我丈夫去年也去世了。所以,我想找一个寄宿者。
A: A nice, quiet house. That's what I'm looking for.	A:我想找一间好的,安静的房间。
B: This way, sir.	B:先生请这边走。
A: This is a very pleasant room. How much is the rent?	A:这房间很舒适。房租是多少?
B: Fifty dollars a week if you think that's OK. I won't charge you anything for electricity, gas and heat. Oh, yes, you can use the kitchen and refrigerator too.	B:如果您能接受,每周50美元。我不收您电、煤气和暖气费。哦,对了,您也能用厨房和冰箱。
A: Well, I like this place very much. But, you know, I don't have much money.	A:我很喜欢这个房间,但是,我没有多少钱。
B: You seem like a very nice young man. What about $40?	B:您看上去是个不错的年轻人。40美元怎么样?
A: That's good. May I move in tomorrow morning?	A:那太好子。明天早上我能搬过来吗?
B: Fine. I'll be expecting you. If you don't mind, I'd	B:当然可以。我会等您的。如果您不介意的话,您

like to have the first two weeks' rent in advance. | 要预付两周的租金。

Conversation 6

A: What apartment type is still available?
A:你们还有什么房型可供选择?

B: We've sold out all the units in the East Tower. Only design B and C remain in the West Tower and those are selling very fast. The B design is 90 square meters and the C style with double bath is 135 square meters.
B:东楼所有单元已售完,西楼的B型和C型也卖得很快。B型有90平方米,C型有两个卫生间,共135平方米。

A: I definitely like the larger. My bank has cleared a mortgage of 300, 000 Yuan. Does C have two balconies?
A:我比较喜欢大的。我有30万元银行贷款,当然想买C型。C型有没有两个阳台?

B: Yes, both face south, the best position to be in, I might add.
B:有,都是朝南阳台,可以说是目前朝向最好的。

A: You mentioned that the building had several amenities including a swimming pool, gym and... did I miss anything?
A:你提到大楼还提供一些便利设施,如游泳池,健身房……我还遗漏了什么?

B: 24hr building management.
B:24小时物业服务。

A: Yes. How much is the deposit for the one on the 9th floor?
A:对。九楼那间的定金要多少?

B: They are all 15% down, and with another 10% payable on completion in six months.
B:先付15%,六个月完工后再付10%。

A: May I have a look at the contract and the house floor plan?
A:我能看一下合同和房型图吗?

B: Of course. Here you are.
B:当然,给你。

On the Scene 身临其境 面面俱到

主题:莫莉来到约克家,对他家的家具及起居室进行了一番评价。请你看图,根据如下提供的关键词,将他们的对话写出来。

关键词语:living room 起居室　　square meter 平方米
comfortable *adj.* 舒适的　　especially *adv.* 特别

参考答案

Molly: How large the living room is!
York: Yes, about fifty square meters.
Molly: Your curtain is quite beautiful, too.
York: Thank you.
Molly: And the sofa looks comfortable just like a bed.
York: Yes, especially when sitting there and watching TV.
Molly: It would be better if you put a pot of flower here.
York: You are right.

莫莉:起居室真宽敞!
约克:是的,有50平米。
莫莉:你的窗帘也很漂亮。
约克:谢谢。
莫莉:沙发就像床一样的舒服。
约克:是的,特别是坐在那里看电视时。
莫莉:这儿要是放瓶花就好了。
约克:对。

Jobs

CHAPTER

3

人在职场

★招聘人才★ 1 Recruiting

Words and Phrases 闪亮词语 点滴积累

ill-paid(/underpaid) work(/job) 报酬低的工作
highly-paid (/well-paid) job (/work) 报酬优厚的工作
duty work; labour of duty 本职工作
superficial work 表面工作
horse work 吃力而单调的工作
continued unemployment 持续失业现象
creative work 创造性工作
beneficent(/charity) work 慈善工作
rough work(/labour) 粗活
large-scale unemployment 大规模失业
mass unemployment 大量失业
collar(/uphill/heavy) work 繁重的工作

Useful Sentences 七彩精句 连点成线

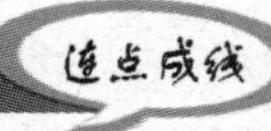

Interview 面试用语

1. *What's the salary?* 薪水是多少?
2. *Is it salaried or hourly?* 是固定薪水还是按小时算?
3. *Is it part-time or full-time?* 兼职还是专职的?
4. *What are the hours?* 工作时间有多长?
5. *What are the benefits?* 福利待遇如何?
6. *Do I get insurance?* 给我上保险吗?
7. *What would be expected of me?* 期望我做出什么样的业绩?
8. *What are you looking for(in an employee)?* 你要求雇员做到什么?
9. *What are your qualifications?* 你的资历如何?
10. *What is your degree in?* 你得过什么样的学位?
11. *Where did you go to school?* 你在哪儿上的学?
12. *What sort of salary do you expect?* 你期望的薪水是多少?
13. *Let me see your resume.* 让我看一下你的简历。
14. *Let me see your dossier.* 让我看一下你的材料。
15. *Let me see your references.* 让我看一下你的推荐信。
16. *Why did you leave your last job?* 你为什么辞掉了一个工作?
17. *When can you start?* 你什么时候能开始上班?
18. *We will call you if we need you.* 如果我们录用你,会打电话给你的。
19. *Don't call us; we'll call you.* 不用给我们打电话,我们会打给你的。

Green hand 新手

1. *I haven't had much experience (in this line of work).* 我(在这个行当)没有多少经验。
2. *I am still a little new to all this.* 我对这一切还有些陌生。
3. *You're a little green. (idiomatic)* 你还嫩着点。(习惯用语)
4. *You're still wet behind the ears.* 你乳臭未干呢。
5. *You're still young.* 你还年轻。
6. *I'm still new.* 我还是个新手。
7. *You'll catch on.* 你会慢慢懂的。
8. *Give it time.* 慢慢来吧。

Veteran 老手

1. *I wrote the book on that.* 我是这方面的权威。
2. *I know it like a book.* 我通晓那方面的问题。
3. *I know it like the back of my hand.* 我对这方面了如指掌。
4. *I know whereof I speak.* 我对我听讲的东西很内行。
5. *I know all the tricks of the trade.* 我深谙此道。
6. *I know it backwards and forwards.* 我对此事了如指掌。
7. *I know it inside and outside.* 我对此事完全清楚。

8. *I know my math.* 这一行当我很熟。

9. *It's my job.* 这是我的本行。

10. *I'm a professional.* 我就是吃这一碗饭的。

11. *I'm an old hand at this.* 在这方面我是老手了。

12. *I've been there.* 我干过那个行当。

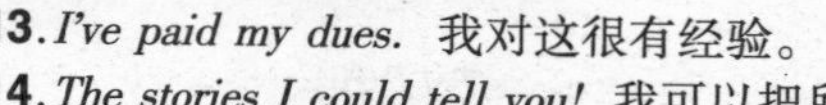

13. *I've paid my dues.* 我对这很有经验。

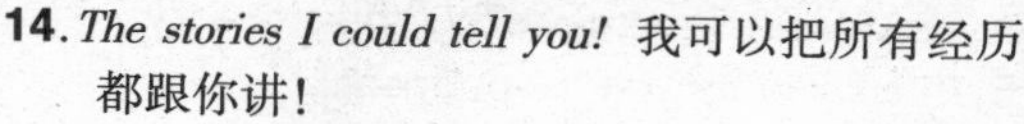

14. *The stories I could tell you!* 我可以把所有经历都跟你讲!

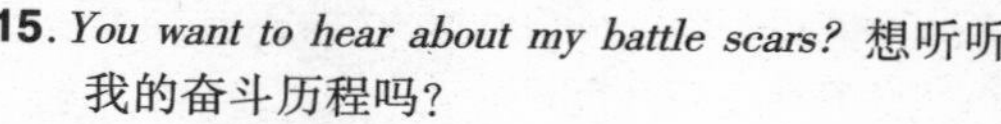

15. *You want to hear about my battle scars?* 想听听我的奋斗历程吗?

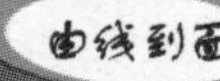

Fashion Conversation 鲜活会话 曲线到面

Conversation 1

A: Would you tell me what educational background you have?

B: Yes, sir. I graduated from high school in 2000, then I entered Changchun University. I graduated in 2004. I have a B. S. degree.

A: What department did you study in?

B: I was in Physics.

A: Why are you so interested in English?

B: Because I have been good at English since primary school and I have developed a strong interest in it. I think it is a very useful international language, especially when working with foreigners.

A:请告诉我你的教育背景好吗?

B:好的,先生。我于2000年高中毕业,然后进入了长春大学。2004年毕业,获得了理学学士学位。

A:你就读的是哪个系?

B:我读的是物理。

A:为什么你对英文这样感兴趣?

B:因为我自小学开始英文就很好,便渐渐培养出了对这个科目的兴趣。而且我认为英文是很重要的国际语言,尤其是和外国人工作的时候。

Conversation 2

A: We are considering several other applicants. No matter whether you are hired or not, we will notify you of our final decision next week.

B: I'm sorry to have taken up so much of your time. Thank you for all you've done for me.

A: Thank you for your cooperation. Good luck to you. Please give us your telephone number before you leave. We will call you if anything comes up.

B: Here is my home phone number.

A: Fine, we will give you the result of the interview next week.

B: Thank you very much. I expect to get a piece of good news soon. Good-bye!

A:我们正在考虑其他几位应聘者。不管你是否会被录用,我们都会在下周内告诉你我们最后的决定。

B:很抱歉占用您这么长的时间。感谢您为我所做的一切。

A:谢谢你的合作。祝你好运。临走之前请将你的电话号码留下来,如果有什么事我们就给你打电话。

B:这是我家的电话号码。

A:好的,下个星期我们就会通知你面试的结果。

B:非常感谢,我期盼早日获得佳音。再见!

Conversation 3

A: What can I do for you?

B: I have come at your invitation for an interview.

A: Nice to meet you. Please sit down.

B: Thank you, sir.

A: I've invited several candidates to come today. You are the first one to have arrived. What was your major in the university?

A:能为你做些什么吗?

B:我是应邀来参加面试的。

A:很高兴见到你。请坐。

B:谢谢您,先生。

A:我今天邀请了好几个面试者,你是第一个到的。你在大学里学习什么专业?

B:My major was English.
B:我主修英语。
A:No wonder you speak English so fluently.
A:难怪你的英语说得如此流利。
B:Thank you for your compliment.
B:谢谢您的夸奖。
A:Where are you working now?
A:你现在在什么地方工作?
B:I'm working at a hotel.
B:我在饭店工作。
A:How long have you been working there?
A:你在那里工作多长时间了?
B:Nearly three years.
B:将近3年了。
A:Could you tell me your expectation in salary?
A:你能告诉我你期望的薪水吗?
B:At present I get 5000 yuan per month.
B:我目前的月薪是5000元。
A:OK. How can we contact you about our final decision?
A:好的。我们怎样告知你我们最后的决定?
B:You can call me at your convenience by dialing the number 5373251.
B:你们方便的时候打电话5373251找我。

Conversation 4

A:Sit down, please. Welcome to our hotel.
A:请坐。欢迎你的到来。
B:Thank you very much.
B:多谢了。
A:First of all, tell me a little bit about yourself.
A:首先,请介绍一下你自己。
B:My name is Li Lei. I'm a sophomore.
B:我的名字叫李雷。大学二年级的学生。
A:Why do you want to work here as a part-ime?
A:为何你想在这儿打工?
B:First, I want to get some money to support my study. Second, I can also practise my spoken English with the foreign tourists.
B:首先,我想挣点钱来支助我的学习。第二,我也想同外国游客练习一下我的英语口语。
A:Are you sure you can do the job well?
A:你坚信你能做好这份工作吗?
B:Yes, I'm sure I can be a good waiter and offer my best service to people.
B:是的,我相信我肯定是个好服务员,并且我要提供最优质的服务给顾客。
A:Good, I'm impressed.
A:好,我很感动。
B:Thank you very much for giving me such a chance.
B:非常感谢你能给我这个机会。

Conversation 5

A:Hello, I'm John. I read in the poster that you're looking for a student to work as a language assistant.
A:嗨,你好,我叫约翰。我看了你们要找学生作语言助手的海报。
B:Yes, we are. Are you interested in the job?
B:是的,是我们的。你对这个工作感兴趣吗?
A:I think so. But before I apply, could you tell me more about the work?
A:是的,我很感兴趣。但在我申请之前,你能否让我了解更多的情况?
B:Have you ever worked with tape recorders before?
B:你以前曾做过磁带录音工作吗?
A:I used cassette recorders a lot when I studied English in junior middle school.
A:在初中我学习英语时,我用过很多盒式磁带。
B:Good. If you decide to take the job, I'll explain how to operate the system. Are you sure?
B:好。假如你决定干这份工作,我将给你解说怎样操作系统,怎么样?
A:How many hours would I work?
A:要工作多少小时?
B:Ten hours a week. Monday through Friday from 4 to 6 pm. And 150 yuan a week.
B:每周10个小时。星期一至星期五的下午4点到6点。每周150元。

A: OK, I'll take the job. A: 好吧,我做这份工作。

B: Fine. Please fill out this application form. B: 行。请填一下这张申请表。

On the Scene 身临其境 面面俱到

主题:韦德来到一家大公司面试。请你看图,根据如下提供的关键词,将他们的对话写出来。

关键词语:application *n.* 申请,请求　corp *n.* 公司
position *n.* 职位　advancement *n.* 前进,进步
opportunity *n.* 机会,时机

参考答案

Wade: Hi, I'm here to fill out an application for the job you advertised in the paper.
Interviewer: What is your name?
Wade: My name is Wade.
Interviewer: What kind of work experience do you have?
Wade: I have worked with the ABC Corp. for 2 years as a Sales Reporter.
Interviewer: Why are you looking to change jobs?
Wade: I am looking for a position with advancement opportunities.
Interviewer: Well, we certainly have that here.

韦德:你好,我来这儿填写您在报纸上登的招聘信息的申请表。
面试接待人:你叫什么名字?
韦德:我叫韦德。
面试接待人:你有什么工作经验?
韦德:我在ABC公司干了两年销售调查员。
面试接待人:你为什么换工作?
韦德:为了寻找更好的机会。
面试接待人:嗯,我们倒是有很好机会。

★银行职员★ 2 Bank Clerk

Words and Phrases 闪亮词语 点滴积累

correspondent bank 代理银行
branch 分行
savings bank 储蓄所
credit union 信用社
cash machine/cash dispenser/cashomat 自动提款机
bank clerk 银行职员
senior clerk 高级职员
loan record keeper 信贷记账员
paying teller 出纳员
foreign exchange teller 外汇出纳员
runner 收账员
checker 审核员
payee 收款人
payer 支付人
guard/security officer 警卫人员
banking hours 银行营业时间
paying-in counter 存款柜台
waiting room 等候厅
cheque/check 支票
bank account 银行存款
total savings deposits 储蓄额
open an account 开户头
withdrawal slip 取款单
credit card 信用卡
foreign exchange rate 汇率

Useful Sentences 七彩精句 连点成线

Something about savings 有关储蓄的事务

1. *Your balance at this bank is 620 yuan.* 您在银行的结余金额为620元。
2. *You have to deposit enough money before you can write out your checks.* 您必须有足够的存款才能开支票。
3. *The annual interest rate is 2.25% at present.* 现在年利率是2.25%。
4. *It's payable within half a year.* 这在半年内有效。
5. *We honored the check as the overdraft was only 30 yuan.* 我们承兑支票的透支额只有30元。
6. *Cheques issued must be made payable to a specified person only.* 签发的支票必须由指定的人支取。
7. *The interest is added to your account every year.* 利息每年都加到您的存款中。
8. *The interest on term deposit is only due at maturity.* 定期存款利息必须到期支付。
9. *Your deposit is exhausted.* 您的存款支完了。
10. *Here's your bankbook, sir. Just sign your name on it.* 这是您的存折,先生。只要在上面签上您的姓名就行了。
11. *Your fixed account is mature and can be withdrawn any time.* 您的定期存款已经到期了,随时可以提取。
12. *You can draw on this account by cheque in payment of goods.* 您可以用支票从这账上支付货款。

Money convertion 有关货币兑换

1. *The rate for traveler's checks is 827 yuan against $100.* 旅行支票的比率是827元人民币兑换100美元。
2. *How much do you want to convert?* 您想要换多少?
3. *The traveler's checks service charge is one per cent of the total amount.* 旅行支票的手续费是总额的百分之一。
4. *What currency do you want?* 您要哪国货币?
5. *In what denominations?* 要什么票面的?

Basic request to a bank clerk 办理基本业务

1. *I'd like to cash a check.* 我想兑现一张支票。
2. *I'd like to cash these traveler's checks.* 我想兑现这些旅行支票。
3. *I'd like to cash these savings bonds.* 我想把这些储蓄债券兑换成现金。
4. *I'd like to make a deposit.* 我想存一笔钱。
5. *I'd like to transfer money into savings account.* 我想把钱转到储蓄账户上。
6. *I'd like to withdraw money from my account.* 我想把钱从我的账户上取出来。
7. *I'd like to make a withdrawal.* 我想取钱。

Requesting a loan 要求准予贷款

1. *I'd like to apply for a loan.* 我想申请一笔贷款。
2. *I'd like to apply for a mortgage.* 我想申请抵押贷款。
3. *I'd like to apply for a home equity loan.* 我想申请一笔住宅抵押贷款。
4. *I need to mortgage my home.* 我要把住宅作为抵押。
5. *I need a second mortgage.* 我需要第二笔抵押贷款。
6. *I'd like a self-amortizing loan term.* 我想要一笔自动分期偿还贷款。
7. *I'd like a variable interest rate mortgage.* 我想要一笔可变利率抵押贷款。
8. *I'd like an adjustable rate mortgage.* 我想要一笔可调利率抵押贷款。

Fashion Conversation 鲜活会话 由线到面

Conversation 1

A: What can I do for you, sir? | A:先生,能为你做什么吗?

B: Yeah, I would like to open a new account. I want to deposit 500 dollars. | B:嗯,我想新开一个户头,存500美元。

A: Very good, sir. What kind would you like? | A:很好,先生。你要存哪一种?

B: Could you tell me how many kinds there are in your bank? | B:请告诉我你们银行有些什么类型的存款方式?

A: Besides the checking account, there's a monthly savings account and a daily interest account. | A:除了支票存款户头外,还有按月计息和按日计息的户头。

B: Could you tell me something about the differences of the three accounts? | B:你能告诉我这三个户头有什么区别吗?

A: Yeah, first, different accounts carry different rates of interests. Then, you may write checks against a checking account, and this you may know according to its name. But you can't write checks against a monthly savings account or daily savings account; you can only make withdraws from them. | A:好的。首先,不同的存款户头有不同的利率;其次,顾名思义,你可以用支票户头开支票。但按月计息和按日计息的存款就不能开支票,只能取款。

B: I won't write any checks, I think. So I'd like to take the monthly savings account, then. | B:我想我不用开支票。因此我就开按月计息的存款户头吧。

A: Would you fill out this form? | A:请填好这张表好吗?

B: OK... Here you are. | B:好的……给你表。

A: All right. And here's your deposit book. | A:很好。这是你的存折。

Conversation 2

A: I'm sorry. Do you have another card? | A:抱歉,您是否有其他信用卡?

B: What's wrong?
B：怎么了？

A: The computer says that you're over your limit. Would you like to call and find out what the problem is?
A：电脑显示您的余额不足，您是否要打电话查一下？

B: There shouldn't be any problem. Try the card again.
B：应该没有问题才对，再刷一次。

A: I've already tried it several times.
A：我已经试过很多次了。

B: That's the only credit card I own.
B：我只有这张信用卡。

A: Would you like to pay cash or would you like me to hold this for you?
A：您要改付现金，还是要我帮您保留？

B: I don't have enough cash on me right now. If you could hold it until tomorrow, that would be great!
B：我身上现金不够。若能帮我留到明天当然最好。

A: OK. When will you come?
A：没问题。你什么时候来？

B: I'll come back around noon tomorrow.
B：我明天大约中午来。

A: Anytime tomorrow is fine. I'll hold it until 9:00 p.m..
A：明天随时都可以来。我会帮您保留到晚上9点。

Conversation 3

A: I need to report a stolen card.
A：我的信用卡要挂失。

B: I need your name, account No., and the card's expiration date.
B：我需要你的名字、卡号，还有信用卡到期日。

A: Lisa Miles. 006239983746, 5/30/07.
A：莉莎·麦尔斯。006239983746，2007年5月30日。

B: And your mother's maiden name... just to verify your identity.
B：还有你母亲娘家的姓……只是为了确定你的身份。

A: Jenny.
A：珍妮。

B: I canceled your card, Miss Miles. No charges have been made today.
B：我已经取消了你的卡，麦尔斯小姐。今天并没有刷卡纪录。

A: Can you send a new card to my home address?
A：你能把新卡寄到我家吗？

B: Yes, but the card number will be different.
B：可以，不过卡号会变了。

Conversation 4

A: Good afternoon, sir. What can I do for you?
A：下午好，先生。我能为你做些什么吗？

B: Good afternoon, miss. I'd like to open a checking account for my firm.
B：下午好，小姐。我想为我的公司开一个支票账户。

A: OK. You need a current account, right?
A：好的。你需要开立一个往来账户，对吗？

B: No, I said I'd like to open a checking account.
B：不，我是想开一个支票账户。

A: You're right, sir. But we usually use the term current account when we talk about checking account kept by a business firm. It is often called a demand account as well. So they mean the same thing.
A：先生，您说得对。不过，当我们谈到企业持有的支票账户时，我们通常用往来账户这个术语。而且，它还常常被称为活期账户。所以，它们实际上指的是同一件事。

B: I see. But how come it is often called a demand account?
B：我明白了。但它为什么常常被称为活期账户？

A: That's because the balance in the accounts can
A：这是因为账户上的余额可以在需要时随时提

be withdrawn on demand at any time. You need only write a demand or a check to make a withdrawal from the account.

取。你只需填写一张用款需求单或一张支票就可以提款。

B: Aren't all account like that?

B:并非所有的账户都是这样的吧?

A: No, sir. Most banks may require a notice usually at least seven days before the withdrawal on savings or other interest bearing accounts.

A:不是的,先生。大部分银行都可能要求储蓄账户和其他付息账户至少在提款七天前通知银行。

B: Really? But I've never been asked for such a notice.

B:真的吗?可我从来也没有被要求提款前事先通知银行。

A: Well, in actual practice, most banks rarely invoke that regulation. The bank, however, has the option of enforcing the regulation if it considers it necessary.

A:嗯,在实际工作中,大部分银行很少实行那条规定。然而,如果银行认为必要的话,有权照章办理。

B: Oh, I've never noticed this before. Thank you very much for your information.

B:噢,我可从来也没注意到这点。十分感谢你介绍的情况。

A: It's my pleasure.

A:很高兴能为你服务。

B: Now, could you please tell me how to open a current account?

B:现在你能不能告诉我怎么开立往来账户?

A: Of course. All you need to do is to fill out this signature card and pay your first deposit.

A:当然可以。你要做的是填写这张签名卡并存入第一笔存款。

B: How much is it, please?

B:多少?

A: $5,000 or over, sir.

A:5000 美元以上,先生。

B: All right, here is $5,000, and here is the filled out signature card.

B:好的,这是 5000 美元,这是填好的签名卡。

A: Thank you. Five thousand dollars, sir?

A:谢谢。是 5000 美元吧,先生?

B: That's right.

B:是的。

A: By the way, would you like to have the name and address of your firm printed on the checks?

A:顺便问问,你喜欢把你公司的名字和地址印在支票上吗?

B: Yes, that'll be great. Can that be done?

B:是的,那太好了。可以印上去吗?

A: Yes. Just put a "√" here, please.

A:可以,请在这打个"√"。

B: OK.

B:好的。

A: May I have your ID please, sir?

A:先生,我可以看看你的身份证吗?

B: Sure, here it is.

B:当然可以,在这。

A: Now please sign the card.

A:现在请签名。

B: OK.

B:好的。

A: All right, sir. Here is the receipt, your ID and a check-book.

A:好了,先生。这是你的收据、身份证和支票本。

B: Thank you very much.

B:十分感谢。

A: You're welcome.

A:不必客气。

B: Good-bye.

B:再见。

A: Good-bye.

A:再见。

On the Scene 身临其境 面面俱到

主题:张先生来到银行申请贷款买车,一位职员热情地接待了他。请你看图,根据如下提供的关键词，将他们的对话写出来。

关键词语：loan *n.* 贷款；借出　　purchase *v.* 买；购买
sit down 坐下

参考答案

Mr. Zhang: Are you the loans-officer?
Clerk: I certainly am. May I help you?
Mr. Zhang: Yes. I'd like to make a loan.
Clerk: Alright. Please sit down.
Mr. Zhang: It's a loan for a car I'd like to purchase.
张先生：你是贷款部负责人吗？
职员：我是，我能帮您什么忙吗？
张先生：是的，我想办一笔贷款。
职员：好的，请坐下。
张先生：我想贷款买辆汽车。

★邮政人员★ 3 Post-office Clerk

Words and Phrases 闪亮词语 点滴积累

POB(Post Office Box) 邮政信箱
mail box;postbox 信箱
carrier mailman 邮差
stamp 邮票
mail bag 邮件袋
postage 邮资
memorial stamp 纪念邮票
stamp duty 印花
local mail 本地邮件
outgoing mail 外埠邮件
international mail 国际邮件
parcel post 包裹邮件
mail 邮件
letter 信件
printed matter 印刷品
postmark 邮戳
postage due 邮资不足
ordinary mail 平信
express 快信

Useful Sentences 七彩精句 连点成线

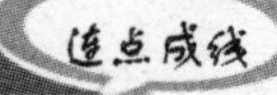

A postal clerk greeting a customer 邮局职员招呼顾客

1. *Next.* 下一位。
2. *Who's next?* 下一位到谁了？
3. *Can I help someone?* 谁要办什么？
4. *How may I help you?* 您有什么事？
5. *How can I help you?* 您有什么事？

Buying stamps 买邮票

1. *I need some stamps, please.* 请给我一些邮票。
2. *I'd like to buy a stamp, please.* 我想买一张邮票。
3. *I'd like to buy a book of stamps, please.* 我想买一本邮票。
4. *I'd like to buy a roll of stamps, please.* 我想买一卷邮票。
5. *I'd like to buy a sheet of stamps, please.* 我想买一版邮票。

Post 投寄

1. *This needs to go first class.* 这邮件需要以优先投递方式发送。
2. *First class, please.* 请给予优先投递方式发送。
3. *Air mail, please.* 请用航空投寄。
4. *I need this to go express mail.* 我需要以快件投寄。
5. *I need to send this overnight.* 我需要当晚就要发送。
6. *I need to send this second-day mail.* 我需要第二天就要送出。
7. *I need to send this parcel post.* 我需要以邮包方式投寄。
8. *I need to send this by certified mail.* 我需要以保证邮件投寄。
9. *I need to send this by registered mail.* 我需以挂号件投寄。
10. *Return receipt requested, please.* 请给回执。

Asking questions at a post office 在邮局里顾客提问题

1. *How much postage do I need for this?* 这邮件邮资是多少？
2. *How much postage does this need?* 这邮件需多少邮资？
3. *How much postage do I need to send this air mail?* 这个航空邮件的邮资是多少？
4. *Can you weigh this?* 您能称一下这邮件吗？
5. *How do I get my mail forwarded?* 你怎样才能把

我的邮件转发出去？

6. *Do you have any envelopes I could buy?* 有信封卖吗？

7. *How long will it take?* 邮件到达目的地要多长时间？

8. *Can I have the ZIP code for Chicago?* 能把芝加哥的邮政编码告诉我吗？

9. *May I have the ZIP code for Chicago?* 能把芝加哥的邮政编码告诉我吗？

10. *Can I have a change-of-address form?* 能给我一张更改地址的表格吗？

Questions a postal clerk might ask a customer 邮局职员可能会问顾客的问题

1. *First class?* 要优先投递吗？
2. *How many stamps do you need?* 您要多少张邮票？
3. *A sheet or a roll?* 要一整版还是要一卷？
4. *How many?* 要多少？
5. *Any particular style?* 有没有特殊要求？

Other expressions used by a postal clerk 邮局职员的其他用语

1. *We're out of those.* 对那事我们都不清楚。
2. *That should arrive on Monday.* 邮件该在周一到达。
3. *That ought to arrive on Monday.* 邮件该在周一到达。
4. *Let's hope that arrives on Monday.* 咱们希望周一能到达。
5. *Sorry, you will have to stand in a line.* 对不起，你该排队等候。
6. *Sorry, you will have to keep a place in line.* 对不起，你该排队等候。
7. *I'm sorry, I can only release the package to the person it is addressed to.* 对不起，我只能把邮包交付收件人。
8. *The forms are over there.* 表格在那里。
9. *Please fill out a form and bring it back to me.* 请把表格填好后拿来给我。
10. *Please show me your identification.* 请出示您的身份证。

A postal clerk bringing a transaction to an end 邮局职员结束收发业务

1. *Would you like anything else?* 您还有其他的事吗？
2. *Do you need anything else?* 您还有其他事情吗？
3. *Anything else?* 还有其他事吗？
4. *Will that be all?* 就这些事吗？
5. *Is that all?* 就这些事吗？

Fashion Conversation 鲜活会话 由线到面

Conversation 1

A: Excuse me. I'd like to send this letter to the United States. Can you tell me the postage?	A：劳驾，我想把这封信寄去美国，请问邮费多少？
B: I'll have to weigh the letter. It's overweight. You'll have to pay extra.	B：我得称一称重量。超重了，你得另付超重费。
A: How much is it altogether?	A：一共多少钱？
B: It comes to 3 yuan and 50 fen.	B：一共3.5元。
A: All right. Here is a 5 yuan bill.	A：那好。这是5元。
B: Here's your change. It would be best if you stick on this airmail label.	B：这是找您的钱。你最好将航空标签贴上。
A: I'm sorry, but I can't seem to get this label stuck.	A：对不起，这标签贴不上。
B: I'm sorry. I should have told you. You must paste	B：很抱歉！我本应告诉你的，你必须用浆糊贴。那

it on. There is a bottle of glue on that table over there.

边桌上有瓶胶水。

A: No wonder it wouldn't stick! I should have known. Thanks... Oh, where do I mail it?

A:难怪贴不住!我早应想到。谢谢!信投在哪里?

B: There's a mailbox just outside.

B:门口有个邮筒。

Conversation 2

A: I want to mail this parcel to Beijing.
B: Do you want to register and insure it?
A: Register is enough. I really don't want insurance.
B: Please, put the box on this scale.
A: No problem, it's not that heavy.
B: Well, it is a little overweight. It weighs more than the post office will accept.
A: Then what am I supposed to do?
B: You could repack it into two boxes, or you can take this box to the railroad station. They will ship it like this.

A:我要往北京寄一个包裹。
B:你要挂号和保险吗?
A:挂号就够了,不必保险。
B:请把盒子放在天平秤上。
A:没问题,不会那么重。
B:哦,有点超重。重量超过邮局的限度。
A:那我该怎么办呢?
B:你可以重新把它分成两包,或者拿到火车站去,不用分包可以寄。

Conversation 3

A: I need to pay this bill.
B: The payee's name is on the form, but you have to write in your own name and address. If you don't do that, they won't know who the money is from.
A: Do I need any identification?
B: No, that's not necessary.
A: Here you are then.
B: I see that this is a magazine subscription form. You'd better put your subscription number on it.
A: Why do I need to do that?
B: That way you can be sure that they know you paid and they won't cancel your subscription.
A: Thanks for the advice. I'll do that.

A:我要付这个账单。
B:收款人姓名在这个单子上,但你要把你的姓名、地址写上。如果你没写名字,他们将无法知道钱是谁寄的。
A:我需要写住址身份证明吗?
B:不,不需要。
A:给你单子。
B:我看这是份杂志订单,你最好把你订阅的号码写下来。
A:为什么要这么做呢?
B:这样才可以让他们知道你已付款,他们就不会取消你的订阅。
A:多谢你的建议,我会照你所说去做。

Conversation 4

A: Can I have this money order cashed, please?
B: Yes, sir. But you'll have to endorse at first.
A: Yes, of course.
B: Can I see your ID?
A: Is a student ID card enough?
B: Yes, that's fine. Here you are, five hundred yuan.
A: Thank you. By the way, can I buy a money order?
B: Domestic or international?
A: International.

A:请把这汇票兑换一下。
B:好的,先生。请你在汇票背面上签名。
A:好的,好的。
B:能出示一下你的身份证吗?
A:学生证行吗?
B:可以。你的钱,500元。
A:谢谢。顺便问一下,能买一张汇款单子吗?
B:国内的还是国际的?
A:国际的。

B: You have to fill out this application form first.
B：你要先填一份申请表格。
A: Thanks. (*filling out the form*)
A：谢谢。(*填表格*)
B: You are welcome.
B：别客气。

Conversation 5

A: Excuse me! Could you tell me where I can get a registered envelope and some stamps?
A：请问！在哪儿(我)可以买到挂号信封和邮票？
B: At that counter.
B：在那个柜台。
A: Excuse me! How much does it cost to send an air mail letter from here to Guangzhou?
A：请问！从这寄到广州一封航空信要多少钱？
C: Eighty cents.
C：80分。
A: Do you have any registered envelopes?
A：你有挂号信封吗？
C: Yes, a large one or small one? Is this one OK?
C：有。大的还是小的？这个大小合适吗？
A: Too large, I am afraid. Do you have a smaller one?
A：太大了。还有小的吗？
C: Certainly. What about this one?
C：有。这个怎么样？
A: That's OK. Would you mind telling me what the cost of the postage on this registered letter and two 80-cent stamps will be?
A：正合适。你能告诉我寄这封挂号信再加两张80分的邮票一共多少钱？
C: Just a moment. I'll have to check. All together you should pay three yuan and one mao.
C：等一下，让我算一下。噢，总共是3块1毛钱。

A: Here you are. Thank you very much.
A：给你钱。谢谢。
C: You are welcome.
C：欢迎您再来(不客气)。

Conversation 6

A: Excuse me! Where can I send a parcel?
A：请问！寄包裹在哪儿？
B: At that counter over there.
B：在那边的柜台。
A: Hello. May I send a parcel to Zhengzhou here?
A：你好，往郑州寄包裹是在这儿吗？
C: Yes. what is inside your parcel?
C：对。你的包裹里装的是什么？
A: Two shirts, a pair of shoes and a suit.
A：两件衬衫，一双鞋子和一套西服。
C: By regular (ordinary post) mail or air mail?
C：普通邮件还是航空邮件？
A: How long does it take for it to go by regular mail from here to Zhengzhou? And how long to go by air mail?
A：从此地到郑州普通邮件需多久，航空呢？
C: Ah..., it takes one weeks by regular mail, while it takes one or two days by air mail.
C：普通的要一周，航空只需1-2天。
A: How much for regular mail?
A：普通邮件要多少邮资？
C: It depends on the weight of your parcel, let me weigh it first. It's three kg, so it costs eighteen yuan and a quarter by regular mail (ordinary post).
C：要看你的包裹有多重了。让我先称一下。3千克，普通邮件要花18元25分。
A: What about air mail?
A：航空邮寄呢？
C: You'll have to add twenty yuan more. Which way do you prefer?
C：再加20元。你要普通邮件还是航空？
A: By air mail, please. Here is the money.
A：航空吧。给你钱。
C: Keep the receipt, please.
C：请保存好收据。

A: Many thanks. | A: 谢谢。
C: It's my pleasure. | C: 不客气。

On the Scene 身临其境 面面俱到

主题：洛拉来到邮局寄两封到中国的邮件，邮政人员称好重量为195克。请你看图，根据如下提供的关键词，将他们的对话写出来。

关键词语：express *n.* 快递；快件　　postage *n.* 邮资
urgent *adj.* 急迫的；紧急的　　register *v.* 注册；挂号

参考答案

Lora: Excuse me... but I'd like to have these two letters posted back to China. This one as express mail, and this one as registered.

Clerk: So, that's express mail special delivery for that one and registered for the other. Is that right?

Lora: Exactly. This one is urgent.

Clerk: Then please fill in this form.

Lora: OK. I hope it is all correct.

Clerk: Correct and clear. And it's 195 grams... that'll be \$1.95 for postage.

洛拉：打扰了，我想寄两封邮件到中国。这封寄快件，这封寄挂号。

职员：那么，这封寄特快专递，另一封挂号，是吗？

洛拉：对，这封很急。

职员：请填一下这张表。

洛拉：好了，但愿都填对了。

职员：填对了，而且很清楚。信重195克，邮资为1.95美元。

★办公文秘★ 4 Office Secretary

Words and Phrases 闪亮词语 点滴积累

cellophane tape 透明胶带
calculator 计算器
computer 电脑
carbon paper 复写纸
correction fluid 涂改液
eraser 橡皮擦
graph 图表
ink 墨水
notebook 笔记本
pencil sharpener 削铅笔机
staple 订书针
ball-point pen 圆珠笔
coffee pot 咖啡壶
gel ink pen 中性笔
fountain pen 钢笔
glue 胶水
paper clip 纸夹
stapler 钉书机
scissors 剪刀
waste basket 废纸篓
time card 出勤卡
time sheet 出勤表

Useful Sentences 七彩精句 连点成线

Filing 归档

1. *Would you like me to file them according to dates?* 你要我依日期顺序归档吗?
2. *I'll copy them and file them both ways.* 我会复制一份,然后两种方式各存一份。
3. *I'm going to clean out all the old files.* 我将把所有旧的档案都清理掉。
4. *The rule of file-keeping is "one customer – one file".* 存档管理的立案规则是"一户一卷"。
5. *My secretarial duties includes taking shorthand, typing and filing.* 我作为秘书的职务包括:速记、打字和整理档案。
6. *Please file all these reports for me.* 请替我把这些报告归档。
7. *I can't find the document I was working on yesterday.* 我找不到昨天做的那个文件了。
8. *Did you look up those files I requested?* 我要的那些档案资料都找到了吗?
9. *But first of all, fetch me those Brown files right now.* 但是首先帮我找到布朗名下的文件夹。
10. *File the reports in alphabetical order.* 将报告依字母顺序归档。
11. *File the letters according to dates.* 将信件依照日期顺序归档。
12. *File the reports both ways.* 将报告按两种方式各归档一份。

Report the meeting 报告会议过程

1. *Here's the minutes of the meeting.* 这就是会议记录。
2. *Here are all the reports and materials handed out in the meeting.* 这是在会议中分发的报告和资料。
3. *I think you'll have to do some replies.* 我想你将需要做些回答。
4. *Can you tell me a bit more about it?* 你能讲得稍微详细些吗?
5. *How long did the meeting last?* 会议进行了多久?
6. *Did the chairman ask for me?* 会议主席问起我了吗?
7. *You've done an excellent job.* 你做得非常好。

The reception wording 接待员用语

1. *I'll tell Mr. White you're here.* 我马上告诉怀特先生,说您来了。

2. *I'll show you the way.* 我来领路。

3. *Would you come this way, please?* 请这边走。

4. *May I tell him what you wish to see him about?* 请问您找他有什么事？

The reception secretary wording 前台文秘用语

1. *May I have your name, please?* 请问尊姓大名？

2. *Would you please have a seat and wait for a few moments?* 请坐下来稍等片刻。

3. *What can I do for you, sir?* 先生我能为你做点什么？

4. *Would you tell me what you wish to see him about?* 能告诉我您见他有什么事情吗？

5. *Do you have an appointment, sir?* 你事先有预约吗？

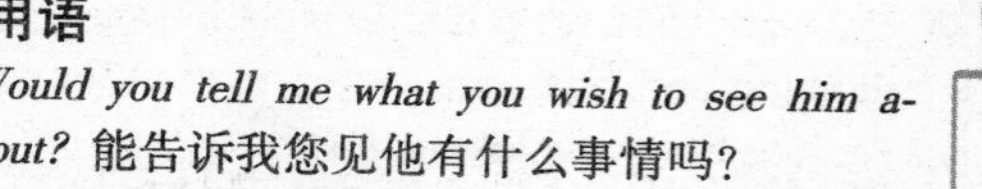

Conversation 1

A: Miss Wang, did you look up those files I requested?

A：王小姐，我要的那些档案资料都找到了吗？

B: I'm sorry, Mr. Steven. I couldn't find any information on that company, even though I checked all the cross-references. I don't think it's there.

B：很抱歉，史蒂文先生，尽管我查了全部的对照表，但仍未找到有关那个公司的资料。我想它不在那儿。

A: I'm almost sure that information was filed.

A：我几乎可以肯定那份资料已经存档了。

B: Would you like me to check again under a different heading?

B：让我在别的项目下再查一查，好吗？

A: Yes, in fact I believe I asked you to put it in Mr. Brown's file.

A：好的，事实上我相信已让你在布朗先生那里存档了。

B: Maybe that's why I couldn't find it. All the information on the Brown correspondence is filed under "B".

B：也许这就是我为什么找不着的原因了。所有与布朗往来信件都归在"B"字母下。

A: Do you still remember how our filing system works?

A：你还记得我们的归档系统是如何操作的吗？

B: Yes, I do. All files are arranged alphabetically.

B：记得，所有文件都是按字母顺序排列的。

A: That's right.

A：对了。

B: And outgoing and incoming correspondence is kept in the file, reports and business documents in this one, and customer's information in that one.

B：发出和收到的信函都存在那个文件夹里了，报告与公司文件在这里，客户资料在那里。

A: Great.

A：很好。

B: By the way, I'm going to clean out all the old files by tomorrow. Would you like to look through before I throw them away?

B：顺便说一下，我准备明天把所有的档案都清理一下。在我把它们处理掉之前，你还要仔细地检查一遍吗？

A: Of course. But first of all, fetch me those Brown files right now.

A：当然了。但是首先帮我马上找到布朗名下的文件夹。

B: Yes, Mr. Steven.

B：好的，史蒂文先生。

Conversation 2

A: Miss Liu, you are going to take over my job as secretary here from next Monday. Now let me tell you the office rules first.

A：刘小姐，从下周一开始，你将接替我在这儿的秘书职位。让我先给你讲一下办公制度。

B: Thank you. It's very important for me to know about them.

B:谢谢你。懂得这些对我来说很重要。

A: The working hours are from eight to twelve in the morning and from one to five in the afternoon. Be sure not to be late or absent.

A:工作时间是从上午 8 点到 12 点,下午从 1 点到 5 点。务必不要迟到或旷工。

B: I'll do my duty.

B:我会忠于职守的。

A: To be a good secretary, you'll have to be quite familiar with office routine and try to learn to do a bit of everything.

A:要想成为一个好秘书,你就得对办公室的日常事务非常熟悉,并试着学做每一件事。

B: Yes, I'll try my best.

B:好的,我会尽力的。

A: Come here please, Miss Liu. I'd like to explain the filing system to you.

A:请到这边来,刘小姐。我想跟你讲讲档案管理系统。

B: All right.

B:好的。

A: This is your filing cabinet and all the documents must be filed alphabetically.

A:这是文件柜,所有的文件都必须按字母顺序存档。

B: Yes, I understand.

B:是的,我知道。

A: And this is a safe. The confidential files are kept in it. You'll have the key to it. Please keep in mind that you must be very careful with it.

A:这是保险柜,机密档案都存放在这里。这是钥匙。记住你必须好好保管它。

B: Yes, I will.

B:好的,我会的。

A: And one more thing, our boss makes a point of keeping everything in order. So you'd better be careful about this and don't throw things about. Otherwise, he'll be mad at you.

A:对了,还有一件事,我们的老板认为一切井然有序是很重要的。所以你最好仔细些,不要乱丢东西。要不然,他会对你非常生气的。

B: OK. I'll bear that in mind. Thanks a lot for what you have told me.

B:好的,我会记住这些的。谢谢你所告诉我的一切。

Conversation 3

A: Molly, have you received the fax from the Sunshine Company?

A:莫莉,你有没有收到阳光公司发来的传真?

B: No, sir. I have called Lois and she told me that their fax machine was out of order and she would send us the fax this afternoon.

B:没有。我已经打电话给洛伊丝,她告诉我她们的传真机坏了。下午她会给我们发传真。

(*in the afternoon*)

(*下午*)

B: I have received the fax from Sunshine Company. Here it is, sir.

B:我已经收到了阳光公司发来的传真。给您,先生。

A: Oh, that is terrible. The fax has been muddled. What's worse, page three is missing. Would you please ask them to send us the fax again?

A:太糟糕了。传真的字模糊不清,更糟糕的是,第三页没有。请你让他们再传一份。

B: All right, sir.

B:好的,先生。

(***Molly then calls Lois***)

(***莫莉打电话给洛伊丝***)

B: Hello. This is Molly. May I speak to Lois, please?

B:你好。我是莫莉。请问洛伊丝在吗?

C: This is Lois.

C:我就是。

B: Lois, would you please send me the fax again. The fax you sent me just now was very unclear and page three is missing.

B:洛伊丝,请你再传一次。刚才你发的传真模糊不清,而且第三页没有。

C:I am sorry. I will send you the fax again right now.

C:很抱歉。我会马上给你再传一次。

B:Thank you so much.

B:非常感谢。

C:You are welcome. Bye.

C:不用谢。再见。

Conversation 4

A:Good morning, Mr. Smith. Would you like me to brief your schedule for today?

A:早晨好,史密斯先生,要我对您今天的日程安排做个简短的报告吗?

B:Yes.

B:好的。

A:You are scheduled to meet Mr. Thompson of ABC Company at eleven this morning. Then, you have a lunch appointment with Mr. Li. And this afternoon at four you will attend a press conference.

A:今天上午十一点你要与ABC公司的汤姆森先生会面。然后,午餐时间与李先生有约。下午四点出席一个新闻发布会。

B:I'm afraid I can't attend the press conference due to an urgent conference with the Board of Directors at half past four.

B:我恐怕不能出席新闻发布会,因为在四点半我要与董事局开一个紧急会议。

A:All right. Do you want me to cancel the reservation for you?

A:好的。您要我为您取消预约吗?

B:Yes, thank you very much. In addition, do you have the marketing proposal ready?

B:是的,谢谢。另外,那份市场建议书准备好了吗?

A:The proposal is being repaired right now and I think it will be ready by tomorrow morning.

A:那份建议书正在修改,我想明早便可准备好。

Conversation 5

A:Anne, would you please come in for a while? Please also bring along the minutes of yesterday's management meeting.

A:安妮,你能进来一下吗?同时,请带上昨天的高层会议记录。

B:Of course, sir... Here's the minutes of the meeting.

B:当然可以,先生……这就是会议记录。

A:How long did the meeting last?

A:会议进行了多久?

B:The meeting was delayed by twenty minutes and it lasted for one and a half hours.

B:会议推迟了20分钟,进行了一个半小时。

A:Did the chairman ask for me?

A:会议主席问起我吗?

B:Yes, I told him that you were very ill and couldn't attend.

B:是的,我告诉他你病了,所以无法出席。

A:All right. Have you handed in my report to him?

A:好的,你把我的报告交给他了吗?

B:Yes, I did. Besides, here are all the reports and materials handed out in the meeting. I think you'll have to do some replies.

B:是的,此外,这是在会议中分发的报告和资料,你也许要做些回答。

A:Thank you, Anne. You've done an excellent job. Did they mention the date for the next meeting?

A:谢谢你,安妮,你做得非常好。他们提及下次会议的日期了吗?

B:No, they didn't. The chairman said he would send a memo to all managers by the end of this week informing them of the date of the next meeting.

B:没有,主席说将在本星期内发一份备忘录给各位经理,通知下次开会的日期。

Conversation 6

A: Mr. Jackson, I've drafted a schedule for your business trip next week. You may have a look.

B: Oh, great! Let's discuss it together. Now, when am I off then?

A: You're leaving on Tuesday morning.

B: What time exactly?

A: Your flight takes off at 8:10 a.m.. And you arrive in Shanghai at 10:40. Mr. Yang is meeting you at the airport. Wednesday's a busy day. You're attending the conference in the morning and in the afternoon you're going to the exhibition.

B: Oh, am I seeing Mr. Li?

A: Yes, you're seeing him on Thursday. You're inspecting the factory in the morning and having dinner with him in the evening.

B: I've got a schedule!

A: Oh, that's not everything. You're free on Friday and then on Saturday you're catching the 9 o'clock plane back to Guangzhou.

A:杰克逊先生,我为你下周的商务旅行作了一下安排。你可以看一下。

B:噢,好的!我们一起讨论一下吧。那么,我什么时候离开?

A:你星期二上午离开。

B:确切是什么时间?

A:你的飞机上午8:10起飞,10:40到达上海。杨先生会在机场接你。星期三是忙碌的一天。你上午参加会议,下午去展览会。

B:噢,我见李先生吗?

A:是的,你星期四见他。你上午视察工厂,晚上与他一起吃晚餐。

B:行程真满。

A:噢,这还不是所有的事。你星期五有空,星期六你乘9点钟的飞机回广州。

On the Scene 身临其境 面面俱到

主题:杨先生来找王先生,王先生的秘书严华接待了他。请你看图,根据如下提供的关键词,将他们的对话写出来。

关键词语:secretary *n.* 秘书
conclude *v.* 终止,结束
common *adj.* 共同的
flexible *adj.* 柔韧性
seeing is believing 眼见为实
representative *n.* 代表
expand *vt.* 扩张
desire *v.* 要求
foreign trade 对外贸易

参考答案

Yan Hua: Welcome to our company, Mr. Yang. My name is Yan Hua, the secretary of Mr. Wang.
Mr. Yang: Nice to see you!
Yan Hua: Would you like to have a cup of tea or coffee?
Mr. Yang: Thanks, I like Chinese tea very much.
Yan Hua: Glad you like it. By the way, is this your first visit to China, Mr. Yang?
Mr. Yang: Yes, as a representative of IBM, I hope to conclude some business with you?
Yan Hua: We also hope to expand our business with you.
Mr. Yang: This is our common desire.
Yan Hua: I think you probably know China has adopted a flexible policy in her foreign trade.
Mr. Yang: Yes, I've read about it, but I'd like to know more about it.
Yan Hua: Right. Seeing is believing.
Mr. Yang: Sure.
严华:杨先生,欢迎光临。我叫严华,是王先生的秘书。
杨先生:见到你很高兴。
严华:您想喝茶还是咖啡?
杨先生:谢谢,我很喜欢中国茶。
严华:很高兴您喜欢中国茶。顺便问一下,您是首次访问中国吗,约翰逊先生?
杨先生:是的,作为国际商用机器公司的代表,我希望与贵公司做成几笔生意。
严华:我们也希望与贵公司扩大贸易往来。
杨先生:这是我们的共同愿望。
严华:我想你也许已经了解到中国在对外贸易中采取了灵活的政策。
杨先生:是的,我已经知道了一点,但我还想多了解一些。
严华:对,眼见为实。
杨先生:的确如此。

★人民警察★ 5 Police

Words and Phrases 闪亮词语 点滴积累

double criminality 双重罪
illegal gold importing 私运黄金罪
conviction 判罪
condemn 定罪
misdemeanor 轻罪
felony 重罪
innocent 无罪
false crime 顶罪
murderer; homicide 杀人犯
criminal 犯人
principal 主犯
accessory 从犯
accomplice 共犯
abettor 教唆犯
repetition offence 屡犯
prisoner awaiting trial 未决犯
loser 刑事犯
political offender 政治犯
war criminal 战犯
unintentional crime 过失犯
culprit 嫌疑犯
parolee 假释犯
first crime 初犯
ex-convict 前科犯

Useful Sentences 七彩精句 连点成线

A police officer seeking information 警官了解情况

1. *What seems to be the problem here?* 这里出了什么事？
2. *Tell me exactly what happened.* 跟我讲清楚，究竟发生了什么事？
3. *Are you lost?* 你迷路啦？
4. *Can you provide a description of the missing person?* 你能给我描述一下那个失踪者的特征吗？
5. *Can you describe the assailant?* 你能描述一下那个袭击者吗？
6. *Do you have a permit to do that?* 你做这种事，有许可证吗？
7. *What's going on here?* 这里发生了什么事？

Fashion Conversation 鲜活会话 由线到面

Conversation 1

A: Sir, I want to report a case of theft to you.
B: Theft of what?
A: A wallet.
B: What does it contain?
A: Money, my passport, a ruby ring for my fiancée and a Master Credit Card.
B: Have you reported your loss of your card to the relevant bank?
A: Yes, I've done that.
B: How much money was stolen?
A: About six hundred dollars.

A：警官，我想向你们报告一桩偷窃案。
B：什么东西被偷了？
A：一个钱包。
B：钱包里有什么？
A：钱、护照、给我未婚妻的红宝石戒指及一张万事达卡。
B：关于丢失的信用卡，你是否向有关银行报告了？
A：我已经做了。
B：被偷了多少钱？
A：大约600美金。

Conversation 2

A: Where was your wallet stolen?

B: On a crowded bus during the rush hour, maybe on a Bus No. 112.

A: Have you seen the suspected pickpocket?

B: Not clearly. While I was standing in the front enjoying the passing beautiful scenes, I vaguely felt someone touching the back pocket of my pants. I thought the fast bus might throw the passengers off balance so he unconsciously touched it, which I paid no attention to.

A: What did he look like?

B: It seems to me all the Chinese look same. In my eyes, he was a man of medium height, well shaved and cleanly dressed.

A: What was he wearing then?

B: Blue jeans and a gray jacket.

A: Would you mind writing down what you've told us above, including your name, nationality, the number of your passport and temporary residential address so that we can keep a record?

B: No, of course not. Do you think it possible for me to retrieve my stolen articles?

A: I am not so sure, but my colleague and I will strain to crack down the case and return them to you as soon as we can.

A:你的钱包在哪里被偷的?

B:在上下班高峰时期拥挤不堪的公交车上,可能是112路公共汽车上吧。

A:你有没有看见那个扒窃嫌疑人?

B:没有看仔细。我站在车里,欣赏着外面的美景,模模糊糊觉得有人碰了我的裤子后袋。我以为高速行驶的汽车使乘客失去平衡,使他无意识地碰了我的裤子后袋。对此我也没在意。

A:他长得什么样?

B:对我而言,中国人的长相都几乎一样。依我看来,他是中等个子、脸面修得干净、穿着整洁的男人。

A:那么他穿什么衣服?

B:蓝色的牛仔裤和灰色的夹克衣。

A:你介意把你以上对我说的话写下吗?这包括你的姓名、国籍、护照号码和暂住地,以便我们备案。

B:当然不介意。你认为我有可能重新得到我的被扒窃的物品吗?

A:我不敢确定。我和我的同事将尽力侦破此案,尽早地归还你的物品。

Conversation 3

A: Are you Mr. Thomson who called for emergency police service?

B: Yes, I am.

A: She may be Mary, your girlfriend?

B: Yes, she is.

A: We've caught the two suspects and found Mary's handbag.

B: How efficient and magic the Shanghai police are!

A: Thank you for your praise. Can you go with us to our police station to help identify the suspects, check up your stolen things and make a record of your case?

B: Yes. By the way, what measures have you taken to enable you to work too efficiently?

A: That's because the Shanghai police have acted on the direction of Mr. Wu, municipal bureau's

A:你是刚刚打过应急电话的汤姆森吗?

B:是的。

A:这位就是玛丽,你的女朋友?

B:是的。

A:我们已经抓获了两名嫌疑人并找到了玛丽的包。

B:上海警察真有效率和神奇!

A:谢谢你的赞扬。你能不能和我们一起去警署帮助辨认嫌疑人、核查被盗的东西并做有关这件案子的笔录。

B:好的。顺便问一下,你们采用什么方法使你们警方工作如此有效率?

A:这是因为上海警方依照市公安局吴局长的指示,开展了网络化巡逻。

director, to go on net-like patrol.

B: What do you mean by going on net-like patrol?

A: It means at any time of the day and night there're policemen patrolling around on foot or on bikes or in vehicles.

B: How can you make such a quick response to my call?

A: Because our police cars are equipped with two-way radios and GPS, communication between the headquarters and patrolmen is made quite convenient and efficient. Once something happens, it's easy to give orders. To meet the needs of crime prevention in Shanghai, different patterns of patrol have been established, such as regular patrol, random patrol, nighttime patrol, daytime patrol, bike patrol, vehicle patrol and so on. The police act as a net covering every corner of Shanghai.

B: 你说的网络化巡逻是什么意思?

A: 它指的是不论白天黑夜都有警察或步行,或骑车或开车巡逻。

B: 那么你们怎么对我的求援电话作出反应的?

A: 因为我们的警车都配备了无线电双向通讯系统和全球定位系统。总部和巡警之间的通讯就变得相当的方便有效。一旦有事发生,发指令很方便。为了迎合上海防范犯罪的需要,我们采取了各种巡逻方式,例如定期巡逻、乱线巡逻、夜间巡逻、白天巡逻、自行车巡逻和机动车巡逻,等等。警察像一张网覆盖着上海的各个角落。

On the Scene 身临其境 面面俱到

主题:杨先生因为醉酒驾车被交警拦下。请你看图,根据如下提供的关键词,将他们的对话写出来。

关键词语:driving license 驾驶证
zigzag *n.* 摇晃
protest against 抗议
admit to 承认
regulation *n.* 规则
whiskey *n.* 威士忌酒
alcohol *n.* 酒精
blood *n.* 血液
suspend *v.* 延缓

参考答案

Policeman: Stop, sir. Can you show me your driving license, please?

Mr. Yang: Why?

Policeman: You may have drunk wine.

Mr. Yang: How do you know that? I've drunk only a little whiskey, which I don't think makes me drunk.

Policeman: I've noticed you driving zigzag and now your breath smells of alcohol.

Mr. Yang: Sir, I must protest against your distorting the fact.

Policeman: Let's wait and see. Please follow me to the hospital to have a blood test.

Mr. Yang: Oh, it's not necessary. I have to admit to having drunk half a bottle of whiskey at my friend's birthday party.

Policeman: You have to be fined and your driving license will be suspended for your drunk driving, running the red traffic light and ignoring the policeman's directions.

Mr. Yang: Don't you think you've punished me so seriously?

Policeman: No, I've done so just according to the regulations.

警察:停车,先生! 请出示你的驾驶证。

杨先生:为什么叫我停车?

警察:你可能喝过酒了。

杨先生:你怎么知道的? 我只喝了点威士忌酒,我想这不会让我喝醉吧。

警察:我看到你歪歪斜斜地开车,又闻到了你呼出的酒气。

杨先生:警官,我必须抗议你歪曲事实。

警察:让我们等着瞧吧。请跟我去医院验血。

杨先生:那就不必了。我承认在朋友的生日晚会上,喝了瓶威士忌酒。

警察:对于你的酒后驾车、闯红灯和无视警察的指挥,你必须遭到罚款和吊销驾驶证。

杨先生:难道你不认为你的处罚太重了吗?

警察:不,我是按照规章办事。

★物业管理★ 6 Property Management Clerk

Words and Phrases 闪亮词语 点滴积累

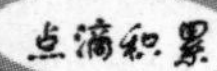

central heating and air-conditioning 冷暖中央空调
fitness center 健身中心
membership card 会员卡
public facilities 公物
maintenance department 维修部
villa 别墅
style 风格
enviroment 环境
location 坐落位置
for rent 出租
tenant 租户,租赁者
square meter 平方米
rental 租费
management fee 管理费
recreational facilities 娱乐设施
garage 车库
security system 安全系统
be equipped with 装配有
common area 公共区域
service center 服务中心
inform 通知
dial 拨号
compensation 赔偿
on duty 值班
patrol 巡逻
smoke detector 报警器

Useful Sentences 七彩精句 连点成线

About property management clerks 物业管理员用语

1. *I'd like to give you a brief introduction to our villa and give you some literature about the villa for your reference.* 我把我们的别墅向您作个简要介绍,给您一些资料供参考。
2. *May I give you my business card? Could I get yours?* 给您一张我的名片好吗?您可否也给我一张?
3. *Our houses are only for rent.* 我们的房屋仅供出租。
4. *From which date do you want to rent the house?* 你们愿意什么时候租用房屋?
5. *We happen to have a three-bedroom house available for rent beginning on October 1.* 正巧我们有一套有三个卧室的房子可在10月1日起租。
6. *Our villa is managed by the Nanyang Group.* 我们的别墅隶属于南洋集团管理。
7. *Let's go to see the house, shall we?* 我们一起去看看房子好吗?
8. *You can enjoy many recreational facilities here.* 这里有许多康乐设施供您享用。
9. *Its location is nice with a lot of privacy.* 这幢房子的方位非常好,很幽静。
10. *The monthly rental is 1000 dollars for this house, including basic furniture, management fee, local telephone fee, school shuttle and domestic newspapers.* 这幢房子的月租是1000美元,包括基本家具、管理费、本地电话费、校车、国内报纸。
11. *The biggest house is 200 square meters with an attached garage.* 最大的房子有200平方米并配有车库。
12. *We provide on TV set with 22 channels, including satellite programs.* 我们提供一台可接收22个频道的(包括卫星节目)电视机。
13. *Each house has central heating and air-conditioning.* 每幢房屋都有冷暖中央空调。
14. *Guards are on duty 24 hours.* 保安人员24小时值班。
15. *We hold a safety first policy.* 我们坚持安全第一的原则。
16. *It has graceful environment and large green areas.* 住宅区环境幽雅,有大片绿地。
17. *Each house is equipped with a full-size washer and a dryer.* 每幢房屋配有大容量洗衣机和干

衣机。

18. *You are responsible for your own linens, lamps, kitchen ware and additional furniture.* 你要自备床上用品、台灯、厨房用具、额外家具等等。

19. *There is a Jacuzzi bathtub and a shower-stall in the master bedroom's bathroom.* 主卧室的卫生间内有一个按摩浴缸和一个淋浴室。

20. *All window of the house have curtains or window blinds. The sliding glass doors have vertical blinds.* 所有玻璃窗都有窗帘或百叶窗，落地玻璃门有垂直帘。

21. *It is better to make reservations for certain activities, such as tennis, in order to ensure availability.* 有些活动最好预约，如网球之类，以确保（场地的）使用。

22. *Tenants of the villa can use their VIP cards to use the Fitness Center.* 别墅的住客可使用贵宾卡去健身中心健身。

23. *Kitchen appliances include a hoodfan, a dish washer, a large refrigerator and a garbage disposal.* 厨房配有抽油烟机、洗碗机、大冰箱和垃圾处理机。

24. *You can put foil paper on the bottom of your oven to help keep it clean.* 您可在烤箱底部放锡纸以便保洁。

25. *The garage door is remote-controlled for your convenience.* 为方便您使用，车库门是遥控的。

26. *Please tell your children to be careful not to damage the flowers, trees, lawn and other public facilities.* 请告诉您的孩子要爱护花草树木及公物。

27. *If you need to move anything in the house, please contact the reception desk. We will send someone to help you.* 如果您需要搬动房内的东西，请与服务台联系，我们会派人来帮忙。

28. *Would you please fill out the registration forms and sign the receipt?* 请您填写一下住宿登记单并在收据上签一下字好吗？

29. *We will do our best to respond immediately.* 我们会尽快提供帮助。

30. *The water faucet in your house is dripping. We will send a maintenance man to fix it.* 您家水龙头正在滴水，我们会派维修人员来修复。

31. *The garbage disposal can only handle small amounts at one time.* 垃圾处理机每次只能处理少量垃圾。

32. *Please be careful not to overload it.* 请小心别超负荷使用。

33. *We are very sorry for the water stains on your ceiling.* 非常抱歉您家天花板上有水迹。

34. *These can be caused by leak in the roof.* 这可能是由于屋顶有渗漏。

35. *We will repair it after fixing it.* 修整后我们将重新粉刷。

36. *We will have a thorough check.* 我们将做彻底的检查。

37. *Sometimes this work may cause a temporary disruption to your TV cable.* 可能有时会干扰您的电视线路。

38. *Our service center is open round the clock. If you need any help please dial 9 at any time.* 我们服务中心昼夜开放。您有任何需求请随时拨打9。

39. *This is the service center. What can I do for you? Would you please tell me your house number?* 这是服务中心，能为您效劳吗？请告诉我您的住房号码。

40. *Our service center has the functions of the business center and front desk of the hotel.* 我们服务中心具有宾馆商务中心及总台的各种功能。

Fashion Conversation 鲜活会话 曲线到面

Conversation 1

A: Plumbing company. Can I help you?
B: Yes, please. We have a leaky faucet. Could you send someone to repair it?
A: Your address and phone number, please?
B: 216 People Street, Phone number is 5373106.

A：管道公司，您有什么事吗？
B：哦，是的，我家的水龙头漏水了，能否派人去修一下？
A：请说您的地址和电话。
B：人民大街216号，电话是5373106。

A: Name, please?
B: Jim Green.
A: OK, our plumber will be there to help as soon as possible.
B: Thank you very much.
A: You are welcome.

A：姓名？
B：吉姆格林。
A：我们的水暖工会尽快赶到修理。
B：非常感谢。
A：不客气。

Conversation 2

A: Excuse me. Is a plumber available now?
B: Sorry, sir. They are all in the field.
A: So when are they available?
B: Let me check the schedule. The nearest one is in the afternoon.
A: Could you tell me the exact time?
B: About 2 o'clock.
A: Can you manage it earlier?
B: We'll do our best. The repair man will call first. Your address, telephone number and name, please?

A：请问有管道修理工在吗？
B：对不起，先生。他们都出去工作了。
A：那什么时候能回来？
B：让我看看工作日程。最早的一个在今天下午。
A：能否告诉我具体是什么时间？
B：大约两点钟。
A：能不能早点？
B：我们会尽力的。去之前我们的工作人员会先打电话给您的。请留下您的地址、电话和姓名。

Conversation 3

A: Excuse me, sir. I am looking for a plumber to take a look at my kitchen drain.
B: What's wrong with it?
A: The water can't get through.
B: Whether it is blocked by some waste?
A: No, I have checked it.
B: OK, I'll send a person to have a look right now.

A：先生，打扰一下。我想找一位修理工帮我看看我们家厨房的下水道。
B：什么情况？
A：水流不出去。
B：是不是给什么垃圾塞住了？
A：没有，我已经检查过了。
B：好吧，我马上派个人去看看。

Conversation 4

A: Hello. Is this Domestic Electrical Appliances Repairing Center?
B: Yes, it is. What can I do for you, Madam?
A: Well, I've got a problem with my refrigerator.
B: What's wrong with it?
A: I think it simply doesn't work, because everything in it has gone bad.
B: Has there been an electricity cut?
A: No, my air conditioning is on all the time and I'm watching TV now. Can you send someone round to look at it?
B: I'll send someone to look at it immediately. What's the name and address, please?
A: My name is Ellen White. That's E-L-L-E-N, Ellen, W-H-I-T-E, White. And My address is 203 Chinese Rose Villas.

A：喂，是家电维修中心吗？
B：是的，您有什么事吗，夫人？
A：我的电冰箱出了点毛病。
B：怎么回事？
A：我想它就是不制冷了，因为里面放的东西都坏了。
B：有没有停电？
A：没有，我的空调一直开着而且我现在正在看电视。你能不能派个人来给看一看？
B：我马上就派人去看看。请问您的姓名与地址？
A：我叫爱伦·怀特。就是E-L-L-E-N，爱伦，W-H-I-T-E，怀特。我的地址是月季别墅203号。

B: Your telephone number?
A: My phone number is 23356665.
B: OK. Thank you. I think our repairman will get to your place in an hour or so. Will you be at home then?
A: Yes, of course I will. Thank you very much. Goodbye.
B: Goodbye.

B：您的电话号码是多少？
A：我的电话号码是23356665。
B：好。谢谢您。我想我们的修理工将在一小时左右赶到您家。您到时候在家吗？
A：我当然会在家。非常感谢您。再见。
B：再见。

On the Scene 身临其境 面面俱到

主题：张先生向物业人员了解他将要入住的房子的设施。请你看图，根据如下提供的关键词，将他们的对话写出来。

关键词语：facility *n.* 设施　　central heating 中央供暖
appliance *n.* 用具　　oven *n.* 烤箱
garbage disposal 垃圾处理系统

参考答案

Mr. Zhang: Well, how about the house facilities?
Receptor: Each house has central heating and air-conditioning. Besides, they are all equipped with a full-size washer and a dryer, kitchen appliances include an electric range with oven, a hoodfan, a dish washer, a large refrigerator and a garbage disposal.
Mr. Zhang: Are there smoke detectors in the house?
Receptor: Of course. In each room there is a smoke detector on the ceiling. In addition, we provide one safe for each house.
Mr. Zhang: I think there must be a clothes closet in each room, isn't there?
Receptor: Yes, you are right, sir. But I'm afraid you are responsible for your own linens, lamps, kitchen ware, and additional furniture.
Mr. Zhang: That's OK. I thought so.
张先生：那房屋的设施怎么样？
接待员：每幢房屋有自己的冷暖中央空调，此外，还配有大容量洗衣机和干衣机。厨房设备有带烤箱的电炉、抽油烟机、洗碗机、大冰箱和垃圾处理机。

张先生:房屋里有报警器吗?

接待员:当然有了,每个房间的天花板上都有报警器。另外,我们还为每家提供一个保险箱。

张先生:我想每个房间都有衣橱,对吗?

接待员:您说得的对,先生。不过您恐怕要自备床上用品、台灯、厨房用具和额外家具。

张先生:那没关系。我就是这么想的。

★推销人员★ 7 Salesman

Words and Phrases 闪亮词语 点滴积累

floor-polisher 地板打蜡机
carpet shampooer 地毯洗涤机
refrigerator; fridge; freezer 电冰箱
electric vacuum cleaner 电除尘器
electric typewriter 电动打字机
electric fan 电风扇
telephone set 电话机
electric radiator 电暖炉
electric blanket 电热毯
television camera; telecamera 电视摄像机
electric iron 电熨斗
sewing machine 缝纫机
dry battery(/cell) 干电池
dryer; drier 烘干机
air-cooler 冷风机
water meter 水表
desk fan 台扇

Useful Sentences 七彩精句 连点成线

Sell insurance 推销保险

1. *Could I have a few minutes of your time to tell you about our new comprehensive insurance plans?* 我可以用几分钟时间向你介绍我们最新的全面保险计划吗?
2. *How about I meet with you tomorrow and we can discuss Phoenix's plans in person?* 那么明天我亲身来向你介绍凤凰保险的计划,好吗?
3. *Mr Brow, it would only take about fifteen minutes of your time.* 布朗先生,我只会用大约十五分钟。
4. *Did you know that you can leave the money to a friend or relative?* 你知不知道保额是可以留给朋友或亲属的?
5. *This year Fortune is offering several new plans.* 今年幸运推出了几个新计划。
6. *One is designed specifically for single people.* 有一个专为单身人士而设的。
7. *I'll leave this pamphlet with you, and if you'd like more information, here's my card, you can call me any time.* 我把这个简介留给你看,如果你想得到更多资料,这是我的名片,你可以随时找我。

Sell estate 地产推销

1. *Are you selling your flat?* 你想把房子卖掉吗?
2. *Those are very popular sellers in this area. How long have you been living there?* 这类房子在这区很受欢迎。你在那里住了多久?
3. *Oh! It must be very hard to leave.* 噢!那么你一定很舍不得了。
4. *I've brought along some samples of what we can do to sell your home. We have several different plans depending on the type of home you have and how quickly you want to sell it.* 我带了几个放盘的计划,是应房子的种类和你想何时售出而定的。
5. *My family is moving by next month at the latest because I got a job in another country, so the quicker I sell this place the better.* 我们最迟在下个月要搬家了,因为我在另外一个国家找到工作,所以越快售出越好。
6. *How much will this package cost?* 这套计划要多少钱?
7. *It is cheaper, but it might take longer for your house to sell.* 这个便宜一些,但亦可能需要较长时间才能售出房子。

Advertisement 广告推销

1. *Miss Green, this is Bart from the "Elite Journal".* 格林小姐,我是《精英杂志》的巴特。

2. *I'm sorry, I've already done all my advertising with the "Star Magazine".* 对不起，我早已在《巨星杂志》刊登了广告。

3. *Maybe we can find something that'd better suit the needs of your business.* 或许我们能为你提供更合适的服务。

4. *And we'll sit down with you at your convenience and help you create an advertisement that you are satisfied with.* 我们可以在你方便的时间商讨，保证会制作一个令你满意的广告。

5. *Yes, our readers are mostly business people.* 是的，我们的读者大部分是商界人士。

6. *But the newspaper only reaches a certain clientele, especially those right in the city.* 但报纸只能接触到一部分客户，而且局限于本市。

7. *Our magazine is international and it reaches a particular clientele, business people, who tend to travel more than people in other professions.* 我们的杂志则是国际性的，而且可接触到特定的顾客，就是比其他行业更常出国的商界人士。

Bagman 旅游推销

1. *Mrs. Green, the reason I'm calling is to let you know about a special package tour to Europe for senior citizens.* 格林太太，我来电的原因是想为你介绍一个为中老年人而设的欧洲旅游套餐。

2. *The price includes travel and lodging as well as several tours, but not food.* 价钱包括交通、住宿和观光，但不包括食物。

3. *What countries will the tour be going to?* 那么旅游地点包括哪些国家？

4. *That's quite a trip! How long is it?* 这个行程不错，为时多久？

5. *It's a month-long tour. So far a lot of people have been interested in it.* 这个旅程为期一个月，现时已有不少人报名参加。

6. *How much does the whole package cost?* 整个套餐需多少钱？

7. *I can send you some information if you like.* 如果需要的话，我可以寄一些资料给你。

Fashion Conversation 鲜活会话 由线到面

Conversation 1

A: Hello, is Mr. Tom Ervine at home?
A：你好，汤姆·欧文先生在家吗？

B: I'm Tom Ervine.
B：我是汤姆·欧文。

A: Mr. Ervine, I'm Rose from Oceanview Realty, we talked on the phone yesterday about putting your house on the market.
A：欧文先生，我是海景地产公司的罗斯，我们昨天曾通过电话谈及把你的房子放盘一事。

B: Oh yes, of course, come on in.
B：噢，是的，请进来。

A: I've brought along some samples of what we can do to sell your home. We have several different plans depending on the type of home you have and how quickly you want to sell it.
A：我带了几个放盘的计划，是应房子的种类和你想何时售出而定的。

B: My family is moving by next month at the latest because I got a job in another city, so the quicker I sell this place the better.
B：我们最迟在下个月要搬家了，因为我在另外一个城市找到工作，所以越快售出越好。

A: All right, you might want to go with our most aggressive selling plan then. Your house will be included weekly in our for sale advertisements in the newspaper and it will be put on our web site in addition to having it featured in our office and suggesting it to potential clients.
A：好的，那么你应该想看看我们最积极的一个计划。你售房的广告会放在我们每星期刊登于报纸的广告内，也会放在电脑网页上，而我们公司的地产代理也会向客户介绍你的楼盘。

B: How much will this package cost?
B：这套计划要多少钱？

A: It will be six hundred dollars per month.
A：每月 600 元。

B: Is there anything cheaper than that?
B:还有没有比较便宜的?

A: We have another plan that has all the same components except instead of having weekly advertising in the newspaper, you get one advertisement a month. It costs two hundred dollars.
A:我们有另一个计划,就是每月刊登一次,其他的条件一样,价钱是200元。

B: That sounds more in my price range.
B:这个比较符合我的预算。

A: It is cheaper, but it might take longer for your house to sell. In the long run, the first plan may end up being cheaper if your house sells within the first month because of it. You can change plans as you go along. For instance, you could start with the first plan and change it to the second after one month. It's really up to you, we're very flexible.
A:这个是便宜一些,但亦可能需要较长时间才能售出房子。长远来说,第一个计划可能更便宜,因为你的房子可能在第一个月内便能售出。但其实你选择了以后亦可以改变计划,例如在第一个月后改为另一个计划,这是很有弹性的。

B: Sounds good, but I'll have to discuss it with my wife when she gets home from work.
B:很好,但我要等太太回家后再商谈一下。

A: No problem. Before I go, let me show you some of the different advertising schemes we have. You can pick which type of advertisement you would like to have. Also, I'm going to take some pictures of the house before I leave if that's okay with you, so if you decide to go with one of our plans, we can get started right away.
A:没有问题,在我离开之前,让我为你介绍不同的广告计划,你可选择任何一种。此外,如果你不反对,我希望可为房子拍照。当你选定了计划后,我们就可以开始了。

B: All right, let me have a look at what you've got there.
B:好的,让我看看你的资料。

Conversation 2

A: Hi, I'm here to see Mr. Ma.
A:嗨!我是来找马先生的。

B: Right this way, please.
B:请跟我来。

A: Hello, Mr. Ma? I'm Kate Green of "*Success Magazine*".
A:马先生,你好,我是《成功杂志》的凯特·格林。

B: Nice to meet you, Miss Green. What can I do for you this morning?
B:格林小姐,很高兴认识你,我有什么可帮到你吗?

A: Actually, Mr. Ma, I've come to talk to you about advertising in our magazine.
A:马先生,其实我是来看看你是否有兴趣在我们的杂志上刊登广告的。

B: Oh?
B:噢?

A: Yes, our readers are mostly business people. Most of them travel a lot and spend a lot of money on hotels. Advertising with us could be especially beneficial to you because a lot of business people come here for meetings and conferences.
A:是的,我们的读者大部分是商界人士。他们大都时常出差,并花费很多于酒店住宿之上。在我们这里登广告会对你很有帮助,因为很多商界人士会来这里开会。

B: I've already advertised in the newspaper.
B:我已在报纸刊登上广告。

A: Yes, but the newspaper only reaches a certain clientele, especially those right in the city. Our magazine is international and it reaches a parti-
A:是的,但报纸只能接触到一部分客户,而且局限于本市。我们的杂志则是国际性的,而且可接触到特定的顾客,就是比其他行业更常出国的

cular clientele, business people, who tend to travel more than people in other professions. | 商界人士。

B:What is your circulation? | B:你们的销量有多少?

A:Last week, it was over eight hundred thousand. | A:上星期销量超过80万。

B:That's rather impressive. Advertising fee must be quite expensive then. | B:这相当可观,那么广告费一定相当昂贵吧?

A:I think it's pretty reasonable when you take into consideration how many people it reaches. | A:如果你考虑到读者的人数,便会觉得价钱合理了。

B:How much would a full page advertisement be? | B:那么一整页的广告要多少钱?

A:A full page advertisement costs fifty thousand dollars. A half-page is twenty-six thousand dollars. We also have a special section for hotels that lists your name, location and a contact number. It's four thousand dollars. Here are some samples of advertisements we've done for other hotels in the past. | A:整页广告是5万元,而半页则是26000元。我们亦有一个酒店专页,可刊出贵酒店的名字、地址和电话,这个是4000元。这是一些酒店广告的样板。

B:They're very well put together, but it is a little more expensive than I usually put into advertising. | B:看来做得很好,但比我们惯常花在广告上的费用略高。

A:Mr. Ma, think of it this way. If only one percent of our readers saw the advertisement and came to your hotel, that would be eight thousand new customers every week. | A:马先生,你可这样想:只要有百分之一的读者看到广告而到你的酒店的话,那每星期便会有8000个新客人了。

B:That's true, and you do have some really great advertisements here. Tell you what, we have a management board meeting night. I'll talk to them about it then and see what they think. | B:这也有道理,而且你们的广告也做得很好。这样吧,我们明晚有个管理层的会议,我会向他们提出这件事,看看他们有何看法。

A:Okay, I'll come in and see you again on Thursday then. If there's any more information you want between now and then, or if you have any questions, don't hesitate to give me a call. Here's my card. | A:好的,我不如星期四来见你吧。如果这期间你需要什么资料或有什么问题,请与我联络,这是我的名片。

B:Thank you, I'll see you on Thursday. | B:谢谢,我们星期四见。

A:All right, I'll see you then. | A:好的,到时见。

Conversation 3

A:Hello, Mrs. Green? | A:你好,是格林太太吗?

B:Yes, I'm Mrs. Green. You must be the guy from the refrigerator company. | B:是,我是格林太太。你一定是冰箱公司的人吧!

A:Yes. | A:是的。

B:Come on in, the refrigerator is in here. | B:请进来,冰箱就在这里。

A:How long have you had your refrigerator, Mrs. Green? | A:格林太太,你的冰箱用了多久?

B:About fifteen years now. | B:大约15年了。

A:There's a good chance that even if we could fix your refrigerator, the parts will no longer be a- | A:就算我们能够修理你的冰箱,也未必能买到零件,因为冰箱已出厂超过10年了。

vailable because it is more than ten years old.

B: You mean I have to buy a brand-new refrigerator?

B: 你的意思是我要买一个全新的冰箱?

A: Not necessarily, but if you do, Freezone will take your old refrigerator back and give you credit towards a new refrigerator for it.

A: 也未必,但如果你想的话,你可将旧冰箱送到自由圈,便可以折扣优惠购买新冰箱。

B: Really? I didn't know that. Do they do that even if a refrigerator is irreparable?

B: 真的? 我以前并不知道。就算冰箱不能修理也可以吗?

A: Anytime someone buys another Freezone refrigerator from us, we'll take their old Freezone refrigerator on matter if it's still running or not and give them credit on the new one depending on what condition the old one is in.

A: 任何人向我们购买冰箱,我们都会收回旧的,不论性能如何。至于旧冰箱值多少钱就要视乎它的性能而定。

B: In that case, I might just think about getting a new refrigerator. This one hasn't been working very well for the last couple of years, even before it broke down. It's just getting old, that's all.

B: 那么,我还是买一部新的好。这个冰箱在过去几年就算没有故障,性能也不太好,可能是旧了一点。

A: If you'd like some information on our new line of refrigerators, I've got some pamphlets with me that I can leave with you.

A: 如果你想看看新系列冰箱的资料,我可留下一些小册子给你。

B: That would be great. I'll talk to my husband about it when he gets home.

B: 那很好,待我丈夫回家后,我会与他谈谈。

A: No problem. I think I know what's wrong with your refrigerator now, but I'll have to check and see if the part you need is available when I get back to the office. I'll come by tomorrow if we have it, or if not, I'll give you a call to let you know, okay?

A: 没有问题,我大概知道冰箱有什么问题,但我要回公司看看有没有所需的零件。如果有的话,我明天再来;如果没有的话,我致电给你,好吗?

B: Okay, thank you.

B: 好的,谢谢。

A: And if you have any questions about our new refrigerators, here's my card. Give me a call anytime.

A: 如果你对我们的新冰箱有任何问题,这是我的名片,你可随时致电给我。

B: Thanks.

B: 谢谢。

A: No problem. I'll see you tomorrow.

A: 没有问题,明天见。

Conversation 4

A: Hello, my name is Jack. I'm from Winsome Investors Limited. Could I have a few moments of your time to tell you about our investment opportunities?

A: 你好,我名叫杰克,我是威森投资公司的投资顾问。我可否用少许时间向你介绍一下我们的投资方式。

B: I don't really have time right now.

B: 我现在没有时间。

A: It will only take a few minutes, sir. Do you have your money invested in anything now to prepare for the future?

A: 先生,我不会花多过几分钟的。你有没有为将来而作投资呢?

B: Not at the moment.

B: 现在没有。

A: Well, I can lt you know of a few different ways

A: 我可以为你介绍几种投资方式,现在有很多选

that you might want to invest your money. There are so many options out there now, that it's pretty much a full-time job keeping up with all the new things. Now I know you don't have the time to keep up on them, but it's my job to keep up on things for you, so I can tell you just about the options which are most beneficial to you.

择,而管理财务差不多已是一份全职工作。我知道你并没有时间去管理所有资金,但我能替你处理投资事宜,并给你提供一些最有利的投资组合。

B: Will you be long?　B:你会用很多时间吗?

A: It really depends on how many questions you have, Mr. . . .　A:看你的问题多少,阁下是……

B: Taylor Asser.　B:泰勒·亚塞。

A: It really depends on you, Mr. Asser. It can take less than ten minutes for me to present several different options to you.　A:亚塞先生,看你想知道什么,十分钟内我就可以为你介绍几种最基本的投资选择。

B: Well, all right, come in then.　B:好的,请进来。

A: Thank you.　A:谢谢。

Conversation 5

A: Hello, I'm Mary, can I help you with anything?　A:你好,我是玛丽,可以为你效劳吗?

B: I'm looking around for a new car, my old one is in pretty bad shape, but I'm not sure exactly what I'm looking for..　B:我想找一部新车,因旧车已很残旧,但我并未决定购买哪种类型的汽车。

A: What kind of car do you have now?　A:你现在的是什么汽车?

B: It's a 1989 Ford.　B:是1989年的福特。

A: Were you looking for something along the same line or something different?　A:那么你想找一部相似的汽车,抑或一部完全不同的?

B: I'm not sure really.　B:我也不太肯定。

A: May I ask what your name is?　A:我可以怎样称呼你?

B: Oh, it's William Caesar.　B:噢,是威廉凯撒。

A: Okay, Mr Caesar, do you have any children?　A:好的,凯撒先生,你有子女吗?

B: Yes, my wife and I have three kids.　B:有,我太太和我有三名子女。

A: Have you considered buying a mini-van?　A:你是否想过买一部小型客货车?

B: No, I'd never really thought about it.　B:我从来都没有想过。

A: They're quite roomy and nice for any family with more than two kids. With a mini-van, every kid gets to sit next to a window.　A:这种车很宽敞,最适合有超过两个孩子的家庭,而且每个孩子也可坐在窗旁。

B: That would certainly stop a lot of the fighting in our family every time we get in the car!　B:那么可大大减少小孩子争执的次数!

A: Most mini-vans today come fully equipped as well, automatic windows, air-conditioning, stereo. You can get automatic sliding doors as well, but they have to be specially ordered. If you like I can let you test drive the Grand Star, Mr Caesar. It's one of our most popular models. You might find it hard to get used to at first because it's bigger than your car, but really it's quite easy to

A:现时大部分的小型客货车都设备齐全:自动窗、冷气和音响。如有需要,你亦可预订自动门。凯撒先生,我可让你试试“巨星”,这是最受欢迎的款式之一。你最初可能觉得它体积较大,不过它是很容易上手的。

drive.

B: I'd love to test drive one to see what it's like. A mini-van makes a lot more sense for my family than a car.

B: 我也很想试试这车,对于我的家庭来说,小型客货车似乎比一般房车实用。

A: When you get back, I'll show you some of our other models as well, and I'll let you see what kind of options and colours you can get with each model. You'll find that there's a pretty extensive choice.

A: 当你试车后,我会让你看看其他款式以及每个款式可供选择的设备和颜色。你会发现选择多得很呢!

B: Okay, we'll talk when I get back.

B: 好的,我们试车后再说吧。

Conversation 6

A: Hello, can I speak to the head of the household?

A: 喂,我可以跟户主讲话吗?

B: May I ask who's calling?

B: 请问你是谁?

A: This is Jiang Ping with Children's Publishing Company. May I have your name, sir?

A: 我是儿童出版公司的江平。先生,可以告诉我您的姓名吗?

B: My name is Chen.

B: 我姓陈。

A: Thank you, Mr. Chen, do you have children?

A: 谢谢您,陈先生,您有孩子吗?

B: Yes.

B: 有。

A: Great! I think you must care for the children's education.

A: 太好了! 我想您一定很关心孩子的教育问题吧。

B: Certainly.

B: 当然了。

A: Mr. Chen, maybe you have heard about it already that Children's Publishing Company has the most successful Children's English Learning Books in the market. These books will help your children a lot in learning English.

A: 陈先生,您或许听说过儿童出版公司有许多市场上最优秀的儿童英语学习读物,这些读物将对您的孩子学英语大有帮助。

B: Yes.

B: 是的。

A: And we are running a special offer on the books now. I would like to tell you more about it.

A: 现在我们这些读物正特价优惠销售。我很乐意给您详细说一下。

B: Oh, I'm sorry, I am kind of busy and my…

B: 啊,对不起,我现在有点儿忙……

A: Mr. Chen, you can have savings up to 50 percent, and this offer will expire in two days.

A: 陈先生,您可以节省50%,这个特价优惠两天就结束了。

B: Oh, sorry, Miss Jiang. As a matter of fact, my daughter is only eleven months old.

B: 啊,很抱歉,江小姐,事实上,我的女儿才11个月大呢。

A: Oh, all right. Mr. Chen, you may find out you need it in the future, please don't hesitate to call me. Thank you for your time.

A: 啊,好的,陈先生,您可能会发现将来会需要它,到时请尽管打电话给我。谢谢您,占用了您这么多时间。

B: I appreciate your calling. Goodbye.

B: 我很感谢你打电话给我。再见。

A: Goodbye, have a nice day.

A: 再见,祝您愉快。

On the Scene 身临其境 面面俱到

主题:怀特先生接到了电话推销员丹·摩尔推销便携式录音机的电话。请你看图,根据如下提供的关键词,将他们的对话写出来。

关键词语: Hited Electronics Company 海德电器公司
a great discount 大幅度打折出售
portable type recorder 便携式录音机

参考答案

Dan: Hello, may I speak to Mr. White?
Mr. White: This is he speaking.
Dan: How are you doing this evening, Mr. White?
Mr. White: I am fine. Who's this?
Dan: This is Dan, Dan Moore. I'm calling on behalf of Hited Electronics Company. Mr. White, as you know, everything now is offered with a great discount in our company.
Mr. White: Yes, I know.
Dan: Now, I'm calling to recommend you a new style of portable type recorder.
Mr. White: Oh? Can you give me more detail, then?
Dan: Certainly, sir. This kind of recorder is completely portable and very light in weight.
Mr. White: What about the quality of the sound? Sometimes these portables sound very tiny.
Dan: It's pretty good. And it'll open up a whole new world of pleasure for you and your family. You can have a free trial for two weeks, and if you are not satisfied, you may return it.
Mr. White: How much is it?
Dan: We'll give you a 50 percent discount. It's only 169 dollars now.
Mr. White: Your offer sounds interesting.
Dan: Yes, Mr. White. It'll save you a lot of money and virtually it's risk-free for you. We will take your order over the phone.
Mr. White: OK, I'll take it.

丹:喂,可以让怀特先生接电话吗?
怀特先生:我就是。
丹:怀特先生,今晚你好吗?
怀特先生:很好。你是哪位?
丹:我是丹,丹·摩尔。我代表海德电器公司打电话来。怀特先生,你知道,我们公司所有的东西都在大幅度打折出售。

怀特先生:是的,我知道。

丹:现在我打电话向您推荐一种新款式的便携式录音机。

怀特先生:哦?那么你能详细说明一下吗?

丹:可以,先生。这种录音机是便携式的,重量很轻。

怀特先生:音质怎么样?这种便携式录音机有时音量很小。

丹:质量很好。它将为您和您的家庭开辟一个全新的娱乐天地。您可以免费试用两个星期,如果不满意,你可以退货。

怀特先生:多少钱?

丹:我们给您打五折,仅169美元。

怀特先生:听起来挺吸引人的。

丹:是的,怀特先生,这可以为您节省很多钱,而且实际上对您而言是完全没有风险的。我们可以用电话接受订购。

怀特先生:好的,我买了。

Entertainment

CHAPTE

4

消遣娱乐

★报刊杂志★ 1 Newspaper and Magazine

Words and Phrases 闪亮词语 点滴积累

newspaper 报纸
extra issue 号外
daily; daily paper 日报
evening paper 晚报
morning paper 晨报
Chinese paper 中文报纸
English paper 英文报纸
political news 政治新闻
big news 头条新闻
hot news 最新新闻
exclusive news 独家新闻
journal 日刊
weekly 周刊
monthly 月刊
bimonthly 双月刊
quarterly 季刊
semiyearly; semiannually 半年刊
biyearly; biannually 双年刊
almanac 年鉴
supplementary issue 增刊
special issue 特刊
memorial volume 纪念刊
illustrated periodical 画刊

Useful Sentences 七彩精句 连点成线

Requesting a subscription from a magazine agent 订期刊

1. *I'd like to subscribe.* 我想订一份杂志。
2. *I'd like a subscription.* 我想订阅杂志。
3. *Give me a subscription to **News week**.* 给我订一份《新闻周刊》。
4. *I'd like to renew my subscription.* 我想延长订阅期限。
5. *I'd like to cancel my subscription.* 我想取消订阅。
6. *I'd like to change my subscription to weekends only.* 我想把订单改一下，只要周末版就可以了。
7. *I'd like to take advantage of your special offer for new subscribers.* 我想享受你们给新订户的优惠。

Making a complaint to a newspaper agent 向报纸代理商投诉

1. *I didn't receive a newspaper this morning.* 今天早上我没有收到报纸。
2. *I didn't get today's paper.* 我没有今天的报纸。
3. *My paper has been arriving late.* 我的报纸来得不及时。
4. *They always throw my paper in the yard.* 他们总是把我的报纸扔在院子里。
5. *My paper today is missing the additional section.* 我今天报纸中的附加版不见了。

Responses to complaints 对投诉的回复

1. *I apologize for the inconvenience.* 我对给您带来的不便表示歉意。
2. *I'm terribly sorry for the inconvenience.* 我请您原谅由此给您带来的不便。
3. *We'll have a paper sent out to you right now.* 我们立刻就给您送去一份报纸。
4. *I'll send out the missing section right away.* 我马上就把您缺少的那版给您送去。
5. *I assure you the matter is being taken care of.* 我保证我们会解决问题的。

Request to a newspaper agent 向送报人提出要求

1. *Could you please leave the paper on the hall ?* 您能把报纸放在前厅里吗？

2. *I'm moving. I'd like to give you my new address.* 我要搬家了，给您一个我的新地址。

3. *I'm going on vacation. Can you hold my paper for two weeks?* 我去度假，您能把我的报纸代为保存两星期吗？

4. *I'd like to order a back issue.* 我想订一份过期杂志。

Expressions used by a magazine agent 杂志代理商用语

1. *May I have your name, address and ZIP code?* 请告诉我您的姓名，地址和邮编好吗？

2. *Give me your name, address and ZIP code.* 请您把您的姓名，地址和邮编给我。

3. *Would you like a six-month or one-year subscription?* 您要订半年还是一年？

4. *May I ask why you wish to cancel?* 我可以问一下您为什么取消订阅？

Fashion Conversation 鲜活会话 由线到面

Conversation 1

A: Where's today's papers? | A：今天的报纸在哪儿？
B: On the table, Tom. | B：在桌子上，汤姆。
A: Anything important in the news today? | A：今天有什么重要新闻吗？
B: The same old stories, some one robbed a jewellery store, another murdered his wife, It's too silly. | B：老一套，有人抢了珠宝店，还有人杀了他老婆，太无聊了。
A: I think you're right. Well, you see the sun appears. | A：不错。噢，你看，太阳出来了。
B: Have a nice day! Let's go out for a walk. | B：天气不错。出去走走吧。

Conversation 2

A: What's your favorite magazine? | A：你最喜欢的杂志是什么？
B: I'd say it's ***the Reader's Digest***. It's the most famous monthly published one in the U. S. A. | B：要我说是《读者文摘》，在美国是最有名的月刊。
A: Why do you like it best? | A：为什么你觉得是最好的？
B: It's got many years of experience and prestige and extensive coverage. | B：有多年的出版史，新闻报道方面很有权威，内容也很广泛。
A: Well, I think it's extremely informative and interesting. The articles in it help me understand your people and culture much better. I always enjoy reading them. | A：我想它极富有知识性和趣味性，里面的文章帮助我更好地了解那里的人情与文化，我一直喜爱阅读。
B: I can see you're a careful reader as well as an observer. You know that's why so many people like reading it. And one more thing, language succinct, it's a very good magazine to read, especially for you people. | B：我看得出你是个细心读者，同时善于观察，你知道这么多人为什么喜欢读这杂志。还有，这本杂志语言精炼，这是本供读者阅读的好杂志，尤其对于你们。
A: You're right. | A：你说得对。

Conversation 3

A: I've been reading a lot lately about the issue of women's rights. | A：我最近阅读了大量关于女权问题的文章。
B: That is hot topic now. | B：那可是当今的热门话题。
A: I find a lot of different points of view depending | A：根据我读的不同杂志或报纸，我发现有许多种

on which magazine or paper I read.

不同的观点。

B: How true! If you read a women's magazine, just about every article has that as a topic in one way or another.

B:一点不错!如果你读一本妇女杂志,几乎每篇文章在某种程度上都谈论这个问题。

A: Yes, and if you read a conservative paper or magazine, they cover many of the same issues but from a different point of view.

A:是的,如果你读的是保守主义的报纸或杂志,它们也报道许多同样的问题,但观点却不一样。

B: A person has to know that the publisher has his or her own opinions and that is the viewpoint that will be expressed in that publication.

B:谁都明白,出版者有自己的观点,而他们的出版物所表达的就是他们的观点。

A: I guess it would help if I knew something about the background of the publishers of the materials I read.

A:我想,如果我了解一些出版者的背景,对我会有些帮助。

B: Yes, but not many people have the time or interest in doing that.

B:是的,不过不会有很多人有空或有兴趣去做那种了解。

A: What do you think is the best way for a person to get unbiased information on a subject?

A:要获得关于一个问题的不带偏见的信息,你觉得最好的方法是什么?

B: It would help to do a lot of reading. You should make sure that you read articles from several points of view. Then you have to realize that no one is completely unbiased, not even yourself.

B:多读多看有好处。你应该看各种观点的文章。然后你要明白,没有一个人是完全没有偏见的,甚至你自己也是这样。

A: I know that's true. I have definite opinions on that subject and many others.

A:这我知道。我对这个问题和许多其他问题有明确的观点。

B: With that in mind, you have to make a judgment. Look at all the facts and decide for yourself which viewpoint is most nearly correct.

B:这一点搞清楚以后,你还要做出判断。了解所有的事实,然后判断哪一种观点最正确。

A: You're saying, then, that the final opinion should be my own opinion.

A:那么,你是说最终还是要以我自己的观点为准了。

B: That's correct. It should be made, however, after a careful consideration of all you have read.

B:对。不过,要仔细考虑你所读过的所有材料之后再确定你的观点。

Conversation 4

A: What's the date today?

A:今天几号?

B: It's September 22, 1996.

B:1996年9月22日。

A: Where's today's newspapers?

A:今天的报纸在哪儿?

B: They're on the office desk.

B:在办公桌上。

A: Is there anything startling in the news today?

A:有什么惊人消息吗?

B: Yes, the Ship "Safeguarding Diaoyu Island" left Hong Kong for Diaoyu Island this morning.

B:有,"保钓号"船离开香港开赴钓鱼岛。

A: Who is the captain?

A:谁是船长?

B: Wei Lizhi is the captain.

B:魏立志是船长。

A: Diaoyu Island belongs to China. I wish them success. Any other important news?

A:钓鱼岛属于中国。祝他们成功。还有其他什么重要消息吗?

B: Yes, our Foreign Affairs Minister Mr. Qian Qi-chen has left for New York to attend the 51th session of the United Nations.

B:有,我们的钱其琛外长已前往纽约参加第51届联合国大会。

A: Oh, it's a good chance to make the problem of Diaoyu Island solved sooner.

A:哦,这是争取早日解决钓鱼岛问题的好机会。

Conversation 5

A: What can I do for you?
B: Do you have the latest issue of ***National Geography***?
A: Why certainly, you'll see it in the racks for Newspapers. Just keep on going straight until you meet the dead end. You can't miss it.
B: Thank you.
A: You're welcome.
B: I'll get this one. Can you change my bill to coins? I need to make a few phone calls.
A: All right, here it is.

A:有什么能为您效劳吗?
B:你们有最近一期的《国家地理》吗?
A:当然有,您可以在报纸架上找到。一直走到底就会看到,不会错过的。
B:谢谢。
A:不客气。
B:我买了。你可不可以把我的纸币换成硬币?我需要打几个电话。
A:好的,给您。

On the Scene 身临其境 面面俱到

主题:安在看报纸,威廉问她报纸上的新闻有什么。请你看图,根据如下提供的关键词,将他们的对话写出来。

关键词语:section *n.* 部分 item *n.* 项目 apartment *n.* 公寓住宅 editorial *n.* 社论

参考答案

William: Anything interesting in the papers?
Ann: Umm. Nothing special in the foreign section.
William: How about home news?
Ann: Let me see. Here's a news item about some key universities.
William: What's that?
Ann: Some apartment buildings for their students are being built now. Oh, there is an editorial about the poor and wealthy.

威廉:报纸上有什么有趣的新闻?
安:嗯,国外版没什么。
威廉:国内的呢?
安:我看看,有一些关于重点大学的事儿。
威廉:怎么了?
安:一些新教学楼建成了。哦,这儿有一个关于贫富的专题报导。

★电视电影★ 2 TV Program and Film

Words and Phrases 闪亮词语 点滴积累

movie; film; motion picture 电影
musicals 音乐片
animated cartoon/animation; cartoon 卡通片;动画片
documentary film 纪录片
literary film 文艺片
newsreel 新闻片
comedy 喜剧片
swordsmen film 武侠片
detective film; mystery 侦探片
ethical film 爱情片
western movies 西部片
science fiction 科幻片
feature 故事片
adventure story 冒险故事片
spy story 反特片;间谍片
leading man; screen actor; film star; the hero 男主角
leading lady; screen actress; film star; the heroine 女主角
film star 电影明星
film actor 电影男明星
film actress 电影女明星
lengthy motion pictures 长片
shorter feature 短片
trailer; preview 预告片
thriller 惊险刺激片
nouvelle vague 新潮派影片
tragedy 悲剧片
dracula movie 恐怖片

Useful Sentences 七彩精句 连点成线

TV 电视

1. *Do you watch the 7 o'clock news on TV?* 你看七点的新闻报道吗?
2. *Which do you watch most often, game shows, sitcomes or soaps?* 你经常看什么电视节目,机智问答、情景喜剧还是肥皂剧?
3. *What is your favorite talk show?* 你最喜欢的谈话节目是什么?
4. *I like to watch the Tonight Show with Jay Leno.* 我喜欢 Jay Leno 主持的今夜星空。
5. *Hurry up! I'm going to miss the hockey game on ESPN!* 快点!我快要错过 ESPN 的曲棍球赛了。
6. *Awesome! My show's starting!* 哦!我的节目要开始了!
7. *This episode is really interesting/funny/exciting.* 这一集实在太精彩了。
8. *This plot is too ridiculous!* 这个剧情太胡扯了。
9. *Stop flipping channels all the time!* 不要随便乱转台!

Film 电影

1. *Would you like to see the movie* ***Gone with the Wind?*** 你想看《飘》这部电影吗?
2. *Who plays the part of heroine in the movie?* 这部电影里,谁担任女主角?
3. *What did the media say about the movie?* 媒体是如何评论这部片子的?
4. *The movie has got this year's Oscar Award. It's really worth seeing.* 这部电影获得了今年的奥斯卡奖,它是一部真正值得看的片子。
5. *The Hollywood pictures are popular to the people throughout the world.* 好莱坞电影受到世界人民的欢迎。
6. *What do you think of her acting?* 你认为她演技如何?
7. *Can you tell me the story of the film?* 你能给我讲讲这部电影的故事吗?
8. *Tom Cruise is my favorite actor. I must go and see it.* 汤姆·克鲁斯是我最喜欢的演员,我一定要

去看这部片子。

9. *Who is the star in the film?* 这部电影主演是谁?

10. *Does that film have both Chinese and English subtitles?* 那部电影有中英文字幕吗?

11. *It was a touching movie.* 这部影片太让人感动了。

12. *It's a great movie and performed by Henry Fondar and Katharine Hepburn.* 电影很棒,是由亨利·方达和凯瑟琳·赫本出演。

Fashion Conversation 鲜活会话 由线到面

Conversation 1

A: Hello, Mary, do you like watching TV?
B: Yes, very much. My mother always says I spend too much time in doing it.
A: So do my parents. We should finish our homework, and then help our parents with housework.
B: Maybe you are right. But sometimes it's too hard for me. I even can't help thinking of those good TV programs when I have to do my homework.
A: Really? You are keen on TV. What kind of programs do you like to watch?
B: My favorite programs are some interesting English movies.
A: It will benefit you a lot from TV set programs.
B: Maybe you can say that.

A:嗨,玛丽,你喜欢看电视吗?
B:是的,非常喜欢。我妈妈说我把太多的时间都花费在看电视上。
A:我的父母也这么说我。我们应该完成我们的家庭作业,接着帮父母做些家务。
B:也许你说得对。但有时对我来说太难了。我甚至在做作业时,都禁不住想那些好的电视节目。
A:真的吗?你对电视太着迷了。你喜欢什么样的电视节目?
B:我喜欢一些有趣的英语电影。
A:你会在电视节目中受益颇丰。
B:或许真的会。

Conversation 2

A: What do you usually watch at home?
B: Almost everything. I'm a couch-potato.
A: I love quiz shows and talk shows.
B: I think quiz shows are too much complicated for me. The hosts speak too fast.
A: Could I switch to Channel 3, if you don't mind?
B: Not at all. What's Channel 3?
A: It's the musical channel. Can I turn up the volume a little bit?
B: Go ahead.

A:你常在家看些什么电视?
B:几乎都看。我是个电视迷。
A:我喜欢看智力竞赛节目和谈话类节目。
B:我觉得看智力竞赛节目挺费劲的,主持人语速太快。
A:我想看一下3频道,可以吗?
B:当然。什么节目?
A:音乐频道,我可以把声音开得再大一点吗?
B:可以。

Conversation 3

A: What are you doing, brat?
B: Watching the spoilers online for ***Buffy the Vampire Slayer*** and waiting for mom to get off the couch.
A: TV blues? Tell me about it. Hey, let me use your computer to see the spoiler for ***the next Survivor*** show...
B: No... I need to find out what's happening to

A:小家伙,你在干嘛呢?
B:我在网络上看《魔法奇兵》的剧情介绍啊,还有等妈从沙发上离开。
A:电视忧郁症吗?我跟你同病相怜。嘿,让我用你的电脑看下一集《我要活下去》的剧情介绍吧……
B:不要……我要查查现在《魔法奇兵》在演什么。

Buffy the Vampire Slayer now.

A: Geez, you watch it on TV, watch it on the Net, talk about it online, subscribe to the magazine — you're ill!

A: 天啊,你在电视上看、在网络上看、又在线上讨论、还订它的杂志——你有病啊!

B: Well, I'm not ill enough to torture myself in some desert and fight with people just for money.

B: 呃,我还没病到为了钱,在沙漠里折磨自己,跟人斗来斗去。

A: Hey! Learned a lot about psychology from that show!

A: 嘿!从那个节目里学到了很多心理学的东西耶!

B: Well, fine. You know how to survive. And I'm a part of *Buffy the Vampire Slayer* pop culture. So?

B: 那好吧。那你就该知道怎么活下去了。而我是《魔法奇兵》流行文化的一份子。那又怎样?

A: At least you're not dressing up like a *Star Trek geek*. Did you see Tommy?

A: 至少你不会穿得像一个《星舰迷航记》的怪胎。你看到汤米了吗?

B: I know. He's a major sci-fi geek.

B: 我知道。他是一个无药可救的科幻怪胎。

A: Oh! The lights! Did you hear that? Mom's screaming!

A: 哦!灯怎么了!你听到了吗?妈在尖叫!

Conversation 4

A: Hey, if you're not busy this weekend, would you like to go see a movie?

A: 嘿,周末没事的话,愿意去看电影吗?

B: Sounds good. What should we see?

B: 主意不错,看什么呢?

A: How about that European movie?

A: 欧片如何?

B: You mean the one starring John Travollta?

B: 你指的是约翰·特拉沃尔塔主演的那部吗?

A: Yeah, that's the one. I've heard the special effects and the plot are outstanding.

A: 对,就是它。我听说特技和情节都属一流。

B: Sounds like an interesting film. Let's meet at five o'clock on Saturday.

B: 听起来像是部很有趣的电影。我们约星期六5点见面。

A: Okay, see you then.

A: 好,到时见。

Conversation 5

A: Wasn't that a great flick? I was on the edge of my seat through the whole movie.

A: 那部片子是不是很棒?我从头到尾一口气都没松过。

B: I would say it was a typical run-of-the-mill Hollywood thriller.

B: 我觉得它是典型的常见好莱坞恐怖电影。

A: Well, I'm no movie expert, but those special effects were impressive by any standards.

A: 我不是电影专家。但是那些特效不管用什么标准来衡量都是吸引人的。

B: Special effects? Baloney! That movie was made on a shoestring budget. They've been using trick photography like that for years.

B: 特效?胡说!那个电影是用低成本制作的。像这种摄影技巧人家已经用了很久了。

A: Okay. But you have to admit that it was an exciting story, especially with that surprise ending.

A: 好吧,不过你得承认故事很感人,尤其是那出人意料的结局。

B: You should read the book. The original story is much better and has a different twist at the end.

B: 你应该看看那本书。原来的故事更好而且是不同的结局。

A: Oh, really? How does the book end?

A: 哦,是吗?书里的结局如何?

B: Read it yourself and find out!

B: 你自己去看,自己去找。

On the Scene 身临其境 面面俱到

主题:洛依斯与艾米莉在谈论电影《卧虎藏龙》和《角斗士》。请你看图,根据如下提供的关键词,将他们的对话写出来。

关键词语:nomination *n.* 任命　Crouching Tiger, Hidden Dragon《卧虎藏龙》
female *n.* 女性　outrageous *adj.* 蛮横的
totally *adv.* 完全地

参考答案

Emily: What did you think of the nominations for best movie?

Lois: I was just knocked out that a Chinese film got so many nominations!

Emily: Yeah, well no surprise. ***Crouching Tiger***, ***Hidden Dragon*** was awesome!

Lois: Like I was on the edge of my seat the whole time I was watching it.

Emily: I know what you mean! Some of those fight scenes were jaw-dropping. And it was so cool to see the women. They really kicked ass.

Lois: What is so great is that the film has three generations of female stars, Cheng Peipei from the 60s, Michelle Yeoh from the 80s, and this newcomer Zhang Ziyi.

Emily: It's inspiring, isn't it?

Lois: What do you think of ***Gladiator***?

Emily: Absolutely outrageous! The fight scenes were full of heart-stopping action.

Lois: But wouldn't you say it was more for guys?

Emily: Oh, totally! It's all about guys and fighting. But I really go for action flicks.

艾米莉:你是怎么看最佳影片提名的?

洛依斯:我没想到一部中国影片获得了那么多提名。

艾米莉:也不算太令人惊讶。《卧虎藏龙》拍得太好了。

洛依斯:看这部片子的时候我的屁股都悬在椅子上。

艾米莉:我明白你的意思。有些武打场面让人惊叹不已。看那些女演员真带劲,她们简直太厉害了。

洛依斯:尤其是该片汇集了三代女明星,60年代的程佩佩,80年代的杨紫琼,加上新人章子怡。

艾米莉:挺激励人的,对吧?

洛依斯:你觉得《角斗士》怎么样?

艾米莉:非常棒。搏斗的场面惊心动魄。

洛依斯:你是否觉得这部片子更适合男人?

艾米莉:没错。一帮男的在那儿打来打去的。可是我真的很喜欢动作片。

★饲养宠物★ 3 Feeding Pets

Words and Phrases 闪亮词语 点滴积累

howler monkey 吼猴
leaf monkey 叶猴
dhole 豺
sea otter 海獭
fox 狐(赤狐)
racoon-dog 貉(狗獾)
cat 家猫
wolf 狼
hyena 鬣狗
civet 灵猫
dog 犬
lion 狮
mink 水貂
otter 水獭
panda 熊猫
snow leopard 雪豹
zebra 斑马
Tibetan gazelle 藏羚
hippopotamus 河马
ox 公牛
rabbit 野兔
takin 羚牛(扭角羚)
deer 鹿

Useful Sentences 七彩精句 连点成线

Words of playing with pets 玩赏宠物用语

1. *What's your pet's name?* 你的宠物叫什么名字?
2. *What kind of pet do you have?* 你的宠物是什么?
3. *What breed is your dog?* 你的狗什么血统?
4. *How long have you had your pet?* 你养宠物多久了?
5. *How many pets do you have?* 你养了多少宠物?
6. *What do you feed your pet?* 你喂什么给宠物吃?
7. *When do you feed your dog?* 你几时给你的狗喂食?
8. *What kind of tricks can your dog do?* 你的狗可以玩什么把戏?
9. *He just learned how to shake hands.* 他刚学会怎么握手。
10. *Does your dog get a lot of exercise?* 你的狗经常锻炼吗?
11. *We let him run around the yard everyday.* 我们每天都让它绕着院子跑几圈。
12. *Can your parrot talk?* 你的鹦鹉会说话吗?
13. *How often do you take your pet to the vet?* 你多长时间带它看一次兽医?
14. *Are your pet's molts up to date?* 你的宠物换毛了吗?
15. *Is your dog housebroken?* 你的狗会弄乱家里吗?
16. *Does your puppy always chew up your shoes?* 你的小狗总是啃你的鞋吗?
17. *I brush my Yorkshire every day.* 我每天都会帮我家的约克郡犬梳毛。
18. *I take my cocker spaniel to be groomed once a week.* 我每星期都带我的科卡犬去美容呢。
19. *When a dog's happy, it wags its tail.* 狗高兴的时候会摇尾巴。
20. *Our cat is really fat! It just eats and sleeps all day.* 我家的猫很肥!一天到晚就知道吃饭睡觉。
21. *My myna bird can imitate what people say.* 我家的八哥会学舌。

Conversation 1

A: I heard you bought a new dog. What kind is it?
B: It's a Dalmatian.
A: Is it the kind with black and white spots?
B: That's right. When he gets older, he'll be a really good guard dog.
A: My aunt has dog called Sunny, but she's not a good guard dog. She wouldn't hurt a soul.
B: Most dogs have to be trained in order to become good guard dogs.
A: Sunny is pretty spoiled. When she's hungry, she'll whine until you give her food.
B: Will she take any orders?
A: No, she won't listen to any orders people give her.
B: What good is she then?
A: Whenever my aunt gets home, Sunny knows it and will run to the door to meet her.
B: I need a wife like Sunny.

A：我听说你新买了一只狗。是什么品种的？
B：是达尔马提亚狗。
A：就是身上有黑白斑点的那种吗？
B：没错。等他长大一点，就会变成非常好的看门狗。
A：我姑姑有一只狗叫桑妮，但她不是只看门狗。她不会伤害任何人。
B：大多数的狗在成为好的看门狗之前，都要先经过训练。
A：可是桑妮被宠坏了。她饿的时候就会一直哀叫，直到你给她东西吃才罢休。
B：她听命令吗？
A：不，她谁的命令都不听。
B：那她有啥好的？
A：无论我的阿姨何时回家，桑妮都会知道，而且还会跑到门口去迎接她。
B：我需要一个像桑妮一样的太太。

Conversation 2

A: Can your dog do any tricks?
B: Sure he can. He can shake hands, roll over, and even play dead.
A: I wish I had a dog. My cat can't do any tricks.
B: Yeah, but sometimes he wants to play with me, but I don't have time.
A: So who takes care of him then?
B: My little brother likes to play with him. He even gives him a bath every week.
A: I can't do that with my cat. She hates water.
B: You're right. Maybe you should get a dog.

A：你的狗会一点小把戏吗？
B：当然会。他会握手，打滚，还会装死。
A：我也想养条狗。我的猫什么也不会。
B：是啊，不过有时他想跟我玩，我却没时间。
A：那谁照顾他呢？
B：我的小弟弟喜欢跟他玩。他甚至每星期给它洗澡。
A：我不能给我的猫洗澡。它讨厌水。
B：对，也许你应该也养只狗。

Conversation 3

A: Mary, can your dog do any tricks yet?
B: Oh, yeah! He can sit down, roll over, and even play dead.
A: Really? Does he chase balls?
B: Yup. Hey, do you want to see a picture? See, he's eating lunch.
A: This can't be the same dog. He's so clean, he shines.
B: See, he's wagging his tail.

A：玛丽，你的狗会做什么表演了吗？
B：喔，会啊！它会坐下、打滚，还有装死。
A：真的？它会追球吗？
B：当然。嘿，你要看照片吗？看，它正在吃午餐。
A：这绝不是那只狗。这么干净，它的毛还闪闪发光呢。
B：你瞧，它正在摇尾巴。

A: He's really cute. His bowl even has his name on it.

A: 它真的很可爱。它的碗上还有它的名字呢。

Conversation 4

A: She's a Persian. She has papers and everything. Not like a street dog.
B: Cats chase mice, don't they?
A: And bugs. They can catch anything.
B: Do you have to walk a cat?
A: No, they use litter boxes or go outside by themselves. They're so smart.
B: But then you have to change the litter box.
A: It's better than picking up dog poop.

A: 它是只波斯猫。血统证明等文件全都有。不像流浪街头的狗。
B: 猫会捉老鼠,是吧?
A: 还有虫子。猫什么东西都能捉得到。
B: 你得去遛猫吗?
A: 不用,它们都会用猫沙盆,要不就自己到外面解决。它们是很聪明的。
B: 但这样你就得换猫沙啦。
A: 这总比收拾狗屎强。

On the Scene 身临其境 面面俱到

主题:杰克与安吉在谈论安吉的小狗宾果。请你看图,根据如下提供的关键词,将他们的对话写出来。

关键词语:cute *adj.* 可爱的
well-behaved *adj.* 行为端正的
scratch *n.*,*v.* 抓痕,抓
claw *n.*,*v.* 爪,用爪抓
move away 搬走
puppy *n.* 小动物,小狗
couch *n.* 床
house-cat 家猫

参考答案

Jack: Your dog is really cute. What's his name?
Angie: His name is Bingo.
Jack: What kind of dog is he?
Angie: We're not sure because the neighbors gave him to us after they moved away.
Jack: Well, he sure likes to run around a lot. Is he well-behaved?

Angie: Oh yes, he is. When he was a puppy, he liked to chew my father's shoes, but he's okay now.
Jack: That sounds like my cat. She likes to scratch the couch with her claws.
Angie: I didn't know that you had a cat. When did you get her?
Jack: About a year ago actually. You've probably never seen her though.
Angie: Really? Why is that?
Jack: She's not a house-cat. She stays outside most of the time.
Angie: Bingo could never do that. He stays in the house except when we take him to the park.

杰克:你的狗真可爱。它叫什么名字?
安吉:宾果。
杰克:它是什么狗?
安吉:我们也不清楚,是邻居搬家时送给我们的。
杰克:它总是喜欢不停地跑圈,有规矩吗?
安吉:哦,有的。它还是小狗时喜欢啃我父亲的鞋,不过现在好了。
杰克:跟我家的猫一样。它喜欢用爪子抓沙发。
安吉:我不知道你养了猫。什么时候养的?
杰克:大约一年前。不过你可能看不到它。
安吉:是吗?为什么?
杰克:它不是家猫。它大部分时间都在外面。
安吉:宾果可不会这样。除了我们带它去公园,它总待在家里。

★网上玩乐★ 4 Enjoy oneself Online

Words and Phrases 闪亮词语 点滴积累

surf 冲浪
navigate 浏览
search engine 搜索引擎
specialized search engine 专业搜索引擎
Internet Relay Chat 因特网多线聊天系统
web address 网址
online forum 在线论坛
Bulletin Board System 电子公告系统
download 下载
upload 上传
post 张贴
hacker 电脑黑客
firewall 防火墙
netiquette 网络礼节
snail mail 传统邮件
newbie 网络新手
lurk 隐身
troll 旋转
flame 火焰
shopping cart 购物车
chat room 聊天室
host 主机
encryption 加密
decryption 解密
electronic mail 电子邮件
spam 垃圾邮件
keyboard 键盘
mouse 鼠标
printer 打印机
click 点击
double click 双击
graph 图像
cursor 光标
re-boot 重新启动
software 软件
multimedia 多媒体
monitor 显示器

Useful Sentences 七彩精句 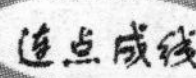 连点成线

New games 新潮电玩

1. *Don't you like games?* 难道你不喜欢玩游戏吗？
2. *The most advanced is the* ***Sanguo series*** 三国志系列是最先进的游戏。
3. *I prefer to play* ***Red Alert*** 我更喜欢玩红色警戒。
4. *To me getting in touch with each other has more fun than the coolest computer games or the hottest information.* 对我来说，人与人之间的相互联系比最酷的电脑游戏或是热点信息有趣多了。
5. *He has turned his computer into an electronic playground.* 他已把他的电脑变成了电子游乐场。
6. *We come here every other day to play computer games.* 我们隔天就来玩电脑游戏。
7. *We are hooked on strategy games.* 现在对策略游戏都上瘾了。
8. *I used to play arcade games a lot. Now I don't have much time.* 我以前也常玩巷战游戏，不过现在实在没空了。
9. *They have the latest machines and lots of new games.* 该处有最新的游戏机和许多新游戏。
10. *Before you drop the ball into the spinning well, you bet a number on the layout.* 在你把小球投入转盘之前，先在布局上赌个号码。
11. *If the ball falls and stops on the number you bet on, you win.* 如果小球停落在你下赌注的号码上，你就赢了。
12. *These days my son has turned his computer into an electronic playground. He plays football, rides horses, drives racing cars, and does a whole bunch of other things on the computer.* 最近我那儿子把他的计算机变成电子游乐场了。他在

电脑上踢足球，骑马，开赛车，还玩其他的游戏。

13. *Most male customers choose first person shooting, real time strategy, action or sports, while female customers prefer simulating, action or role playing.* 大多数男性顾客会选择第一人称射击，实时战略，动作和运动类，而女性喜欢动作，模拟和角色扮演类。

14. *Shooting, action and sports games require flexible movements and real time strategy usually needs overall consideration.* 射击，动作和运动类大多需要灵活的身手，实时战略则需要全局的统筹。

15. ***Counter Strike** is one of the hottest shooting games and **Might & Magic** series are popular among girls because the game has attractive plot and interesting scenes.* 反恐精英是现在最热门的射击游戏，魔法门系列有很有意思的情节和场景，很受女孩的欢迎。

16. *If your computer runs fast, I think the latest editions are better, because although old editions are cheaper, they are less exciting and attractive.* 如果您的机子很快的话，还是最新的版本比较好，因为旧版虽然便宜，可没有新版那么激烈和有趣。

17. ***Mechwarrior** is such a good game. The graphics are awesome!* 麦克战士是一个非常好玩的游戏，画面十分漂亮！

Meeting online 网上见面

1. *Hello. how are you?* 哈罗，你好吗？
2. *Hello. A/S/L?* 哈罗，请告知你的年龄、性别和所在地？
3. *Hi, are you online?* 你好，你在线吗？
4. *How's life?* 过得如何？
5. *Are you there?* 你在吗？
6. *How is today?* 今天好吗？
7. *Hi, boy or girl/male or female?* 嗨，男的还是女的？
8. *Hi, where are you from?* 嗨，你从哪里来的？
9. *Hello!* 你好！
10. *Haven't seen you for ages!* 好久不见了！
11. *Glad to see you.* 见到你很高兴。

News online 网上新闻

1. *Is there a set of news about education of all-around development?* 有关素质教育的一组新闻？
2. *Will the browser allow me to read news freely?* 浏览器会允许我随意翻看新闻吗？
3. *I'm reading the news on the Internet.* 我正在读网上新闻。
4. *I often get the news on the Internet.* 我一般在网上看新闻。
5. *You can get more information on the Internet than in newspaper.* 你可以在网上获得比报上更多的信息。
6. *There are over 10000 news online everyday.* 每天网上有上万则新闻。
7. *Newsgroup can therefore form a particularly useful source of information, news or views.* 新闻组可以成为你的特别有用的信息、新闻和观点的来源。
8. *From the online news get this news?* 从网上新闻得到的消息？
9. *The online news spread more quickly than the newspaper.* 网上新闻的传播速度要比报纸快得多。
10. *The browser will present you with an option to move on to the next news.* 浏览器会向你提示选择，问你是否阅读一下篇新闻。
11. *It will be very convenient if the articles are connected by explicit "threads".* 如果各类文章都按明显的线索串起来，阅读起来会很方便。

Online Auction 网上竞拍

1. *All sales are final.* 拍卖结束后，交易不得取消。
2. *Don't bid if you can't pay.* 如果你付不起，请不要叫价。
3. *If eBay crashes within 24 hours of the close of the auction, I reserve the right to cancel the auction.* 如果 eBay 在结束拍卖 24 小时内关机，我保留取消拍卖的权利。
4. *If you do not honor your bid, I will leave negative feedback.* 如果你不把你的叫价当作一回事，我将给你负面回馈评价。
5. *No deadbeat bidders.* 标下物品又不买的竞标者请勿叫价。

6. *Can you tell me what your reserve price is?* 你能告诉我你的保留底价是多少吗？
7. *After you post feedback for me, I'll do so for you.* 你给我回馈评价后，我也会给你回馈评价。
8. *Congratulations on being the winner for this auction.* 恭喜你成为这次拍卖的赢家。
9. *Before I bid on your auction, I was wondering what forms of payment you accept.* 在竞价你的拍卖项目前，我想先了解你会接受何种付款方式。
10. *I won this auction, final price $24.73.* 我赢了这个拍卖，最后价格是24.73美金。
11. *I noticed your auction on eBay for a gold ring.* 我注意到您在eBay上有个黄金戒指的拍卖。
12. *I won several of your auctions. Please tell me what the total cost of it is.* 我赢了你的好几个拍卖物品。请告诉我的总价是多少？
13. *Terrific! Very satisfied with purchase, Extremely friendly! Recommended!!!!* 非常棒！我对这次交易非常满意，极度友善！向大家推荐!!!!

Online stock 网上股票

1. *What if I want to seek some share's tendency on Internet?* 我要在网上查看某个股的走势怎么办？
2. *Is it simple to buy in and sell out stocks on line?* 网上买卖股票，操作容易吗？
3. *Is it risky to invest money in the stock market?* 投资股票市场是有风险的吗？
4. *How to seek the stock quotations on Internet?* 那我怎么能在网上查看股市行情？
5. *Do you know anything about the stock market?* 您知道关于股票市场的事吗？
6. *Over the Internet I can buy stock and check my stock value.* 在网上我可买股票，查看股票行情。
7. *You have got your own stockholder account and capital account, so you only need apply for the online trust function.* 你已有股东账户和资金账户，只要申请开通网上委托功能就行。
8. *If you want to handle and use this with skill in the stock market, you have to take good advantage of the resources on the Internet.* 要想在股市中应对自如，必须要利用好这些互联网上的资源。
9. *Please enter your demand into a computer or you may telephone your stockbroker.* 请往电脑里输入你的指令或打电话给您的经纪人。
10. *We will offer you the best service here.* 我们可以向您提供最优质的服务。
11. *They pay around $2 a share in dividends.* 他们每一股约付两美元红利。
12. *Investors want a high return on their money.* 投资者希望他们的钱有高收益。
13. *Common sense tells you that sooner or later the market will fall sharply.* 常识告诉你，行市迟早会大幅下跌。

Fashion Conversation 鲜活会话 由线到面

Conversation 1

A: Have you bought "*War Craft* Ⅲ" yet?
B: Yeah! I bought it the day it was released.
A: How do you like it?
B: It's a great game. There are a lot of new characters.
A: Did it cost very much?
B: It cost about thirty. Most games cost about that much.
A: "*Mechwarrior*" is such a good game. The graphics are awesome!
B: Oh, I know what you mean. I'm addicted to that game.

A：你买了“战争三代”没有？
B：买了！它发行的当天我就买了。
A：你喜欢它吗？
B：这个电脑游戏棒极了。有很多新的人物。
A：很贵吧？
B：大约30美元。大部分电脑游戏差不多都是这个价儿。
A：电脑游戏“麦克战士”真好玩！画面可漂亮了！
B：哦，我明白你说的意思。我已经迷上那个游戏啦！

A: My roommate always wants to play it. But I told her to buy her own game.
A: 我的室友总想玩它，但我让她自己去买一个。

B: Yeah, my roommate likes to watch me play. He says it's like watching a movie.
B: 是吗！我的室友也喜欢看我玩。他说就像是看电影一样。

A: I've never seen such good graphics.
A: 我从来没有看过这么好的画面。

B: And I've never heard such good sound in a game.
B: 我在电脑游戏里也从来没有听过这么好的音乐。

Conversation 2

A: Do you know Yahoo Greetings, Jack?
A: 杰克，你知道雅虎的贺卡网站吗？

B: Sure. It's a popular e-card website.
B: 当然，它是一个很受欢迎的贺卡网站。

A: Can you tell me how to send one on it?
A: 你可以教我怎样发送吗？

B: Okay. Did you get the Yahoo ID?
B: 好的，你在雅虎上有 ID 没有？

A: ID? What's that?
A: ID？是什么？

B: I mean, you must register first before you send a card.
B: 我的意思是说，在你发送贺卡前，一定要注册。

A: Oh, I see. But I have done it.
A: 我知道了，但是我已注册过了。

B: Ok. Choose the card which you like best, and fill in the following blanks with both you and your friend's names and e-mail addresses.
B: 那好。选一张你喜欢的贺卡，在下面的空白栏中，填入你和你朋友的名字和电邮地址。

A: Is that all?
A: 这就完了吗？

B: Don't forget to send.
B: 别忘了发送。

A: Oh, I see. Thanks.
A: 哦，我知道了，谢谢。

Conversation 3

A: Hi, there!
A: 大家好！

B: Hi, Tom.
B: 你好，汤姆。

A: You look happy today.
A: 你今天看起来挺开心的呀。

B: Yeah, I'm happy with my computer. I can do lots of things with it: e-mail, chat, or travel worldwide. That's amazing!
B: 是啊，跟电脑一起我很开心。我可以用它来做许许多多的事：发电子邮啦，聊天啦，或者周游世界。这简直太奇妙了！

A: Good on you! I have lots of fun with the Web, too. I take the email off the computer in the morning, print it out, and deliver it. I get e-mail from other countries for our classroom pen pals.
A: 你真行！我在网络中也得到了好多乐趣。我早上先从电脑上把电邮弄出来，打印好，然后再分送出去。我帮我们同班的笔友们接收从其他国家发来的电邮。

B: This is a lot more fun than just sitting at a desk, looking at a book. I first discovered the Internet on my home computer and I said, "Boy! There's a lot of great information out there." And best of all it's fun, interesting, and very graphic.
B: 这比干坐在书桌前对着书本有趣多了。当我在我家的电脑上第一次发现互联网的时候，我对自己说，"好家伙！有这么多绝妙的信息在这儿呀。"最绝妙的是，它好玩、有趣，并且很形象。

A: The Web is a great resource for finding any kind of information you can think of. When you research a topic, the secret of success is focus. By now, there are hundreds of thousands of Web sites online.
A: 网络是一个绝佳的资源，能查找到你能想到的任何种类的资讯。在你搜索一个主题时，成功的秘诀是目标不宜过于宽泛。现如今，网络上有成千上万的网址呢。

B: That's right. In my opinion, the trick is how to fo-
B: 不错。在我看来，窍门是如何把焦点集中在你

cus on what you're looking for, and to pare down your thoughts.

所要寻找的主题上，理清思路，不要让其他的想法扰乱你。

Conversation 4

A: Is it simple to buy in and sell out stocks on line?

B: Yes it is. You should login the server, and fill in the account, password, etc.

A: Is the procedure complex to entrust after logging in successfully?

B: No, it isn't. When we buy in stocks, we need to input the stock code. The system will fill in the price "the trust price item" automatically and give you the number of stocks that can be bought.

A: If I don't want to invest all my capital, can I change the trust amount?

B: Certainly. You can change both the trust price and the trust amount.

A: Isn't selling out similar to buying in?

B: Yes, it's simpler than buying in. You can see the list you hold on the interface, and you only need to double click the stock to be sold.

A: Can I cancel the bill?

B: Yes. After the system carried out the cancel, you should double click some trust item to decide whether to cancel or not. You should know that if you have struck a bargain, you should't cancel it.

A：网上买卖股票，操作容易吗？

B：容易，您要先登录服务器，并填好账号、密码等信息。

A：登录成功后委托过程复杂吗？

B：不复杂。买入时我们需要输入证券代码。系统会自动在"委托价格"项填入价格，并给出可买股数。

A：那我不想把资金全部用完，可以改变委托数量吗？

B：当然。委托价格和委托数量都可以更改。

A：卖出与买入应该差不多吧！

B：是，比买入还容易。界面上展示了你现在持股列表，双击你卖出的股票即可。

A：也可以撤单吗？

B：可以，执行撤单选项后，双击某一项委托则决定是否进行撤单，要注意，已成交的不可撤单哦。

Conversation 5

A: Fancy meeting you here at this moment! It's 5 a.m. at your local time, isn't it? You got up so early in the morning?

B: Actually, I sit up throughout the night. I haven't gone to bed yet.

A: You spent almost a whole night staying online?

B: You bet.

A: Didn't you feel sleepy?

B: No, not at all. It's weird, isn't it?

A: It's like you are kind of addicted to internet.

B: I am?

A: Yes, you are. OK, I'd like ask you some questions which can determine whether you are hooked on the net? but you are supposed to answer my questions honestly. OK?

B: OK, no problem.

A: OK, here we go. No. 1, do you feel a need to use

A：真想不到在这个时候在这儿碰上你，你的当地时间是早上5点，是吗？你这么早就起床了吗？

B：实际上，我熬了一个通宵。我还没上床睡觉呢。

A：你几乎在网上呆了一整夜？

B：当然。

A：难道你不觉得困吗？

B：不，一点儿也不。有点怪，是吧？

A：好像你有点上网成瘾了。

B：我吗？

A：是的，就是你。我来问你一些问题。这些问题可以决定你是否已经迷上网络了。但是你应该诚实地回答我的问题。

B：好的。没问题。

A：好吧。开始了。第一个问题，为了获得满足，你

the internet for longer amounts of time in order to achieve satisfaction?	是否觉得有需要花更长的时间上网呢?
B:Yes,I do.	B:是的。
A:Do you feel restless and irritable when attempting to cut down or stop internet usage?	A:当试图减少或停止上网时,你是否会感到不安和易怒呢?
B:Sometimes.	B:有时候是这样。
A:Do you use the internet to escape from problems or relieve a poor mood?	A:你会通过上网来逃避问题或者缓解糟糕的心情吗?
B:Yes,right. absolutely,that is what I do.	B:是的,对。完全是这样。我就是这样做的。
A:Ok,the last question goes like this,do you risk the loss of significant relationships,your job or education or career opportunities because of the internet?	A:好了,最后一个问题是这样的,你会因为上网而甘愿冒着失去重要的关系、工作或教育机会的危险吗?
B:No. I can't be that stupid.	B:不会。我不可能那么傻。
A:Maybe you are not an internet addict yet,but I should say you are very close,because you have had some symptoms of internet addition. You'd better not be lost in the cyberspace. You know,spending to much time on net will not only do harm to your health,but also destroy everything in your life.	A:也许你还不是一个网络瘾君子,但我要说你已经很接近了,因为你已经有一些"网瘾"的症状了。你最好是不要迷失在网络世界里了。你知道,在网上花太多的时间不仅对你的身体有危害,而且还会毁掉你生活中的一切。
B:Thanks for your sincere concern.	B:谢谢你真诚的关心。

Conversation 6

A:There are millions of web pages on the net. How do I find what I'm looking for?	A:网上有数百万的网页,我怎样才能找到我想要的东西呢?
B:Use a search engine like Baidu and Yahoo.	B:用搜索引擎,比如:百度和雅虎。
A:How does it work?	A:它是如何工作的呢?
B:You enter the name or topic you are interested in,then ask the search engine to find pages about your topic.	B:你输入你感兴趣的名字或话题,让搜索引擎查找有关此话题的网页。
A:How to use the search engine?	A:如何使用搜索引擎呢?
B:Let me tell you step by step.	B:让我一步步地告诉你。
A:OK!	A:好!
B:At first,we can click www. yahoo. com. cn.	B:首先,我们可以点击雅虎网站。
A:Shall we use the search engine on it?	A:我们要用它上面的搜索引擎吗?
B:Yes,we type into the key words.	B:是的,我们输入关键单词。
A:Then it will search automatically?	A:然后它就会自动搜索了?
B:Yes,it will show a lot of websites about the key words.	B:是的,它会列举一系列与关键词有关的网址。
A:If I find the website I need,what shall I do?	A:如我找到我所需的网站,我该怎么做?
B:That's easy,click the website,and you can enter.	B:很好办,你可点击网站,你就可以进入了。
A:Thank you for your help!	A:谢谢你的帮助。

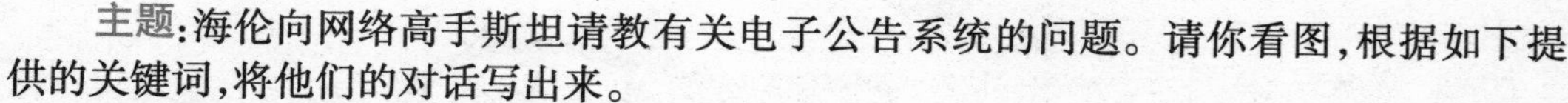

主题:海伦向网络高手斯坦请教有关电子公告系统的问题。请你看图,根据如下提供的关键词,将他们的对话写出来。

关键词语:BBS 论坛(电子公告系统)

参考答案

Helen:Do you know what the BBS is?
Stan:Sure.
Helen:Tell me then.
Stan:BBS means Bulletin Board Service.
Helen:Oh, I see, but what's it used for?
Stan:A lot of things!
Helen:Tell me in details.
Stan:Okay. BBS, an online service offers a wide variety of online games, files, one-on-one chat, message areas, private mail, and participatory forums.
Helen:Oh, that's great. I want to try later.
Stan:Why not?
海伦:你知道什么是 BBS 吗?
斯坦:当然知道。
海伦:那么请告诉我。
斯坦:BBS 的意思是电子公告系统。
海伦:哦,我知道了。但它是用来干什么的?
斯坦:很多用处。
海伦:告诉我详细一些。
斯坦:好的,BBS 是一种广泛提供在线游戏、文件、一对一聊天、留言区、个人信箱和参与性论坛的在线服务。
海伦:哦,那太棒了,我想一会儿试一下。
斯坦:为什么不呢?

★快乐假日★ 5 In Holidays

Words and Phrases 闪亮词语 点滴积累

hiker/wayfarer 徒步旅行者
holiday inn 度假村
scenic spots 景点
picnic 郊游野餐
excursion/go for an outing 远足
holiday maker 度假游客
weekend trip 周末旅游
holiday camp 假日野营地
summer vacation spot 消暑度假场所
camping trip 野营
rock climbing 攀岩
mountain climbing 登山
drifting;floating tour 漂流
surf culture 冲浪运动
roll coaster 坐过山车
bungee jumping 蹦极跳
sleeping bag 睡袋
travelling-rug 旅行毯
dance 舞蹈
dancing party;ball 舞会
social dance 交际舞
samba 桑巴舞
waltz 华尔兹舞
tango 探戈舞
ballet 芭蕾舞
folk dance 民间舞

Useful Sentences 七彩精句 连点成线

Dancing 舞会用语

1. *Would you have a dance with me?* 能和你跳个舞吗?
2. *May I have the honor of engaging you for the next dance?* 能赏光请你跳下曲舞吗?
3. *Let's do the disco.* 我们去蹦迪吧!
4. *How many kinds of dance have you learnt?* 你学会跳几种舞?
5. *I've just learned how to dance this new step.* 我刚学会跳这种新舞步。
6. *Sorry, I am engaged for the social dance.* 抱歉,这交际舞我有约在先了。
7. *May I have the pleasure for the next tango or waltz?* 下一个的探戈或华尔兹可以和我跳吗?
8. *The music is going on again. Will you accept my arm?* 音乐又响起来了,请和我跳支舞好吗?
9. *This piece of music is suitable for waltz.* 这支曲子适合跳华尔兹。
10. *Why don't we have one more dance?* 为什么我们不再跳一曲呢?
11. *You must be rather thirsty. Let's go to the buffet and have some drinks?* 你一定口渴了,我们去柜台喝点饮料好吗?
12. *Most young people like modern dances, such as rock and roll, the twist, and especially the break dancing.* 年轻人大都喜欢跳现代舞,比如摇滚舞、扭摆舞,尤其喜欢霹雳舞。
13. *Good. I hope no one else lets the cat out of the bag. I want her to be really surprised.* 很好,我希望不会有人泄漏这个秘密。我想让她大吃一惊。

On holidays 度假

1. *What a vast lake! The water extends as far as the eyes can reach.* 多么大的湖啊!这湖水一望无际。
2. *What a beautiful and pacific place this is!* 多么平静而美丽的地方啊!
3. *It is wonderful sitting by the lakeside angling.* 坐在湖边钓鱼真是好极了。
4. *What a beautiful beach!* 多漂亮的海滩呀!
5. *We can get a good tan today.* 我们今天可以好好享受一下日光浴了。
6. *You really enjoyed the ferry ride, didn't you?* 你真的很喜欢坐渡船吧!

7. *It's fun playing on the sand.* 在沙滩上玩真带劲。

8. *I want to go and stretch out in a hammock.* 我想在吊床上躺一下。

Picnic supper 野炊

1. *Can you come on a picnic this Sunday?* 星期天你能来参加野餐吗?
2. *We are going to the beach and have lunch there.* 我们准备去海滩并在那儿吃午饭。
3. *I'm looking forward to the picnic.* 我盼望着去野餐。
4. *What a beautiful view! Why don't we have a picnic there?* 多美的景色! 我们为什么不在那儿进行一次野餐呢?
5. *We have a good time today.* 我们今天玩得很高兴。
6. *It's very cold today. You'd better wear more clothes to have a picnic.* 今天很冷,你最好多穿些衣服去野餐。
7. *We should get up very early and gather at the school gate.* 我们应该早起在学校门口集合。
8. *What should we take when we are going to have a picnic?* 去野餐时我们应该带些什么?
9. *I feel tired. Let's sit down under the big tree with luxuriant foliage.* 我感觉很累。咱们坐在那棵枝繁叶茂的大树下吧。
10. *Before we have our picnic, we have to climb the high mountain.* 在进行野餐前,我们得爬上那座高山。
11. *If I could live in such a beautiful place, I would be on top of the world.* 若我能居住在如此美丽的地方,我会是世界上最快乐的人。
12. *Would you like some hamburgers?* 你想来些汉堡包吗?
13. *I don't feel like drinking Coca-Cola.* 我不喜欢喝可口可乐。
14. *I'm really very satisfied with the picnic.* 我真的对这次野餐很满意。
15. *Would you please sing a song for us, Emma?* 爱玛,你能给我们唱首歌吗?

Outing 郊游

1. *Do you know of any good hiking trails around here?* 你知道这附近不错的远足小路吗?
2. *Have you already decided the course of your hike?* 你已经决定好远足的路线了吗?
3. *How many members were there in your party in all?* 和你同行的人共有多少?
4. *Please put the water into the canteen.* 请把水注入水壶里。
5. *We went down the hill.* 我们下了山。
6. *What is written on that guidepost?* 路标上写的是什么?
7. *Weren't you caught rainy shower on the way?* 在路上你没有遇上下雨吗?
8. *You got very tired, didn't you?* 你很累,是不是?

Fishing 钓鱼

1. *What pound test-line are you using?* 你用的是什么磅数的线?
2. *Did you have any luck today?* 今天运气如何?
3. *How many fish did you catch?* 你钓到多少鱼?
4. *Do you have any extra hooks?* 你还有多余的鱼钩吗?
5. *Do you prefer fresh water or salt water fishing?* 你是喜欢湖钓,还是海钓?
6. *Of course, I would never go fishing without my bass boat.* 当然,我总是坐我的鲈鱼船去钓鱼的。
7. *Could you lend me fishing tackle?* 能借个钓具吗?
8. *What kind of fish is the most difficult to catch?* 哪一种鱼最难钓?

Fashion Conversation 鲜活会话 由线到面

Conversation 1

A: This is the good life—no work, no cell phone, no stress.

A: 这才是生活呢——没有工作,没有电话,没有压力。

B: Too bad it's just for a week. It's hardly long enough to put all that out of my mind.	B:就是一个星期太短了。我还没有把这些全放下,它就结束了。
A: Cheer up. A lot of people don't even get a week's vacation.	A:振作起来吧,很多人还没有一个星期的假期呢。
B: I don't get it. How can you always look on the bright side? Doesn't anything bother you?	B:我还是理解不了,为什么你总是往好处想呢?难道没有任何事让你感到烦心?
A: Sure, but I don't let it get to me. Life's too short for that.	A:当然有,只是我不让它来影响我,和它相比,生命太短暂了。
B: I need to learn to think like that. Wanna teach me?	B:我应该学会像你那样想,能教教我吗?
A: It would be my pleasure. Lesson one, close your eyes and relax.	A:我很荣幸。第一课,闭上眼睛,放松下来。

Conversation 2

A: Hey, homes! I thought that was you walling over here. Gimme some skin! How about your living?	A:嘿,老兄!我想在这儿靠墙根站着的肯定是你。来,拍个手吧!你好吗?
B: Yo! Good to go, man. I was just maxing and relaxing here. Hey, you're sure sporting some fly gear. You must be living large? You used to tell everyone you were always taped out all the time.	B:嗨!很好,老兄。我不过是在这里歇一会儿。嘿,你穿得蛮讲究的,一定混得不错吧!过去你可是对每个人都哭穷。
A: I just started minting last year. I like those dead presidents! I just gotta be careful not to get jacked when I walk outside!	A:我只是去年开始才赚了些钱。钱这玩意儿我真是喜欢!我在外面走都是小心翼翼的,生怕被人打劫!
B: You're not just talking outside your neck. You know, you're the first person I've recognized since I fell in at this reunion and I've been clocking everyone for an hour.	B:别胡扯了!你知道吗,你是我在这里碰到的第一个熟人,我张望了都有一个小时了。
A: Well, see that freak over there cresting at you? Remember her? That's Kim. She used to be a real duck but now she's too cold!	A:哎,有没有看到那边有个美人儿正在向你微笑?还记得她吗?她叫金。她过去可是个丑八怪,现在却这么漂亮!
B: Yeah, she could really bust a move. I don't mean to be cracking on her, but every time I tried jaw jacking with Miss Thang, she got so frosted that I finally just folded.	B:是呀,她的舞跳得也很棒。不是我有意要贬她,她架子好大,每次我想和她搭讪,她都爱理不理的样子,我只好作罢。
A: She was gissing you bad, homes. I got benched by her tonight, too. You know, this party's played. I've been waiting for them to pump it up for an hour. I'm breaking out. Peace up!	A:她对你看不上眼,老兄。我今晚也受到了她的冷遇。这个聚会没什么戏唱了。我等了都一个钟头了,还没把音响的音量开大点。我要走了。再见!

Conversation 3

A: Mr. Taylor, please sit here. This is our traditional seat for the guest of honour.	A:泰勒先生,请这儿坐。这是我国传统的贵宾席。
B: Don't tell me I'm the guest of honour this evening.	B:不敢相信我竟是今晚的贵宾。

A: Precisely so.

A:正是如此。

B: I'm much honoured to be given so much attention. But I'm really a bit nervous.

B:你们这样尊敬我,我感到很荣幸,但又感到很不安。

A: Would you like to use the chopsticks or the fork and knife?

A:您喜欢用筷子,还是用刀、叉?

B: When you are in China, do as the Chinese do. I'll take the chopsticks and learn the art.

B:入乡随俗,就用筷子吧,正好借此学学用筷子的技艺。

A: Don't worry about that. I'll be your tutor. And in case, there still are the fork and knife to resort to.

A:别担心。我来当您的老师,万一不行,还可用刀叉。

B: Well, I must warn you beforehand, I'm not much of a bright student. You must be patient with me.

B:不过我得事先告诉您,我可不是聪明的学生,您得耐心些。

A: Well, Mr. Taylor, what would you have for a drink? Rice wine or Mao Tai?

A:泰勒先生,您喝什么酒?黄酒还是茅台?

B: I think I will have the famed Maotai. I know it is one of the best liquors in the world.

B:我想喝点有名的茅台,我知道那是世界名酒之一。

A: Maotai doesn't go to the head as most liquors do.

A:茅台不像别的酒,喝了不头晕。

B: How nice.

B:那太好了。

A: Mr. Taylor, to our friendship and to your health.

A:为我们的友谊,为泰勒先生的健康干一杯。

B: To your health, and to the health of all the gentlemen present.

B:为主人的健康,为在座各位先生的健康干一杯。

A: Try some of the cold dishes.

A:尝尝凉菜。

B: Very delicious. I see your cuisine takes care of colour, flavour and taste all at the same time.

B:很好吃,我注意到,你们做的菜对色、香、味都考虑到了。

A: May I help you to some of the Beijing roast duck? This is a Beijing speciality.

A:来一点北京烤鸭,好吗?这是北京名菜。

B: How delicious! Tender and crisp. I've never tasted anything like that.

B:真好吃!又嫩又脆。我从来还没有吃过这样好吃的菜。

A: Do you care for sea-food? Help yourself to the sweet and sour bass if you care for it.

A:您爱吃海味吗?随便吃点糖醋鲈鱼吧。

B: The bass is fresh and tasty. I have never tasted better.

B:这鲈鱼新鲜可口,我还没有尝到过比这更好的鱼。

Conversation 4

A: May I have the first dance?

A:我可以和您跳第一支舞吗?

B: With pleasure!

B:非常荣幸!

A: I know that you are a good dancer. What dances do you like?

A:我知道您是跳舞高手。您喜欢什么舞?

B: I like the old styles of dance, such as fox-trot, waltz, rumba, tango and so on. They're all so graceful.

B:我喜欢老式舞,像狐步舞、华尔兹、伦巴、探戈等等。这些舞都非常优美。

A: Why do you like the old styles of dance?

A:您为什么喜欢老式舞呢?

B: Do you think I should like modern dances?

B:您认为我应该喜欢现代舞?

A: I think so, because most young people like mod-

A:我认为应该是,因为大多数年轻人喜欢跳现代

ern dances, such as rock and roll, the twist, and especially break dancing.
舞，比如摇滚舞、扭摆舞，尤其是喜欢跳霹雳舞。

B: Oh, sorry, I don't dance rumba. Rose can do it well. Why not ask her?
B：噢，对不起，我不会跳伦巴舞。罗斯跳得很好。您为什么不去请她呢？

A: Yes, I will. Thank you.
A：是的，我会去的。谢谢您。

B: You are welcome.
B：不客气。

A: I admire your gracefulness.
A：我欣赏您的优美舞姿。

B: That's very kind of you to say so.
B：您对我说这些，您太好了。

A: Thanks. I'll go to ask her.
A：谢谢。我去请她。

B: Enjoy yourself!
B：玩得开心！

Conversation 5

A: Where are you going to play this weekend?
A：这个周末你打算去哪儿玩？

B: I have not given it much thought. Do you have any good suggestions?
B：还没想好，你有什么好建议？

A: I want to spend two days in the mountains with friends. The city is too noisy. Do you know Tanzhe Temple?
A：我和朋友想去山里玩两天，城里太闹腾了。知道潭柘寺吗？

B: I have been there. It is in the middle of the mountains. It is not noisy there and you have to be a vegetarian.
B：我去过，在半山腰上。那儿可不"闹腾"，而且还要"吃素"。

A: Do you want to climb the mountain with us?
A：你们愿意跟我们一起去爬山吗？

B: Does it have enough lodging?
B：能住得下？

A: No problem. The temple is quite large.
A：没问题，寺里很大。

B: There are many ancient pine trees there. It is especially quiet at night. It is wonderful to listen to the monks chanting while listening to the soothing sound of the winds in the pine trees.
B：那儿有很多古松，晚上特别幽静，一边听着和尚念经书，一边听着松涛声，可真妙极了！

A: I'm getting a little excited now. What clothes should I wear?
A：我现在就有点儿激动了。穿什么衣服呢？

B: Take some thick clothes with you. It is rather cold there at night. If you wear the T-shirt you're wearing, you will become a "popsicle".
B：带点厚衣服，那里晚上是很凉的。再穿现在的T恤，非冻成"冰棍"不可。

A: Anything else I should bring?
A：还要带别的吗？

B: If you like taking pictures, you may bring a camera with you.
B：如果你喜欢照相，可以带上照相机。

A: Needless to say.
A：这还用你说！

Conversation 6

A: Wow! What a beautiful scenic spot. It's so open. And just breathe that fresh air, you can almost taste its freshness.
A：哇！多么漂亮的观光胜地，这么宽广。只要呼吸一下这儿的空气，几乎就能尝到它的新鲜味道。

B: You can have a bird view of Guilin City from the top of the mountain.
B：你从山顶可以俯瞰桂林城。

A: Wonderful! I'll often come here for mountain climbing.
A：太棒了！以后我要经常来这儿爬山。

B: You should. Many Guiliners, especially the old and the young, will climb mountains here in the morning.

B:你应该来。每天早上这都有很多桂林人来爬山,尤其是老人和年轻人。

A: No wonder people say: Even the immortals would rather be Guiliners.

A:难怪人们说:宁做桂林人,不做神仙。

B:... Quick! Pass me your binoculars. Look at that bird... I've never seen one of those before. It's indigenous to Guilin, and an endangered species too. This is lucky.

B:……赶快!把你的望远镜给我,看看那只鸟……我从来没见过那种鸟类,它是桂林本土的鸟类,而且是濒临灭绝的一种。我们运气真好。

A: I didn't know you liked bird watching.

A:我以前不知道你喜欢观察鸟。

B: I don't really. I just like wildlife, and you don't get to see too much of it in the city. This place is full of it.

B:也不尽然,我只是喜欢野生动物,在城市里你根本没机会看到它们,而这里竟有这么多。

On the Scene 身临其境 面面俱到

主题:卡尔与哥们尼克一起来河边钓鱼。请你看图,根据如下提供的关键词,将他们的对话写出来。

关键词语:bait *n.* 诱饵　　fish with 用……钓鱼
lure *n.* 诱饵;引诱　　seem to 似乎
look like 看来　　bite *v.* 咬

参考答案

Carl: What are you using for bait today?
Nick: I'm fishing with worms. The fish seem to like them.
Carl: Is that so? I'm using lures, and the fish are biting those too.
Nick: Looks like a lucky day for us.
卡尔:你今天用什么做饵?
尼克:用毛虫。鱼好像很喜欢吃毛虫。
卡尔:是吗?我用诱饵,鱼也喜欢吃这些。
尼克:看来今天我们运气都不错。

★健身运动★ 6 Working out

Words and Phrases 闪亮词语 点滴积累

safety belt 保护带
bounding bed 蹦床
wall ladder 壁梯
auxiliary apparatus 辅助体操器械
balancing ladder 杠梯
rebound tumbling apparatus 技巧弹跳器械
chest expander(/developer) 拉力器
wall bars;rung 肋木
long pole 练习用长杆
horizontal ladder 平梯
medicine ball 实心球
gym ladder 体操梯
spring-grip 握力器
sandbag 小沙袋
handing apparatus 悬挂器械
hanging ladder 悬梯
dump-bell 哑铃

Useful Sentences 七彩精句 连点成线

Words at the gym 健身房用语

1. *How much can you bench?* 躺举你能举多重?
2. *How often do you work out?* 你多长时间训练一次?
3. *Do you know how to do this exercise correctly?* 你知道怎么正确做这项锻炼吗?
4. *Does the trainer at the gym give good advice?* 健身房的教练教导有方吗?
5. *Why do you work out at that gym?* 你为什么到那个健身房锻炼?
6. *How much does it cost to work out there?* 在那训练要花费多少钱?
7. *Is the equipment at the gym new?* 健身房的设备是新的吗?
8. *Do they offer any aerobic classes?* 他们提供有氧健身课吗?
9. *Do you use any muscle enhancers?* 你使用任何健肌药吗?
10. *What muscle groups are you planning to exercise today?* 你今天打算锻炼哪些肌肉?
11. *What time does the gym open?* 健身房几点开门?
12. *Can you see any improvement in your physique since you started lifting weights?* 从你练举重以来,你的体格是否变强壮了?
13. *Do you belong to a fitness club?* 你是健身俱乐部的成员吗?
14. *Do you like to jog?* 你喜欢慢跑吗?
15. *I've been running every morning.* 我每天早上都跑步。
16. *My muscles are so sore today!* 我的肌肉今天酸得要死!
17. *That's because you ran too far yesterday.* 那是因为你昨天跑的距离太长了。
18. *I try to work out at least three times a week.* 我努力做到一星期至少健身三次。
19. *How can I avoid injuring myself during exercise?* 在运动时如何避免伤害?
20. *How do I know if I'm exercising long enough to burn fat?* 要怎么样我才知道我的运动时间长得能够燃烧脂肪?

Climb mountains 爬山

1. *Now is the best season for mountaineering.* 现在是登山的最佳季节。
2. *Mountaineering is very popular among young people.* 登山在年轻人当中非常流行。
3. *Did you climb during the vacation?* 假期里,你爬过山吗?
4. *Did you enjoy the mountaineering trip?* 你很喜欢登山旅行吗?
5. *The view from the top was quite beyond description.* 山顶的景色难以描述。

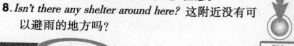

6. *I climbed Mont Blanc in Switzerland with my friend.* 我跟朋友爬过瑞士的勃朗峰。

7. *Take care as the weather is very changeable on the mountain.* 山上的天气多变,要多注意。

8. *Isn't there any shelter around here?* 这附近没有可以避雨的地方吗?

Fashion Conversation 鲜活会话 由线到面

Conversation 1

A: Do you have a gym? I'd like to work out.
A:你们有健身房吗? 我想健身。

B: Our fitness center is on the first floor, next to the sauna.
B:我们的健身中心在一楼,就在桑拿浴室的隔壁。

A: Sounds great. I'll go after I get changed. Is there an extra charge for the gym?
A:听起来不错。我换好衣服再去。健身房需要另外付费吗?

B: No, it's included. But there's a charge for the in-house masseuse and beautician.
B:不用,都包括在房价里了。但饭店里的女按摩师跟美容师服务要另外计费。

A: I'll keep that in mind.
A:我记住了。

B: Just call if you want an appointment. I'll have your bags sent up to your room.
B:要预约的话,打个电话来就好了。我会把行李送到你的房间。

Conversation 2

A: Now let's use the weight machines.
A:现在我们来用用重量训练器材吧。

B: How about the rowing machine?
B:用划船器怎么样?

A: Great. They've all got built-in TVs.
A:好极了。它们上面都装了电视。

B: Cool! We can watch ***Ally Mcbeal***!
B:酷!我们可以看《艾丽的异想世界》!

A: But we could just stay there for 20 minutes.
A:可是机器有20分钟的使用时限。

B: What exercises can I do to firm up my backside?
B:要做什么运动才能让我的臀部结实呢?

A: I would recommend doing some squats. Spread your feet about shoulder-length apart, toes facing forward, and slowly bend at your knees.
A:我建议你做些下蹲运动。双脚张开与肩同宽,脚趾向前,膝盖慢慢弯曲。

B: Like this?
B:像这样!

A: Keep your back straight and look forward. Good. Do about 3 sets of 20.
A:背部挺直,眼睛正视前方。好,做3次,每次20下。

B: Are there any other exercises I can do?
B:我还可以做些什么运动?

A: Ride the bike for at least 20 minutes.
A:骑至少二十分钟自行车。

Conversation 3

A: What is my ideal weight?
A:我的理想体重是多少?

B: If depends on your height and body type.
B:这取决于你的身高与体型。

A: How can I avoid injuring myself during exercise?
A:在运动时如何避免运动伤害?

B: By warming up before and cooling down after your workout.
B:健身前要热身,健身后要做放松运动。

A: Sir, tell us about your experience with Super Bulk-up.
A:您给我们讲一讲使用"超健肌"的经验吧。

B: Well, it's completely changed my life.
B:它彻底地改变了我的生活。

A: Tell us how.
A:告诉我们是怎么改变的。

B: Well, before, I was the skinniest guy on the beach.
B:嗯,我以前是海滩上最瘦弱的男人。

A: And now?
A：那现在呢？

B: Just look! In six short weeks I've put on 30 pounds of pure muscle.
B：众位瞧瞧！在短短的六个星期之内我就多了30磅的精壮肌肉。

A: Wow! All because of Super Bulk-Up.
A：哇！这全是因为“超健肌”。

Conversation 4

A: You look fresh recently. And... What's your weight now?
A：你近来看起来精神很好。还有……你现在的体重是多少？

B: 110 pounds.
B：110磅。

A: Really? Congratulations! That's really something beyond my imagination. How did you make it? Did you keep on a diet?
A：真的。恭喜！真难以想象。你怎么减肥的？是节食吗？

B: No, you know I can't bear eating less.
B：不是。你知道少吃东西我可受不了。

A: Then do the slim pills take effect on you?
A：那，是减肥药起作用了？

B: I've quit it already. I go to aerobics class every day instead.
B：我早就已经停用了。我现在每天参加健美班锻炼。

A: How's it going on?
A：怎么样？

B: You see. I've lost my weight in spite of my good appetite.
B：你看，我的体重下降了，但食欲仍很好。

A: I'd better exercise my body too. My limbs are rusty now.
A：我最好也锻炼锻炼身体，我的胳膊腿都不灵活了。

B: I don't think so. You look full of energy every day. Time has stood still with you?
B：我没觉得。你每天看起来精力都很充沛，真是青春常驻啊。

A: Thank you.
A：谢谢。

On the Scene 身临其境 面面俱到

主题：费伊在健身房教洛拉做健身运动。请你看图，根据如下提供的关键词，将她们的对话写出来。

关键词语：burning *adj.* 酸痛　　backside *n.* 臀部
tight *adj.* 结实的　　trainer *n.* 教练

参考答案

Lora: Yes. Do 12 to 25 reps and then stop. Rest a bit. And then do another set. Rest. And do a third set.
Fay: Oh! My arms are already burning!
Lora: Then rest. You don't want to hurt yourself.
Fay: Now you can help me firm up my backside. Yours are so tight!
Lora: I think you should ask the trainer about that. I was born with mine!
洛拉:对。做12到25下后停下来休息片刻,然后再做一次。休息,然后做第三次。
费伊:噢!我的手臂已经酸痛了!
洛拉:那就休息。不要伤到自己。
费伊:你可以教我如何收紧臀部。你的臀部好结实!
洛拉:我觉得你该问问教练如何做。我的臀部是天生的!

Vehicles

CHAPTE

5

四通八达

★海港航行★ 1 By Ship

Words and Phrases 闪亮词语 点滴积累

channel 航道
speed (of a ship) 航速
stateroom 特等舱(包舱,包房)
second-class 二等舱
third-class cabin 三等舱
captain's cabin 船长室
head 船上厕所
hull 船身
prow; bow; stem 船头
stern 船尾
cabin 船舱
gangway; accommodation ladder 舷梯
deck 甲板
mast 船桅
feeder service ship 货柜集合船
cargo vessel 货轮
semi-cargo liner 客货轮,客货船
passenger liner 定期班轮
ocean-going freighter 远洋货轮
side-wheel steamer 侧轮蒸汽船
double-ended ferry 两头型轮
super tank 超级油轮
motor boat 汽艇
yacht 游艇
cutter 小汽艇
rowboat 划艇
canoe 独木舟
sampan 舢板
gondola 吊舟
cord 木排
bamboo raft 竹筏

Useful Sentences 七彩精句 连点成线

Onboard a ship 搭船

1. *Could you help me with my bag?* 请帮我提一下袋子好吗?
2. *Now you may go on board with your hand baggage, your other suitcases will be carried by the porters.* 现在,你可提着行李袋上船,其他的旅行箱可由搬运工帮你搬运。
3. *Here is your cabin madam. You're on the C-deck, this is your berth, the upper one is for your friend Mrs. Jackson.* 夫人,你的舱位到了,你在C甲板,这是你的床位,你的朋友杰克森太太睡上层。
4. *I hear the gong, I'd better go ashore now.* 铜锣声响了,我想我现在最好上岸。
5. *You better do, thank you very much for having come all the way to the port to see me off.* 我想也是,很感谢你老远跑来码头为我送行。

Conversation aboard a ship 上船后的会话用语

1. *When will we arrive in Honolulu/Sydney?* 我们什么时候可抵达檀香山/悉尼?
2. *How long are we going to stay there?* 我们要在那儿逗留多久?
3. *What time should we be back on board?* 我们什么时候得回到船上?
4. *My cabin is leaking, would you please fix it for me?* 我的舱位漏水了,请你帮我修理一下好吗?

Fashion Conversation 鲜活会话 由线到面

Conversation 1

A: How many ports do we call at on our passage?

A:我们一路上要在几个港口停留?

B: Four ports.	B:4个港口。
A: The ship is going very fast.	A:船走得真快。
B: Perhaps she makes about 25 knots an hour.	B:每小时大约行驶25海里。
A: You look pale. Are you seasick?	A:您脸色不好。是不是晕船?
B: I don't feel very good.	B:我感到不太舒服。
A: I have some tablets for seasickness.	A:我有治晕船的药。
B: They give me no help at all.	B:它们对我一点用都没有。
A: Then we'd better go back to our cabin.	A:那我们最好回到船舱里吧。

Conversation 2

A: Let's go for a walk on the deck.	A:我们到甲板上走走去吧。
B: OK. Is the wind in our favour?	B:好啊。是顺风吗?
A: I'm afraid it'll be rather rough.	A:恐怕有点儿风浪。
B: Which way is the wind now?	B:现在是什么风向?
A: It's the east wind. Take care, you'll fall down the hatch. Grasp the handrail firmly.	A:是东风。小心点儿,不要跌下舱口去。握紧栏杆!
B: I think we'd better go below.	B:我看我们最好还是下去吧!

Conversation 3

A: We'll embark tomorrow at noon. Are you ready?	A:明天中午就要上船了,你都准备好了吗?
B: Almost. The only thing left is the troublesome packing.	B:差不多了。只剩下一件事,就是令人头痛的打包。
A: What's the problem?	A:有什么问题吗?
B: It is said that all the ladies have to wear evening dresses at the Gala Dinner.	B:我听说在船长晚宴上所有女士都要穿着晚礼服。
A: Don't worry! If you have nothing to wear, my sister can lend you her pink one.	A:不必担心,如果你没有的话,我妹妹可以把粉红色的那件借给你。
B: Thanks. And I wonder if I have to pack the beach sandals, umbrella and straw hat.	B:谢啦!我还在想要不要带海滩鞋、阳伞和草帽。
A: All that stuff is available at the shop on board, so I won't be taking them with me myself.	A:那些都可在船上商店买到,我自己不带的。
B: Then, how about some snacks and drinks?	B:那带些零食和饮料怎么样?
A: Sure. But you have to pay a beverage charge!	A:当然可以。不过饮料是要付开瓶费的喔!
B: Really? Then I'd rather bring some magazines for onboard reading.	B:真的吗?那我还是改带几本杂志在船上看好了。
A: The most important thing is to bring your swimming suit and sports wear.	A:更重要的,是要记得带你的泳装和休闲服。
B: That's right. I also have many cosmetics and skincare products to take along. How about you?	B:没错!我还得带一大堆的化妆保养品,你呢?
A: I've bought a travel set of skincare products. It's much lighter!	A:我买了一组旅行保养品,轻省多了。
B: Look at how many things!	B:你看!我要带的东西真多啊!
A: You can make them fit into two pieces of baggage, the large one and the small one.	A:你可以把它们分减至两个行李,一大一小。
B: Really? And how?	B:真的吗?怎么分呢?
A: Different uses for each bag's contents.	A:你可以依袋子的不同用途分类装东西啊!

B: That's a smart idea! I didn't think of it.
A: Finally, don't forget to bring along your passport and Access Card.
B: I won't. Thanks for reminding me.

B:好聪明的办法!我没想到这点呢。
A:然后,别忘了携带你的护照和登船卡喔!
B:我不会的,多谢提醒。

On the Scene 身临其境 面面俱到

主题:轮船因为大雾而晚点了,两个陌生的同船者开始聊上了关于海上出行的事儿。请你看图,根据如下提供的关键词,将他们的对话写出来。

关键词语:on time 及时　　fog *n.* 烟雾
unpleasant *adj.* 讨厌的　　foggy *adj.* 模糊的

参考答案

Jack: Can this ship sail on time?
Mary: I'm afraid not. There'll be some delay because of the fog.
Jack: It's unpleasant to be out on a foggy day.
Mary: Yes. Are you going to travel by ship?
Jack: Yes. It's the most comfortable way to travel by ship.
杰克:这趟船没晚点吧?
玛丽:我想大概是晚点了。可能因为大雾有一些延迟。
杰克:大雾天出行真让人不愉快。
玛丽:是的。你打算坐船出行吗?
杰克:是的。坐船是一种比较舒服的旅行方式。

★乘坐飞机★ 2 By Plane

Words and Phrases 闪亮词语 点滴积累

to check in 办理乘机手续
plane ticket 飞机票
boarding card 登机牌
to board a plane 登机
date 班期
flight 航线;航班
first class 头等舱
business class 公务舱
economic class 经济舱
special price 特价
to book a ticket 预订机票
to reserve a seat in advance 提前订座
to cancel the reservation 取消订座
return ticket(英) 往返票
round-trip ticket(美) 往返票

Useful Sentences 七彩精句 连点成线

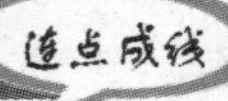

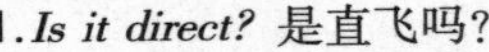

Questions passengers might ask about the airline flight 乘客对航班可能提的问题

1. *Is it direct?* 是直飞吗?
2. *Is there a layover?* 中途要停留吗?
3. *How long is the layover?* 中途要停留多久?
4. *Do I have to change planes?* 我需要换机吗?
5. *Is a meal served?* 有餐点供应吗?
6. *Do you have my frequent flyer number?* 有我的常乘客优惠活动号吗?
7. *How much carry-on luggage is permitted?* 允许随身带多少行李?

Describing airline flights 讲述航班情况

1. *It's non-stop.* 这是直达飞行。
2. *You'll change planes in Denver.* 你将在丹佛换机。
3. *You have a layover in Chicago.* 你要在芝加哥作短暂停留。
4. *There's a one-hour layover in Dallas.* 在达拉斯停留一个小时。
5. *You only have 20 minutes to make your connection.* 你只有二十分钟时间去搭乘联运班机。
6. *All domestic flights are nonsmoking.* 国内班机都禁止吸烟。
7. *To be eligible for the lower fare, you have to stay over Saturday night.* 要买到打折扣的机票,必须过了星期六晚上再走。
8. *The State Department has issued a travel warning in that area.* 国务院已对该地区发出了旅行警告。

Rescheduling an airline flight 更改航班

1. *I need to cancel my flight.* 我要取消航班。
2. *I need to reschedule my flight.* 我要更改航班。
3. *Can I change my flight schedule?* 我可以更改航班吗?
4. *Is there a penalty for changing my plans?* 我改变计划要被罚款吗?

At the airport boarding gate 在机场登机口

1. *At this time we'd like to pre-board those passengers with young children or those needing extra assistance.* 现在我们想让这些带小孩的乘客或需要特殊帮助的乘客先登机。
2. *We are now boarding passengers in rows 24 through 36.* 现在从第 24 排到第 36 排的乘客登机。
3. *We are now boarding all rows on Flight 1234 to Columbus.* 现在所有乘坐飞往哥伦布第 1234 航班的乘客登机。

4. *May I see your boarding card?* 我可以看一下您的登机牌吗？

5. *You're permitted two carry-on items.* 你可以随身携带两件行李。

In an airplane 在飞机上

1. *Please observe the no smoking signs.* 请遵守不准吸烟的告示。
2. *The emergency exits are located on either side of the plane over the wings.* 紧急出口设在两边机翼的上方。
3. *Please locate the exit nearest you.* 请看清离你最近的安全门。
4. *Please keep your seat belts fastened until the captain has turned off the seat belt sign.* 机长将安全带信号熄灭后才能将你的安全带解开。
5. *Please remain in your seat until the plane has come to a complete stop.* 飞机尚未完全停稳前，请勿离开你的座位。
6. *Please return to your seat.* 请回到您的座位上去。
7. *Please bring your seat back to its full upright position.* 请将您的椅背回复到垂直的位置。

Fashion Conversation 鲜活会话 由线到面

Conversation 1

A: Good morning. Can I help you?
B: Good morning. I'd like to make a reservation to Guangzhou for August 2.
A: Just a moment, please. I'm sorry, sir. There is no ticket available on that day. But we have flights for Guangzhou the next day.
B: May I inquire about the departure time?
A: A 9:12 flight in the morning and a 14:00 flight in the afternoon.
B: When will the plane reach for the morning flight?
A: At 6:15.
B: OK. I'd like to book a ticket for this one.
A: All right, sir. Please reconfirm your ticket no later than 12 o'clock two days before the flight; otherwise, your reservation will automatically cancelled.
B: Yes, I know. What's the fare?
A: It's 870 RMB, not including ground transportation fares between the airport and downtown.
B: I see. Will it be doubled for the round trip?
A: Right, sir. And please do not forget to bring a valid travel document with you when you buy the tickets.
B: I will.

A:您早，能为您做些什么？
B:早，我想订一张8月2日去广州的机票。
A:请稍等。对不起，先生，8月2日的票已订完了，但第二天有去广州的航班。
B:请问飞机都什么时候起飞？
A:早上航班9:12起飞，下午航班14:00起飞。
B:早上班机什么时候到达？
A:6:15。
B:好吧，我订一张这次班机的票。
A:好的，先生。请最好在起飞前两天的中午12点前再确认一下机票，否则预订会自动取消。
B:是的，我知道。票价多少？
A:870元，不包括市区到机场的地面交通费。
B:明白了，往返票是不是加倍？
A:是的，先生。请别忘了带您有效旅行证件来买票。
B:好的。

Conversation 2

A: Good morning. Welcome aboard! This way, please.
B: Thank you. Stewardess, can you direct me to my seat?

A:早安，欢迎登机！请这边走。
B:谢谢，空中小姐，您能带我到我的座位上去吗？

A: Certainly. May I see your boarding pass, please?

A:当然。请让我看看您的登机证好吗?

B: Sure, here it is.

B:好的,在这里。

A: Thank you. Come this way, please. Your seat is in the middle of the cabin on the left.

A:谢谢。请这边走。您的座位在机舱中间的左侧。

Conversation 3

A: Have some champagne and Belgian chocolates.

A:要来点香槟和比利时巧克力吗?

B: Well, thank you. And could you bring us a deck of cards?

B:呃,谢谢。你可以拿一副纸牌给我们吗?

A: Certainly.

A:当然。

C: Do you have anything to read?

C:你们有什么可以看的吗?

A: Yes... We have these magazines and newspapers.

A:有的……我们有这些杂志和报纸。

C: Cool! Vogue, GQ! and Elle! Thanks.

C:酷! Vogue, GQ 还有 ELLe! 谢谢。

D: What's the meal on this flight?

D:飞机上提供什么餐点?

A: Here's the menu. You have three choices.

A:这是菜单。您有三项选择。

D: Wow! Filet Mignon! Peking Duck! Lobster!

D:哇! 菲力牛排! 北京烤鸭! 龙虾!

A: All first class meals are gourmet. We'll service you in an hour, but you can order now.

A:所有头等舱的餐点都是美食。我们将在一小时内供餐,可是您可以现在点餐。

D: We'll have the filet and the duck, thanks.

D:我们要菲力牛排及烤鸭,谢谢。

A: Great. Just sit back and prepare for takeoff.

A:好的。请坐好准备起飞。

Conversation 4

A: Please place your seats in the upright position.

A:请将你的座椅扶正。

B: What's happening? It's getting worse!

B:发生什么事了? 越来越糟。

A: There's no need for alarm. It's just bad turbulence... and...

A:没有必要惊慌。只是一股强烈的气流……而且……

B: And what?

B:而且怎样?

A: Some technical problems. But they're working on it right now.

A:有点机械上的问题。不过他们正在设法解决。

B: But I have to go to the bathroom!

B:可是我得去上厕所!

A: I'm sorry, but you'll have to stay in your seat.

A:很抱歉,但您必须待在座位上。

B: I'm going to explode. Whoa! Oh, my god!

B:我快憋不住了。哇! 喔,我的天啊!

A: This isn't so much fun after all. This is the worse I've ever experienced.

A:这下可不好玩了。这是我经历过最糟糕的。

B: I think I'm going to be sick.

B:我想我要吐了。

A: Here. Here's a barf bag.

A:给,呕吐袋在这儿。

B: Oh! I'm so scared!

B:喔! 我好害怕!

A: Don't worry. I'll protect you even better than Jack protected Rose in ***Titanic***!

A:别担心。我会比《泰坦尼克号》中的杰克保护罗斯做得更好来保护你!

Conversation 5

A: Hello. May I see your boarding pass, please?

A:你们好,我可以看一下你们的登机卡吗?

B: Here you are.

B:给您。

A:18A and 18B are right back here. Please stow your carry-on baggage in the overhead compartment. If I can be of assistance, just let me know.

A:18A 和 18B 就在这儿后面。请把随身行李放在上面的行李柜里。如果需要我帮忙的话,请尽管告诉我。

B:Thanks. Uh, would my camera be all right in the overhead compartment? I don't want it to get broken.

B:谢谢。呃,我的照相机放在上面行李柜里没事吧?我可不希望它被摔坏了。

A:It should be fine there. If you feel more comfortable about it, you can stow it beneath the seat in front of you.

A:应该没问题的。但如果您觉得放在您前面座位底下比较放心的话,就放在那儿好了。

B:I think I'll do that instead, thanks.

B:我想我会放在座位底下,谢谢。

A:Don't mention it. Please be seated and fasten your seat belts.

A:不客气。请坐好,系好安全带。

On the Scene 身临其境 面面俱到

主题:飞机刚刚起飞,机长正向全体乘客致辞,汤姆开始小声的插话,他的朋友玛丽不让他吱声。请你看图,根据如下提供的关键词,将他们的对话写出来。

关键词语:captain *n.* 机长　　crew *n.* 机组人员
cabin *n.* 机舱　　sense 清楚
altitude *n.* 高度,高处　　relax *v.* 放松

参考答案

Captain: Good afternoon, everyone. This is your captain speaking. I'm Captain Li Lin and my crew and I will be piloting this 535 aircraft from New York to Amsterdam, Holland.

Tom: I can't believe we're on our way!

Captain: You may have noticed that I turned off the "fasten seat belt" sign a few moments ago. If you like, you may get up and move about the cabin. However, the crew and I advise you to keep that seat belt fastened, in case of turbulence. We keep ours fastened, and we hope you will, too.

Tom: That makes sense, doesn't it?

Mary: Shh!

Captain: After we reach our cruising altitude, I'll give you the weather report for Amsterdam. Until then, relax and enjoy our famous KLM service. Thank you and out.

机长:各位中午好。这是机长报告,我是李林机长,我和本班机全体乘务人员将驾驶这班535客机从纽约飞往荷兰阿姆斯特丹。

汤姆:真不敢相信我们已经上路了!

机长:诸位可能已注意到我在几分钟前关掉了"系好安全带"的指示灯。如果诸位愿意的话,可以起身在机舱内走动。不过,我和全体机员建议您就座时系好安全带以免突然遇到气流。我们自己系着安全带,希望诸位也能这样做。

汤姆:很有道理,对吗?

玛丽:嘘!

机长:在我们攀升至巡航高度时,我会向诸位报告阿姆斯特丹的天气状况。到那时您就可以放松自己享受我们著名的荷兰皇家航空公司的服务。播报完毕,谢谢。

★铁路之旅★ 3 By Train

Words and Phrases 闪亮词语 点滴积累

parcels office 承运包裹处
luggage counter 行车柜台
platform scale with dial 有刻度盘的台秤
suitcase 手提箱
luggage sticker 行李标签
luggage receipt 行李收据
luggage clerk 行李员
poster 招贴
advertisement 广告
station mailbox 车站邮箱
station restaurant 车站餐厅
waiting room 候车室
schedule 时刻表
porter 搬运工
left luggage lockers 寄存行李锁柜
tunnel to the platforms 通向站台的地道
steps to the platforms 通向站台的台阶
station bookstand 车站报刊柜
information office 问讯处
station clock 车站大钟
railway map 铁路地图
ticket office 售票处
ticket counter 售票柜台

Useful Sentences 七彩精句 连点成线

Instructions from a commuter train conductor 短途往返列车车长的指示语

1. *Stand clear of the doors.* 不要站在门口。
2. *For your safety, don't lean on the doors.* 为了您的安全，别靠在门上。
3. *No smoking, littering, or radio playing.* 禁止吸烟，禁止乱扔杂物，禁止打开无线电。
4. *Please have your tickets ready for the conductor.* 请将您的车票准备好让检票员检票。
5. *Next stop is St. Louis.* 下一站是圣路易斯站。

Asking about a long train trip 询问有关长途火车旅行事宜

1. *Is it direct?* 是直达吗？
2. *Do I have to change trains?* 我得转车吗？
3. *Is there a dining car?* 有餐车吗？
4. *Can I order a special meal?* 我可以叫份特做的膳食吗？
5. *Can I check my baggage through?* 我的行李可以托运到目的地吗？
6. *When does the next train leave?* 下一班火车什么时候开？
7. *Are there seats still available?* 还有座位吗？
8. *Is the train on time?* 火车准点吗？
9. *What's the departure time?* 火车出发是几点？
10. *When does the train get in?* 火车什么时候进站？
11. *What's the arrival time?* 到达时间是几点？

Fashion Conversation 鲜活会话 由线到面

Conversation 1

A: How shall we go to Amsterdam?
B: I prefer to travel by train.
A: By train? It'll take us a much longer time than by air.
B: I've never made any long distance travel by train

A：我们怎样去阿姆斯特丹？
B：我想乘火车去。
A：乘火车？那路途时间可就比乘飞机长多了。
B：我在欧洲还从未乘火车长途旅行过，每次我都

in Europe. Each time I take a plane, so I want to change. I believe that'll be more exciting. I want to see more of the continental landscape.

乘飞机，所以这次我想换一下。我相信乘火车更令人激动，我想看看欧洲大陆的风光。

A: Yes, it's nice indeed. The view along the railway is wonderful as the train passes farmland, mountains, rivers and woods, and you'll see the variation of the landscape.

A：是的，确实不错。火车驶过农田，穿过山区、树林，跨过河流，沿途的景色变化无穷，这主意真不错。

B: I feel very excited already. But I'm a little bit worried about the luggage.

B：我已经很兴奋了，但我还是有点担心行李。

A: Don't worry. The continental rail system has a perfect luggage service. The only thing you have to do is to claim your luggage at the destination.

A：不用担心。欧洲大陆的铁路行李托运服务很好。您只需要在目的地取行李就是了。

B: Oh, is it? When shall we leave?

B：哦，是吗？我们什么时候出发？

A: Take your time. We'll have to book our tickets first.

A：别着急。我们还得先订票呢。

Conversation 2

A: Let's go into this car, shall we?

A：我们进这个车厢好吗？

B: All right. So crowded today.

B：好吧，看来今天车厢太挤。

A: Now let me settle the luggage. This suitcase should go on the rack. Could you give me a hand?

A：现在让我把行李放好，这只箱子应放在行李架上，帮我一下好吗？

B: Sure. Here it is... Oh, this is really heavy.

B：可以。来……，噢，好重啊！

A: I'm sorry. You know my wife always packs in a lot of things for me when I travel.

A：对不起。您知道每次我旅行，我妻子都要给我装上许多东西。

B: Well, it's nice to have somebody to worry about you all the time. But I prefer to travel light. Look, this suitcase is all I've got when I travel, and I always have everything I need.

B：有人总在惦记着您，那当然好，不过我喜欢轻装旅行。瞧，我外出旅行就这么一只箱子，而且需要的东西也都有了。

A: I guess you're right. Now we can make ourselves comfortable.

A：我想您说得倒也是。好了，现在我们可以放松放松了。

Conversation 3

A: We're about to miss the train. Hurry up!

A：我们要赶不上火车了，快点儿。

B: Hold on. I haven't heard the whistle, so there's time.

B：别着急，我还没有听到鸣笛，还有时间。

A: Which train are we in?

A：我们乘哪班车？

B: Let me see. Oh, No. 14.

B：让我看看。哦，14 次。

A: Oh, bother! It's the very end of the train.

A：哦，麻烦了，这是最后一班了。

B: We have no choice.

B：我们别无选择。

A: Here we are, Train 14. Let's get in.

A：来了，14 次车。我们上去。

B: Seats No. 20 and 21. It's nice that we've got a window seat.

B：20 号和 21 号座。太好了，我们的座位在窗口。

A: But I prefer the aisle seat here. I feel sick with a seat back to the engine.

A：可我宁愿要过道旁的座位，我坐在引擎发动机后面会感到恶心。

B: Take whichever you like. Let's put our suitcases on the rack.
B: 随您的便吧。让我们把旅行箱放在架子上。

A: Oh, the baggage rack is full. Put them under the seat for the time being.
A: 哦,行李架满了。暂时放在座位下面吧。

B: All right. But I must take my camera out.
B: 好的,不过我必须拿出照相机。

A: Well, there goes the whistle. We're leaving. Do you know when the train is due in New York?
A: 哦,鸣笛了,就要走了。您知道火车什么时候到纽约吗?

B: I'm not quite sure. But it takes about 15 hours, so we'll arrive around 10 o'clock tomorrow morning.
B: 我也不太清楚。大约15个小时吧,我们明天上午10点左右能到。

Conversation 4

A: Here we are at last. Let me put our baggage on the rack.
A: 咱们终于上来了。让我把咱们的行李放到行李架上。

B: Thank you. It's so cool inside the train. I was almost hit by heatstroke in Shanghai.
B: 谢谢。车上真凉快。在上海我差一点中暑。

A: Yes, weren't you! The temperature went to 38℃ and it was wet, too.
A: 可不是嘛! 气温高达摄氏38度,而且又很潮湿。

B: This is your sleeping bed and the upper one is mine.
B: 这是你的卧铺,上面那个是我的。

A: Good. There is a sheet and a blanket on the sleeping bed. The bedding is so clean.
A: 好。卧铺上有一个床单,还有一个毯子。卧具很干净。

B: We'll be warm at night.
B: 我们夜里就不会冷了。

A: Yes. Here comes the train attendant.
A: 是的。列车乘务员来了。

C: Ladies and gentlemen, who'd like some warm water?
C: 女士们,先生们,谁要开水?

A: Some warm water, sir, please.
A: 先生,我要一点开水。

C: Alright, put the cup on the table, or you'll burn your hand.
C: 好的,把杯子放到桌子上。否则你的手会烫伤的。

A: Thank you.
A: 谢谢。

B: I saw the auto water boiler at the end of the car. Can we get the water ourselves?
B: 我在车厢的尽头那边看到有一个自动热水器。我们可以自己去打水吗?

C: Yes, madam. When I'm not available, you can help yourselves there. But be sure not to throw the leftovers there.
C: 可以,夫人。我不在的时候你们可以自己去打水。但是请注意不要把剩饭菜倒在那儿。

A: No, we won't.
A: 我们不会往那儿倒剩饭菜的。

Conversation 5

A: Magazines and newspapers. Who'd like a copy?
A: 报纸杂志来了。谁想看看?

B: Let's read magazines.
B: 咱们看看杂志吧。

C: Good idea! A copy of "***China Wealth***", please.
C: 好主意,请给我一本《中国财富》。

A: Here you are. $9.80 please.
A: 请拿着,9.8美元。

C: Do I have to pay for it?
C: 我得买下来吗?

A: Yes, madam, they're new.
A: 是的,夫人,这些是新出杂志。

B: But we used to be free of charge.
B: 但是,以前这些是免费阅读的。

A: Things have changed, you know.
A: 情况不同了,你知道。

B: Alright, alright. Here is $9.80.
B: 好吧,好吧,给你9.8美元。

On the Scene 身临其境 面面俱到

主题:杰克想乘火车到上海,他来到售票处。请你看图,根据如下提供的关键词,将他们的对话写出来。

关键词语:express *n.* 快车　　straight *adj.* 整齐的
berth *n.* 停泊处　　fee *n.* 费,酬金
upper *adj.* 上面的,上部的　　conductor *n.* 领导者,经理

参考答案

Jack:How long will this express take to go to Shanghai?
Ticket Seller:About 20 hours.
Jack:How many stations will it stop at?
Ticket Seller:This express will go straight from Beijing to Shanghai without a stop.
Jack:Oh. Is there a train that leaves in the afternoon?
Ticket Seller:Yes, there is one. Do you need a ticket?
Jack:I'd like to have two soft berth to Shanghai for tomorrow.
Ticket Seller:OK. It comes to 1,400 yuan including service fee.
Jack:May I have two lower berths?
Ticket Seller:Sorry. We usually pair the upper and lower together to sell. You may ask the conductor to change it for you.
Jack:I see. Thanks a lot.
Ticket Seller:Have a nice trip.
杰克:这辆快车将用多少时间到达上海?
售票员:大约20个小时。

杰克:它将在多少站点停车?
售票员:这辆特快将从北京直达上海,中途不停车。
杰克:噢,有下午发车的列车吗?
售票员:有,有一列,你想买票吗?
杰克:我想要两张明天到上海的软卧票。
售票员:好。含服务费在内,共1400元。
杰克:我能买两张下铺的吗?
售票员:对不起。我们通常都是上下铺成对一块卖。你可以找列车员给你换票。
杰克:我知道了。多谢。
售票员:祝你旅途愉快。

★乘汽车★ 4 By Bus

Words and Phrases 闪亮词语 点滴积累

bus route 公共汽车路线
license plate 汽车牌照
car make 汽车牌子
vehicle registration certificate 机动车行驶证
driving license 机动车驾驶证
bus;omnibus 公共汽车
trolleybus 无轨电车
dining car;restaurant car 餐车
sightseeing bus 观光汽车
motorcoach 大轿车(游览车)
open car 敞篷车
phaeton 敞篷旅行汽车
shuttle bus 接送车
baggage car 行李车厢
cable car 缆车
electric locomotive 电力机车
steam locomotive 蒸汽机车
diesel locomotive 柴油机车
through train 直达快车
express train;fast train 特别快车

Useful Sentences 七彩精句 连点成线

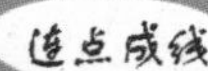

Asking about a long bus trip 询问有关乘坐长途汽车旅行事宜

1. *How long is the layover?* 中途要停留多久?
2. *Do I have to change buses?* 我需要转车吗?
3. *Can I check my baggage through?* 我可以托运行李直到目的地吗?
4. *How much luggage can I carry on?* 我可以携带多少行李?
5. *Is the bus on time?* 这班公共汽车准点吗?
6. *What's the departure time?* 什么时候发车?
7. *When does the bus get in?* 公共汽车什么时候进站?

Asking about bus routes 打听公共汽车路线

1. *Is this the bus to Linden Avenue?* 这是去林敦大街的公共汽车吗?
2. *Does this bus go to Howard Street?* 这车开往霍华德街吗?
3. *Could you let me know when we get to Davis Street?* 到了戴维斯街时,请告诉我一声好吗?
4. *Can you tell me where to get off?* 到站请叫我一声好吗?

Instructions when boarding a bus 上公共汽车时的指示语

1. *Step up, please.* 请上来吧。
2. *Watch your step.* 当心脚下。
3. *I cannot make change.* 恕不找零。
4. *You must have the correct change.* 自备零钱。
5. *Move to the rear(, please).* (请)到后车厢去。
6. *There's plenty of room in the rear.* 后车厢有许多空地方。
7. *Another quarter, please.* 请再投一枚25分的硬币。
8. *Keep your arms and head inside the bus.* 别把头和手臂伸出车外。
9. *Please exit through the rear door.* 请从后门下车。

Asking about a bus seat you want to sit in 汽车上询问可否坐你想坐的座位

1. *Is anyone sitting here?* 这儿有人坐吗?
2. *Is this seat taken?* 这个位子有人坐吗?
3. *Is this space taken?* 这个位子有人坐吗?
4. *Is this seat occupied?* 这个位子有人坐吗?

Fashion Conversation 鲜活会话 由线到面

Conversation 1

A: Is this the right bus for San Francisco?

B: It sure is. Can I see your ticket? OK, fine.

A: When's the first stop?

B: About two hours out of Los Angeles. Give me the bags, I'll put in on the bus. Here's your claim tag. Don't lose it. When you get off the bus, give it to me.

A: Thank you. Is it all right to smoke on the bus?

B: Sure, but only in the rear, and only cigarettes. And alcohol is not allowed.

A: I see. Thank you.

A:这是到旧金山的巴士吗?

B:正是,我可以看你的车票吗?好了,没问题。

A:第一站什么时候到?

B:大约出洛杉矶后2小时。袋子给我,我会放在车上。这是你的签条。不要丢了,下车时给我。

A:谢谢。车上可以抽烟吗?

B:可以,但是只能在后座,而且只能抽香烟,车上也不能喝酒。

A:我知道了,谢谢你。

Conversation 2

A: Let's move to the rear of the bus, we'll get off at the back. Oh yes, before we move to the rear, you have to get an add-a-fare from the driver for the No. 10 at Troost Avenue?

B: (*Overhears it*) Drop a quarter in the box, sir.

C: Driver, could you please let me know when I arrive at Troost Avenue?

B: Sure thing, sir.

A: (Whispers to C) He may forget. Don't worry. I'll remind you.

C: You're very kind indeed.

(*The bus approaches the Troost Avenue bus-stop*)

A: Pull the buzzer which is strung across the bus above the windows. Otherwise the driver will go right past the stop if he finds no one waiting there. Don't forget to transfer to the east — bound No. 10.

A:我们到车厢后边去吧,我们得在后边下车。对了,我们去后边之前,您应该向司机买一张在土斯特大街换乘10路车的追加车票。

B:(*偶然听到了*)往箱子放25美分,先生。

C:司机,车到土斯特大街时您告诉我一声好吗?

B:当然可以,先生。

A:(对C耳语)他可能会忘掉,别着急,我会提醒您。

C:您真太好了。

(*车快到土斯特大街的车站了*)

A:拉一下在车窗上面与蜂音器相连接的绳子,否则司机看到站上没人等车的话就一直开过去了,别忘了换乘往东行驶的10路公共汽车。

Conversation 3

A: Sir, please pay for you trip.

B: Do I need exact change to ride the bus?

A: No, but if you don't you must pay extra.

B: Could you explain carefully?

A: Okay. It's \$3. If you give \$5, without change returned.

B: Can I use my commuter's pass?

A: I'm afraid you can't.

A:先生,请买票。

B:我要搭公共汽车需要准备好零钱吗?

A:不需要,但是如果没有正好的零钱,你必须多付。

B:你能细说一下吗?

A:好的,搭车需要付三元,但如果你付五元。不找零。

B:可以用月票吗?

A:恐怕不行。

Conversation 4

A: Stand back from the door, please. Let the passengers off. You can't get on until the other passengers get off.
A:请别站在车门口,让车上乘客先下去。车上乘客不下车,你也没法上车。

B: How much is the fare, please?
B:要多少车钱?

A: One dollar. Drop it in the box. Move to the rear of the bus. There are plenty of seats in the rear.
A:一元。把钱放进这只收银箱。到车厢后面去吧,那里有很多座位。

B: Wait. I want to ask you if this bus goes down Fifth Avenue as far as Greenwich Village.
B:等一下,这车是不是经过第五大道,一直到格林尼治村那儿?

A: That's right. Move along, please. There are more people waiting to get on. Move to the rear.
A:是的。请走开些。这里有很多乘客都要上车。走到后面去。

B: I thought this bus went down Park Avenue.
B:我觉得这车是开往派克大道的。

A: No, that's the Number 1. That goes down Park Avenue. This is the Number 2.
A:不,那是1路公共汽车。1路车去派克大道。我们这是2路车。

B: But I thought this was the right bus to go to Washington Square Park.
B:不过我认为这车是去华盛顿广场公园的。

A: It is. Get in, please. You're holding everyone up. You can't miss Washington Square Park.
A:没错。请往里边一点。你把别人的路挡了。你会找到华盛顿广场公园的。

B: Would you tell me when we get there?
B:到了那里时,能告诉我吗?

A: It would be better if you watched out for yourself. I might forget.
A:恐怕还是你自己留神更好些,我可能会忘记的。

B: Well, how will I recognize it?
B:哎呀,那我怎么知道呢?

A: Just watch for the big arch and all the trees. Get off the bus when we get there.
A:留神看,前面会有一座大型拱门,周围还有不少树木。车到了那里时你就下去。

Conversation 5

A: I am looking for a comfortable convenient way to see the country.
A:我想找一种舒适方便的方法来游览这个国家。

B: Have you heard of motor coaching? It's one of the fastest-growing segments for the travel industry.
B:你听说过乘大客车旅行吗?这是旅行业增长最快的一个部门。

A: No, I've not heard of it. Tell me about it.
A:我没听说过。给我介绍一下吧。

B: It's almost like going on an ocean cruise except that you go by land. Everything is planned for you from the moment you step on board a luxury coach.
B:那就像乘海轮旅行,只是你在陆地上进行。从你登上豪华大客车开始,每样事都为你安排好了。

A: Is it just a bus?
A:是不是普通大客车?

B: Oh, no. The motor coach is air-conditioned, there is a galley for food preparation, movies or music are available for your entertainment and attendants are there to take care of your every need.
B:不是的。客车上有空调,由厨房准备食品,有电影和音乐供你欣赏,还有服务员为你提供无微不至的服务。

A: Wow! That sounds like pure luxury.
A:嚯,听上去真是非常豪华呀。

B: All tours are planned to make sure the guests are able to do all the shopping they want. Stores
B:旅行团有周密安排,确保游客可以尽情购物。商店和购物中心已经认识到客车旅行团的价

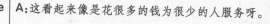

and shopping centers have recognized the value of motor-coach tours by having convenient accommodations for the driver, tours of the centers, lunches and goodie bags for those on the tour. Some centers even have interpreters representing 22 languages available to serve tourists.

值。它们为司机提供方便的食宿，为游客提供参观、午餐和小礼品包。有些购物中心还配有翻译，用22种语言为游客服务。

A: That looks like a lot of expense to accommodate just a few people.

A: 这看起来像是花很多的钱为很少的人服务呀。

B: There is a lot of money involved in this industry. The city of Denver, for instance, says the motor-coach industry brings \$26.6 million a year to their city. They figure each passenger brings at least \$156 a day to the local economy.

B: 这门生意里可有不少钱可赚呢。例如丹佛市说客车旅行行业一年为该市带来2,660万美元。根据他们的计算，每一个旅客为当地经济每天至少带来156美元。

A: I can see why cities like tis tourist industry.

A: 现在我明白了各城市为什么喜欢旅行业了。

B: Yes, and the tourists themselves fine it a very comfortable, relaxing way to see the sights they are interested in with not much effort on their part except for parting with the money.

B: 正是这样，旅游者自己也觉得这是一种舒适轻松的方法，可以观赏他们感兴趣的地方，而他们自己并不用费力，只要花些钱就行了。

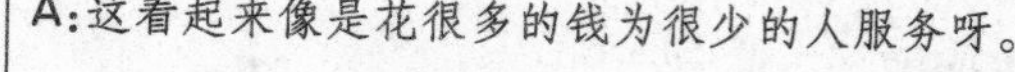

On the Scene 身临其境 面面俱到

主题：公交车里，欧文在买车票的同时寻问到国家公园还有几站地。请你看图，根据如下提供的关键词，将他们的对话写出来。

关键词语：fare *n.* 费用，旅客　　altogether *adv.* 完全地
remind *vt.* 提醒，使想起

参考答案

Conductor: All, fares, please.
Owen: How much is the fare to the National Park?
Conductor: Where did you get on?
Owen: J. H. Building.
Conductor: A half dollar.
Owen: How many stops are there to the National Park?
Conductor: Six altogether. Don't worry, I will remind you.
Owen: Thanks a lot.
车长:大家请买票了。
欧文:到国家公园多少钱?
车长:您从哪里上的?
欧文:JH 大厦。
车长:50 美分。
欧文:共有几站啊?
车长:6 站。别担心,到站时我告诉你。
欧文:太谢谢了。

★乘出租车★ 5 Taxi

Words and Phrases 闪亮词语 点滴积累

go straight on 直行
turn left 向左转
turn right 向右转
drive slowly 慢行
beware 注意行人
prepared to stop 准备停车
no parking;no stopping 禁止停车
no passing;no overtaking 禁止超车
no entry 禁止驶入
no horn;no hooter;no tooting 禁止鸣笛
no thoroughfare;road closed 此路不通
roadwork ahead 前方施工
slow down, look around and cross 一慢二看三通过
give way;yield 让路
traffic light 红绿灯
red light 红灯
green light 绿灯

Useful Sentences 七彩精句 连点成线

Basic instructions to a cab driver 对出租车司机的基本指示语

1. *Take me a the airport.* 送我去机场。
2. *I need to go to Fifth and Main.* 我要去第五街缅因街路口。
3. *Fifth and Main, please.* 请送我去第五街缅因街路口。

A taxi driver asking where to go 出租车司机询问去何处

1. *Where to?* 去哪儿?
2. *Where to, friend?* 去哪儿,朋友?
3. *Where to, chief?* 去哪儿,先生?
4. *Where to, Bud?* 去哪儿,老兄?
5. *Where to, lady?* 去哪儿,夫人?
6. *What intersection is that near?* 哪个十字路口近?
7. *Where is that?* 在哪儿?
8. *Which airport?* 哪个机场?

A taxi driver asking general questions 出租车司机的一般问话

1. *You in a hurry?* 你急吗?
2. *Which way do you want me to go?* 你要我走哪条路线?
3. *I don't go there.* 我不去那儿。
4. *It's rush hour, I don't go to the airport.* 现在是高峰时间,我不去机场。
5. *I'm not on duty.* 我不当班。
6. *Is the radio too loud?* 收音机太响吗?
7. *It will cost you double fare to leave the city.* 开出城市你要加倍付车费。
8. *Mind if I smoke?* 我抽烟你介意吗?
9. *I'm going to smoke.* 我要抽烟了。
10. *Please don't smoke.* 请不要抽烟。

A taxi driver identifying the final destination 出租汽车司机确认最后目的地

1. *Which corner?* 哪个拐角?
2. *Which side of the street?* 马路哪一边?
3. *Which side of the intersection?* 十字路口的哪一边?
4. *Want me to drop you at the door?* 要我把你送到门口吗?
5. *That house (over) there?* 那边的那座房子吗?
6. *Is here okay?* 这里下车好吗?

Paying a taxi fare 付出租车车费

1. *Do you have change for a twenty?* 你能把一张20元的钞票兑开吗?
2. *Can you break a twenty?* 你能把一张20元的钞票兑开吗?
3. *All I have is a twenty.* 我只有一张20元的。
4. *Keep the change.* 不用找钱了。
5. *I need a receipt.* 我要一张发票。
6. *Give me a receipt.* 给我一张发票。

A taxi driver discussing payment 出租车司机谈付费

1. *Do you have smaller bills?* 你有小面额的钞票吗?
2. *Don't you have anything smaller?* 你有小面额的钞票吗?
3. *I can't break that.* 我兑不开。
4. *I'm sorry; I don't have (any) change.* 很抱歉,我没有零钱。
5. *Do you need a receipt?* 你需要发票吗?

Fashion Conversation 鲜活会话

Conversation 1

A: Hi, taxi!	A:嗨,出租车!
B: Please get in... Where to, ma'am?	B:请上车……女士,去哪里?
A: The railway station, please.	A:火车站。
B: OK. Here we go.	B:好的。我们走吧。
A: Excuse me. Do you think I can get there in time to catch the 11:30 train?	A:请问,我能赶上11点半的那班火车吗?
B: Well, let me see. Now it's 11:00 sharp. It's a long way to go. If I take the shortest route, we may come across a traffic jam. If I take a less heavy route, it will save us 10 or more minutes, but you'll have to pay more. Which do you prefer?	B:嗯,让我想想。现在正好是11点,这儿离火车站很远。如果走最近的路,可能会遇上交通堵塞。如果走不那么拥挤的路的话,可以节省10分钟甚至更多的时间,但您得多付些钱。您想走哪条路?
A: Are you sure that I can get there in time if we take the less heavy route?	A:如果走不那么拥挤的路,您敢肯定我能赶得上吗?
B: Generally speaking, we can if we go at this speed and nothing unexpected happens.	B:一般说来,如果按现在这个速度,路上又没有其他意外的事发生的话,能赶上。
A: How much more do I have to pay?	A:我得多付多少钱?
B: Compared to the shortest route, you may pay around 5 Euro more.	B:与走最近的路相比,您可得多付大约5欧元。
A: That's acceptable. No one wants to miss a train.	A:那行。没有人愿意赶不上火车。
B: OK... Here we are. We'll turn left at this cross. To go straight ahead is the shortest route.	B:那好……您看,我们在这个十字路口得往左拐了,直走到最近的路。
A: Thank you.	A:谢谢。

Conversation 2

A: Where is that?	A:请问去哪里?
B: Take me to the airport, please.	B:请带我去机场。
A: (*while driving*) Are you in a hurry?	A:(*驾驶中*)您赶时间吗?
B: I have to be there before 17:00.	B:我得在下午五点之前赶到那儿。
A: We'll make it except a jam. You know it's rush hour.	A:不塞车的话就能赶到,要知道现在可是高峰期。
B: There's an extra ten in it for you if you can get	B:如果您能让我准时赶到,我可以多给您10美元。

me there on time.

A: I'll do my best. | A:我尽力吧。

Conversation 3

A: You're new here, aren't you? | A:你初次到这里,对不对?

B: Yeah. How did you know? | B:是的,你是怎么知道的?

A: I can tell by your accent and you don't seem sure of where you are going. | A:我是根据你的口音,以及你似乎不太确定要到哪儿去判断出来的。

B: I have to admit I really don't know where I am going. I just want to visit some place here. | B:我不得不承认,我实在不知道要去哪儿。我只是想参观此地的某些地方。

A: Do you want my advice? | A:需要我的建议吗?

B: Sure. Where do you think I can go? | B:当然,你认为我可以到什么地方去呢?

A: Why not go to the shore. It's a great day to be in the beach. Lots of people there. | A:不妨去海边。今天到海边去最好了,那里有许多人。

Conversation 4

A: Taxi, Taxi. | A:出租车,出租车。

B: Yes, madam, where are you going? | B:好的,夫人,你去哪儿?

A: I am going to the Chinese Consulate General at 520, 12th Ave. | A:我到第12条大街520号的中国总领事馆。

B: Get in, please. | B:请上车。

A: Thank you. Can we get there in half an hour, sir? | A:谢谢。我们可以在半小时之内赶到吗,先生?

B: I am not sure, madam. Generally we can, but look at the traffic. It's the rush hour at noon. | B:说不定,夫人。一般来讲,可以在半小时内到达。但是你看现在的交通,正是中午最拥挤的时候。

A: I am leaving for Boston at 1:20 p.m. on a Greyhound. I'll have to go back to the Consulate General to pick up my baggage. | A:我将乘1:20的灰狗汽车去波士顿。我必须先回总领事馆取行李。

B: Goodness me. We are really in a hurry. | B:天哪,时间还真的很紧呢。

A: Can't we go faster? | A:能开快一点儿吗?

B: I am afraid not, madam. We'll have to observe the speed limit. We are in the center of town, you know. | B:恐怕不行,夫人。我们必须在限速内行驶。你知道,我们现在是在市中心。

On the Scene 身临其境 面面俱到

主题:埃伦乘坐出租车去上班,司机走的不是她通常所走的路线。请你看图,根据如下提供的关键词,将他们的对话写出来。

关键词语:short cut 捷径　　way *n.* 路;路线

trust *v.* 信任;信赖　　area *n.* 范围;区域

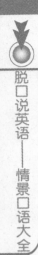

参考答案

Ellen: Where are you going?
Driver: I'm taking a short cut.
Ellen: But I don't usually go this way.
Driver: It's faster.
Ellen: I'm not sure.
Driver: Trust me. I know this area very well.
Ellen: Is it going to cost more?
Driver: Actually, it will be cheaper for you.
埃伦:您要开到哪里去?
司机:我是在抄近路。
埃伦:可是我通常不走这条路。
司机:走这条路比较快。
埃伦:我可不太确定。
司机:相信我。我对这一带很熟。
埃伦:这样车费会比较贵吗?
司机:其实会更便宜些。

★租车出行★ 6 Rent a Car

Words and Phrases 闪亮词语 点滴积累

price list 价目表
van 厢型车
full coverage 全险
a full tank of gas 一满箱的油
rent 租用，租借，租价
mileage 里程数
driver's license 驾驶执照
gallon 加仑
insurance 保险
receipt 收据
rental term 租期
service charge 手续费
renter 求租人
deposit 保证金
medium-sized 中型的
cost of gasoline 汽油费
rent-a-car office 租车行
manual transmission 手动档
automatic transmission 自动档

Useful Sentences 七彩精句 连点成线

Rent a car 租车

1. *I'd like to rent a car for a week.* 我想租辆车子，租1星期。
2. *I'd like to rent a car for three days.* 我想租辆车子，租3天。
3. *Something not too large.* 不要太大的。
4. *I'd like a car that's economical on gas.* 我要一辆省油的。
5. *I'll take the Buick.* 我要别克车。
6. *What are the rates per day?* 每天租金多少？
7. *What does this insurance cover?* 这项保险包括什么内容？

Return 还车

1. *Do I have to return the car here?* 在这里还车吗？
2. *Where are your other branches located?* 你们其他的分店在哪里？
3. *I will return it here.* 我会在这里还。
4. *I am here to return the car.* 我来这里还车。
5. *I am returning the car. My name is You-xin Li.* 我来还车，我叫李又新。
6. *Here's the car I rented last week. Sorry about the big dent in the door.* 这是我上星期租的车，很抱歉车门上有个大凹洞。

Checking a Car 检查汽车

1. *What's the problem?* 什么问题？
2. *Brakes are grabbing.* 刹车吱吱作响。
3. *Brakes aren't working very well.* 刹车不灵。
4. *The car is hard to start.* 汽车很难发动。
5. *The engine keeps backfiring all the time.* 发动机老是回火。
6. *The automatic window control doesn't work.* 自动窗户控制器坏了。
7. *The window won't wind up and down.* 这窗子摇不上也摇不下。
8. *My engine stalled.* 发动机发动不起来了。
9. *Could you do something about the clutch?* 你能不能修一下离合器？

Problems on the highway 车在公路上出了问题

1. *I need a tow truck.* 我需要牵引车把我的车拖走。
2. *I need a tow.* 我需要牵引车把我的车拖走。
3. *My car is a mile away.* 我的车在离这一英里的

地方。

4. *My car is near the interchange.* 我的车在立交桥附近。

5. *Do you know what the problem is?* 你知道问题出在哪里吗？

6. *When can you give me an estimate?* 你什么时候能告诉我大致的费用？

7. *When will it be ready?* 什么时候可把车修好？

When someone is arrested 某人被拘留时

1. *I didn't see a stop sign.* 我没有看到停车标志。
2. *I was only five(miles) over the limit.* 我只是超过限速五英里。
3. *What charge are you taking me in on?* 你指控我什么？
4. *What am I charged with?* 我犯了什么错？
5. *I demand to see my lawyer.* 我要见我的律师。
6. *You can't arrest me!* 你不能拘留我！
7. *What's the charge?* 你指控我什么？
8. *What's the rap?* 我错在哪里？
9. *What's the beef?* 你指控我什么？
10. *I didn't do anything.* 我什么错也没有。
11. *I didn't do anything wrong.* 我什么过失也没有。

Fashion Conversation 鲜活会话 由线到面

Conversation 1

A: Hi. I'm looking to rent a car for a week.
B: Are you at least 25 with a valid driver's license and a valid credit card?
A: Yes. And yes.
B: What model were you thinking about?
A: What's your economy model?
B: The Hyundai Accent. It's $ 135.99 per week plus taxes. All cars come with unlimited mileage.
A: Not bad. What's your high-end car?
B: A Ford Mustang convertible. It would suit you two young ladies very well!
A: Hmm. How much with taxes?
B: The base price for one week is $288.95. Plus two dollars per day for the license fee, and local taxes. The total is $327.94.

A：嗨。我想要租辆车，租一个星期。
B：你有25岁吗？带着有效的驾照跟有效的信用卡吗？
A：有，都带着呢。
B：你想要租什么款式的？
A：你们的经济型汽车是什么车？
B：现代汽车。一星期135.99美元，税另算。所有的车都没有里程限制。
A：不错。你们最好的车是什么车？
B：福特野马敞篷车。正好配你们两位年轻小姐。
A：嗯。连税多少钱？
B：基本的价钱是一个星期288.95美元。再加每天两美元的执照费，外加当地税，总共是327.94美元。

Conversation 2

A: Is the van ready?
B: Yes. We have it all ready for you. It's parked right outside. Come have a look.
A: Okay. Hey, this is really nice!
B: Yes, this is the Ford Windstar. It's very popular!
C: Yeah, I've seen them advertised.
B: Now, make a note here if you find any dents or scratches.
A: Well, it all looks pretty good, uh, there's small scratch right here.
B: Okay, just mark that on the form, and that way, we know when you return the car that you didn't

A：旅行车准备好了吗？
B：是的，已经全都为你们准备好了。就停在外边。过来看看吧。
A：好，嘿，真是不错。
B：对，这是一辆福特“风之星”，很流行的。
C：嗯，我在广告上见到过。
B：好，要是你找到任何划痕或刮伤的，就在这儿注明一下。
A：啊，看着都很不错，呃，这儿有一小道刮伤。
B：好，请在表格上注明一下，这样一来，等你还车的时候我们就知道你没有把车弄坏了。

cause the damage.

C: Oh, good idea. Well, I can't find anything else.

B: Good. Now, here's the key — and take a look inside and make sure everything's working alright.

A: Okay... Hey, it's got a full tank of gas!

B: Yes, we fill all the cars before they leave. But be sure you bring it back filled, because we charge you two dollars a gallon to fill it here.

A: Very good.

C:好主意,好了,别的找不到什么了。

B:好,现在给你钥匙,让你们到里面看看,确认一下每样东西是否都运行正常。

A:好的,嘿,油箱里的油加得满满的!

B:对,车辆离开前我们都把油加满的。不过,你还车的时候也得把它加满,因为你要是到这儿再加的话,就得花两块每加仑了。

A:很好。

Conversation 3

A: Where can I hire a limousine?

B: Over there on the left, ma'am. At the booth with the poster.

A: Oh, I see. ... Excuse me, could you call a limousine? I'd like to see the sights of the city.

B: With or without an interpreter?

A: Without, thank you.

A:我到哪儿可以租一辆高级轿车呢?

B:夫人,在左边那儿。就在海报的票亭那边。

A:哦,我懂了。……你可以叫一部高级轿车吗?我想到城里观光。

B:要不要一位翻译呢?

A:不用了,谢谢您。

Conversation 4

A: May I help you, sir?

B: Can I rent a car for just one day?

A: Yes, sir. What kind of car would you like?

B: I'd like a compact car that gets good mileage.

A: Yes, I see. Please fill out this form.

B: How much will you charge for the car?

A: It is $50 a day 11 cents a mile after the first 100 miles.

B: OK, I'll take it.

A: These are your keys. The car is parked over there. Spot No. 50.

A:你要租车吗,先生?

B:我想租辆车用一天,行吗?

A:行,先生。你想租哪种车?

B:一辆省油的小型车。

A:明白了。请你填好这张表格。

B:你怎么收费?

A:每一天收50美元,超过100英里每英里加11美分。

B:行,就这样吧。

A:给你车钥匙。车子停放在50号车位。

On the Scene 身临其境 面面俱到

主题:汤姆来到租车处想租一辆结实的小汽车。接待员向他推荐了一辆。请你看图,根据如下提供的关键词,将他们的对话写出来。

关键词语:reserve *n.* 储备　　recommend *v.* 推荐,介绍

compact *adj.* 结实的　　mileage *n.* 里程

参考答案

Receptor: May I help you?
Tom: Yes, I'd like to rent a car for the weekend.
Receptor: Have you already reserve one?
Tom: No, I haven't.
Receptor: OK. What kind of car would you like?
Tom: I want to rent a small compact car. Would you please recommend one that is cheap and easy to drive?
Receptor: Fine. Here you are.
Tom: Can you tell me the rate per day?
Receptor: Here is a list of our rates. It's $ 23 with unlimited mileage.

接待员:有什么可以效劳?
汤姆:我想租辆车过周末。
接待员:您有预约吗?
汤姆:没有。
接待员:好的。您想租什么样的?
汤姆:结实点儿的小车。您给我推荐一辆又便宜又好驾驶的好吗?
接待员:好的。您看这辆。
汤姆:每天租金多少?
接待员:这是我们的价目单,不限里程每天23美元。

★私人汽车★ 7 Private Car

Words and Phrases 闪亮词语 点滴积累

parking garage 停车库
car park; parking lot 停车场
indoor car park 室内停车场
washing bay; washing area 洗车场
bus station 公共汽车站
terminus; terminal 终点站
the departure station; station at the beginning of a bus line 始发站
car; sedan 小轿车
minibus 面包车(小型公共汽车)
jeep 吉普车
motor vehicle 机动车
chartered bus 包车
motorcycle 摩托车
three-wheeled automobile 三轮汽车
pedicab 人力三轮车
bike; bicycle 自行车
moped 两用车(机器,脚踏)
cart 手推车(两轮马车)

Useful Sentences 七彩精句 连点成线

Traffic rules 交规

1. *I had no problem with the U-turn?* 我调头做得也没问题。
2. *It is important to parallel park in the crowded city.* 在拥挤的城市,路边停车是很重要的。
3. *The DMV must treat you the same regardless of age, gender or race.* 车管所对待你必须与别人一样,不管年龄、性别和种族。
4. *If you have one serious mistake, or 5 small mistakes on your scorecard, you will fail the driving test.* 如果你路考的记分卡上记录一个严重错误或超过5个小错误,这次考试你就通不过了。
5. *You must turn on your turn signal at least 100 feet before the turn.* 在转弯之前至少100码处就应该打转向灯。
6. *Make a U-turn and go back the other way.* 掉个头往回走。
7. *Did you use the turn signals properly?* 你正确使用转向灯了吗?
8. *Not this time, but my tire hit the curb during a right turn.* 这次没有,但在我右拐弯的时蹭到了路沿。

About studying driver 关于学驾驶

1. *Are you going to teach me to drive soon?* 你打算很快教我开车吗?
2. *When I pull this knob, the engine starts.* 当我拉这个把手时,发动机就启动了。
3. *I'm going to my driver's course.* 我要去上驾驶员培训课。
4. *I'll register for driver's course right away.* 我马上就去报名参加驾驶员培训班。
5. *The insurance premiums are considerably lower if you take a driver's course.* 经过驾驶员培训班学习,要交的保险费就少多了。
6. *When you see a "STOP" sign, you have to come to a complete stop.* 看到"停车"标记时,必须完全停下来。
7. *You didn't observe the traffic light. You ran through the yellow light.* 你没遵守红绿灯,抢了黄灯。
8. *When a yellow light is shown, traffic which has not already entered the intersection must stop.* 当黄色号志灯亮时,车子未进入十字路口时,就必须停车了。
9. *You didn't put on the signal before you made the turn.* 转弯前,你没打方向灯。
10. *You cut the corner too short and ran over the curb.* 你转的弯太小,所以压到了安全岛。
11. *You need a little more practice.* 您需要多多练

习。

12. *You didn't look into the rear-view mirror before you moved into another lane.* 在你变换车道时，没有看后视镜。

13. *You should have made sure no car was coming from behind.* 一定要确定后面没有其他的汽车驶过来。

Talking about driving 谈开车

1. *We'll have to make a U-turn here.* 我们只好在这里掉头了。

2. *I'm trying to make up the twenty minutes.* 我想把耽搁的20分钟补回来。

3. *We've got to be careful. The road ahead is pretty icy/slippery.* 我们要小心点，前面的路面结满了冰/很滑。

4. *We'll have to slow down, the road ahead is under construction.* 我们要开慢一点，前面正在施工。

5. *I have been driving for 5 years.* 我开车已经有5年了。

6. *Let's find a car park nearby.* 在附近找个停车场吧。

7. *I've turned the front lights on, it's getting dark.* 天色暗了，我把前车灯打开。

8. *We'll have to keep to the right.* 我们必须靠右行驶。

9. *I always drive to work.* 我一直都是开车上班。

10. *I do a lot of city driving.* 我常在市内开车。

11. *I do a lot of country driving.* 我常在郊外开车。

12. *I'll slow down now.* 我要减速了。

13. *Do you like driving?* 你喜欢开车吗？

14. *How long have you been driving?* 你开车有多久了？

15. *What's the speed limit in the city?* 市区限速是多少？

16. *When did you learn to drive?* 你是什么时候学开车的？

17. *Are you sure we're on the right route?* 你确定我们没走错路？

Fashion Conversation 鲜活会话 由线到面

Conversation 1

A: Watch where you're going. You almost killed me! I'm learning to drive!

B: You turned right in front of me. Try using your turn signals next time.

A: Not so fast. You can't put this on me. You drive like a maniac.

B: Look, buddy, nobody got hurt, so drop it, OK? No harm, no foul.

A: You're lucky I'm short on time, or I'd... I'd...

B: You'd what?

A: I'd give you a piece of my mind.

B: Yeah, whatever.

A：开车的时候注意点儿，你差一点儿撞到我。我正在学车过程中。

B：你是在我前面右转的，下次转弯的时候记得用转向灯。

A：我速度又不快，你不能把责任归咎到我头上。你开起车来像个疯子。

B：嘿，朋友，我们都没有受伤，没出什么事比什么都好，你就别再说了，好吗？

A：算你走运，我没有时间与你理论了，否则我就……我就……

B：你就怎么样？

A：我就跟你好好理论理论。

B：是啊，随便你怎么样。

Conversation 2

A: This is my fitness certificate and this is my trainee's permit, sir.

B: OK. Come tomorrow to attend a lecture about driving rules. Then come here three times a week to learn basic skills of driving. Our course is from four to five every afternoon. Are Mon-

A：先生，这是我的健康证，这张是我的受训许可证。

B：好，明天来参加驾驶规则讲座，以后每周来这里3次学开车的基本技巧，我们每天下午4点到5点上课。星期一、四、五，你方便吗？

day, Thursday and Friday convenient to you?

A: Yes. That's a good time for me. What are you teaching me in addition to fundamental techniques of car operation?

B: Defensive driving, on-the-road driving, anticipation of possible dangerous acts by others, hazardous situations and special techniques to avoid them.

A: I see.

B: In this city you will be fined 200 yuan for a number of traffic violations.

A: What are they?

B: Driving with no lights at night, failing to heed traffic lights and speeding in excess of 60 kilometers per hour.

A: How do they know that I am not following the speed limit?

B: They have installed radar on the road.

A: Anything else?

B: You must keep in mind these interrelated parts and systems: the engine, fuel system, cooling system, electrical system, transmission system and suspension system.

A: Where is the brake and steering gear?

B: This is the steering gear and this is the brake.

A: I see. Should I inspect each part carefully each time before I drive?

B: Yes. That ensures safety.

A:方便,时间很合适,除了基本的行车操作技巧外,你还要教我什么?

B:防卫驾驶,路面驾驶,司机危险动作预知警讯,特殊情况及闪避的特殊技巧。

A:我知道了。

B:在本市内许多交通违规都要罚200元。

A:哪些违规?

B:夜间驾驶不开灯;不看红绿灯;时速超过60公里/小时。

A:他们怎样知道我超速?

B:在路旁装有测速器。

A:还有呢?

B:你必须记住这些相关部分及各种系统。这是引擎,燃油系统,冷却系统,通电系统,传递系统和悬置系统。

A:刹车和方向盘在哪里?

B:这是方向盘,这是刹车。

A:我明白了。开车之前,每个部位都要检查吗?

B:对,这样可以确保安全。

Conversation 3

A: I passed my driving test! The DMV gave me a real license. Now I can throw away my learner's permit!

B: Congratulations! BTW, is the parallel parking part of the test as hard as people say?

A: Not really. I still have trouble with the turn signals and doing the U-turn in a small space.

B: I heard it through the grape vine that you hit a lot of cones last time. Did you hit any orange safety cones this time?

A: Not this time, but my tire hit the curb during a right turn.

B: Did the tester let you keep the scorecard?

A: No, but that would be cool if she had.

B: Your tester was a woman?

A: Yeah, she liked my voice and said I was cute.

A:我通过了路考!车管所给我发了驾照。现在我可以把我的学车证扔掉了。

B:恭喜!顺便问一下,路边停车真的像人们说的那么难考吗?

A:不一定。我在打转弯灯和在窄的地方调头时还有点小毛病。

B:我听说你上次碰了好多隔离墩。这次你碰到橘黄色隔离墩了吗?

A:这次没有,但在我右拐弯时蹭到了路沿。

B:考官给你保留记分吗?

A:没有,但如果她记了那会很酷的。

B:考官是个女的?

A:是的,她喜欢我的声音还说我很可爱。

B: No wonder you passed! I have to go to help Jack pick out a dress for his big date with Ray.
A: Can I give you a lift?
B: Out of the question! Your driving tester girlfriend may get jealous!

B:怪不得你通过了!我得帮杰克去取衣服,他跟雷有重要约会。
A:我能送你去吗?
B:别想!你的考官女朋友也许会吃醋的!

On the Scene 身临其境 面面俱到

主题:夫妻俩人开车到城里买菜。半路上他们来到了加油站。请你看图,根据如下提供的关键词,将他们的对话写出来。

关键词语:gallon *n.* 加仑　　super *adv.* 非常　　coolant *n.* 冷冻剂

参考答案

Husband: Hi, darling, today is Independence Day. Let me take you to town for a look and then do the week's shopping.
Wife: Great! (*They get in their car*)
Husband: Oh, we need to go to the gas station first.
Wife: All right. Let's go to the Shell.
Husband: OK. 10 gallons of super, please.
Receptor: Yes, sir. 10 gallons of super. Oh, you need some coolant as well.
Husband: Fill it in, please.
Receptor: $ 18 in all.
Husband: Here is $ 20. Keep the change.
Receptor: Thank you.

丈夫:嗨,亲爱的,今天是独立日。我带你到城里看看,然后咱们去买下周的菜。
妻子:好极了。(*他们上了自己的汽车*)
丈夫:哎,咱们得先去一趟加油站。
妻子:好吧。咱们去贝壳加油站吧。
丈夫:好吧,请加10个加仑的高级汽油。
接待人员:好的,先生,10个加仑的高级汽油。哎呀,您也需要加些冷却剂了。
丈夫:请加吧。
接待人员:总共18美元。
丈夫:这是20美元。不用找零钱了。
接待人员:谢谢。

Travelling

CHAPTER

6

行者无疆

★旅行计划★ 1 Travelling Plan

Words and Phrases 闪亮词语 点滴积累

sightseeing trip 观光旅游
conducted tour 有导游的旅游
coach tour 乘游览车旅游
group tourist 团体旅游者
individual tourist 单个旅游者
escort 陪同人员
interpreter 翻译
local guide 地陪
national guide 全陪
sightseeing route 旅游路线
city tour 城市游
country tour 乡下游
natural scenery tour 自然景观游
departure 启程
itinerary 旅游线路
group size 组团人数
package tour 包价旅游

Useful Sentences 七彩精句 连点成线

Tour arrangement 旅游安排

1. *Can you arrange a trip for us?* 你能为我们安排一次旅行吗?
2. *How long would you like your trip?* 你们希望旅行多少天呢?
3. *There is a four-day tour to these cities.* 有一趟到这些城市的四日游。
4. *The tour includes the places of interest such as Window of the World and Chen Clan Academy.* 这个旅行包括世界之窗、陈家祠这样的名胜古迹。
5. *What is the price of the tour?* 旅行费用是多少?
6. *The tour includes the air fare, hotel accommodations and three meals each day.* 这次旅行包括了机票、旅馆住宿和每日三餐。
7. *Would you take a package tour or travel alone?* 你是参加包价旅行还是单独去?
8. *I can only be away for a week for a trip.* 我只有一周的时间进行一次旅行。
9. *How are you going, by air or by train?* 你准备怎么走,是乘飞机还是乘火车?
10. *Can I recommend the Ocean Tour to you? The places are worth seeing.* 我给你推荐海洋游好吗?那些地方值得一看。
11. *Can you give me a sightseeing guide book?* 能给我一本观光指南吗?
12. *What is the fee of guide per day?* 一天导游费是多少?

More about pleasure trips 关于娱乐旅行的另一些话

1. *I'll go on a tour of China during the first two weeks of May.* 在5月份前两星期我将去中国旅游。
2. *I'm going to fly to Beijing on May first.* 我5月1日飞往北京。
3. *I'll stay four days in Beijing to visit all the famous tourist attractions.* 我将在北京住四天,参观所有著名的旅游景点。
4. *I'm going to have one and half days in the biggest city of China.* 我在中国最大的城市要待一天半。
5. *I'll fly first class on a Boeing 747 from Beijing to Shanghai.* 我将坐波音747型飞机的一等舱从北京到上海。
6. *I'll take a 4-hour train ride from Shanghai to Nanjing.* 我将坐四个小时的火车从上海到南京。
7. *I've booked a room for three nights at the Jin Ling Hotel in the downtown area.* 我已经在市中心的金陵饭店订了房间,住三个晚上。
8. *After my visit to the ancient city, I'll sail down the Yangtse River and then along the Grand Canal to Hangzhou.* 访问古城以后,我将乘船沿长江航行,然后沿大运河航行去杭州。

9. *I'll have two days to do sightseeing in that beautiful city.* 我将在那个美丽的城市游览两天。

10. *After Hangzhou, I'll go straight to Hong Kong by air.* 游览过杭州后，我将坐飞机直接飞往香港。

11. *The flight will take about two hours and I'll arrive in Hong Kong for dinner.* 飞行大约需要两个小时，我将到香港吃晚饭。

12. *I'll spend the last two days shopping and visiting some friends in Hong Kong.* 最后两天时间，我将在香港买点东西，看看朋友。

13. *I'll leave for home on May 14th and arrive in San Francisco on the same day.* 5月14日我动身回国，并在同一天到达旧金山。

More about business trips 关于工作旅行的另一些话

1. *She plans to go to the annual industrial exposition in Shanghai in April.* 她计划参加4月份在上海举行的一年一度的工业博览会。

2. *On her way to China, she's going to stop in Tokyo to visit he firm's office there.* 去中国的途中，她将在东京停留，访问公司在那里的办事处。

3. *During her stay in Shanghai, she's going to conduct a training program for her firm's local staff.* 在上海期间，她将为公司的当地雇员举办培训班。

4. *After her visit in Shanghai, she's going to meet with some government officials in Beijing.* 在上海访问以后，她将去北京会见一些政府官员。

5. *Since she's been to Beijing quite a few times, she has no plans for sightseeing on this trip.* 因为她已去过北京许多次了，所以这次她不打算进行参观游览。

6. *She will return to the U. S. by way of Seoul.* 她将经由汉城回美国。

Fashion Conversation 鲜活会话 由线到面

Conversation 1

A: I want to travel around Europe for a week. I know where to go, but I do not know how to get there.

B: Would you like to call my travel agent? She can arrange an itinerary for you very nicely. Just tell her where you want to go, and she will take care of how to get you to each destination.

A: Thanks. What's her phone number?

B: 88129607.

A：我要去欧洲旅行一星期。虽然我知道要去哪里，但我不知道怎么去。

B：你要不要打电话给我的旅行代理人？她可以帮你把行程安排好。只要告诉她你要去哪里，她就会帮你把每个目的地的行程安排好。

A：谢谢。她的电话号码是多少？

B：88129607。

Conversation 2

A: Hello, Tom! I need you to book me up with a tour.

B: Where do you want to go this time?

A: My girlfriend want to go somewhere exotic.

B: Well, it's peak season, but we do have some good 4 and 5-day tours.

A: We're into tropical islands.

B: There's a tour to Cebu in the Philippines.

A: But don't we have to go through Manila?

B: Yeah. You can catch a flight from Manila to Cebu.

A: Sounds complicated. I'd rather just take one

A：你好，汤姆！我需要你帮我安排旅游行程。

B：你这次想去哪里？

A：我女友想要去个有异国情调的地方。

B：嗯，现在是旅游旺季，但我们的确有些不错的为期四、五天的行程。

A：我们都喜欢热带的岛屿。

B：有个行程是到菲律宾的宿务。

A：那我们不是要经过马尼拉吗？

B：是的。你们要从马尼拉转机到宿务。

A：听起来挺麻烦的，我宁可到不需要转机的地方。

flight.

B: Why not go to Bali? It's cheap right now.
B:那为何不去巴厘岛？现在去那儿玩很便宜。

A: But Indonesia is dangerous right now.
A:但印尼现在很危险。

B: Bali hasn't been affected at all. It's business as usual.
B:巴厘岛一点也没受到影响。观光业一切如常。

A: Tell me more.
A:说详细点。

B: It's a 4-night, 5-day tour including a five-star hotel and a half-day spa experience.
B:这是个五天四夜的行程,包括五星级饭店住宿以及半天的温泉之旅。

A: Wow! I bet my girlfriend would like that.
A:哇！我敢打赌我女朋友一定会喜欢的。

B: Don't tell her about it. Surprise her.
B:不要告诉她,给她个惊喜。

Conversation 3

A: Good morning!
A:上午好！

B: Good morning!
B:上午好！

A: What can I do for you?
A:需要帮忙吗？

B: My wife and I want to see the places of interest in Shenzhen, Guangzhou and Zhuhai. Can you arrange a tour for us?
B:我和我的夫人想看看深圳、广州和珠海的名胜古迹,你能为我们安排一次旅行吗？

A: How long would you like to stay in these cities?
A:你们愿意在这些城市待几天？

B: Well, three days.
B:嗯,三天。

A: There is three-day package tour. You will have 3 full days in the cities. It is a general tour of the cities. The itinerary includes the places of interest such as Window of the World, China Folk Culture Village, Chen Clan Academy, Southern Yue Tomb, and Gongbei Market.
A:有一个三天的包价旅游。你们将在这些城市里待满三天,是对整个城市进行游览的旅行。旅行路线包括像世界之窗、中国民俗文化村、陈家祠、南越王墓、拱北市场等名胜古迹。

B: That sounds good. How much is the tour?
B:听起来不错,这个旅行多少钱？

A: 2000 for each person.
A:每人2000元？

B: What does it include?
B:它包括什么？

A: It includes your air fare, your hotel accommodations and three meals each day.
A:它包括机票、旅馆住宿和每日三餐。

B: Could we have you make all the necessary plane, hotel, and tour reservations?
B:我们能让你们安排预订必要的飞机,饭店和旅程吗？

A: Yes, We could do that for you.
A:是的,我们可以为你们做这一切。

Conversation 4

A: When do you plan to go to the fair in China.
A:你计划什么时候去中国的交易会？

B: I will leave for the Guangzhou Fair for Export Commodities in the second week of October. I've already faxed my arrival date and time to Ms. Tan in our office in Hong Kong. She will take care of my hotel reservations and transportation both in Hong Kong and in Guangzhou.
B:我将在10月第二个星期动身去参加广州出口商品交易会。我已经把我的到达日期和时间传真给我们香港办事处的谭女士了。她会为我预订好在香港和广州的旅馆房间以及安排交通往返。

A: Is Ms. Tan going to accompany you on your visit to Guangzhou?
A:谭女士将陪你去广州访问吗？

B: Yes, she is. It's she who has been in day-to-day contact with our Chinese suppliers and trade officials there. She's going to participate in all my business meetings in China. As you know, she speaks perfect Cantonese and Mandarin. I'd have a hard time there without her assistance.

B: 她陪我去。我们与中国供货商和贸易官员的日常联系都是由她负责的。我在中国的所有业务会见她都要参加。你知道,她的广东话和普通话都讲得很好。没有她的帮助,我在那儿会很困难的。

A: She's the kind of person who never neglects any details. I remember very well how she made my visit to China last year so fruitful. With her at your side, you won't have to worry about a thing.

A: 她是那种从不忽略任何细节的人。去年她使我访问中国时收获很大,我记忆犹新。有她在你身边,你什么也不用担心。

Conversation 5

A: How many times have you been to China, Mr. Frazer?

A: 弗雷泽先生,你来中国多少次了?

B: It's my third trip to China this year.

B: 这次是我今年第三次来中国了。

A: How long are you going to stay in this country this time?

A: 这次你打算在中国住多久?

B: My tentative plan is to stay ten to fifteen days. After our talks, I'm going to Dalian to make a presentation about a new process for industrial waste water treatment. My company hopes to get the contract for the building of a plant in that city.

B: 我目前的计划是住10到15天。我们会谈结束后,我将去大连做一个有关工业废水处理新工艺的报告。我的公司希望获得在那个城市建厂的合同。

A: Are you going to visit your joint venture in Jinan?

A: 你准备去看看你们在济南的合资企业吗?

B: Yes. That'll be my third stop. I'm going to help them solve some problems with the plant's control system. After Jinan, I'm going to Wuxi to have a meeting with a design institute there to discuss some technical matters concerning the design of a pharmaceutical plant.

B: 去的。那是我的第三站。我要去帮助他们解决工厂控制系统的一些问题。济南之后,我要去无锡和那儿一所设计院举行会议,讨论有关一家制药厂设计的技术问题。

A: It's a busy schedule. I wonder if you've had any chance to do some sightseeing in this country.

A: 你的时候很紧啊。不知道你有没有机会在这个国家游览过?

B: It's a shame I haven't. On my last two trips here, I barely had enough time to finish my business. And then I had to catch some meetings in other countries.

B: 可惜得很,我还没游览过。我上两次来的时候,只有时间办完公务,然后还得赶到其他国家开些会。

A: As you know, there are so many things to see in China that I think you should take advantage of the chance while you're here. It might be a good thing for you to combine business with some pleasure.

A: 你知道,中国有许多可看的东西,趁你在这儿,应该利用这个机会。把你的业务和旅游结合起来是个好主意。

B: I will. As a matter of fact, I plan to do a little sightseeing in Wuxi and Suzhou when I finish my work. I've heard so much about Taihu Lake and the extraordinary gardens there. I'm not going to let myself leave without seeing them this time.

B: 我会的。实际上,我打算完成工作后在无锡和苏州游览参观一下。我听到过许多关于太湖和那儿美丽庭院的介绍。这回我不会不参观一下就走的。

A: That's good. Autumn is the best time of the year for you to enjoy the scenery in the area south of the Yangtse River. I hope you'll have an enjoyable as well as a successful trip in China.

B: Thank you, Mr. Mao.

A:好。秋天是一年之中欣赏江南美景的最佳时间。我希望你在中国的旅行既成功又愉快。

B:谢谢你,毛先生。

On the Scene 身临其境 面面俱到

主题:杰克向玛丽打听那个城市的名胜。玛丽建议他坐车去博物馆。请你看图,根据如下提供的关键词,将他们的对话写出来。

关键词语:museum *n.* 博物馆　　be interested in 对……感兴趣

参考答案

Jack: Can you tell me something about interesting places in this city?
Mary: Well, what kind of things are you interested in?
Jack: I'm interested in history.
Mary: Why not go to the museum?
Jack: Good idea. Can I walk there?
Mary: You'd better take a bus or take a taxi. It's about one hour's walk from here.
Jack: Oh, thank you.

杰克:跟我说说这个城市的名胜好吗?
玛丽:嗯,你对什么感兴趣?
杰克:历史。
玛丽:为什么不去博物馆?
杰克:好主意。我能步行到那儿吗?
玛丽:你最好坐公交车或者打车。差不多得走1小时呢。
杰克:谢谢。

★下榻宾馆★ 2 Live in Hotel

Words and Phrases 闪亮词语 点滴积累

five-star hotel 五星饭店
four-star hotel 四星饭店
three-star hotel 三星饭店
first-class hotel 高级饭店
luxurious hotel 豪华级饭店
super deluxe hotel 超豪华级饭店
average hotel 中等饭店
apartment hotel 公寓式饭店
tourist hotel 旅游饭店
economy hotel 经济饭店
holiday hotel 假日饭店
vacationing hotel 度假饭店
family hotel 家庭饭店
all-suite hotel 全套房饭店
up-to-date hotel 现代化饭店
garden hotel 花园饭店
hotspring hotel 温泉饭店
floating hotel 水上饭店
beach hotel 海滩饭店
airport hotel 机场饭店
railway station hotel 车站旅馆
residential hotel 住家旅馆
yacht hotel 游艇旅馆
bungalow hotel 平房旅馆
motor hotel; motel 汽车旅馆
parador（西班牙）古建筑式旅馆
mom-and-pop hotel 夫妻旅馆
all-couples resort 情侣旅馆
youth hotel 青年旅馆
convention hotel 会议旅馆

Useful Sentences 七彩精句 连点成线

Special requests at a hotel 向旅馆提出具体要求

1. *I'd like a room at the front.* 我想要一间在旅馆正面的客房。
2. *I'd like a suite.* 我想要一个套间。
3. *I'd like a wake-up call, please.* 请给我安排叫醒电话。
4. *I'm staying the weekend.* 我要在这过周末。

Checking in 登记入住

1. *Could I extend my stay here for another night/until next Tuesday?* 我能在这里多住一晚吗/住到下星期二吗?
2. *May I deposit my valuables with your safe?* 我可把贵重物品存放在你们的保险箱吗?
3. *Will you please fill in this registration card?* 请你填张住宿登记卡好吗?
4. *Excuse me, sir. You have missed your passport number here, please complete it.* 抱歉,先生,你这里忘了填护照号码,请补上去。
5. *Your room is 1513, the bellboy will take your luggages and show you the way.* 你的房间是1513号,服务生会替你提行李,带你过去。
6. *I am terribly sorry about that, but we really can't help.* 我感到非常抱歉,但我们实在是爱莫能助。
7. *I wish we could help you, but during this peak season, most hotels find it difficult to accommodate all their guests.* 我希望我们能帮得上忙,现在是旺季,大多数的饭店实在无法容纳它们所有的客人。

Completing the hotel check-in 办完住店手续

1. *Here is your key.* 这是您客房的钥匙。
2. *Do you need a bellboy?* 你要侍者替你搬行李吗?
3. *I'll have someone bring your luggage up.* 我叫人把您的行李搬上去。
4. *Enjoy your stay.* 希望您过得愉快。

Checking out 结账离开旅馆

1. *The front desk manager has agreed to extend a 10% discount for me when I checked in.* 那位前台经理在我住进来时，答应算我九折。
2. *Excuse me sir, we don't accept personal check.* 抱歉，先生，我们不接受个人支票。
3. *Your credit card has expired/is too blur, we have to check the Card's Agent for their authorization.* 你的信用卡已过期/字迹模糊，我们得送往信用卡代理商，请他们检查认可。
4. *Please arrange transport for me to go to the airport at 11:00 a.m..* 请为我准备护照，我早上11点要到机场。
5. *Please have my luggage brought down.* 请把我的行李搬下去。
6. *Please call me a taxi.* 请给我叫一辆出租车。
7. *Thank you for staying at our hotel, sir. We hope you will stay with us again on your next trip.* 先生，谢谢您对我们旅馆的惠顾，希望您下次重游此地时，仍再予惠顾！

Fashion Conversation 鲜活会话 由线到面

Conversation 1

A: When I came back to my room today, my key wouldn't work.
A：今天回房间的时候，我的钥匙不能用。

B: That happens sometimes. I'll re-code it.
B：偶尔会发生这种情况。我会重新编码的。

A: Thanks. While I'm here, I'd like to change some money, too.
A：谢谢。既然来了，我还想换一些钱。

B: Certainly. Do you have cash or traveler's checks?
B：可以。你是现金还是旅行支票？

A: Traveler's checks. One more thing. Can I stay an extra night?
A：旅行支票。还有一件事。我可以多住一晚吗？

B: Let me see if the room is open... yes, it is. I'll change your reservation.
B：我看看这个房间有没有空着……，有，有的。我会更改你的订房记录。

A: Hello, I was wondering how I could get an outside line.
A：喂，我想知道怎么打外线电话。

B: For a local number, just dial nine, and then the number.
B：拨本地电话，先拨9，然后再拨电话号码就行了。

A: And if it's long-distance?
A：如果是长途呢？

B: You can dial directly by dialing nine, one, and then the area code and number.
B：你可以直拨9、1，然后拨区号和电话号码。

A: Actually, I want to use a calling card.
A：事实上，我想用电话卡。

B: No problem. Dial nine, one, and then your calling card number.
B：没问题。拨9、1，然后拨你的电话卡号码。

Conversation 2

A: What time is check-out?
A：退房时间是几点？

B: Noon.
B：中午12点。

A: OK. Is breakfast included with the room?
A：好。早餐含在房价里吗？

B: No, I'm afraid not. Here's your key. You'll be in room twelve-o-three.
B：恐怕没有。这是你的钥匙。你的房间号是1203。

A: My friend is coming later this afternoon. Could you leave a key for her, in case I'm not here?
A：我朋友下午会晚点儿到。你可以留把钥匙给她吗，以免我不在这里？

B:Sure. Just write her name and your room number on this envelope, and I'll see that she gets it.

B:当然。把她的名字跟你的房间号码写在这信封上,我会亲自交给她。

Conversation 3

A:Good afternoon! Welcome to our hotel.

B:Good afternoon! I'd like to have two suites and ten single rooms, please.

A:Have you made a reservation?

B:Yes, we have booked them for our tour group from the United States. I'm Wang Hai. I'm from China International Travel Service.

A:Oh, I'm sorry. There is no reservation from your service.

B:I'm sure we have made a reservation. Could you check again a reservation for Friday for the tour group from the United States?

A:All right, Let me check again. Ah, yes, two suits and ten single rooms from China International Travel Service.

C:Do the rooms have a bath? I feel like taking a bath right now.

A:Yes, every room is equipped with a bath, a telephone and an air-conditioner.

C:That's good!

A:Can I see your passports, please?

C:Yes, there are our passports.

A:Thank you. Here are your passports. Please fill in these registration forms.

C:The registration forms are finished. Shall we have our keys to the rooms.

A:Of course. Here are the keys to your rooms. Your rooms are on the 3rd floor. The bellboy will take you to your rooms.

C:Thanks.

B:I guess you must be tired after a long trip. If there's nothing else you want, I will be leaving. I will meet you at the lobby on the ground floor at seven o'clock tomorrow morning for your breakfast. You can take a good rest tonight.

C:I don't think there is anything else. You have been very considerate. Thank you very much.

B:You are welcome. Enjoy your stay. See you tomorrow.

C:See you tomorrow.

A:下午好,欢迎光临我们酒店。

B:下午好,我想要两个套间,10个单人房。

A:你们预定了吗?

B:是的,我们已经为我们来自美国的旅游团预订了房间,我是王海,是中国国际旅行社的工作人员。

A:噢,对不起,贵旅行社没有预订。

B:我确信我们预订了。请再查一查,是为来自美国旅行团预订的,时间是星期五。

A:好吧,让我再查一查,啊,是的,中国国际旅行预订了两个套间,10个单人间。

C:房间带有浴室吗?我现在就想洗个澡。

A:有,每个房间带有浴室、电话和空调。

C:太好了!

A:可以看一看你们的护照吗?

C:可以,这是我们的护照。

A:谢谢,护照还给你们。请填写登记表。

C:登记表填完了,我们可以拿钥匙了吗?

A:当然可以。这些是你们房间的钥匙。你们的房间在3楼,服务员会把你们带到你们的房间。

C:谢谢!

B:我想经过一段长距离旅程之后,你们一定感到很疲倦吧,如果没有什么事情可以帮忙的话,我要走了。我会在明天早上7点钟在一楼大厅等待大家去进早餐,你们今晚可以好好休息一下。

C:我想没有什么事情了,你想得非常周到,谢谢你!

B:不客气,祝你们过得愉快,明天见。

C:明天见。

Conversation 4

A: Good morning. The Wang Fujing Hotel. How may I help you?	A: 早上好！王府井酒店。请问有什么需要吗？
B: Good morning. I'd like to book a room for Friday night and Saturday night.	B: 早上好！我想预订周五和周六两晚的房间。
A: Certainly. What kind of room would you like?	A: 当然可以。请问你想订什么样的房间？
B: A single room please. I hope you're not fully booked.	B: 一个单人间。房间没有订满吧？
A: A single room? That's fine. In whose name shall I make the booking?	A: 一个单人间，是吗？好的。用谁的名字预订呢？
B: Jones. According to your website, the nightly rate is $50, including breakfast.	B: 琼斯。你们网站上说，一夜的费用是50美元，包括早餐。
A: We offer a 20% discount for guests staying on Friday and Saturday. The total cost will be $80, including breakfast.	A: 对周五和周六的客人，我们打8折。总费用是80美元，包括早餐。
B: Thank you very much. I look forward to seeing you on Friday.	B: 非常感谢。希望周五能见到你。
A: Could I just take your credit cad number please? I should mention that there is a cancellation charge of $20.	A: 能给我你的信用卡号吗？我要说一下，如果取消预订的话，要收取消费20美元。
B: That's fine. My credit card number is...	B: 没问题。我的信用卡号是……

Conversation 5

A: I'll put your bags down here. Now let me show you some of the features of this room.	A: 我把行李放在这里。现在让我来介绍一下房间的设施。
B: OK.	B: 好。
A: Your room safe is in here. We suggest you keep all your valuables in the safe.	A: 房间的保险柜在这里。我们建议你把贵重的东西放在保险柜里。
B: I'll put them in right now. How does it work?	B: 我现在就放进去。这要怎么用？
A: Close the door, and input a four number code. That will lock it, and you input the code again to open it.	A: 关门，然后输入四位数字的密码。保险柜就锁起来了，你再输入一次密码就可以开了。
B: How about TV?	B: 电视呢？
A: The TV is here. Basic cable is included, and we have pay-per-view movies as well.	A: 电视在这里。包含了基本的有线频道，还有按次计费的电影频道。
B: Is there anywhere I can check my e-mail?	B: 我可以在哪里查我的电子邮件？
A: There is a high-speed Internet connection in the room.	A: 房间内有一条高速的因特网联接。
B: I don't have a computer.	B: 我没有电脑。
A: In that case, you can use our business center. There are computers there.	A: 那样的话，你可以使用我们的商务中心。那里有很多电脑。
B: I assume it has a fax machine as well.	B: 我想那里应该也有传真机。
A: Yes, everything you need. Now let me explain about the sheets.	A: 是的，你需要的都有。现在我说一下这些床单。
B: Is there something special?	B: 有什么特别之处吗？

A:To conserve water, you can put this car on your bed if you don't want the sheets washed.
A:为了节约用水,如果你不想洗床单的话,就把这张卡放在床上。

B:You'll change the sheets otherwise?
B:否则就会换洗床单?

A:That's right.
A:没错。

B:I see... All part of saving the environment! Here's something for you. Thanks for your help.
B:我懂了……这都是为了保护环境!这是给你的(给他小费)。谢谢你的帮忙。

Conversation 6

A:Good Evening, sir. May I help you?
A:你好,先生。我能帮助你吗?

B:Yes, do you have a room for two people?
B:你们有双人房间吗?

A:Surely. Would you like a king or queen-sized beds?
A:当然有。你要特大号还是大号床?

B:A queen-sized bed would be fine. It's just for my wife and myself. How much will the room be?
B:大号床就行。只有我太太和我两个人。房间多少钱?

A:That will be $48 plus tax.
A:48 美元外加税。

B:Does that include a Senior Discount?
B:老年人折扣包括在内吗?

A:No, it doesn't. That discount applies to those who are 60 years or older.
A:不包括。这个折扣只适用于60岁或60岁以上的人。

B:That's us. We are both over 60.
B:我们就是。我们俩都过60岁了。

A:I would never have guessed you're that old! Of course, you'll be given the Senior Discount of 10%. That would make the cost of your room $43.20.
A:真看不出您那么大年纪了。当然,你们享受10%的老年人折扣。这样你们的房费是43.20美元。

B:That's very reasonable. Is it a non-smoking room?
B:这很合理。是禁烟房间吗?

A:Yes. We have a non-smoking room with a queen-sized bed. The control for the climate control system is beside the entry door, and there is a refrigerator with beverages and snacks for your enjoyment. Will you pay by cash or credit card?
A:是的。这是一间大号床的禁烟房。室温环境控制系统调节器在进门旁边,冰箱里有饮料、小食品供取用。您是付现金还是用信用卡付款?

B:Credit Card. Here it is. I'll be making some phone calls this evening. Does the room have a direct-dial phone?
B:信用卡。这就是我的卡。今晚我要打几个电话。房间里有直拨电话吗?

A:Yes. You can call anywhere in the world from your room. The instructions are on the desk by the telephone. For long distant calls you can either use your phone company charge card or you can charge it to your room. All local calls are free. I'll keep an open ticket on your credit card and you can settle the account when you check out in the morning. Please fill out this registration card for me and we will get you right up to your room.
A:有的。你可以从房间里给世界各地打电话。使用说明在电话旁边的桌子上。打长途电话,你可以用你的电话公司计费卡,也可以计入房费。本地电话免费。我给你写一份空白信用卡付费单,明天早上你离店时再结清账。请填一下这份登记单,我们马上送你去房间。

B:(*After a pause*) There, that's complete. Do I sign it here?
B:(*稍后*)好了,填全了。我要在这儿签名吗?

A: Yes, right on that line. Thank you. And now sign this credit card ticket, please. Thank you again. Here's the key to your room. Take the elevator right over there and go to the tenth floor. The room will be down the hall to your right after you exit the elevator. Enjoy your stay with us, Mr. Johnson.

B: Thank you. You have been very helpful.

A:对,就在那条线上,谢谢。现在请签一下这张信用卡付费单,谢谢。这是你的房间钥匙。坐那边的电梯到十层,出电梯向右,房间就在楼厅前面。祝你们在我们旅馆愉快,约翰逊先生。

B:谢谢,麻烦你了。

On the Scene 身临其境 面面俱到

主题:格林先生来到阳光大酒店入住。接待员热情地接待了他。请你看图,根据如下提供的关键词,将他们的对话写出来。

关键词语:reasonably *adv.* 适度地　　parlour *n.* 营业室
staff *n.* 全体职员　　discount *n.* 折扣
access *n.* 入门　　bar *n.* 障碍物

参考答案

Receptor: Good afternoon. Welcome to Sunshine Hotel.
Mr. Green: Thank you.
Receptor: How many pieces of luggage do you have?
Mr. Green: Just these three.
Receptor: Two suitcases and an attache case. Is that right?
Mr. Green: Yes, that's all.
Receptor: May I help you to your room?
Mr. Green: Yes.
Receptor: May I help you with your attache case?
Mr. Green: Well, I'll take that case myself.
Receptor: Yes. May I have your room number, sir?
Mr. Green: Room 1201.

Receptor: Thanks. Please follow me and come this way. This is your room. After you, sir. May I put your suitcases here?

Mr. Green: Sure. Just put them anywhere.

Receptor: Here is your room key. Anything else I can do for you, sir?

Mr. Green: No, thanks. If I need any help, I will call you.

接待员:下午好。欢迎光临阳光大酒店。

格林先生:谢谢。

接待员:您有几件行李?

格林先生:只有这3件。

接待员:两个旅行箱和一个公文包,对吗?

格林先生:是的,就这些。

接待员:我送您去房间好吗?

格林先生:好的。

接待员:您的公文包要我拿吗?

格林先生:噢,我自己来吧。

接待员:好的。先生,您的房间号是多少?

格林先生:1201房间。

接待员:谢谢。请跟着我走这边。这是您的房间。先生,您先走。我可以把旅行箱放在这儿吗?

格林先生:当然可以。随便放吧。

接待员:这是房间的钥匙。还有别的事吗,先生?

格林先生:没有了,谢谢。如果需要帮助,我将叫你。

★宾馆服务★ 3 Hotel Service

Words and Phrases 闪亮词语 点滴积累

registration card 登记卡
reception counter 前台
room service 房间服务
limousine service 接送服务
call a cab 叫计程车
double bed 双人床
twin beds 两张单人床
single room 单人间
suite 套房
bellboy 男侍,侍者
maid 女侍
bell captain 侍者的领班
with bath 有淋浴设备
first-rate hotel 一流旅馆
emergency exit 紧急出口
local call 市内电话
long distance call 长途电话
main dining 主要餐厅
quilt 被子
blanket 毛毯;毯子
sheet 床单
bedspread 床罩
pillow 枕头
pillowcase;pillowslip 枕套
slippers 拖鞋
bath room 浴室
bath tub 浴缸
toilet paper 手纸
mirror 镜子
flush toilet 抽水马桶

Useful Sentences 七彩精句 连点成线

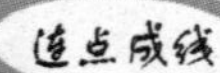

Having breakfast in one's room 在个人的房间用早餐

1. *I would like to have breakfast served in my room.* 我想要在我的房间里用早点。
2. *I want to see a menu/have both jam and butter with my toast.* 我要看一下菜单/我的土司要夹果酱和奶油。
3. *Come in, the door isn't locked.* 请进,门没锁。
4. *Please put everything on this table.* 请把所有的餐点放在这张餐桌上。
5. *Your tea is in this electric percolator, if you plug this cord into the wall socket, it will stay hot.* 你的茶在电动过滤器里面,若你把这个插头插入墙上的插座,它就会保温。
6. *Would you please sign this chit ma'am?* 太太,请你在这张账单上签一下名好吗?

Availing oneself of a hotel's assorted facilities 利用旅馆的各种设备

1. *Could I buy some stamps for my letters and postcards?* 我能买一些贴在信封和风景明信片上面用的邮票吗?
2. *I would like to have my shoes polished/my coat pressed.* 我想找人擦皮鞋/熨西装。
3. *I want to rent a TV set/cash my traveler's checks.* 我想要租一台电视机/把旅行支票兑换成现金。
4. *Could you wake me up at six tomorrow morning.* 请你明早六点叫我起床。
5. *Room service, please bring me another blanket.* 房间服务部,请给我另外送来一条毯子。

Fashion Conversation 鲜活会话 由线到面

Conversation 1

A: Good morning, sir. May I help you?
B: Yes. I'd like to send a fax to China. Do you have such kind of service?
A: Of course.
B: That's great! This is the main message.
A: Is this the code number of the receiver?
B: Yes. Will you please put on the code number of your center? In case they want to send me a fax.
A: Yes, I will. Would you please tell me what your room number is?
B: Room 201.
A: Just a moment, sir.
...
A: Thank you for waiting, sir. It is 60 yuan. Overseas fax rate are 20 yuan per minute with a minimum three-minute charge. This is your receipt.
B: Thank you very much.
A: You are welcome, sir.

A:早上好,先生。我能为您做点什么?
B:我想发一个传真到中国。你们有这种服务吗?
A:有的。
B:太好了!这是正文。
A:这是接收方的传真号码吗?
B:是的。你能把你们中心的传真号码写上吗?以免他们要给我发传真。
A:好的,我会的。您能告诉我您的房间号码是多少吗?
B:201 房间。
A:请稍等,先生。
……
A:谢谢您等了那么久,先生。一共 60 元。海外传真费用为每分钟 20 元,最低按三分钟收费。这是您的收据。
B:非常感谢。
A:不用谢,欢迎下次再来,先生。

Conversation 2

A: I've locked myself out of the room. May I borrow a duplicate key?
B: Don't worry, sir. I'll open the door for you.
(*She opens the door with a reserve key*)
A: Thank you very much. Sometimes I'm quite absentminded.
B: It doesn't matter, sir. What else can I do for you?
A: Ah, I'm afraid there's coming wrong with the TV set. The picture is wobbly. And I had called the maintenance department yesterday evening. They said they would send a electrician in ten minutes. And I had waited till this morning, and the repairman didn't come. I don't know how they could explain this. But if they don't repair the TV set by this noon, I'll call the manager.
B: I'm sorry to hear that. May I have a look at it?
A: Here it is.
B: (*Tries to fix it, but in vain*) I'll call the maintenace department for you. Please wait just a few

A:我把我自己锁在门外了。你能借给我备用的钥匙吗?
B:不要着急,先生。我给您开门。
(*她用备用钥匙打开了门*)
A:非常感谢!有时我真是心不在焉的。
B:没关系,先生。我还能为您做些什么吗?
A:噢,恐怕我的电视机出了点儿问题。画面摇摆,不稳定。我昨天晚上给维修部打了电话,他们说过十分钟就来一位电工。结果我等到今天早上,修理工都还没来。我不知道他们怎么解释这事。但是如果他们中午之前还不修电视的话,我就打电话给他们的经理。
B:听到这件事真对不起。我可以看一下电视机吗?
A:你看吧。
B:(*想修好它,但无济于事*)我替您给维修部打个电话。请等几分钟。

minutes.	
A: OK. I trust you.	A:好。我相信你。
(*Ten minutes later, there is a knock on the door*)	(*十分钟以后,有人敲门*)
C: May I come in?	C:可以进来吗?
A: Come in, please.	A:请进。
C: The TV set is not working well. Is that right, sir?	C:电视机坏了,是吗,先生?
A: No, it isn't.	A:是的。
C: Let me have a look. (*Finishes the repairing and checks other electric facilities in the room*) Sir, everything is OK now.	C:让我看一看。(*修理完了又检查了房里的其他电器设备*)现在一切都好了,先生。
A: What efficiency! Thanks a lot. But why you didn't come yesterday evening?	A:效率真高!多谢了。但是你们为什么昨天晚上不来呢?
C: I'm awfully sorry for that. We got the wrong room number. Sorry!	C:实在是太抱歉了。我们记错了房间号码。对不起。
A: That's OK.	A:没关系。

Conversation 3

A: Good morning, madam. I'm the bellman. I'll get the baggage up to your room.	A:早上好,夫人。我是行李员。我会把行李送到您的房间去的。
B: Thank you very much.	B:非常感谢。
A: Are these three pieces all yours?	A:这三件行李都是您的吗?
B: Yes.	B:是的。
A: Let me carry them for you.	A:让我来搬。
B: Thanks. I can take this briefcase.	B:谢谢。我可以拿这个手提箱。
A: Oh, leave it to me. I'll do that for you. This way, please. Here we are. Please take this elevator to the seventh floor. The floor attendant will meet you at your elevator entrance there and show you to Room 720. I'll take the baggage elevator and get your baggage up to your room.	A:噢,我来吧。我会替您搬的。请走这边。我们到了。请乘这部电梯上七楼。楼面服务员会在电梯门口迎接您,领您到720房间的。我乘行李电梯,把您的行李送到房间去。
B: Very good. See you then.	B:很好。回头见。
A: See you in a minute.	A:一会儿见。

Conversation 4

A: Housekeeping.	A:客房服务。
B: Come in, please.	B:请进。
A: Good morning, madam.	A:夫人,早上好。
B: Good morning. It seems that you are a little bit late today.	B:早上好。今天你来得好像有点儿晚。
A: I'm sorry for that. There are too many check-out rooms to do this morning. You know I always do the check-outs first unless there is a request. Next time, if you want me to make up your room early, just let me know. I am always at your service.	A:实在对不起。今天上午结账离店客人的房间太多了。您知道,除非有人提出要求,我通常总是先整理那些客人刚结账离去的房间。下回如果您要我早一点儿收拾您的房间,尽管吩咐,我随时愿为您服务。
B: Thanks a lot. I should like to have a nap after	B:多谢。午饭后我想打个盹。

lunch.

A: Yes, I see. Your room will be ready in half an hour, madam.

B: Thank you for your kindness.

A: My pleasure.

A:我知道了。您的房间将在半小时内整理好,夫人。

B:谢谢你的热情服务。

A:愿意为您效劳。

Conversation 5

A: I'd like to have breakfast in our room tomorrow morning. Could you bring it here?

B: Yes, of course. We provide very good room service.

A: Very good. When should we order our breakfast?

B: This is your doorknob menu. Just check the items you would like for breakfast, mark down the time, and hang it outside your door before you go to bed tonight.

A: Is there any other way to have room service?

B: Yes, sir. You may dial "1" to call the room service section directly to order your meal.

A: By the way, what should we do with the dishes when we finish eating?

B: Please leave them outside your room.

A:我们明天想在房间里用早餐。您能否把早餐送到房间来?

B:当然可以。我们提供非常好的客房送餐服务。

A:好极了。我们什么时候可以预订早餐?

B:这是挂门餐牌。您只需在您想用的早餐项上打上记号,注明用餐时间,然后在今晚就寝前把牌挂在门外就可以了。

A:还可以用什么方式得到客房送餐服务?

B:您可以拨"1"直接打电话到客房送餐服务部订餐。

A:顺便问一下,我们吃晚饭后那些盘子怎么处理?

B:请把它们放在房间外。

Conversation 6

A: I'd like to ask the laundry service.

B: Well, just put your stuff in the laundry bag and put it outside your room.

A: How soon can I have them back?

B: Usually in a day. If you give it in the morning, maybe you'll get it by evening.

A: How much is it?

B: The rate chart is contained in the stationery folder in your dresser's drawer.

A: Oh, I see. Well, would you please send someone to Room 511 to pick up some laundry for me?

B: Yes, sir. The chambermaid will be there in a few minutes.

A: Thank you.

B: You are welcome.

A:麻烦你替我把衣服拿去洗一下。

B:好的,请把衣服放到洗衣袋内,然后把洗衣袋放到门外。

A:大概要多久才能洗好?

B:通常一天就可以洗好。如果你早上拿出来洗的话,或许傍晚就可以拿回来。

A:洗衣价格是多少?

B:价格表在抽屉里的信件夹里。

A:噢,我知道了。嗯,你能派人到511房间来把我要洗的衣服拿走吗?

B:可以,先生。一会儿服务员就会去。

A:谢谢你。

B:不用客气。

On the Scene 身临其境 面面俱到

主题:清洁工来到南希住的房间里,要求为她打扫卫生,南希让清洁工人半小时后再来。请你看图,根据如下提供的关键词,将她们的对话写出来。

关键词语：madam *n.* 女士　　make your bed 替您收拾床铺
buzzer *n.* 铃

参考答案

Cleaner: May I clean your room now, madam?
Nancy: No. Will you come back in about half an hour?
Cleaner: Tell me when make your bed, please?
Nancy: You may make all of them in about half an hour.
Cleaner: Is it warm enough in your room, ma'am?
Nancy: It is just right.
Cleaner: Thank you. Ring the buzzer if you want anything.
清洁工：女士，我现在可打扫您的房间吗？
南希：现在不行。您半小时后来好吗？
清洁工：请问我何时替您收拾床铺？
南希：您可以在半小时后来一起收拾。
清洁工：您房间够暖和吗？
南希：刚刚好。
清洁工：谢谢。假使您需要任何东西，请按铃。

★国内之游★ 4 Travelling Inland

Words and Phrases 闪亮词语 点滴积累

the Great Wall of China 中国万里长城
embrasured watchtower over the city gate 箭楼
bell tower; clock tower 钟楼
turret; corner tower 角楼
side tower 阙楼
memorial archway 牌坊
waterside pavilion; pavilion on water 水榭
pond 池塘
long corridor 长廊
Emperor's Audience Hall; Throne Hall 金銮殿
imperial palace for short stay away from the capital; imperial abode 行宫
(imperial) palace 皇宫
front palace 正宫
western palace 西宫
eastern palace; crown palace 东宫
gate of palace 天门
Meridian Gate 午门
the Gate of Supreme Harmony 太和门
Gate of Divine Might 神午门

Useful Sentences 七彩精句 连点成线

North of China 华北地区

1. *You need at least six days to cover the important attractions in Beijing.* 要想游遍北京的重要景点,至少需要6天时间。
2. *The most luxurious and classy hotel with top services is the Beijing International Club Hotel.* 最豪华、最上档次的宾馆要数北京国际大饭店。
3. *You do have to try good local dishes in Beijing.* 您确实应该品味一下地道的北京菜。
4. *The Great Wall meanders from east to west for about 6,350 kilometers or 12,700 Li.* 长城从东到西蜿蜒约6350公里,也就是12700里。
5. *The Great Wall is indeed the crystallization of the industry and wisdom of the Chinese people and also a symbol of the ancient Chinese culture.* 长城的确是中国人民劳动和智慧的结晶,也是古代中国文化的象征。
6. *Tianjin is a good shopping city as well as a museum of 19th European architecture.* 天津是个很好的购物城市,也是一个19世纪欧洲建筑博物馆。
7. *Tianjin also has sea passenger routes with Dalian and other ports in South Korea and Japan.* 天津也有去大连和韩国及日本港口的海运航线。
8. *Shijiazhuang, the capital of He Bei province, with a total population of six million, is an industry city.* 石家庄,河北省的省会,有600万人口,是一座工业城市。
9. *Qinhuangdao is one of China's busiest harbors, with an urban population of about 448,000, it is one of the 14 Open Coastal Cities.* 秦皇岛是中国最繁忙的港口之一,也是14个沿海开放城市之一。拥有城市人口大约44.8万。
10. *Dong Shan is where the Qin emperor searched for the pills of longevity and boarded his ships. There's a good view of the sea and the sunrise.* 东山是一个观海和看日出的好地方,秦始皇曾遣人在此泊船求取长生不老之药。

East of China 华东地区

1. *Jinan is at the junction of the Beijing-Shanghai and the Qingdao-Jinan railways.* 济南位于京沪铁路线和青济线的交汇处。
2. *Mountain Tai is 2.5 million years old.* 泰山已有250万年的历史了。
3. *Qingdao is an important manufacturing center, ice-free port and pretty summer resort.* 青岛是重要的制造中心、不冻港和避暑圣地。
4. *Weifang is named for its international Kite Festival every year.* 潍坊每年举行的风筝节很有名。

5. *Marco Polo visited Suzhou in the latter half of the 13th century and proclaimed it another Venice.* 马可·波罗13世纪下半叶曾游历过苏州，并盛赞其为另一个威尼斯。

6. *The most important spots in Nanjing are Sun Yat-sen Mausoleum and Soul Valley Temple.* 南京最著名的景点是中山陵和灵谷寺。

7. *In Zhouzhuang, history and culture are so well blended with nature.* 在周庄，历史和文化同自然完美地结合在一起。

8. *Suzhou embroidery is famous for its delicate workmanship, beautiful designs and tasteful colors.* 苏绣以其精致的工艺、漂亮的设计和雅致的色彩而举世闻名。

9. *It is experiencing double-digit economic growth and its average per capita income is one of China's highest.* 上海经济正以两位数的增长速度发展，人均收入居中国之最。

10. *Shanghai's urban population is approximately 7.5 million plus three million "Floaters".* 上海市区人口约750万，另外还有300万"流动的弄潮儿"。

11. *In Shanghai, the hottest temperature is 40℃ in July and August, and the coldest is -5℃ in January and February.* 上海天气最热是在七八月间，气温最高可达摄氏40度，最冷则在一二月间，气温降至摄氏零下5度。

12. *After the opening of the Pudong International airport, international Flights will gradually shift to the new airport, and only domestic flights will go from Hongqiao Airport.* 浦东国际机场启用后，国际航班将陆续移向新机场，而虹桥机场只起落国内航班。

North-east 东北地区

1. *The average daytime temperature in January in Harbin is -15℃.* 哈尔滨1月份白天平均气温为摄氏零下15度。

2. *Harbin's major tourist attraction is Ice Sculpture Festival.* 哈尔滨吸引旅游者的主要景致是冰雕节。

3. *The annual Harbin Summer Music Festival is held in July.* 每年一度的哈尔滨夏季音乐节在7月举行。

4. *The Sun Island is an ideal place for summer holiday.* 太阳岛是夏日度假的理想去处。

5. *Dream World is a great place to swim all year round.* 梦世界是常年可游泳的好地方。

6. *Harbin's pine nuts and ginseng are good to taste.* 哈尔滨的松果和人参值得一尝。

7. *Changchun is noted for a city of forests.* 长春素有"森林之城"的美称。

8. *Changchun is also famous for a city of everlasting spring beyond the Great Wall.* 长春还有"塞外春城"的美誉。

9. *The province of Jilin borders on Korea and Russia.* 吉林省与朝鲜和俄罗斯接壤。

10. *On summer evenings you can find dancers in costume in People's Square.* 夏日傍晚您会看到许多人身穿民族服装在人民广场翩翩起舞。

11. *The meteorite in Jilin Exhibition Hall is believed to be the largest in the world.* 吉林展览馆的陨石被认为是世界上最大的。

12. *The famous Crater Lake in Changbai Mountains is beautiful Heaven Lake.* 长白山区最著名的火山口湖是美丽的天池。

13. *The Former Palaces of the Last Emperor was looted after the Japanese surrender.* 末代皇帝以前的宫殿在日本投降后被劫掠一空。

North-west 西北地区

1. *Xinjiang Uigur autonomous Region is the largest region in China.* 新疆维吾尔自治区是中国最大的自治区。

2. *Xinjiang produces oil, ketchup, sheep, pears, grapes and grain.* 新疆出产石油、番茄酱、绵羊、珍珠、葡萄和谷物。

3. *The Flaming mountain is so named because the incessant sun is supposed to make the rocks seem on fire from a distance.* 火焰山之所以得名是因为太阳光连续照耀，使得岩石从远处看，就像在着火一般。

4. *The area on the Silk Road is extremely dry and cold even on summer nights.* 丝绸之路所经区域非常干燥，即使在夏天，夜晚也很冷。

5. *You can identify people's nationality from their facial features and their distinctive dress in Kashi.*

在喀什,您可以从人们的脸部表情和他们独特的衣着辨别他们的民族。

6. *Lanzhou was called "Gold City" after gold was found here.* 兰州发现金子后曾被称作"金城"。
7. *Bingling Si Grottoes are 129 km southwest of Lanzhou.* 炳灵寺石窟在兰州城西南 129 公里处。
8. *Many caves in Mogao Grottoes have a series of pictures telling stories.* 莫高窟的许多洞窟内有一系列记事壁画。
9. *Some of the colors in the grottoes are still original and vivid.* 窟内的一些颜色仍旧保持原样,栩栩如生。
10. *White Horse Pagoda commemorates the horse of the Indian monk Jiumoluoshi.* 白马塔是纪念印度和尚鸠摩罗什的马而建的。
11. *The Yangguan Pass is Just a beacon tower now.* 阳关现在只是一个烽火台。
12. *Qinghai's ninety-six percent land is pasture.* 青海 96% 的土地是草原。
13. *Qinghai is famous for the Tear Lamasery and the Bird Island in Qinghai Lake.* 青海以塔尔寺和青海湖上的鸟岛而闻名。
14. *Qinghai is the source of both the Yellow and Yangtze rivers.* 青海既是黄河的源头,也是长江的源头。
15. *Xining has a nickname of "World of Salt."* 西宁俗称"盐的世界"。
16. *Qinghai Lake is China's largest saltwater lake.* 青海湖是中国最大的咸水湖。

South-west 西南地区

1. *Tibet is an important touring place because of its unique culture, its celebrated monasteries, and its stark, spectacular scenery.* 西藏独特的文化、有名的寺院以及庄严、壮观的景色使其成为了一个重要的旅游胜地。
2. *Lhasa, the capital of Tibet, is the main point of entry to the roof of the world.* 拉萨,西藏的首府,是走进"世界屋脊"的主要通道。
3. *The Tibetan people are brave, strong and forthright, very kind and hospitable.* 藏族人民勇敢、刚毅、豪爽,又十分善良好客。
4. *Tashi delek is the Tibetan greeting. It means "good luck".* 扎西德勒是藏族的问候语,它的意思是"吉祥如意"。
5. *Buttered tea is a unique drink in Tibetan regions, it's also the main drink for the guests.* 酥油茶是西藏地区独具风味的饮料,同时也是藏族人待客必备饮料。
6. *For many people, Yunnan is a land of mystery.* 对许多人来说,云南是一片神秘的土地。
7. *Yunnan has not only a variety of magnificent highland scene, but also charming frontier landscapes.* 云南既有雄伟壮丽的高原景观,又有妩媚迷人的边塞风光。
8. *The Stone Forest in Lunan, Yunnan, enjoys a high reputation in the world. Every year over one million people, both from abroad and at home, come here to visit it.* 云南的路南石林享誉世界,每年要接待国内外游客百万余人。
9. *Dali is a world-renowned tourist attraction. It is widely acclaimed as "the Oriental Switzerland", "the Chinese Geneva" and "the Pearl on the Yungui Plateau".* 大理是举世闻名的旅游胜地,被称为"东方瑞士"、"中国的日内瓦"和"云贵高原上的一颗明珠"。
10. *For centuries, Xishuangbanna had been a hidden land and it was almost inaccessible.* 多少世纪以来,西双版纳一直都是一片鲜为人知的土地,要抵达西双版纳几乎难于上青天。

South of China 华南地区

1. *Hunan's embroidery is one of the four famous in China.* 湖南的湘绣是中国四大名绣之一。
2. *Shaoshan is 104km southwest of Changsha.* 韶山在长沙西南 104 公里的地方。
3. *Dongting Lake is the largest lake in China.* 洞庭湖是中国最大的湖泊。
4. *Hunan Huagu opera originated from local folk songs and ditties.* 湖南花鼓戏起源于当地民歌和小调。
5. *Junshan Silver Needles tea enjoys a good reputation across China.* 君山毛尖茶在全中国都享有盛名。
6. *Shennongjia Prime Forest in Hubei province attracts eco-travelers.* 湖北省的神农架原始森林

吸引着生态旅游者。

7. *Wudang Mountain is the home of the Wudang style of martial arts.* 武当山是武术武当派的祖庭。

8. *Hankou, Hanyang, and Wuchang are separated from each other by the Yangtze and Han rivers.* 汉口、汉阳和武昌被长江和汉江彼此分开。

9. *Wuhan Yangtze River Bridge is the first bridge for both railway and highway on Yangtze River.* 武汉长江大桥是长江上第一座铁路、公路两用桥。

10. *Yellow Crane Tower is the symbol of Wuhan.* 黄鹤楼是武汉的象征。

Fashion Conversation 鲜活会话

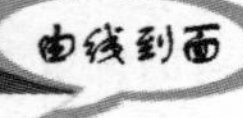

Conversation 1

A: Ladies and gentlemen, now, we have arrived at the Dunhuang Mogao Grottoes.
A: 女士们、先生们，现在我们已到达敦煌莫高窟了。

B: I have heard that it is one of the famous sites in China. But I know only this. Can you tell me more about it?
B: 我听说过它是中国名胜之一。但是我仅知道这么多。您能再告诉我多一些吗？

A: OK, Dunhuang in western Gansu Province was an important town on the Silk Road in ancient times. The Dunhuang Mogao Grottoes or Caves of One Thousand Buddhas is one of the three famous grottoes in China.
A: 好的，敦煌在西北部的甘肃省，在古代它是丝绸之路上重要的小镇。敦煌莫高窟，俗称千佛洞，是中国三大宝窟之一。

B: It sounds very exciting. Why do we call it Caves of One Thousand Buddhas?
B: 听起来很有趣，我们为什么称它为千佛洞？

A: There are altogether 493 caves, 2400 sculptures and murals of 45,000 square metres in Mogao Grottoes. In the China grotto art, Mogao Grottoes is the largest in scale, richest in content, highest in artistic value, longest in its gallery, and most widespread in its reputation.
A: 这里总共有 493 个洞窟，彩塑 2400 尊，壁画 45,000 平方米。在中国的石窟艺术中，莫高窟的规模最大，内容最丰富，艺术价值最高，画廊最长，名声传播最远。

B: Oh, thank you.
B: 哦，谢谢。

Conversation 2

A: Jiuzhaigou is well known across the world. What does Jiuzhaigou mean in Chinese?
A: 九寨沟闻名世界。九寨沟在汉语中是什么意思呢？

B: Jiuzhaigou means Nine Stockades Canyon. It is a nature preserve.
B: 九寨沟意思是九个山区的寨子。它是一个自然保护区。

A: Oh, very interesting. Can you tell me more about it?
A: 噢，真有趣。您能多介绍些情况吗？

B: Well, this preserve comprises 60,000 hectares of primitive forest with species earlier thought to be extinct.
B: 呃，这个保护区有 6 万公顷原始森林，内有早期的物种，有的被认为濒临灭绝。

A: It is worthy of adventures.
A: 那可真值得去探险。

B: Yes. It is called a fairyland because it is covered with green trees, carpets of flowers, lakes and waterfalls.
B: 是的，它被称作“童话世界”，因为它遍地是绿树、鲜花、湖泊和瀑布。

Conversation 3

A: This is the Museum of the Former Palaces of the Last Emperor Pu Yi.
A: 这就是末代皇帝溥仪皇宫博物馆。

B: Oh, I have seen a movie named "*The Last Emperor.*"
B: 噢，我看过一部电影叫《末代皇帝》。

A: Yes, some of the sets are shot here. Let's visit Ton De Palace.
A: 是的，其中的一些镜头就是在这儿拍摄的，我们去参观通德宫吧。

B: Did the last emperor live here?
B: 末代皇帝在这个宫殿里住过吗？

A: No, only one of his wives lived in this palace although it was built for the last emperor.
A: 没有，只有他的一个妃子在这里住过，尽管这个宫殿是给他修建的。

B: Why didn't he live in this palace?
B: 为什么他不住在这个宫殿呢？

A: Because it was built by the Japanese and Pu Yi suspected it was bugged.
A: 因为这是日本人修建的，溥仪怀疑里面安装有窃听器。

B: Oh. Where did he live?
B: 噢。那他住哪里呢？

A: Pu Yi himself lived in the neighboring building over there.
A: 溥仪自己住在旁边的那栋楼里。

Conversation 4

A: Here we are on the top of the Oriental Pearl TV Tower. We can not only have a bird's-eye view of the whole city, but also have a glimpse of Shanghai's past and present.
A: 我们现在来到了东方明珠电视塔上。我们不仅可以鸟瞰整个上海市，而且可以看一看上海的过去和现在。

B: My god, this view is really breathtaking.
B: 我的天哪，这景色真令人太兴奋了。

C: Look at those boats that we saw a moment ago. They seem so small now.
C: 瞧那些我们刚才见到的那些船，现在那么小。

D: Wu, I didn't quite catch that. How tall is this tower?
D: 吴，我刚才没有听清楚，这座塔有多高？

A: It is 468 meters high and is the world's third tallest TV tower, after only the 553-meter CN Tower of Toronto and the 535-meter Moscow TV tower.
A: 这座塔高468米，是世界第三高电视塔，仅次于553米高的多伦多CN电视塔和535米高的莫斯科电视塔。

E: Miss Wu, why is this tower shaped like this, with all these globes?
E: 吴小姐，这座塔为什么要采用这样的造型，要用这么多球？

A: The eight globes were designed in a special way to remind one of a Tang dynasty poem that compares sounds played on a plucked instrument to "a string of pearls dropping onto a jade plate".
A: 这八个球是特别设计的，为的是让人们联想到一首唐诗，即把琵琶声形容为"大珠小珠落玉盘"。

E: Very romantic.
E: 真的很浪漫。

A: These globes are actually built for sightseeing, dining and hotel accommodations. The 20-room Space Hotel is located in the five small balls between the two large globes. Each ball has a suite and three standard rooms on two levels, which are connected by a winding stairway.
A: 这些圆球实际上被用作观景、就餐和住宿。拥有20个房间的"太空宾馆"就位于两个大球之间的五个小球中。每个小球分别有一个套间和三个标准间，由一个旋转式楼梯相连。

E: It's really unbelievable.
E: 这真令人难以相信。

A: If you look to the east, you can see the Yangpu Bridge, which is the longest cable-stayed suspension bridge in China. You can also see a lot of modern buildings not far from here in Lujiazui area. That is the 88-storey Jin Mao Building and over there is the Shanghai Stock Exchange.

A: 大家如果向东看就能看到杨浦大桥，这是中国最长的悬索桥。大家还能看到陆家嘴区离这里不远处的一群现代建筑。那是 88 层高的金贸大厦，那边是上海证券交易所。

B: I think that soaring Jin Mao Building can stand for Shanghai's economic boom.

B: 我觉得这直插云天的金贸大厦象征着上海的经济繁荣。

A: I agree with you. Not only is it the tallest skyscraper in China, but also it represents the energy and determination of the people in Shanghai. The design of this gently tapered building embodies China's history and culture.

A: 我同意您的说法。这不仅是中国最高的摩天大楼，而且代表着上海人民的活力和决心。这座逐渐变细的大厦的设计包含着中国的历史和文化。

On the Scene 身临其境 面面俱到

主题：泰德和安正在谈论旅游圣地香港。请你看图，根据如下提供的关键词，将他们的对话写出来。

关键词语：modern *n.* 现代人
financial *adj.* 财政的，金融的
passenger *n.* 乘客，旅客
definitely *adv.* 明确地
tourism *n.* 观光事业

参考答案

Ted: Hong Kong is one of the most modern, most vibrant cities in the world, right?

Ann: It's definitely right. Hong Kong is reputed as an international financial, trading, shipping, tourism and free port.

Ted: Come on. Here are a few lines about Hong Kong. Every minute, a ship enters or leaves Victoria Harbor of Hong Kong.

Ann: A plane takes off or lands at Kai Tak International Airport of Hong Kong every three minutes.

Ted: Oh, here are more. In terms of passenger flow, Kai Tak Airport is one of the three busiest in the world.

Ann: Hong Kong International Airport was also identified by U. S. A '99 Architecture Exposition as one of the top 10 buildings of the 20th century all over the world.

泰德：香港是世界上最现代、最具动感的城市，对吗？

安:绝对正确。香港作为国际金融、贸易、运输、旅游的自由港而声名远播。

泰德:看,这儿有几条有关香港的信息。每一分钟就有一艘船进入或离开香港的维多利亚港。

安:每三分钟就有一架飞机起落香港启德国际机场。

泰德:噢,还有呢。说到旅客流量,启德机场是世界三大最繁忙的机场之一。

安:香港国际机场还被美国'99建筑博览会评为20世纪世界10大建筑之一。

★国外之游★ 5 Travelling Abroad

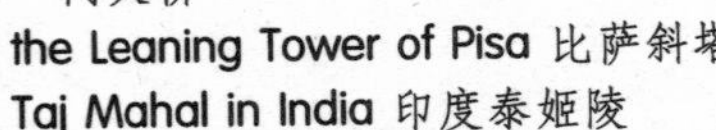

Words and Phrases 闪亮词语

the Pyramids 金字塔
the Sphinx 狮身人面像
the Statue of Liberty 自由女神像
Notre Dame de Paris 巴黎圣母院
the Eiffel Tower in Paris 埃菲尔铁塔
Louvre 卢浮宫
the Arch of Triumph 凯旋门
the Opera House in Sydney 悉尼歌剧院
Big Ben in London 伦敦大本钟
the Tower Bridge in London 伦敦塔桥
the Golden Gate Bridge in San Francisco 旧金山金门大桥
the Leaning Tower of Pisa 比萨斜塔
Taj Mahal in India 印度泰姬陵

Useful Sentences 七彩精句

连点成线

A Trip to Australia 走进澳洲

1. *From up here we can have a bird's-eye view of the city.* 从这上面，我们可以鸟瞰整个城市。
2. *Do you know what that building is?* 您知道那是什么建筑吗？
3. *What a magnificent sight! Oh, darling, do come over here and look at this magnificent view.* 多么壮观的景象啊！啊，亲爱的，快过来看这儿壮丽的景色。
4. *It's so fresh and quiet here. I love it. Let's spread something in the shade here for a picnic.* 这儿空气这么新鲜、这么安静，我很喜欢，让我们在这儿的树阴下铺点东西吃野餐吧。
5. *I can always be your guide.* 我随时愿为你们当向导。
6. *The place is too large for a day's visit.* 那地方太大了，一天根本浏览不过来。
7. *We can watch the sunrise if you wish.* 要是您愿意，我们可以去观看日出。
8. *You won't have fun there at this time of year, believe me.* 相信我，这个季节去那儿没什么好玩的。

A Trip to USA 走进美国

1. *The Great Lakes are the great wonder of Middle America.* 五大湖是中美洲最大的自然景观。
2. *It is also the biggest body of fresh water in the world.* 它也是世界上最大的淡水水体。
3. *Let us approach the lakes by the best way.* 让我们沿着最佳路线去观赏五大湖。
4. *Ontario is more elusive compared with the other lakes.* 与其他湖相比，安大略湖最迷人。
5. *Superior is the worst storm lake.* 苏必利尔湖的风浪最大。
6. *St. Mary's river is at the upper end of Huron.* 圣玛丽河位于休伦湖的上游。

A Trip to England 英国之行

1. *London is the capital city of England and of Britain.* 伦敦是英格兰的首府，也是英国的首都。
2. *London is one of the world's leading commercial and cultural centers.* 伦敦是世界主要的贸易和文化中心之一。
3. *The legislative, executive and judicial branches of government are all situated in London.* 英国政府的立法、行政和司法机构均设在伦敦。
4. *London grew from the Thames.* 伦敦的发展源自泰晤士河。
5. *London is a combination of the past and the present and the future.* 伦敦是往昔、现时和将来三者的融合。
6. *London is a city for explorers.* 伦敦是一座让人们探胜猎奇的城市。

A Trip to Canada 加拿大之行

1. *How high are the mountains in western Newfoundland?* 在西部纽芬兰山有多高？
2. *Where is the highest waterfall in Canada?* 加拿大最高的瀑布在哪儿？
3. *What is the longest river in Canada?* 加拿大最长的河流是哪条？
4. *What is the highest mountain in Canada?* 加拿大最高的山是哪座？
5. *Is Toronto an industrial city?* 多伦多是工业城市吗？
6. *Is it really light at midnight in the north?* 在北部午夜真的有光吗？
7. *What does maple leaf stand for?* 枫叶代表什么？

Sightseeing in South-east Asia 观东南亚

1. *Indonesia is an island country, consisting of as many as 3,000 islands.* 印尼是个岛国，由3000个岛屿所组成的。
2. *You must not fail to visit Bali Island, it is called the "Last Paradise".* 你绝对不能不去巴厘岛，巴厘岛被称为是"最后的乐园"。
3. *One place you should see in Cambodia is Angkor, which contains the ruins of the Khmer dynasty.* 吴哥是柬埔寨一个非参观不可的地方，它保有许多高棉王朝的遗迹。
4. *Bangkok is the capital of Thailand, it is a city with thousands of Buddhist temples.* 曼谷是泰国首都，有着数以千计的佛寺。
5. *Kuala Lumpur is the capital of Malaysia, it is famous for the pewter ware of selangor.* 吉隆坡是马来西亚首都，以雪兰莪制的白镴器具闻名。
6. *Manila is the capital of the Philippines.* 马尼拉是菲律宾首都。
7. *Singapore is called the "Lion City", there are four races of inhabitants, Indian, Malay, Eurasian and Chinese.* 新加坡称为"狮城"，居民包括四种种族：印度人、马来人、欧亚混血人及中国人。

A Trip to East Asia 东亚之游

1. *There are two routes for the pleasure boats on the Lake Ashinoko.* 芦湖游览船共有两条路线。
2. *I took the course that stops at Hakone where the station for the ropeway is located to climb Mt. Komagatake.* 我选择了停靠箱根园的路线，因为在那里有前往驹岳山顶的索道站。
3. *Did you see the small red torii gate(shrine gate)?* 你见到那座小型的红色牌坊——鸟居了吗？
4. *Every April, the Japanese celebrate Cherry Blossoms Festival.* 每年四月，日本人庆祝樱花节。
5. *Now it's the season for cherry blossoms.* 现在正是樱花怒放的季节。
6. *By April, Japan is at the height of its beauty.* 四月的日本，真是美极了。
7. *I wonder how the sakura tea tastes.* 我想知道樱花茶是什么味道。
8. *Do you know the tea ceremonial?* 你懂茶道吗？
9. *Everyone wants a chance to see cherry blossoms while they're the most beautiful.* 每个人都想在樱花开得最美的时候有机会来赏樱花。

Fashion Conversation 鲜活会话 由线到面

Conversation 1

A: Wow! Brisbane is a pretty modern city.

B: Yeah. It combines the vitality of a modern, bustling city with the sociable atmosphere of a country town.

A: Look at the modern glass skyscrapers towering over the old wooden houses perched on stilts. It is a scene of harmony between the old and the new. It's marvelous!

B: It is marvelous!

A：哇！布里斯班真是一座现代城市。

B：是啊。它把现代喧闹城市的生命活力和乡村城镇的社交氛围融为一体。

A：看那座现代的玻璃摩天大楼，它俯瞰着坐落在支柱撑着的古老木屋，构成一幅古老和现代之间的和谐景色。真是太美了！

B：美极了！

A: I was told that Brisbane is best known for the Gold Coast...

A:我听说布里斯班最负盛名的是黄金海岸……

B: And the Great Barrier Reef.

B:还有大堡礁。

A: That's right. I heard of it. Why don't we go there now?

A:是的,我听说过。我们现在为什么不去那儿呢?

B: No hurry. First of all, I want you to see something unique in Australian.

B:不要急。首先,我想让你看看澳大利亚独一无二的东西。

A: What is it?

A:是什么?

B: Warana.

B:蓝天盛会。

Conversation 2

A: Which is the best way approaching the Great Lakes?

A:游览五大湖的最佳路线是什么?

B: Well, we should get on board a ship and start from the Lake Ontario.

B:噢,我们应该登上一艘轮船从安大略湖出发。

A: Lake Ontario?

A:安大略湖?

B: Yes. It's the smallest of the Great Lakes, but it's deep, with a maximum sounding of 802 feet. Compared with the other lakes, Ontario is more elusive.

B:是的。它是五大湖中最小的一个,但水很深,最深处有802英尺。与其他的4个湖相比,安大略湖更加迷人。

A: Is the famous Niagara Falls there?

A:著名的尼亚加拉瀑布是在那儿吗?

B: Yes. Its sheer thunderous drop has been an elusive barrier between the Ontario and other lakes.

B:是的。飞溅直下的瀑布早成了安大略湖和其他湖之间的一座虚幻的屏障。

A: But the Erie Lake is the one that people talk about a lot.

A:但是伊利湖却是人们谈论的对象。

B: That's because it's a killer of small draft. It has a reputation for treacherous flash storms.

B:那是因为它是水浅的船舶的杀手。它以突如其来的暴风雨而闻名。

A: How about others?

A:其他湖呢?

B: Superior is the worst storm lake; Lake Huron is the second largest of the lakes; and Lake Michigan is the only one of the lakes that is entirely within the U.S.

B:苏必利尔湖的风浪最大;休伦湖是五大湖的第二大湖;密执安湖是其中唯一完全位于美国境内的湖。

Conversation 3

A: This is Westminster Abbey. It's one of the oldest buildings in London, and in its architecture you will recognize different styles.

A:这是威斯敏斯特教堂。它是全伦敦最古老的建筑之一。从其建筑设计上,您会看到许多不同的风格。

B: Busts and monuments remind us of William Shakespeare, Walter Scott and many others.

B:铜像和纪念碑使我们想起了威廉·莎士比亚、沃特·斯克特以及其他许多人。

A: To the left you see the House of Parliament with the famous clock tower Big-Ben. In the building there is the House of Commons and the House of Lords.

A:在左边您会看到议会大厦,上面有著名的大本钟塔楼。英国议会上院和下院都在这幢大楼里。

B: There, to the left, you see a small street, called Downing Street. No. 10, the last of its ten hou-

B:快往左看,您会看到一条小街道,叫唐宁街。街上10所住宅的最后一所,唐宁街10号,一直是

ses, has always been the residence of the British prime minister.

英国首相的官邸。

A: Now, we're approaching Trafalgar Square.

A: 现在我们快到特拉法尔加广场了。

B: This is Tower Bridge, the most striking of all London bridges.

B: 这是塔桥，是伦敦最有特色的大桥。

A: Look! The bridge is parting in the middle, and the two halves are moving upwards. A big steamer is passing underneath.

A: 瞧！大桥正从中间分开，两半部分正往上升起，一艘大汽船正从下驶过。

B: Down river stretch the London docks.

B: 顺河直下，可以到达伦敦码头。

Conversation 4

A: Have you visited Niagara Falls?

A: 你游览过尼亚加拉瀑布吗？

B: For several times. It has become a tired old tourist sight.

B: 游览过几次了。尼亚加拉瀑布已经成为一个老掉牙的景点了。

A: But if you look it over in an airplane, becomes something completely new.

A: 但是如果从飞机上鸟瞰的话，尼亚加拉瀑布就成为一个全新的景点了。

B: Really?

B: 真的吗？

A: Yes. You should realize that Niagara Falls is not tired, only the way of looking is tired.

A: 是的。你应该知道尼亚拉加瀑布并没有老，只是我们看的方式陈旧点罢了。

B: You are all right. For the ground tourist, the approach to Niagara is flat, and since an industrial area has grown up around the falls, they are surrounded by concrete, asphalt and a strong chemical smell on both the United States and Canadian sides. Only a stretch of lawn and trees reminds us of the wilderness that once was there.

B: 你说得很对。地面上的观光者视觉是平面的，随着瀑布周围工业区的发展，它们被水泥、沥青和强烈的化学味包围着。唯有一片草坪和树木才让人想起那里曾是荒芜的地方。

A: Can we see its real face at altitude?

A: 我们可以在高空将尼亚加拉瀑布看个一清二楚吗？

B: Of course.

B: 当然了。

A: So, I think we should visit it again.

A: 我想我们得再去游览一次。

B: Thank you very much.

B: 非常感谢您。

A: You're welcome.

A: 不客气。

Conversation 5

A: Have you visited Bangkok?

A: 你参观过曼谷吗？

B: Yes. It's a charming city.

B: 参观过，它是一座迷人的城市。

A: Could you tell me about the Bangkok skytrain?

A: 你能告诉我曼谷空中铁路的事情吗？

B: OK. The light railway consists of two intersecting lines, which link at Siam Square. The Sukhumvit Line enables access to a number of hotels, including the Grand Hyatt Erawan, Le Meridien, Hilton International, Landmark, Amari Boulevard , J. W. Marriott, Sheraton Grande Sukhumvit and Novotel Lotus. The Silom Line serves the Regent Bangkok, Pan Pacific, Holiday Inn Crowne Plaza, Shan-

B: 可以。这个轻轨铁路系统由两条线路交叉而成，会合处在暹罗广场。苏坤维线沿线到达许多饭店，包括凯悦大饭店、美丽殿饭店、喜来登国际饭店、兰马饭店、阿玛里林阴大道饭店、J. W. 马里奥特饭店、喜来登苏坤维大饭店和诺沃特尔洛特斯饭店。席隆线沿线到达曼谷丽晶饭店、泛太平洋饭店、假日皇冠广场饭店、香格里拉饭店和曼谷东方饭店。

griLa and Bangkok Oriental.

A: Which advantages does it have?

B: With a maximum fare of about $1 elevated railway will be an affordable option for city residents who now drive to work. The train will also be much quicker, making a cross town trip in under five minutes. Besides reducing traffic congestion, the system is expected to help decrease Bangkok's air pollution.

A: Thank you for let me know so much things.

B: You're welcome.

A: 它有哪些便利之处呢?

B: 这条高架铁路的最高票价约合1美元,现在开车上下班的市民完全有这个购买能力。铁路的速度也要快许多,环城一周用不了5分钟。这条铁路的修建不仅可以缓解交通拥挤,还有助于改善曼谷的空气污染。

A: 谢谢你,让我知道这么多事情。

B: 别客气。

Conversation 6

A: What do you think has impressed you most in London?

B: I don't think I can say for sure. There are so many things that have left a deep impression on me. Yes, there is one thing worth mentioning at least. Although the buildings here seem old fashioned, they have a peculiar flavor of their own.

A: Look at the nameplate on the wall of the corner building. We're getting near to Trafalgar Square.

B: It's interesting where the British people place the road signs, but what's Trafalgar Square?

A: It's a busy road junction with Nelson's statue.

B: Oh, yes, I know something about British History. He's the admiral that defeated Napoleon.

A: You're right. There may not be much to see on the square itself, but it's easy to get from there to many interesting places in London.

A: 您觉得在伦敦给您印象最深刻的是什么?

B: 很难说,很多东西都给我留下了深刻的印象。至少有一件事值得一提。虽然伦敦的建筑物看上去都是老式的,但它们独具风格。

A: 瞧拐角那幢楼墙上的路牌。我们就要到特拉法尔加广场了。

B: 英国人放置路牌的地方真有意思。什么是特拉法尔加广场?

A: 这是个热闹的交叉路口,有尊纳尔逊的纪念铜像。

B: 噢,是的,我对英国知识也了解一点。他就是打败拿破仑的那位海军将军。

A: 是的。或许特拉法尔加广场没多少可看的,但它离很多伦敦著名的景点很近。

On the Scene 身临其境 面面俱到

主题:导游带着汤姆来到了雅典卫城,并向他讲解了卫城的故事。请你看图,根据如下提供的关键词,将他们的对话写出来。

关键词语:

carver *n.* 雕刻匠
wise *adj.* 明智的,博学的
solemn *adj.* 庄严的,隆重的
statesman *n.* 政治家
grand *adj.* 盛大的
ceremony *n.* 典礼,仪式

参考答案

Tom: I'm very glad. We'll see the Acropolis in Athens soon!

Guidence: Yes. It's a very beautiful place. I have been a full-time guide here for many years.

Tom: It's my honor to have you as my guide.

Guidence: You are flattering me. It's my duty to help you.

Tom: OK. Let's come into our point. Can you tell me something about the Acropolis in Athens?

Guidence: Of course. It contains many buildings, such as Parthenon Temple, Hill Gate, Wisdom Goddess Temple. But the most famous one is Parthenon Temple.

Tom: I've heard that carvings in Parthenon Temple are very successful.

Guidence: Yes. It was directed by a famous carver — Pheidias.

Tom: Who's Pheidias?

Guidence: He was a statesman.

Tom: How about Wisdom Goddess Temple?

Guidence: Wisdom Goddess was called "the giver of victory". She is very wise and clever. Her Temple was damaged by Turk in 1686. In the nineteenth century, it was restored. From then, people in Athens began to hate the Turk.

Tom: Now, I really know the reason why Turk can't be praised here.

Guidence: To express their respect to Wisdom Goddess, in a grand festival, they gave her the Parthenon Temple in a solemn ceremony.

Tom: I wish I want to see her Temple becomes stronger and stronger. I really want to fly there.

Guidence: Take your time. We'll get there right now.

汤姆:我很高兴。很快我们就可以见到雅典卫城了。

导游:是的。那是个好地方。我已成为这儿的专职导游好多年了。

汤姆:能让你做我的导游是我的荣幸。

导游:你过奖了。能帮你是我的职责。

汤姆:那我们就进入正题吧。你能跟我讲些关于雅典卫城的事吗?

导游:当然可以了。它包括许多建筑物,像帕提侬神庙、山门、智慧女神庙等等。但是最著名的要数帕提侬神庙了。

汤姆:我听说那所庙里的雕刻相当成功。

导游:是的。它是在一个著名的雕刻师——菲狄阿斯的指导下进行的。

汤姆:谁是菲狄阿斯?

导游:他是个政治家。

汤姆:那么关于智慧女神庙呢?

导游:智慧女神被称作"胜利的赐予者"。她很有智慧。她的神庙在1686年被土耳其人破坏,在19世纪才被修复。从那时候起,雅典人就开始恨土耳其人了。

汤姆:现在,我才真正明白人们在这儿不能赞扬土耳其人的原因。

导游:为了表达人们对智慧女神的尊敬,在一个盛大的节日里,他们以很隆重的方式把帕提侬神庙赐给她。

汤姆:我想去看神庙的愿望越来越强烈了。我真想飞过去。

导游:别急,我们马上就到了。

Sports

CHAPTER

体育看台

★奥运精神★ 1 Olympism

Words and Phrases 闪亮词语 点滴积累

Olympic Anthem 奥运会会歌
Olympic charter 奥林匹克宪章
Olympic flame 奥运圣火
Olympic Games 奥运会
Olympic Oath 奥运会宣誓词
Olympic theme song 奥运会主题歌
Olympic torch 奥运火炬
Olympic trial 奥运会选拔赛
Olympic village 奥运村
opening ceremony 开幕式
organization committee 组委会
Paralympic Games 残疾人奥运会
podium 颁奖台
preparatory committee 筹委会

Useful Sentences 七彩精句 连点成线

Olympism 奥运精神

1. *The Olympic motto is "Higher, Faster, Stronger".* 奥林匹克的格言是"更高,更快,更强"。
2. *The most important thing in the Olympic Games is not to win but to participate.* 奥林匹克运动会重在参与而不是取胜。
3. *Taking drugs before the Games is considered cheating and against sportsmanship.* 赛前服用药物被视为作弊,且违背运动精神。
4. *The Olympic oath encourages athletes, coaches, and officials to observe the rules and to follow the spirit of sportsmanship.* 奥运会誓言鼓励运动员、教练员和裁判员遵守规则,发扬体育道德精神。
5. *Mutual-understanding, friendship, unity and fair play.* 相互了解、友谊、团结和公平竞争。
6. *The Olympic Games help promote a better an more peaceful world.* 奥林匹克运动会有助于实现一个更美好、更安宁的世界。
7. *The most important thing in the Games is not the triumph but the struggle; not to have conquered but to have fought well.* 比赛中最重要的事情不是胜利,而是奋斗;不是征服,而是奋力拼搏。
8. *By undering the stress and strain of tough competition, the athletes grow in strength, endurance, and discipline.* 在经历了激烈竞争的紧张与压力之后,运动员在力量、耐力和纪律方面都有提高。
9. *The athletes should learn to respect and to cooperate with people from many nations during the Games.* 在比赛中,运动员应该学会尊重与来自许多国家的人们合作。
10. *After the hard training of a long time, every athlete would deserve a medal in the Games no matter he won or not.* 经过长时间的艰苦训练,在奥运会上无论是胜利或失败,每个运动员都应获得一枚奖牌。
11. *Team work is essential to a football match.* 足球比赛最重要的是团队合作。
12. *The victory should owe to my coach's patient instructions and the help of my family and friends.* 我的胜利归功于教练耐心的教诲以及家人和朋友的帮助。

New Beijing, Great Olympics 新北京,新奥运

1. *Beijing's success, economically, will be as big a boost to Beijing as it was in the run up to the Games in Tokyo in 1964, and Seoul in 1988.* 北京申奥的成功,从经济上来说,将是一个极大的促进,正如1964年的东京奥运会和1988年的汉城奥运会带来的经济腾飞。
2. *It will be the first time that Beijing has held the Olympic Games.* 这将是北京第一次举办奥林匹克运动会。
3. *China's successful bid for the 2008 Olympics has given the country the international prestige it has been seeking in recent years.* 申办2008年奥运

会的成功给了中国近年来所寻求的国际声望。

4. *By 2008, the environmental quality in Beijing will be comparable to that of major cities in developed countries.* 到2008年,北京的环境质量将可以和发达国家主要城市的环境质量相媲美。

5. *The dynamic growth of Beijing reflects that of China as a whole.* 北京的不断变化从整体上反映了全中国的变化。

6. *Beijing's second bid again has the full supports of the people of China and the Beijing Municipal Government.* 北京第二次申办奥运会得到了北京市政府和中国人民的全力支持。

7. *The Olympic Games in Beijing will be a bridge of harmony between countries and cultures.* 北京奥运会将成为国家与国家之间、文化与文化之间的交流的桥梁。

8. *"Green Olympics, High-tech Olympics and People's Olympics" are our themes.* "绿色奥运,科技奥运,人文奥运"是我们的主题。

9. *In the minds of millions of young Beijingers, the year 2008 represents dreams, pride and wealth.* 在许多年轻的北京人心目中,2008年代表着梦想、骄傲与财富。

10. *Beijing was competing against Toronto, Osaka, Istanbul and Paris for the right to host the 2008 Summer Olympic Games.* 北京与多伦多、大坂、伊斯坦布尔、巴黎争夺2008年奥运会的举办权。

11. *The results of a Gallup poll showed that 94.9 percent of Beijing's residents supports the Olympic bid.* 根据一项盖洛普民意调查的结果表明,有94.9%的北京市民支持北京申奥。

12. *The evaluation team of IOC will visit all the candidate cities to decide which city can host the Olympics.* 国际奥委会的评估团将访问所有申办城市以决定哪一个城市能够获得举办权。

13. *Why would the 2008 Olympic Games be hosted in Beijing?* 为什么北京能够承办2008年奥运会?

14. *What can the Olympic Games bring Beijing?* 奥运会将给北京带来什么?

15. *If China applies for the Olympic Games successfully, as a host country, which gymnasiums do you prepare for the Olympic Games?* 如果中国申办奥运会成功,作为主办国,你们将为奥运会准备哪些比赛场馆?

Pain and Glory 痛苦与荣耀

1. *Champions keep playing until they get it right.* 冠军就是不停地击球直到打出好球为止。

2. *They carried not so much by their bodies but by pride.* 驱使他们移动脚步的不是他们的身体而是一股傲气。

3. *She knows all well that when she rises gracefully she brings joy to many hearts, and lots of heats are crushed when she lands without style.* 她很清楚:当她优雅地升向空中时可使许多人欣喜若狂,而当她毫无风度地跌落在地时,又会让许多人痛心疾首。

4. *They make us believe immortality exists.* 他们使我们相信确实存在永恒的东西。

5. *An image as intense in its evocation of triumph as the image of his weeping in the dought is in its portrayals of heartache.* 这一形象所激发的胜利感和他在场上替补席上痛哭流涕所表现的心痛欲绝的形象一样深刻!

6. *There will be some performances from individual athletes which will fix those Games forever in the minds of these who watch.* 可能某些运动员的某些表现会使得这次奥运会永远留在观众的脑海中。

7. *As she landed, however, she suddenly fell.* 然而,她落地的时候突然摔倒了。

8. *Kerri could hardly bear to watch as he fell again.* 当他再次摔倒时,Kerri不忍心看了。

9. *It was a very hard work, and she had to live without many of the normal things that other teenagers enjoyed.* 训练是艰苦的,而她的生活中没有了其他少女所喜欢的很普通的东西。

10. *I'm only the underdog, and they're expecting me to lose.* 我是个小角色,他们都认为我会输。

Fashion Conversation 鲜活会话 由线到面

Conversation 1

A: I can her the motto "Swifter, Higher, Stronger" in the sports meeting.	A:在运动会上,我经常听到这样一句话"更快,更高,更强"。
B: Does it belong to the Olympic tenet?	B:这也是奥林匹克的信条吗?
A: Sure. One of these.	A:当然了,是其中的一条。
B: This is also comprised by Coubertin?	B:也是顾拜旦提出的吗?
A: No, by this friend, Henri Martin Didon.	A:不是,是他的朋友 Henri Martin Didon 提出的。
B: Could you introduce me some other words on Olympic spirit?	B:你可以跟我介绍一下其他关于奥运精神的格言吗?
A: Okay. Such as "The most important thing is to participate".	A:好吧。比如说"重在参与"。
B: I know this sentence before, but I don't know it comes from Olympics.	B:我以前就知道"重在参与"这句话了,但不知道它与奥运会有关。
A: Where did you get it?	A:你从哪儿得知的?
B: Once, I'm very shy of speaking before others. My teacher encouraged me by it.	B:以前,我很害羞,不敢在众人面前讲话。我老师就是用这一句话来鼓励我的。
A: It really can encourage people to do things they dare not.	A:它的确可以鼓舞人们去做不敢做的事。
B: No wonder so many people are fond of Olympics.	B:难怪有这么多人喜欢奥运会

Conversation 2

A: Look! So many handicapped people.	A:看,那么多残疾人。
B: Yeah. They talk and laugh. They don't feel self-humiliation a bit.	B:是的。他们有说有笑,一点也不自卑。
A: That's right. The Paralytics will open soon.	A:不错,残奥会不久就要开幕了。
B: Maybe among them there are world champions.	B:或许他们中有世界冠军。
A: Though they are handicapped in the body, the standard of health mainly depends on the inner strength.	A:尽管他们身体残废,但健康的标准主要在于心灵健康。
B: What's the purpose of the Paralytics?	B:残奥会的目的是什么?
A: To help the handicapped people recover physically and mentally.	A:帮助残疾人从身体和心理都得到康复。
B: It's set up in order to better display the Olympic spirit of "impartiality, participation and competition".	B:它的设立充分体现了奥运会"公平、参与、竞争"的原则。
A: Right. If they are able to live optimistically, we healthy people should live an even better life.	A:对,残疾人能这样乐观地生活,我们肢体健全的人更应该好好生活了。
B: We should cherish our daily life.	B:我们应当珍惜每一天的生活。

Conversation 3

A: Once every four years, the greatest athletes from all over the world gather together to take part in	A:每隔四年,世界上最优秀的运动员们都从四面八方汇集到一起参加奥林匹克盛会。

the Olympic Games.

B: I think getting a gold medal is the dream of every competitor.

B:我认为赢得一枚金牌是每一个运动员的梦想。

A: But they have to spend long years training hard and lonely.

A:但是他们必须为此年复一年地进行漫长而且常常是单一枯燥的训练。

B: Of course. After all that hard work, they will go the Olympics to compete against other excellent competitors.

B:当然。付出这些艰辛的劳动之后,他们要到奥运赛场上同其他优秀的选手较量。

A: Besides, each of them has to overcome particular difficulties on their way to success.

A:除此之外,他们中的每一个人还不得不在他们成功的道路上克服许多困难。

B: Yes. Behind success are tears and sweats.

B:对。成功的背后有太多的泪水和汗水。

Conversation 4

A: What a shame!

A:真丢脸!

B: What are you reading?

B:你在看什么呢?

A: Spain's Paralympic basketball team had to hand back gold medals won in Sydney because 10 of their players were found to have no disability.

A:参加残奥会的西班牙篮球队不得不退还了他们在悉尼赢得的金牌,因为他们队中的10名队员被查出没有残疾。

B: You don't say! It's a scandal. The Sydney Games were Spain's most successful Paralympics it has ever taken part in.

B:不会吧!这真是个十足的丑闻。悉尼奥运会是西班牙所参加的最成功的残疾人奥运会。

A: They deserve it.

A:他们活该!

B: I'm just wondering how this could happen. How could those who suffered no handicap participate in the Paralympics? It's really to those disabled ones.

B:我只是奇怪这是怎么会发生的。那些没有残疾的运动员怎么能参加残奥会呢?这对有残疾的运动员来说真是不公平。

A: Exactly! The most important thing in the Olympic Games is not to win but to participate. How dare they do this to bring disgrace on the nobility and purity of the Olympics?

A:你的对极了!在奥运会上最重要的事情是参与而不是取胜。他们怎么敢这样做以至于玷污了奥林匹克精神的崇高与纯洁。

B: So the athletes must be given medical or psychological tests to check their eligibility for the Paralympics. Is there anyone who has been involved in this scandal?

B:所以运动员必须接受体格检查或心理检查以确定他们参加残奥会的资格。在这次丑闻中,有人受到牵连吗?

A: Yes. The scandal has already promoted the resignation of the vice president of the Spanish Paralympic Committee(CPE) and the president of the Spanish Federation of Mentally Handicapped Sports(FEDDI).

A:有。这次丑闻已经促使西班牙残奥委员的副主席和西班牙智力残障运动联合会的主席辞职。

B: I think we all should think deeply about the scandal, and answer the question "What do we participate in the Olympics for?" by ourselves.

B:我觉得我们所有的人都应该对这次的丑闻进行深思,并自己回答"我们为什么要参加奥运会?"这个问题。

Conversation 5

A: Coubertin designed the symbol of the five rings. What do the Olympic five rings represent?

A:顾拜旦设计了五环标志。奥运五环代表什么?

B: The rings symbolize the five continents —— Europe (the blue color ring), Africa (the black), Australia (the green), Asia (the yellow) and America (the red) and five rings or circles linked together represent the sporting friendship of all peoples. Do you know Latin, Miss Wei?

B：五环象征五大洲——欧洲(蓝色环)，非洲(黑色环)，澳洲(绿色环)，亚洲(黄色环)，美洲(红色环)，五环连在一起代表世界各国人民的运动友谊。卫小姐，你懂拉丁语吗？

A: A little.

A：懂一点点。

B: Citius, Altius, Fortius.

B：更快，更高，更强。

A: Latin words meaning: "faster, higher, braver". The modern interpretation of them is "swifter, higher, stronger".

A：拉丁语意思是"更快，更高，更强"，现代的解释是"swifter, higher, stronger"。

B: Quite right! They express the athletes' goal of running faster, jumping higher, and throwing more strongly.

B：太正确了！它表达了运动员的目标，跑得更快，跳得更高，投掷得更有力。

A: I think every athlete can recite the Olympic creed, The most important thing in the Olympic Games is not to win but to take part in. The Olympic spirit is impartiality, participation and competition.

A：我想每个运动员都能背诵奥运信条，奥运会最重要的不是输赢而是参与。奥运精神是公平，参与，竞争。

A: Professor Maclaren, I have learnt a great deal from you. Thank you.

A：麦克拉伦教授，我从您那学到不少东西，谢谢。

B: You are welcome.

B：不客气。

Conversation 6

A: I don't quite understand why people must have all kinds of activities to show their support for Beijing's bid. I heard the residents in Beijing went planting trees to show their support. Has it anything to do with the Olympics?

A：我真是不明白为什么人们必须进行各种各样的活动来表明他们支持北京申奥。我听说北京市民去植树来表示他们的支持，这跟奥运会有关系吗？

B: It certainly has. Because the evaluation team of the IOC will visit the 5 cities bidding for the Olympics to decide which city can host the Games, and the environment is one of the crucial factors.

B：当然有关系了。因为国际奥委会评估团会参观5个申办城市以决定哪一个城市获得举办权，而环境是其中一个关键因素。

A: Really? No wonder people say to host the Olympics is a good chance to develop our country.

A：真的吗？难怪人们说举办奥运会是发展我们国家的一个大好机会。

B: That's true. Beijing will be a big city as the cities in developed countries in 2008. It's not only in the environment, other aspects will also be better.

B：说的没错。到了2008年，北京将能够与发达国家的大多数城市相媲美，这不光是指在环境方面，而且在其他方面也如此。

A: In that case, everyone in China will benefit from it.

A：如果是那样的话，每一个中国人都能够从中受益。

B: Yes. But to take this opportunity, I think we must get ready right now.

B：是的。但要抓住这个机会，我认为我们必须现在就做好准备。

A: And learning English well is the first step.

A：而且学好英语是第一步。

B: I think so.

B：我也这样认为。

主题:内瓦和莉斯正在讨论中国女足的故事。请你看图,根据如下提供的关键词,将他们的对话写出来。

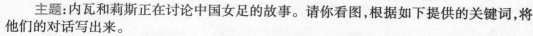

关键词语:FIFA 国际足联　athlete *n.* 运动员　splendent *adj.* 辉煌的
ignore *v.* 忽视　endure *v.* 耐久,忍耐　elect *v.* 选举,推选

参考答案

Neva: Sun Wen was elected as the best football athlete by FIFA, wasn't she?

Liz: Oh! I know. You must be talking about the Chinese woman football?

Neva: Yeah. The splendent achievements of the Chinese woman football team are usually ignored. How unfair it is!

Liz: I feel the same way. We should indeed pay our respect to the Chinese woman football.

Neva: Right. Chinese woman football's characters and the spirits of enduring hardship are more superior than that of the man's.

Liz: Perhaps. It's said that their training conditions are not good enough and their treatments are far from that of the man's.

Neva: Yes. Every girl of the woman football team is very excellent.

Liz: En. They said they couldn't wait for the positive changes passively, but should initially try their best to adapt to the enviroment and create favorable conditions to win the victory.

Neva: They are great.

内瓦:孙雯被国际足联评为了最佳球员,不是吗?

莉斯:噢,我知道了。你是在说中国女足吧?

内瓦:是的。中国女足战果辉煌,却往往不被人关注,真是不公平!

莉斯:我也有同感。我们应该向中国女足致敬。

内瓦:对,中国女足的意志品质、吃苦精神明显优于男足。

莉斯:或许吧。听说她们的训练条件并不好,而且待遇远不如男足。

内瓦:是的。女足姑娘们个个都是好样的。

莉斯:嗯。她们说她们不能消极等待条件好转,而应该主动想办法适应环境,创造有利条件,去夺取每一场比赛胜利。

内瓦:她们真是了不起。

★田径赛事★ 2 Track and Field Events

Words and Phrases 闪亮词语 点滴积累

field event 田赛
countback 平局法
Fosbury Flop 背跃式跳高
takeoff board 起跳板
shot put 铅球投掷
athletic field 田径场
attempt 试跳,试投
balkline 起跳线
circle 投掷圈
discus 铁饼
distance jump 跳远
final jump 最后一次试跳
hammer 链球
hammer thrower 链球运动员
head of javelin 标枪头
high jump 跳高
javelin 标枪
javelin thrower 标枪运动员
judges' stand 裁判台
long approach 长距离助跑
long jump 跳远
pole vault 撑杆跳
putting area 铅球投掷圈
scratch line 起掷线
shot 铅球
shot putter 铅球运动员
standing high jump 立定跳高
straddle 俯卧式跳高
throwing arc 投掷弧
track event 径赛
anchor 末棒队员
breakline 压道线
changeover 交接棒
crouch start 蹲踞式起跑
false start 抢跑
long distance 长跑
marathon 马拉松
middle distance 中跑
on your mark 各就各位
set 预备
sprint 短跑
starter's gun 发令枪
starting block 起跑器
steeplechase 障碍赛
takeover zone 接力区
walk 竞走
abreast start 并排起跑
accelerative running 加速跑
blast 冲刺跑
century sprint 百米跑
curve 弯道
flat-out 全速
hand off 传棒
home bent 最后弯道
hurdle 跨栏
lap judge 计圈裁判
leaving one's own lane 抢道
pace setter 领跑人

Useful Sentences 七彩精句 连点成线

Field events knowledge 田赛知识

1. *Field events can be divided into two major categories: jumping and throwing.* 田赛可分为跳跃和投掷两大类。
2. *Jumping and throwing have different competing arenas.* 跳跃和投掷项目的竞技场所不同。
3. *There is no run-up for throwing events while jumping events require an approach run.* 投掷项目不用助跑,而跳跃项目需要助跑。
4. *We judge the performance of field athletes by distance or height.* 我们用距离或高度来判定田赛成绩。
5. *The women's pole vault world record was broken*

several times in 1995. 女子撑杆跳世界纪录在1995年被打破过几次。

The field contest wording 田赛比赛用语

1. *The jump is declared a foul.* 这次跳跃被判犯规。
2. *What do you think of the jumping and throwing?* 你认为跳跃和投掷的结果如何?
3. *Who broke the record for long jump?* 谁打破了跳远纪录?
4. *Pedroso fouls in the second try. He oversteps the lines.* 佩德罗索第2次试跳犯规,他踏板过线。
5. *Bartova jumps and achieves the records of 4.20 metres.* 芭尔托娃起跳并且达到4.2米的纪录。
6. *Kostadinova fails in her attempt to jump higher than 2.01m.* 科斯塔迪诺娃跳高未能超过2.01米。

Track events knowledge 径赛知识

1. *Events on the track consist of sprints, middle distance races, long distance races, relays, hurdles, barriers, and marathon—the extreme distance race.* 径赛包括短跑、中跑、长跑、接力跑、跨栏跑、障碍跑以及超长跑马拉松等项目。
2. *Track races are measured by time, accurate to one hundredth of a second.* 径赛项目用时间来测定成绩,精确到百分之一秒。
3. *Stride length and frequency are the most important elements of sprinting.* 步长和步频是短跑最重要的因素。
4. *The athletes who will compete in the track events should go to the roll call 20 minutes before the race.* 参加径赛的运动员应在赛前20分钟检录。
5. *Hurdling events are dashes in which competitions must clear a series of ten barriers called hurdles.* 在跨栏项目中,运动员需要跨过十个栏。
6. *The relays are the only true team events in track and field.* 接力赛是田径运动中真正的团体项目。
7. *The standard Olympic distance for men race-walking is 20 000 meters and 50 000 meters.* 正规的奥运会男子竞走比赛有20000米和50000米两种。

The track contest wording 径赛比赛用语

1. *Now the first heat sit on the lane.* 第一组上跑道。
2. *If he commits another false start, he is sure to be disqualified.* 他如果再抢跑,肯定会被取消资格。
3. *He made a fast finishing burst and overtake the leaders on the home straight.* 他快速做最后的冲刺,在冲刺线前超过了领先者。
4. *The runners have been in their lanes. They are doing warming-up exercises.* 选手们已经上跑道了,他们在做准备活动。
5. *He nearly drops the baton at changeover.* 他在交接棒时差点弄丢了接力棒。

Fashion Conversation 鲜活会话 由线到面

Conversation 1

A: What do field events include, Mr. William?
A:威廉先生,田赛项目包括什么比赛?

B: The field events include: high jump, pole vault, long jump, triple jump, shot put, discus throw, javelin throw, hammer throw etc.
B:田赛项目包括:跳高,撑杆跳,跳远,三级跳,推铅球,掷铁饼,投标枪,掷链球等。

A: How many tries is each contestant allowed at each height of the high up event?
A:在跳高比赛中,每一个参赛者在每一高度允许试跳几次?

B: Each contestant is allowed three tries to get over the bar at each height. On a third consecutive miss, the jumper is eliminated. Those who clear a height move on to the next height, until a winner
B:每一高度、每一参赛者允许跳三次,三次连续不过者被淘汰,通过者进行下一个高度,直到决出胜者。

is decided.

A: If two contestants clear the same height in the same number of attempts, who wins?

A:假如两个参赛者以相同的试跳次数跳过同一高度的话,谁是获胜者呢?

B: The one who has fewer misses during the entire competition wins.

B:在整个比赛中,失误较少者胜。

A: If they are still tied, who wins?

A:假如,他们仍然都一样,谁是胜者呢?

B: The competitor with fewer attempts in the competition wins.

B:在比赛中试跳较少者胜。

Conversation 2

A: How many kilograms is the weight of a shot?

A:铅球的重量是多少千克?

B: The men's shot, a solid iron or solid or lead-filled brass ball weighs 16 pounds (7.257kg) and measures 11 to 13 cm in diameter.

B:男子铅球是实心铁球,或者是实心的或用铅灌的铜球,重16磅(7.257公斤),直径为11~13厘米。

A: Where did the shot originate from?

A:铅球源于何地?

B: The shot originated from the European artillerymen's carrying shells in 1440s.

B:铅球起源于15世纪40年代欧洲炮兵搬运炮弹的活动。

A: Was discus throwing a popular activity in ancient Greece?

A:掷铁饼在古代希腊是一种流行的活动吗?

B: Yes, surviving statues can prove it. Performance improved rapidly. The record of discus throw exceeds 200 feet now.

B:是的,幸存下来的塑像可以证明这一点。动作提高很快。现在铁饼纪录已经超过二百英尺。

A: Where did hammer throw originate in?

A:掷链球的起源地是哪里?

B: It originated in Britain. Around the 16th century hammer throw began to prevail among the British blacksmiths, stonemen. They threw their tool-hammer.

B:它起源于英国。在16世纪,掷链球在英国铁匠、石匠中间盛行,他们掷工具锤。

A: Now the hammer is different from the tool-hammer.

A:现在掷链球不同于掷工具锤。

B: The hammer consists of a ball, or head, attached to a long handle by a swivel.

B:链球由一个球体或链头,通过旋转接头连一条长柄。

A: How long is the spring steel wire handle?

A:韧性钢链把手多长?

B: At least 3 feet 10 $\frac{1}{4}$ inches (117.5cm) long.

B:至少3英尺10 $\frac{1}{4}$ 英寸(117.5厘米)长。

A: How does a contestant throw?

A:参赛者怎么掷呢?

B: The contestant swings the hammer around his head several times. Then with the swing of the implement, he makes three turns with his body to gain maximum centrifugal force before he releases it.

B:参赛者在头上方转动链球若干次,然后在掷出链球之前,参赛者的身体随着链球转动三圈得到最大的离心力。

A: Thank you. I can be a hammer thrower after your explanation.

A:谢谢。听了你的介绍,我也能成了链球运动员了。

Conversation 3

A: What races do the track events include?

A:径赛项目包括什么?

B: The track events include: short-distance races or

B:径赛项目包括:短跑、中跑、长跑、竞走、跨栏、接

sprints, middle-distance races, long-distance races, speed walking, hurdle races, relay, steeplechase and marathon.

力赛、障碍赛及马拉松。

A: How many kilometers does a marathon runner cover?

A: 马拉松运动员要跑多少公里?

B: The first marathon race in the 1896 Olympics was a distance of 40 kilometers. The current distance of the marathon isn't 40 kilometers but 42 kilometers and 195 meters.

B: 在1896年奥运会上,首次马拉松赛的距离是40公里。现在马拉松赛的距离不是40公里而是42.195公里。

A: During the short-distance races, the start and the sprint are very important for the runners and results of runners are often just inches apart. What kind of start position is better: standing start or crouch start?

A: 在短跑比赛跑中,起跑和冲刺对运动员尤其重要,往往数英寸定输赢。哪种起跑好些:站立式还是蹲踞式起跑?

B: Nowadays all sprinters start from a crouch position. They get down on all fours, one foot planted ahead of the other in the starting blocks and both hands resting just behind the starting line.

B: 现在所有的短跑运动员起跑都采用蹲踞式,运动员四肢着地,在起跑器上一只脚在另一只的前面,双手在起跑线之后。

A: The crouch start provides a quicker getaway than the standing start.

A: 蹲踞式起跑较之站立式起跑起步快。

B: Contemporaries claimed that the crouch start was the invention of professional track runners.

B: 当代人认为,蹲踞式起跑是专业田径运动员的一个发明。

A: Do hurdles and steeplechase belong to obstacle races?

A: 跨栏和障碍赛属于障碍跑吗?

B: Yes. Obstacle races are of two kinds—hurdles and steeplechase.

B: 属于障碍跑。障碍跑有两种:跨栏和障碍赛。

Conversation 4

A: The women's 100m race is to be broadcast live right away.

A: 马上就要现场直播女子100米比赛了。

B: Really? I won't miss it for anything. It makes me goofy.

B: 真的吗? 我无论如何也不会错过,我简直是痴迷了。

A: Hurry! The sprinters are in their lanes now. They are doing up some warming-up exercises.

A: 快来! 运动员已经上跑道了,他们在做准备活动。

B: The race must be tense and close, I suppose. We get Gail Devers, women's 100m champion of the 26th Olympic Games and the defending champion this time, and. . .

B: 我想这场比赛一定很紧张,很激烈。参加这场比赛的有第26届奥运会女子100米冠军盖尔·德福斯,这次是卫冕冠军,还有……

A: Listen, Gail is in the third lane.

A: 听,盖尔在第三跑道。

B: Who's that woman in the fifth lane?

B: 第五跑道的那位是谁?

A: Marion Jones.

A: 玛里恩·琼斯。

B: Is she an Australian?

B: 她是澳大利亚人吗?

A: No. She is an American. Look. The final is on the line. The starter calls the runners stand behind their blocks. They are to rise to the set position. What's wrong with you?

A: 不,她是美国人。看! 决赛要开始了。发令员把运动员召集到起跑器后面。他们就要起跑了。你怎么了?

B: Oh, nothing. Just nervous.

A: You seem to be more nervous and excited than the sprinters. It fires.

B: Great! Gail takes the lead.

A: But Marion catches up... overtakes Gale... hits the line. Marion ran a perfect race. Terrific!

B: Oh, 10.75 seconds. Incredible!

B:哦,没什么。只是有些紧张。

A:你似乎比运动员更紧张,更兴奋。枪响了。

B:太棒了!盖尔领先了。

A:但玛里恩赶上来了……超过盖尔了……撞线。玛里恩跑得棒极了。太棒了!

B:哦,10.75秒,不可思议!

Conversation 5

A: Chinese sports authorities have given Chinese-born Chen Yueling permission to represent the United States in next month's Olympics.

B: Who's Chen Yueling?

A: She was a national race walker and earned China is first Olympic athletics gold in Barcelona in 1992.

B: Then how can she represent the United States in the Olympics?

A: She retired many years ago. And she's working and studying in the United States now. It's amazing that she can go back to the track after retiring for so many years.

B: Why didn't she just ask for the permission of the United States Olympic Committee?

A: According to the International Olympic Committee's rules, athletes are only eligible to represent adopted countries when they have had that country's nationality for at least three years.

B: How long has Chen had her U.S. nationality?

A: She did not get America's citizenship until 1998.

B: Then, didn't our permission break the IOC rules?

A: We originally said "no" to Chen's issue because we respected the regulations of the IOC and the CAA (the Chinese Athletics Association). But we finally decided to endorse Chen's Olympic trip because we regard "never giving up" as one aspect for the Olympic spirit.

B: All right, let's wish her good luck.

A:中国体育当局已经同意中国出生的陈跃玲代表美国参加下个月的奥运会了。

B:谁是陈跃玲?

A:她以前是一位国家队的竞走运动员,1992年在巴塞罗那为中国队赢得了第一枚奥运会的田径金牌。

B:那她为什么可以代表美国参加奥运会?

A:她很多年前就退役了,现在在美国工作和学习。她在退役了这么多年以后还能重返田径赛场,这真让人惊讶。

B:她为什么不直接征得美国奥委会的同意?

A:根据国际奥委会的规定,运动员只有在取得移居国国籍3年以上时才能代表该国参加比赛。

B:陈获得美国国籍多久了。

A:她直到1998年才获得美国国籍。

B:那么,我们允许她参加比赛不就违反了国际奥委会的规定了吗?

A:最初我们也不同意陈的要求,因为我们尊重国际奥委会和中国田径协会的规定。但后来我们决定认可陈的奥运会之旅,因为我们认为"永不放弃"是奥林匹克精神的一个方面。

B:好吧,让我们祝她好运。

On the Scene 身临其境 面面俱到

主题:田径运动会上,看台上的威尔与琳达正在为大家加油。请你看图,根据如下提供的关键词,将他们的对话写出来。

关键词语:lane *n.* 跑道　　sprint *v.* 疾跑

final *n.* 决赛
precise *n.* 精确
risk *n.* 冒险,风险
theoretically *adv.* 理论上
quickly *adv.* 很快地
palm *n.* 手掌
technique *n.* 技巧,方法
avoid *v.* 避免,消除
baton *n.* 指挥棒;接力棒
hey *int.* 嗨
specific *n.* 细节

参考答案

Will: Come on, York!
Linda: York starts fast. He's in the lead now.
Will: Li Qiang begins to start. York reaches him and passes the baton.
Linda: The third lane drops the baton at changeover.
Will: Lane 4 has caught up.
Linda: Liu Hua takes the baton. He's sprinting.
Will: Lane 4 also completes the changeover. And so do lanes 1 and 3.
Linda: They're now charging for the final sprint.
Will: Lane 3 has caught up with lane 4.
Linda: Liu Hua breasts the tape first.
Will: Lane 3 comes in second. And lane 1 finishes fourth.
Linda: The passing technique is so important. I'm thinking how a team can have a quick and precise passing and avoid the risk of dropping the baton.
Will: It's easy to say theoretically but hard to do.
Linda: As the baton carrier reaches the baton taker, he may call out a short command like "Hey!" or "Get it!", and the taker quickly move his arm back to take the baton.

Will: Quite specific.

Linda: From the point of view of the passing techniques, use the push technique. That is, push the baton forward in a straight line with it s head up and press it into the palm of the extended arm of the receiving runner.

威尔:加油,约克!

琳达:约克起跑很快,他现在领先。

威尔:李强开始起跑,约克赶上他并把棒传给了他。

琳达:第三跑道交接棒时掉棒了。

威尔:第四跑道赶上去了。

琳达:刘华接棒了,他在全速冲刺。

威尔:第四路道也完成了交接棒,第一跑道、第三跑道也完成了。

琳达:他们正在努力做最后的冲刺。

威尔:第三跑道赶上了第四跑道。

琳达:刘华第一个到达终点。

威尔:第三跑道跑了第二名,第一跑道得了第四名。

琳达:传接棒技术太重要了。我现在在想如何才能做到快速、准确地传棒,避免掉棒的危险。

威尔:从理论上说容易,可做起来却很难。

琳达:当传棒人交接棒时,他可以口中发出极短的命令信号,如"嘿!"或"接!",然后接棒人迅速向后伸手接棒。

威尔:说得很具体。

琳达:从传棒的技术角度上说,用手推式。也就是说,接力棒呈直线向前推,棒头朝上,塞入接棒人展开的手掌中。

★水上项目★ 3 Waterside Activities

Words and Phrases 闪亮词语 点滴积累

ten-metre plat form 10 米跳板
degree of difficulty 难度系数
dome of water 水花
armstand dive 臂立跳水
back dive 向后跳水
butterfly dive 蝶式跳水
crouched jump 抱膝跳水
inward dive 向内跳水
jump 直体跳水
spring board dive 跳板跳水
synchronized diving 花样跳水
twist dive 转体跳水
swim lane 泳道
stroke 泳姿
basin 游泳池
back stroke 仰泳
breast stroke 蛙泳
butterfly stroke 蝶泳
free relay 自由泳接力
synchronized swimming 花样游泳
scull 双桨艇
rower 赛艇运动员
blade 桨叶
steer 掌舵
oarsman 桨手
regatta 划船比赛

Useful Sentences 七彩精句 连点成线

Diving knowledge 跳水知识

1. *A diving pool is usually six metres deep.* 跳水池深度一般为 6 米。
2. *The diver should project himself into the air from a high-board or springboard.* 跳水运动员应从跳台或跳板腾空而起。
3. *All feet first entries shall be executed with the arms close to the body and no bending at the elbows.* 脚先入水时,两臂应紧贴身体两侧,手肘不能弯曲。
4. *The entry into water shall in all cases be vertical with the body straight, the feet together and the toes pointed.* 在任何情况下,入水时身体都应伸直,并与水面垂直,两脚并拢,脚尖绷直。
5. *A dive is finished when the whole body is completely under the surface of the water.* 当运动员整个身体浸入水面以下,一个跳水动作才算完成。

The diving contest wording 跳水比赛用语

1. *He excels in opening the water with his palms.* 他擅长用手掌压水花。
2. *She ended with a clean and graceful entry into the water.* 她入水的姿势干净利索而优美。
3. *He achieved a perfectly clean entry, and there is almost no splash.* 他的入水非常漂亮,几乎没有溅起水花。
4. *In spite of the great degree of difficulty, she did a wonderful dive.* 尽管难度系数很大,但她还是跳得非常漂亮。
5. *He has finished the 5 required dives and 6 optional dives quite satisfactorily.* 他非常满意地完成了 5 个规定动作和 6 个自选动作。

Swimming knowledge 游泳知识

1. *Modern competitive swimming originated in the 19th century.* 现代竞技游泳始于 19 世纪。
2. *In the back-stroke, breast stroke, and butterfly a touch by hand is required. The most common turn used in crawl events is the flip turn.* 仰泳,蛙泳和蝶泳要求手触壁。自由泳最常见的转身是筋

斗转。

3. *The first swimmer swims back-stroke, the second breast stroke, the third butterfly, and the fourth freestyle in a medley relay.* 在混合式接力中，第一个运动员用仰泳，第二个运动员用蛙泳，第三个运动员用蝶泳，第四个运动员用自由泳。

4. *In each event the fastest swimmer is placed in the middle lane in the swimming pool.* 在每项比赛中最快的运动员被安置在中间泳道。

5. *In team competition, a team shall consist of at least four but not more than eight members.* 在团体比赛中，团体成员要求在4人以上但不能超过8人。

The swimming contest wording 游泳比赛知识

1. *To get a satisfactory result, racers will always do sufficient warm-up exercises before the race.* 为了取得理想的成绩，选手们在比赛之前总要做充分的热身运动。

2. *It seems that they excel in controlling their breathing.* 他们似乎都很擅长控制呼吸。

3. *How long do you think they can hold their breath?* 你认为他们憋气能憋多久？

4. *He has broken the world record of 100 m freestyle.* 他打破了100米自由泳世界纪录。

5. *He clocked 53.72 seconds in the 100 m back-stroke race.* 他100米仰泳的成绩是53.72秒。

6. *The American swimmer in the fifth lane is the Olympic-record holder in the men's 200 m freestyle, the first one in the heats.* 第五泳道的美国运动员是男子200米自由泳奥运纪录保持者，预赛时他是第一。

Canoeing knowledge 皮划艇知识

1. *The kayak is propelled by kayakers in a sitting position.* 皮艇则是由皮艇桨手用坐姿划行的。

2. *Flat water canoeing was first included in the Olympics at Berlin in 1936.* 皮划艇竞赛在1936年柏林奥运会上第一次被列入比赛项目。

3. *International events are held for one-man, two-man and four-man kayaks.* 国际比赛项目有单人、双人、四人皮艇。

4. *Dominant nations in canoeing include Russia, Germany and East European countries.* 在世界皮划艇运动中居主导地位的国家有俄罗斯、德国和东欧国家。

5. *Slalom canoeing takes place on a rushing-water/wide-water course.* 皮划艇回旋赛是在激流水道中进行的。

6. *Canoeing requires strength, stamina, balance, coordination and great determination.* 皮划艇运动要求运动员具有力量、耐力、平衡性、协调性和巨大的决心。

The canoe contest wording 划艇比赛用语

1. *They draw lots to decide the lanes they should take.* 他们通过抽签来决定道次。

2. *He's got a perfect paddling position.* 他的划桨姿势非常完美。

3. *She takes a "J" stroke.* 她采用的是钩形划法。

4. *Bill ranked second in the semifinal of C-1, 500 meters.* 比尔在1500米单人划艇比赛半决赛中名列第二。

Rowing knowledge 赛艇知识

1. *Rowing is a water sport in which a boat is propelled through the water by means of oars.* 赛艇是用桨作为推动力使船在水上前进的水上运动项目。

2. *A rowing competition is called a regatta.* 赛艇比赛称作赛船会。

3. *A standard men's Olympic course is two thousand meters long.* 奥运会男子水道的标准长度为2000米。

4. *Rowing was officially recognized as an Olympic sport at London in 1908.* 1908年，在伦敦奥运会上赛艇被正式列入奥运会项目。

5. *Women's rowing events were included in the Olympics for the first time at Montreal in 1976.* 女子赛艇项目在1976年蒙特利尔奥运会上第一次被列入奥运会项目。

6. *Dominant nations in the world rowing include Germany, East European countries and the USA.* 在世

界赛艇运动中处于领先地位的国家有德国、东欧国家和美国。

The rowing contest wording 赛艇比赛用语

1. *The German cox steered the boat well and did a good organization job.* 德国队的舵手舵掌得好，组织工作也做得好。
2. *In the first 500 and the last 500 meters, the strike rate has reached as many as 47 strokes a minute.* 在前500米和最后500米，划桨的频率达到了每分钟47次之多。
3. *His sculling rhythm is terrific.* 他的划船节奏太好了。

Fashion Conversation 鲜活会话 由线到面

Conversation 1

A: Diving is an athletic activity. What does diving require as a competitive sport?

B: As a competitive sport, diving requires coordinated movements, expertly timed and controlled.

A: When did diving develop?

B: Diving was developed in the latter part of the 19th century.

A: When was diving accepted as a formal event at the Olympics?

B: Diving has been an Olympic sport for men since 1904 and for women since 1912.

A：跳水是一项竞技运动。作为比赛体育运动，跳水要求什么？

B：作为体育比赛，跳水要求协调的动作、熟练的节奏及控制力。

A：跳水什么时候发展起来的？

B：跳水在19世纪末发展起来的。

A：跳水什么时候作为奥林匹克正式比赛项目被接受的？

B：1904年跳水成为奥运会男子体育比赛项目，从1912年起跳水成为奥林匹克女子比赛项目。

Conversation 2

A: To tell you a secret, I practiced diving for a few years when I was in high school. So I can give you some pointers about the sport.

B: Are you serious? O. K. Why don't we start from the codes divers use for each dive? For example, look at this diver. What does 305C stand for?

A: This stands for reverse 2.5 somersault-tuck (walking approach).

B: What about 405B?

A: Inward 2.5 somersault-pike.

B: I'm wondering what criteria judges use to score a dive?

A: They basically look at the five components of the dive: approach, takeoff, elevation, execution and entry.

B: What do the judges look for while the diver is in the air?

A: The judges look the elevation and execution of the dive. For elevation, they must decide whether the diver has achieved enough height in the air after take-off. For execution, they check the

A：告诉你个秘密，我上高中时练过几年跳水，所以我可以向你介绍一下这项运动。

B：真的吗？好吧，咱们索性从每一跳的代码说起吧。比如说，看这个选手，305C代表什么？

A：反身翻腾两周半抱膝(走板)。

B：405B代表什么？

A：向内翻腾两周半屈体。

B：我想知道裁判给每个动作打分的标准是什么？

A：每一跳裁判基本上会看五个组成部分：准备动作、起跳、腾空、动作完成和入水。

B：那么选手在空中时裁判主要看什么？

A：裁判员要看腾空和动作完成情况。腾空主要看运动员在跳起后是否达到了足够的高度，动作完成情况主要看运动员的技巧和动作是否优雅。

diver's technique and grace in the air.

B: How about entry into the water?

B: 那入水看什么呢?

A: That is the last but not the least important part of a dive. The entry must be vertical, with the body straight and the toes pointed. Moreover, The amount of splashed should be controlled to the minimum.

A: 入水是跳水的结束部分,但也非常的重要。入水时身体要与水面垂直,身体和脚尖绷直,而且溅起的水花要尽可能小。

B: Thanks for your instruction. I have learned a lot from you. With this much knowledge, I will definitely enjoy diving more.

B: 谢谢你的介绍。从你那儿我学到了很多。由此,我更加坚定了喜欢跳水的决心。

Conversation 3

A: What's the spearhead principle in swimming competitions?

A: 什么是游泳比赛的"箭头"原则?

B: In each event the competitor with the fastest entry time is assigned the center lane, or in pools with an even number of lanes, the lane on the right of the center.

B: 每个项目预赛成绩最好的选手在决赛时,被排在最中间的泳道,如泳道数是偶数,就排在中间靠右的泳道。

A: How about the other swimmers?

A: 其他选手呢?

B: They are placed alternately left and right of him in descending order of speed, so that the slowest swimmers are in the two outside lanes.

B: 他们按成绩从快到慢依次左边一个、右边一个地排好泳道,这样成绩最慢的选手就被排在最外面的两个泳道上。

A: What's the order of strokes in medley events?

A: 混合泳的顺序是怎样的?

B: In individual event, competitors swim an equal distance of four strokes: the sequence is butterfly, backstroke, breaststroke and free style.

B: 个人混合泳比赛时,运动员按下列顺序用 4 种姿势游相同的距离:蝶泳、仰泳、蛙泳、自由泳。

Conversation 4

A: Swimming is popular throughout the world both for recreation and as a competitive sport. How many years has man swum for, Mr. Han?

A: 游泳在全世界都是一种大众喜欢的既可娱乐又可作为比赛的体育项目。韩先生,人类游泳已经多少年了?

B: Early pictographs, bas-reliefs and sculptures establish that man has swum for at least 2000 years.

B: 早期象形文字记载,浅浮雕及雕塑证实,人类游泳至少已有两千年了。

A: Swimming ranks as one of man's oldest physical activities. Who developed the modern sport of swimming?

A: 游泳是人类最古老的体育活动之一。谁发展了现代游泳运动?

B: The modern sport of swimming was developed by the English.

B: 英国人发展了现代游泳体育。

A: When were the first swimming contests conducted?

A: 首届游泳竞赛是在什么时候进行的?

B: The first contests, using the breaststroke, were conducted in London in 1837.

B: 首届游泳竞赛,运用蛙泳,于 1837 年在伦敦进行。

A: When was the FINA (Federation Internationale de Natation Amateur) founded?

A: 国际业余游泳协会是什么时候成立的?

B: In 1908.

B: 它成立于 1908 年。

A: When was swimming accepted as a formal event at the Olympics? A:游泳什么时候被列入奥运会正式比赛项目的?

B: At the 1896 Olympic Games men's freestyle was listed in the events. B:在1896年,奥运会男子自由游被列入比赛项目。

Conversation 5

A: What is the main international canoeing competition? A:皮划艇的重要国际比赛有哪些?

B: The main international competition is the World Canoeing Championships. B:重要国际比赛是世界皮划艇锦标赛。

A: Is canoeing included in the Olympics? A:皮划艇是奥运会项目吗?

B: Yes, canoeing is an Olympic sport. B:是的,皮划艇是奥运会项目。

A: When did canoeing become an Olympic sport? A:皮划艇何时成为奥运会项目的?

B: Flat water canoeing became an Olympic sport at Berlin in 1936. B:平静水面皮划艇赛在1936年柏林奥运会上被列入比赛项目。

A: How about slalom canoeing? A:划艇回旋赛的情况如何?

B: Slalom canoeing was first included in the Olympics at Munich in 1972. B:划艇回旋赛第一次被列入奥运会项目是在1972年慕尼黑奥运会上。

Conversation 6

A: Why is rowing in east European countries so strong? A:为什么东欧的赛艇队实力强?

B: They use the squad system instead of the system based on colleges, universities and clubs. B:他们利用集训体制代替大学和俱乐部训练体制。

A: How can we improve the fitness level of our rowers? A:我们如何提高我们赛艇选手的身体素质水平?

B: You should devise some intensive routines of interval training. This should help to improve arm and leg speed. Circuit weight training should help to increase strength. Remember that some training drills should be closely related to actual rowing skills. B:你们应当设计一些常规的强度大的间歇性训练。这有助于提高手臂和腿的速度。循环式的负重训练有助于增强力量。要记住,这些训练必须与赛艇的专项技术紧密结合。

A: How many hours a day should a top rower spend on the water? A:尖子赛艇运动员每天水中训练时间应是几小时?

B: A top rower should spend at least two hours a day on the water. B:高级运动员应至少每天在水中训练2小时。

A: What other forms of exercise do you recommend for the oarsman? A:你还建议对桨手进行哪些其他形式的训练?

B: I also recommend try training in mechanical rowing machines to practise rowing and sculling strokes. This should help to improve technique and rhythm. B:我还建议采用陆上划船练习器进行划船练习,这种方法有助于改进技术和节奏。

On the Scene 身临其境 面面俱到

主题：汤姆教玛丽一些游泳技巧。请你看图，根据如下提供的关键词，将他们的对话写出来。

关键词语：length *n.* 距离　　　　warm-up exercises 热身运动

参考答案

Mary: I can swim only about the length. Then I swim down like a brick. Can you teach me some swimming skills?

Tom: Well, you really need more practice, and a little extra instruction.

Mary: I pulled muscles sometimes, and it was very painful. How can I avoid it?

Tom: You just need some warm-up exercises before beginning swimming.

Mary: You are right. Swimming is a good work-out, it keeps me healthy and fit, and gives me fun, too.

Tom: So you should stick to it.

玛丽：我只能游很近一段距离，然后就会像砖头一样沉下去，你能教我一些游泳技巧吗？

汤姆：哦，你确实需要多加练习和额外辅导。

玛丽：我有时会抽筋，非常痛，我几乎溺水了，怎样才能避免抽筋呢？

汤姆：你只需要在游泳前做些热身运动就行了。

玛丽：你说的对，游泳是一项很好的训练。既保持健康和体形，还有乐趣。

汤姆：所以你要坚持训练哟。

★冰雪运动★ 4 Sports on Snow and Ice

Words and Phrases 闪亮词语 点滴积累

hockey pants 冰球裤
hockey skate 冰球鞋
ice-hockey field 冰球场
ice-hockey stick 冰球杆
ice marking 冰上标记
skate 冰刀
skate land 旱冰场
sudden death 加时赛
anorak 滑雪衣
bob 大雪橇
bob-run 雪橇滑道
boot 滑雪鞋
breakable crust 易碎雪层
cross-country skiing 越野滑雪
downhill race 速降滑雪赛
flat skiing 平地滑雪
luge 短雪橇
mule kick 雪上特技
push off 蹬雪
ski cap 滑雪帽
ski glove 滑雪手套
ski master 滑雪能手

Useful Sentences 七彩精句 连点成线

Hockey 冰球

1. *The hockey player shoot the puck into the goal's net. The team with the most points wins.* 冰球队员将冰球射入守门员的球门，得分最多的队为胜者。
2. *Sometimes the girls play more aggressively than the boys.* 有时女孩比男孩还具有攻击性呢。
3. *In my opinion, the girls skate better than some of the boys.* 依我看，有些女孩比男孩滑冰滑得更好些。
4. *The puck is flat and slides on the ice. The hockey player move it around with his hockey stick.* 冰球是扁圆的，在冰上能滑动。冰球队员用球杆掌握冰球的运动方向。
5. *I'll cheer for you.* 我会为你加油、助威的。
6. *Jean was super; she made a lot of great saves.* 吉恩守门顶呱呱，她救起了好多险球，真了不起。
7. *I really enjoyed watching the game and learning about kids hockey.* 观看比赛、了解儿童冰球赛真使我好高兴。
8. *I move it around with my hockey stick.* 我用球杆掌握冰球的运动方向。

Skiing 滑雪

1. *Skiing originated as a means of everyday winter transportation in Scandinavian countries.* 滑雪最早是斯堪的纳维亚国家常用的冬季交通方法。
2. *When my family went skiing they often rented the equipment-skis, poles, and boots.* 我们一家去滑雪时，通常租用滑雪设备——滑雪板、滑雪杆和滑雪靴。
3. *Grass skiing is popular in some places during the summer when there is no snow on the slopes.* 夏天，有些地方的山坡上没有雪，这时人们喜欢进行滑草运动。
4. *As a sport, skiing compasses downhill skiing, skiing touring, and crosscountry ski racing.* 作为一项体育运动，滑雪包括高山滑雪、滑雪旅行和越野滑雪赛。
5. *Skiing is one of the major events of Winter Olympics.* 滑雪是冬奥会的主要竞赛项目之一。
6. *Alpine skiing consists of downhill, slalom and giant slalom.* 高山滑雪由滑降、小回转和大回转（障碍滑雪）组成。
7. *Generally speaking, the Scandinavian countries dominate the Nordic events. And the Alpine countries dominate the Alpine events.* 一般来说，斯堪的纳维亚国家在北欧滑雪项目上占优势，阿尔

卑斯山脉国家在高山滑雪项目上占优势。

8. *Nordic skiing includes cross country racing, ski jumping and the Nordic Combines.* 北欧滑雪项目包括：越野滑雪、跳台滑雪和北欧混合项目。

9. *When skiing, you need to push on your poles with your body leaning forward and the knees slightly bent to make you move.* 滑雪时，你需要推动你的滑雪杆，同时身体前倾，膝盖微微弯曲来使你移动。

10. *He is hurting down the snow-covered sloped like a missile, making perfect turns and spraying powder against the background of the birch forest below.* 他沿着白雪覆盖的山坡像导弹一样疾驰而下，娴熟地转弯，在山下白桦树林中场起阵阵雪花。

Skating 滑冰

1. *The earliest skaters probably regarded their skates as a means of transport.* 最早的滑冰者可能把溜冰鞋作为一种交通工具。

2. *From its utilitarian origins, skating has developed along several different lines-speed skating, figure skating and skating games.* 从它最初的实用性开始，滑冰沿着不同的形式发展着——速度滑冰、花样滑冰和滑冰游戏。

3. *There's two kinds of speed skating.* 速度滑冰有两种形式。

4. *Long track speed skating usually is an open-air sport with the length of the track 400m.* 在户外进行的长道速滑，通常为400米一圈。

5. *Short track speed skating is an indoor-sport on a rink with the length of the track 200m.* 在室内溜冰场进行的短道速滑，通常为200米一圈。

6. *Modern figure skating is a blend of precision, grace and vigorous athletics —an art and a sport in one.* 现代花样滑冰是一种艺术和体育的融合体，它要求动作精确、优雅并充满生气勃勃的运动气息。

7. *Whether the skater is a veteran or novice, it takes months of work to produce the three to five minutes of heart-sopping leaps, dizzying spins and intricate footwork that keep fans on the edge of their seats.* 无论滑冰选手是老手还是初学者，他们都要花上几个月的时间才能创造出那3到5分钟的令人心跳加速的跳跃、头晕目眩的旋转以及复杂的步法，这一切都让花样滑冰迷们焦急地等待着。

8. *While no competitive skater has ever been killed in a fall, the fear of falling can kill a career.* 尽管还没有一个参加比赛的滑冰运动员死于摔跤，但害怕摔跤的恐惧却可以毁掉一份事业。

9. *The dominant nations in world skating are the USA, Canada, Britain and Russia.* 滑冰运动在世界上居领先地位的国家有美国、加拿大、英国和俄罗斯。

10. *Skaters in speed skating race against the clock and against competitors in other lanes of the rink.* 速度滑冰比赛既要与时间又要与冰场上另一道上的对手比赛。

11. *Figure skating paris perform a wide variety of movements, including many complicated lifts.* 花样滑冰的双人滑动作丰富多彩，包括许多十分复杂的托举和抛接动作。

12. *Ice dancing is basically an adaptation of ballroom dancing.* 冰上舞蹈基本上是舞厅舞蹈的"移植"。

13. *He can perform to a wide range of music, including classical and popular, and let his skating speak for itself.* 他所能表现的音乐范围很广，包括古典音乐和流行音乐，并且能用滑冰来体现音乐的内容。

Fashion Conversation 鲜活会话 由线到面

Conversation 1

A: Tell me something about the game.

B: Well, I pay forward. I get the most chances to score goals. I shoot the puck into the goal's net. The team with the most points wins.

A: Is a puck like a ball?

A：给我讲讲冰球赛吧。

B：我是打前锋的，进球得分的机会最多。我将冰球射入守门员的球门，得分最多的队为胜者。

A：冰球是一个圆球的样子吗？

B: Yeah. Sort of. It's flat and slides on the ice. I move it around with my hockey stick.
B: 是的，有点像。冰球是扁圆的，在冰上能滑动。我用球杆掌握冰球的运动方向。

A: Oh, I see.
A: 我明白了。

B: Our team isn't playing very well this season, but we're playing better than last year.
B: 这个赛季我们队打得不好，但比去年打得好。

A: Who is your favorite hockey player?
A: 你最喜欢的冰球队员是谁？

B: I like Doug Gilmour better than Gretzky.
B: 吉尔蒙和格雷茈相比，我更喜欢吉尔蒙。

A: Doesn't Gilmour play for the Toronto Maple Leafs?
A: 吉尔蒙效力多伦多红叶队，是吧？

B: He played for the Toronto Maple Leafs, he was traded. But I still collect his hockey cards.
B: 他以前曾效力于多伦多红叶队，后来转队了。我收集了与他有关的明信片。

A: Do the girls on the team play as aggressively as the boys?
A: 女孩像男孩一样善战吗？

B: Sure. Sometimes they play more aggressively. In my opinion, the girls skate better than some of the boys.
B: 当然啦，有时女孩比男孩还有攻击性呢。依我看，有些女孩比男孩滑冰滑得更好些。

A: I see.
A: 我明白了。

Conversation 2

A: What is the optimum starting age for a young skier?
A: 少年儿童从事滑雪运动的最佳起始年龄是多大？

B: The optimum age is six. In my country, skiing clubs hold training classes for children aged from six to ten.
B: 最佳起始年龄是6岁。在我国，滑雪俱乐部有为6岁至10岁儿童开设的训练课程。

A: How can we improve the fitness level of our skiers?
A: 我们如何提高我国滑雪运动员的身体素质水平呢？

B: You should devise some intensive routines of interval training. This should help to improve leg speed and stamina.
B: 你们应安排一些强度大的常规间歇性训练，这有助于提高腿的动作速度和耐力。

A: What other forms of exercise do you recommend?
A: 你还能再推荐一些其他形式的训练吗？

B: I also recommend stretching and loosening up. This will help to improve flexibility and suppleness. Remember that some training drills should be closely related to actual skiing skills.
B: 我还建议采用伸展和放松练习，这会有助于提高柔韧性和灵敏度。要记住，这些训练应与滑雪的实用技术紧密结合。

A: How many hours a day should a top class skier spend on the snow?
A: 最高水平的滑雪运动员一天应用几个小时进行雪地训练？

B: A top class skier should spend at least three hours a day training on the piste, the jumping hill, or the cross country trail. Intensive daily training should continue in the summer too.
B: 最高水平的滑雪运动员一天至少应用3个小时在雪场、跳台或越野雪道上进行训练。夏季也应同样进行强度大的日常训练。

Conversation 3

A: Congratulations! It is said that Wang is your second student who has won an Olympic gold medal.
A: 祝贺你！据说王是你所带的第二个在奥运会上获得金牌的弟子。

B: Yes. Wang is one of the cleverest students I've ever taught.

B：是的。王是我所教过的最聪明的弟子之一。

A: Could you say something about Wang's success in the Olympics? What makes her success?

A：你能就王在奥运会上的成功说点什么吗？是什么使得她能够成功？

B: She never gives up. There's nothing a coach can do to give a child that attitude. She either have it or she doesn't.

B：要从不放弃。这种态度并不是一个教练能够灌输给孩子的，她自己要么有，要么没有。

A: So that is why she can perform the perfectly executed Tano triple lutz which is considered unthinkable for a girl young at her age.

A：这就是为什么她可以做非常完美的塔诺空中三周跳，这在她的年龄被认为是不可想象的。

B: She has nearly fallen up to 50 times a day to master the Tano triple lutz. For a young girl at her age, only love of the sport can keep her going. And for a good sportsman like her, the satisfaction is in knowing you've pushing this sport, this art, to the limit.

B：为了掌握塔诺空中三周跳，她每天几乎要摔50次跤。对于她这种年龄的女孩子来说，只有对这项运动的热爱才能促使她继续下去。而且对于她这样一个优秀的运动员来说，成功的满足就在于知道你已经把这项运动、这门艺术推向了极限。

Conversation 4

A: Say, what's you favorite sport?

A：嘿，你最喜欢的运动是什么？

B: Hmmm..., it's hard to say. I like golf a lot — but I guess like skating better.

B：嗯，这很难说。我很喜欢高尔夫球，不过我想我更喜欢滑冰。

A: Do you know how to skate, like a skater?

A：你知道怎样滑冰吗，就像滑冰运动员那样？

B: No, I'm strictly a spectator. I just like watching skating. It's so beautiful.

B：不，我是一个纯粹的观众。我只是喜欢看滑冰，它太美了。

A: Then you must know a lot about skating. Would you tell me some rules about skating in the Olympics?

A：那么你肯定非常了解滑冰。你能告诉我有关奥运会的一些滑冰规则吗？

B: Well, the Olympic competition is divided into two stages: a "short" program, with strictly required moves, and a "long" program, which gives skaters more freedom to choreograph their moves. The short program counts 30 percent and the long 70 percent. And a perfect score is 6.0.

B：哦，奥运会的比赛分为两个阶段：短节目和长节目。短节目有严格规定的动作，而长节目给了选手充分的自由来设计他们的动作。短节目占30%，长节目占70%，满分为6.0分。

A: When will the skaters be given a deduction?

A：选手什么时候会被扣分呢？

B: In the short program, specified tenths of a point must be deducted for a fall and for other mistakes, such as a two footed landing or the omission of a required move. Such deductions are huge in a competition where world standings may be decided by one-tenth of a point. In the long program, the negative effect of a fall may be offset by the artistry and technical difficulty of the overall performance.

B：在短节目当中，选手如果跌倒或者犯了其他错误，比如双足着地或漏做了某个规定动作，都会被扣掉某个零点几分。这样的扣分对于零点一分之差就能决定世界排名的比赛来说是非常重要的。在长节目当中，摔跤的负面影响可以被整套动作的艺术和技术难度所抵消。

A: That is to say, a flawless performance in an Olympic competition is really a difficult goal for a skater.

A：也就是说，在奥运会比赛当中，一套没有失误的表演对于运动员来说是很难达到的。

B: Yes. Skaters often have to practice years to mast-

B：是的。运动员们通常要练习几年才能掌握一个

er a jump with high technical difficulty.
技术难度很高的动作。

A: So people always admire their sportsmanship.
A: 因此人们总是很钦佩他们的运动精神。

Conversation 5

A: Coach, I can't skate at all. I'm keeping falling down all the time.
A: 教练,我根本就滑不了,老是在跌跤。

B: Don't be worried. Remember, don't walk. Learn to balance on one foot and glide over the ice.
B: 别着急,记住,不要在冰上走。学会用一条腿平衡,在冰上溜动。

A: But what causes me to glide?
A: 但怎样才能使自己溜动起来?

B: What enables you to glide is the friction the pressure of the skate and your weight cause.
B: 溜冰鞋和你的体重的压力所引起的摩擦力使你能够在冰上溜动。

A: Then, how to balance on the foot?
A: 那么怎样用一条腿保持平衡?

B: Most of the time your weight should be balanced over the center of blade. When you're skating forward the weight should be slightly to the rear of the center point; when skating backward, slightly to the front of it.
B: 要把你的重心放在冰刀的中心点上。当你想向前滑时,重心稍微向冰刀中心点的后面移一点;当你想向后滑时,稍微向前移一点。

A: I see. Thank you, sir.
A: 我明白了。谢谢你,先生。

On the Scene 身临其境 面面俱到

主题:凯在滑雪过程中摔倒了。韦德赶快过来拉她。请你看图,根据如下提供的关键词,将他们的对话写出来。

关键词语:

ski *n.* 滑雪橇	top-level *adj.* 最高阶层的
smoothly *adv.* 平稳地	icy *adj.* 冰冷的
bat *n.* 球棒	teammate *n.* 队友

参考答案

Kay: Ouch! I'm hurt.
Wade: Are you all right?
Kay: Yes. I'm OK. I just had a tumble. No big deal.
Wade: Good. You scared me.
Kay: Sorry. Can you please help me up! I have trouble standing up by myself with the ice skates on.
Wade: Sure. Is this your first time skating?
Kay: Yes. But I believe I can make it soon.
凯:噢！好痛。
韦德:你还好吗?
凯:我还好,只是摔了一跤,没什么大不了的。
韦德:那就好,你吓了我一跳。
凯:抱歉,能不能麻烦你拉我起来?我穿着滑冰鞋不太容易自己站起来。
韦德:没问题,这是你第一次滑冰吗?
凯:是的。不过我相信不久就会学会。

★球类运动★ 5 Balls

Words and Phrases 闪亮词语 点滴积累

midfield 中场
penalty zone 禁区
back 后卫
half back 前卫
forward striker 前锋
kick-off 开球
corner ball/corner 角球
goal kick 球门球
header 头球
penalty kick 点球
dribbling 带球
pass the ball 传球
take the pass 接球
slide tackle 铲球
intercept 截球
hand ball 手触球
offside 越位
shoot 射门
yellow card 黄牌
red card 红牌
attack 进攻
foul 犯规

Useful Sentences 七彩精句 连点成线

Football game knowledge 足球知识

1. *Football, known as "soccer" in American English, is the most popular sport in the world.* 足球在美国英语中叫 soccer，是世界上最为普及的体育运动。
2. *Women's teams didn't become part of the Olympic program until 1996 at Atlanta.* 女子足球直到 1996 年亚特兰大奥运会才成为奥运比赛项目。
3. *It is now the most popular sport in the world with the major powers concentrated in Europe and South America.* 足球是目前世界上最流行的运动。主要足球强国都分布在欧洲和南美洲。
4. *A game is made up of two teams, each having up to 11 players.* 一场足球比赛有两队参加，每队 11 人。
5. *The team that wins the coin toss may choose to kickoff or defend the goal of its choice.* 掷硬币的胜方有优先权选择开球或选择场地。

Basketball knowledge 篮球知识

1. *A team advances the ball by dribbling and passing, and attempts to score.* 球队的进攻是靠运球和传球，并且试图得分。
2. *One free-throw scores one point, and one shot scores two points.* 罚中一次得 1 分，投中一次得 2 分。
3. *The coach insisted that the team practice the one-three-one defense.* 教练坚持要球队采用 1—3—1 区域联防。
4. *A violation is penalized by one or two free throws from the free throw line.* 对犯规的处罚是在罚球线上罚球一次或二次。
5. *A professional game consists of four quarters of ten minutes each.* 职业篮球队比赛 4 节，每节 10 分钟。

Volleyball knowledge 排球知识

1. *There are at most five sets in a volleyball match.* 一场排球比赛最多有五局。
2. *Volleyball was invented by William G. Morgan.* 威廉·基·摩根发明了排球。
3. *In 1951 each volleyball team adopted a 6-player system.* 在 1951 年，排球队采用六名球员制。
4. *Volleyball was listed in the 18th Olympic Games in Tokyo.* 排球是在第 18 届东京奥运会被列入

比赛项目的。

Table tennis knowledge 乒乓球知识

1. *Table tennis is China's national game.* 乒乓球是中国的国球。
2. *By "rally" I mean the period of time when the ball is in play.* 我所说的"回合"是指球往返回击的那一段时间。
3. *Table tennis became a full Olympic sport in 1992 at Barcelona.* 乒乓球在1992年巴塞罗那奥运会上被列为正式项目。
4. *Table tennis involves such basic skills as those of serving, returning the ball and placing it.* 乒乓球涉及诸如发球、回击球、控制球等基本技术。
5. *Officials of a table tennis tournament include an umpire, service, line umpire and scorer.* 乒乓球比赛的正式工作人员包括:裁判员、发球裁判、司线员和记分员。

Tennis knowledge 网球知识

1. *In international competitions, a match is composed of the best of three sets or five sets.* 国际比赛是三盘两胜或五盘三胜。
2. *An ace is a service which cannot be reached by the opponent with his racket.* 发球得分是指使对方用球拍击不到球。
3. *Units of scoring are points, games, sets and matches.* 记分单位是分局,盘,场。
4. *The first point made is called 15; the second, 30; the third, 40; and the fourth, game.* 取得的第一分为15;第二分为30;第三分40;第四分为局。

Badminton knowledge 羽毛球知识

1. *Badminton has been an Olympic sport since 1992.* 1992年羽毛球成为奥运会的比赛项目。
2. *A game is won by the first player to reach fifteen points for men and eleven points for women.* 男子比赛先得15分者胜,女子先得11分者胜。
3. *Badminton can be played by two people in singles or by four people in doubles or mixed doubles.* 羽毛球可以两人单打或四人双打和混合双打。
4. *The umpire's position is on a high seat above the level of the court.* 裁判员的位置在高于场地的座位上。
5. *The IBF lays down the rules for international competitions.* 国际羽联负责制定国际比赛规则。

Water polo knowledge 水球知识

1. *Water polo is a seven-a-side team game played in a swimming pool.* 水球是7人为一队,在游泳池中进行的集体球类项目。
2. *The game is played in a pool at least 1.8 meters deep.* 进行水球比赛的游泳池最少要有1.8米的深度。
3. *The pool is thirty meters long and twenty meters wide.* 游泳池长30米,宽20米。
4. *Water polo was devised in England in about 1870.* 水球大约是1870年在英国开创的。
5. *Nowadays water polo is included as an event in most major swimming competitions.* 现在凡是重要的比赛都包含水球项目。

Baseball knowledge 棒球知识

1. *Baseball is a game between two teams of nine players each, the team which scores the great number of runs shall be the winner.* 棒球是以九人为一队,两支队参与的比赛,跑垒得分多的一队胜出。
2. *The baseball game has no specific length but lasts until the 9 innings are completed.* 棒球比赛没有固定的时间,但必须打完九局,比赛才算结束。
3. *Half inning is completed when three offensive players are called out.* 当三名防守队员被刺杀出局时,比赛就算完成了半局。
4. *The first batter of the line-up is usually the fastest runner of the team.* 第一位出场的击球员通常是该队中跑得最快的队员。
5. *The field is divided into an infield and an outfield.* 棒球场分为内场和外场。

Field hockey knowledge 曲棍球知识

1. *Hockey was considered the national game of India.* 曲棍球被认为是印度的国球。
2. *The new system which applies to men and women will take effect for the 2000 Olympic in Sydney.* 2000年悉尼奥运会对男女曲棍球赛将采用新的方法。
3. *Field hockey is an outdoor game similar to soccer.* 曲棍球是一种在室外进行的类似足球的运动。
4. *Field hockey is played on a field measuring 46m to 55m by 82m to 91m by two teams of 11 players each.* 曲棍球场宽46米到55米，长82米到91米。比赛时双方各有11人上场。
5. *Teams attempt to advance the ball down the field with their wooden sticks.* 双方用木制球棍将球在场上推进。

Bowling knowledge 保龄球知识

1. *A complete bowling game consists of 10 frames.* 一局完整的保龄球赛包括10轮。
2. *Each player is allowed to bowl 2 ball in each frame.* 每位选手在每轮可以投2球。
3. *If a player scores a strike in the 10th frame, he is entitled to 2 bonus balls.* 如果一位选手在第10轮打了一个全中，他被奖励多打2球。
4. *Ten pin bowling was only an exhibition sport in 1988 Seoul Olympics.* 十瓶式保龄球赛在1988年汉城奥运会上只是一项表演赛。

Fashion Conversation 鲜活会话 由线到面

Conversation 1

A: What is offside, Kerry?

B: A player is offside if he receives a forward pass from a teammate in the opponent's half of the field, with fewer than two opponents between himself and the goal.

A: How is a foul committed?

B: If a player trips, kicks, strikes, obstructs or holds an opponent, he's committed a foul.

A: What's the penalty for it?

B: If it's merely a minor offence, the referee may award a free kick. For an intentional offence, the offender may be shown a yellow card. But if he repeats it intentionally, he may be shown the red card. Then the player is sent off the field.

A: Do you think it a good means to curb violence on the football field?

B: To some extent, yes.

A: When is penalty kick awarded?

B: That's when a serious foul is committed inside the penalty area. Why are you so interested in football today?

A: I've got a ticket for the match between Argentina and Poland.

A：克里，什么叫越位？

B：在对方半场，本方队员向前传球时，接球队员与球门之间少于两名对方队员即为越位。

A：什么情况构成犯规？

B：如果对对方队员采用绊、踢、打、阻挡及拉人等手段即为犯规。

A：如何处罚呢？

B：如果只是一般犯规，裁判员可判罚任意球。如果是故意犯规，犯规队员可能会被亮黄牌。如果再次有意犯规，可能就会被亮红牌，被罚下场。

A：你认为这是阻止球场暴力的有效途径吗？

B：从某种程度上来说，是的。

A：什么时候罚点球？

B：在禁区内严重犯规时，就会被判罚点球。你今天怎么对足球这么感兴趣？

A：我弄到了一张阿根廷队对波兰队的票。

Conversation 2

A: Hello, Huajian. Did you watch the live broadcast

A：你好，华健。你昨天看了女子篮球赛实况转播

for the women's basketball match yesterday? 没有?

B: No. But I've already got the result. I hadn't expected that the Chinese team would be defeated. B:没看,但我知道结果了。我没有想到中国队会输。

A: Nor had I. That means they have no chance to compete for the medals. But the failure doesn't mean the Chinese women basketball team is inferior to the other teams in their abilities, techniques and skills. Still, I think they are great. A:我也没想到。这就意味着中国队失去了争夺奖牌的机会,但这并不意味着中国女篮在能力、技术和技巧方面就比其他队差。我仍然认为中国女篮了不起。

B: I'm proud of them. We have to admit that chance played an important role. What's Chinese women team's best result in the Olympics? B:我为他们感到自豪。我们得承认,偶然性起了很大的作用。中国女篮的最好奥运成绩达到什么名次?

A: They won the silver medal at the Barcelona Olympic Games. They routed Cuba by nearly 40 points and reached the final. A:她们曾在巴塞罗那奥运会上获得过银牌。她们以将近40分的优势淘汰了古巴队,进入了决赛。

B: With which team did they compete for the gold medal? B:她们和哪一个队争夺金牌?

A: The Unified team. A:独联体队。

B: The US women's basketball team seems to be winning the gold medal. B:美国女篮这次似乎要得金牌。

A: It's very hard to predict the result. As a matter of fact, the Australian team can rival the American team in many respects, especially in personal skills and team work. A:结果还很难预料。实际上,澳大利亚队在很多方面都能与美国队媲美,尤其是在个人技术和团队合作方面。

Conversation 3

A: What sports do you go in for, Mr Blair? A:布莱尔先生,你喜欢什么体育运动?

B: I'm absolutely mad about volleyball. B:我酷爱排球。

A: Did the game gain great popularity after it was invented? A:自从这种运动被发明以来,这种运动很盛行吗?

B: No, it didn't. Volleyball became more popular after the International Volleyball Federation (a governing body) was formed in 1947. B:这种运动当时并不盛行。在1947年,成立了管理机构国际排球联合会,排球得到极大普及。

A: Have there been any great changes in the tactics? A:战术上有很大变化吗?

B: Yes, there have been great changes in combination, defensive patterns, offensive patterns and power volleyball. B:是的。在战术组合、防守阵形、进攻阵形及强攻型打法上有很大变化。

A: When was volleyball listed as an Olympic event? A:排球运动什么时候被列入奥运会比赛项目的?

B: It was listed in the 18th Olympic Games in Tokyo. B:排球是在第18届东京奥运会被列入比赛项目的。

Conversation 4

A: How does a table tennis game start? A:比赛如何开始?

B: Players toss a coin. The winner of the toss has the right to serve or to choose ends. B:运动员掷币。胜者有权首先发球或者首先选择场地。

A: What officials are there in a table tennis game? A:乒乓球赛的裁判人员包括哪些人?

B: Officials include an umpire, service judge, scorer and line umpire.

B: 裁判人员包括一名裁判员，一名发球裁判，一名记分员和一名司线员。

A: What is a let?

A: 什么是重新发球？

B: If a service is delivered when the receiver is not ready or if the ball served touches the net.

B: 假如接球方球员尚未准备好球已发出或者发球触网。

A: How many games are there in a match?

A: 一场比赛要打几局？

B: A match consists of the best of five games or the best of seven games.

B: 五局三胜或者七局四胜。

A: Are players required to undergo medical controls?

A: 球员要进行医务监督吗？

B: Doping control tests and gender verification test will be administered according to the ITTF Rules.

B: 依照国际乒联规则要进行兴奋剂和性别检查。

A: What are criteria for participation?

A: 参赛运动员的标准是什么？

B: Criteria for participation will observe the following order of priorities:

1) World ranking: This will be according to the list drawn up by the ITTF Ranking Committee.

2) Continental ranking: According to the six continental areas recognized by the ITTF and the system decided by each continental federation.

3) ITTF invitation: These places will be decided by the ITTF and will include a minimum of 2 men and 2 women players from the NOC of the organizing country if they have not qualified through system 1 and 2.

B: 参赛运动员遵循以下标准排列先后的顺序：

1) 世界级球员：世界级球员由国际乒联名次排列委员会制定名次排列名单。

2) 洲级球员：经国际乒联承认的六大洲比赛确定名次排列。名次排列方法由洲联合会确定。

3) 国际乒联邀请的球员：邀请的名次由国际乒联决定。如果举办国没有运动员通过上述第一类和第二类资格赛，至少可以派男女各两名球员参赛。

A: Now I see. Thank you.

A: 现在我明白了。谢谢。

B: That's all right.

B: 没什么。

Conversation 5

A: Tennis, also known as lawn tennis, is popular among persons of all ages both male and female. The game attracts millions of participants.

A: 网球，又称为草地网球，是深受男女老少欢迎的。这项运动吸引了数以百万计的参与者。

B: Yes, could you please answer a few questions about tennis first.

B: 是啊！请你先回答我一些有关网球的问题好吗？

A: Let me try!

A: 我尽力而为。

B: Where was tennis invented?

B: 网球起源于何地？

A: Tennis was invented in Britain and it owes its origin literally to the church.

A: 网球是在英国发明的，事实上网球的起源与教堂有关。

B: I was told France was the cradle of tennis. So we are two different schools of origin and beginnings of tennis. Another question, when was the ILTF (International Lawn Tennis Federation) founded?

B: 我听说，法国是网球的发源地。看来我们是网球起源的两种不同的学派。另一个问题，国际网球联合会何时成立的？

A: It was founded in Paris, France, in 1912 and its headquarters are now in London.

A: 国际网球联合会于1912年在法国巴黎成立，现在总部设在伦敦。

B: OK. I'll play tennis with you this evening, best of

B: 好，今晚和你打网球，三局二胜还是五局三胜？

three sets or best of five?
A: Whatever you prefer!

A: 听从尊便。

On the Scene 身临其境 面面俱到

主题：伊芙和雷在保龄球馆边玩边聊天。请你看图，根据如下提供的关键词，将他们的对话写出来。

关键词语：bowling *n.* 保龄球　　score *n.* 得分
average *n.* 平均　　seriously *adv.* 认真地，真诚地
frame 轮（保龄球用语）
round 局（保龄球用语，每局有10轮）
take something seriously 把某事当真，认真对待

参考答案

Eve: Do you often play bowling?
Ray: Not very often.
Eve: How often do you play?
Ray: About once a month.
Eve: How about your score?
Ray: Average about 110 and my highest score is 130. How about you?
Eve: About the same. I don't take score too seriously, either. I am playing for fun.
Ray: Have you played bowling before?
Eve: No. Could you tell me something more about it? I want to play well.
Ray: There are 10 frames in a bowling game. Each player is allowed to bowl two balls in each frame.
Eve: You just said 10 rounds.
Ray: "Round" and "frame" are two different terms.
Eve: Perhaps you can tell me a little more about this.
Ray: Hey, slow down. I'll tell you more while playing.
伊芙：你经常打保龄球吗？
雷：我不经常打。
伊芙：你多久打一次？
雷：大约一个月打一次。

伊芙:你一般能打多少分?
雷:大约 110 分左右,我的最高记录是 130 分。你呢?
伊芙:差不多。我对分数不是很看重,我打保龄球只是为了好玩。
雷:你以前打过保龄球吗?
伊芙:没有,你能告诉我更多有关的情况吗?我想打得更好。
雷:保龄球比赛一局有 10 轮,每位选手在每轮可以投两球。
伊芙:你刚才说要打 10 局!
雷:局和轮是两个不同的词。
伊芙:或许你可以再告诉我一些有关的知识。
雷:嘿,别着急,我们边打边说。

★现代五项及铁人三项★ 6 Modern Pentathlon and Triathlon

Words and Phrases 闪亮词语 点滴积累

block chain 车链
brake 刹车
crank shaft 脚蹬轴
false start 抢跑,起跑犯规
individual pursuit race 个人追逐赛
individual time trials 个人计时赛
pacemaker 领先者,领骑者
best six 前6名
blast 冲刺跑
break a record 打破纪录
breast the tape 撞线
build-up to a contest 赛前强化训练
chalk line 场上白线
checkmark flag 标志旗
cinder track 煤渣跑道
come off the hurdle 下栏
come up to the hurdle 上栏

Useful Sentences 七彩精句 连点成线

Modern pentathlon 现代五项

1. *Modern pentathlon used to be held over several days, but it's been compressed into a single day since Atlanta 1996.* 过去,现代五项分几天举行,但自从1996年亚特兰大奥运会以来,这项比赛缩短在一天内完成。
2. *For the first time in Olympic history, Sydney 2000 featured a women's modern pentathlon event.* 2000年悉尼奥运会是历史上第一次设立女子现代五项。
3. *In shooting, competitors have 40 seconds to take each of 20 shots at a 17cm square target.* 射击时,运动员射20发子弹,每射一发用40秒钟,靶子为17平方厘米。
4. *An air pistol is used and shots are fired at a target 10 metres.* 射击采用的是气手枪,射手距靶10米。
5. *Fencing takes place on a piste 14m long and 1.5m wide.* 击剑在长14米、宽1.5米的场地上进行。
6. *In the fencing bout, the first competitor to record a hit is the winner.* 击剑比赛时,首先刺中对手的一方为胜。
7. *The competitors swim freestyle over 200 meters.* 运动员进行200米自由泳比赛。
8. *Forty-point penalties are incurred for two false starts.* 两次抢跳要扣40分。
9. *Runners complete four laps of a 750m course laid out in a stadium.* 运动员要在体育场750米的跑道上跑4圈。
10. *The final event is the 3000m cross-country show-jumping.* 最后一项是3000米越野障碍赛马。

Triathlon 铁人三项

1. *Triathlon became an Olympic event in 2000.* 铁人三项于2000年成为奥运会比赛项目。
2. *Triathlon begins with swimming, followed by cycling and running.* 铁人三项开始是游泳,然后是自行车和赛跑。
3. *Triathlon at the Sydney Games of 2000 involved a 1.5 kilometres swim, a 40 kilometres bike ride and a 10 kilometres run.* 2000年悉尼奥运会的铁人三项游泳为1.5公里,自行车为40公里,长跑为10公里。
4. *Competitors begin the race with a mass start.* 参赛选手比赛时是一起出发的。
5. *Triathletes usually cover a triangular course.* 铁人三项运动员通常所经过的是三角形的赛程。
6. *There are no intervals between the three events of triathlon.* 铁人三项比赛中每两项之间没有时间间隔。
7. *Footwear is not compulsory for cycling, but is a requirement for running.* 在进行自行车阶段的比赛时,选手不一定要穿鞋;但在长跑时,则要求

选手穿鞋。

8. *Helmets must be fastened during the course of cycling.* 在自行车比赛的过程中,必须戴上头盔。

9. *Any swimming stroke can be used in triathlon.* 铁人三项赛的游泳可以采用任何泳姿。

10. *Nothing could be more unfortunate than getting a flat tire when cycling.* 自行车比赛中,最糟的莫过于车胎破了。

Fashion Conversation 鲜活会话 由线到面

Conversation 1

A: When was modern pentathlon introduced to the Olympic Games?

B: It became an Olympic event in 1912. It was designed by Pierre de Coubertin, the chief founder of the modern Olympic Games. But unfortunately, the modern pentathlon's Olympic history has all too often failed to live up to the lofty ideals of its founder.

A: What do you mean by that?

B: In 1968 Swedish competitor Hans Liljeavall was disqualified for consuming alcohol during the competition.

A: Such things have also happened to other events rather than modern pentathlon alone.

B: But the incidence is especially high in case of modern pentathlon.

A: 现代五项是何时成为奥运会比赛项目的?

B: 1912年。这项运动是由现代奥运会的主要创始人皮埃尔·德·顾拜旦设计的。但遗憾的是,奥运会现代五项的历史却频频辜负其创始人的崇高愿望。

A: 你这样说是什么意思?

B: 1968年瑞典选手汉斯·利尔吉瓦尔因在比赛期间喝酒而被取消了比赛资格。

A: 这种事情其他项目也有,又不是只有现代五项才出过这种问题。

B: 但现代五项出现这种问题的概率尤其高。

Conversation 2

A: I want to know some knowledge about the triathlon. Can you tell me?

B: It's a combination of swimming, cycling and running. This event tries the racers' skills, strength, and willpower. They will churn through a 1.5 kilometers swim, cycle through 40 kilometers and finish by pounding their way through a 10 kilometers run.

A: What swimming stroke are the competitors to adopt?

B: Any stroke is allowed.

A: Can the competitors get a substitute if they get a flat tire?

B: No. But they are allowed to run with the bike to one of tire change stations placed around the course. Trained teams then change the tire.

A: How will the competitor be penalized if he or she is found cutting the corner?

B: He or she may be warned or issued a yellow

A: 我想了解一些铁人三项赛的知识。你能告诉我吗?

B: 这是一种由游泳、自行车和赛跑组合而成的比赛。这项比赛很考验选手的技术、力量和毅力。他们要游1.5公里,然后骑40公里的自行车,最后还要跑10公里。

A: 选手在游泳时采用什么泳姿?

B: 任何泳姿都行。

A: 选手的车胎没气时,可以换一辆吗?

B: 不行。但他们可以推着自行车跑到一个设在途中的换胎处去,由经过训练的换胎队换胎。

A: 选手抄捷径,怎样处罚?

B: 可以提出警告或罚黄牌。当然,犯规选手必须

card. Of course the offender will have to cover the corner he or she has cut. And two yellow cards result in disqualification.

补走所抄的捷径。还有，如果被罚两张黄牌就会被取消比赛资格。

A: That sounds fair.

A：这听起来很公平。

Conversation 3

A: What do you think of the standard of the top Chinese fencers?

A：你认为中国顶尖击剑运动员的水平如何？

B: I think they are among the best in Asia.

B：我认为他是亚洲最优秀的运动员。

A: In your opinion, how can we improve the general standard of our fencers?

A：那您认为我们应如何提高我们击剑运动员的水平呢？

B: Firstly, China should have a development program for young fencers.
Secondly, we should study the performance and techniques of the top fencers in the world on film and videotape. Thirdly, we should invite a European coach.

B：第一，中国应有一项培养少儿击剑运动员的发展计划。
第二，我们应从影片和录像中研究世界上最优秀运动员的技术。
第三，我们应当聘请欧洲的教练员。

A: And the fencers themselves should pay attention to the techniques while practicing.

A：击剑运动员本身在训练时应注重技巧。

B: Yes. Improving the standard of the Chinese fencers is not just the coaches' business, nor is just the fencers. Everybody of us should work hard.

B：对。提高中国击剑运动员的水平不仅仅是教练员的事，也不仅仅是击剑运动员的事，我们每个人都应该努力。

Conversation 4

A: Bobby Julich has some very competitive rivals such as Indurain from spain and Laurent Jalabert from France.

A：鲍比·朱利齐有些很强劲的对手，如西班牙的安杜兰、法国的劳伦·加拉伯特。

B: What kind of bicycles do they ride?

B：他们骑的是哪种自行车？

A: Their bicycles are derailleurs, light and strong. They may have 5 to 15 speeds, and each can be applied to a different terrain. In general, low gears for going uphill or against the wind. And high gears for pedaling downhill. And they can be slowed by gripping levers on the handlebars.

A：变速车，又轻又结实，可能有5～15种速度，每种速度可用于不同的地形。一般而言，低速适于上山或逆风行驶，高速适于下山，可通过把手上的握杆减速。

B: The handlebars are different from those of most bikes I saw in China last year which are an important means of transportation for the Chinese.

B：这些自行车的把手不同于我去年在中国看到的多数自行车的把手。自行车是中国人的一种重要交通工作。

A: The drop handlebars of the mountain bikes permit a low and comfortable riding position.

A：山地车的下落式把手可使身子保持低平、舒适。

B: Look, Bobby Julich begins to accelerate.

B：看，鲍比·朱利齐开始加速了。

A: He has to break away from Indurian and Laurent.

A：他得甩开安杜兰和劳伦·加拉伯特。

B: The competition is so fierce.

B：比赛太激烈了。

A: Now, it is a competition between Bobby Julich and Indurian.

A：现在是鲍比·朱利齐和安杜兰在较量了。

B: Indurian is leading. Come on, Bobby. Pedal

B：安杜兰领先。鲍比，加油啊！用力踩呀！太棒

hard. Great! Bobby wins the gold medal. | 了！鲍比夺得了金牌。

On the Scene 身临其境 面面俱到

主题：解说员亚历山大和埃玛在一边欣赏铁人三项比赛中的自行车比赛一边向观众讲解比赛。请你看图，根据如下提供的关键词，将他们的对话写出来。

关键词语：overtake 超越　　14th lap 第14圈
broke the Olympic record 破奥运纪录

参考答案

Alexander: Several cyclists overtake him now. Really intense! The 14th lap. He has broken away from the leading bunch.

Emma: His stamina and speed were tested.

Alexander: In the end, races are all tired out. His heart is willing, but his legs tell us on.

Emma: Even the best engines break down after so many meters.

Alexander: Yes. But he should keep on trying. It's a psychological win.

Emma: He is dashing. He really comes out on top now.

Alexander: There goes the referee's gunshot. The last lap.

Emma: He has turned the home curve and sprint for the finish line on the home straight. And above all, he has broken the Olympic record.

亚历山大：有几个车手又超到他前面了，真紧张！第14圈了，他已经摆脱了领先车群。

埃玛：他的耐力和速度经受住了考验。

亚历山大：到了最后，选手们都累得筋疲力尽。他也是心有余而力不足。

埃玛：跑了那么多米，即使是最好的引擎也会垮的。

亚历山大：是呀，但他还是应该坚持。这是一场心理战的胜利。

埃玛：他冲刺了。现在真的是独占鳌头。

亚历山大：裁判员枪响了，最后一圈了。

埃玛：他转过了最后的弯道，在终点的直道上向终点猛冲。而且最重要的是，他打破了奥运纪录。

Modern Education

CHAPTER

8

现代教育

★注册入学★ 1 Registration

Words and Phrases 闪亮词语 点滴积累

physics 物理学
electrophysics 电子物理学
mathematics & science 数学科学
chemistry 化学
commercial mathematics 商用数学
atmospheric physics 大气物理学
geophysics 地球物理学
power physics 电力物理学
geography 地理学
astronomy 天文学
biology 生物学
zoology 动物学
globe science 地球科学
engineering science 工程科学
chemical engineering 化学工程
control engineering 控制工程
communication engineering 电信工程
electronic engineering 电子工程
electrical engineering 电机工程
mechanical engineering 机械工程
river & harbor engineering 河海工程
aerial engineering 航空工程
industrial engineering 工业工程
civil engineering 土木工程
nuclear engineering 核子工程学
environmental engineering 环境工程
medical engineering 医学工程

Useful Sentences 七彩精句

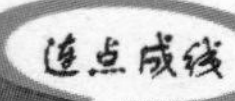

连点成线

Pick out classes 注册选课

1. *Last year, I forgot to bring my picture ID.* 去年我忘了带身份证。
2. *I missed my registration time last year.* 去年我错过了注册时间。
3. *I have to pay my library fines before I can register.* 注册前,我得先交图书馆的罚款。
4. *I check with the records department to make sure they have my transcripts on file.* 我到档案组去确认在档案里是否有我的成绩单。
5. *I call the school when I have questions about registration.* 我打电话给学校,询问有关注册的问题。
6. *I pick out my classes and register for next semester.* 我为下学期选课并注册。
7. *You should select the courses you want to take before you go to register.* 注册前,你要先把课选好。
8. *My advisor told me to have second choices ready.* 我的指导老师告诉我要选好候补的课。
9. *The classes I want are filled.* 我要修的课名额满了。

Choose teachers 选老师

1. *My sister said not to take Professor Lin for English.* 我姐姐说不要修林教授的英文。
2. *Have you heard anything about Dr. Chen?* 你有没有听说过陈博士怎么样?
3. *Would you like me to recommend some good teachers?* 你要不要我介绍一些好老师?
4. *I need to ask someone who has had this teacher if she is good.* 我要问问修过这位老师课的人,看她教得好不好。
5. *My teacher gave me special permission to take his class.* 我的老师特许我修他的课。

Fashion Conversation 鲜活会话 由线到面

Conversation 1

A: Take a seat, please.
A：请坐。

B: Thank you.
B：谢谢。

A: You want to get your Bachelor in education, is that right?
A：你想拿到教育学学士学位，是不是？

B: That's right.
B：是的。

A: You'll need 30 credit hours, 15 from the English Department and 15 from the Education Department.
A：你需要30个学时，英语系15个学时，教育系15个学时。

B: I have no idea about it. Could you explain it in more detail?
B：对此我一点儿都不知道，你能解释得更详细点儿吗？

A: Well, since you have had English Literature, you should also take American Literature. Your transcript indicates that your English background is strong, so I don't think you will have any problem with it.
A：好的，既然你已选修了英国文学，你也应该选美国文学，你的成绩单表明你的英语基础很棒，所以我认为在这方面你不会有什么问题。

B: How many credits can I get for each course?
B：每个课程我能得多少学分？

A: Three credit for each course.
A：每门课3个学分。

Conversation 2

A: Jack Smith, you can come in now. Sorry to keep you waiting. Take a seat .
A：杰克·史密斯，现在你可以进来了。对不起，让你久等了，请坐。

B: Thank you.
B：谢谢。

A: Tell me something about yourself.
A：告诉我一些有关你自己的事情吧。

B: I'm in my last year of high school, taking the college prepare.
B：我在念中学最后的一年，选读大学预修课程。

A: Which is your favorite subject?
A：你最喜欢哪一科？

B: Economics particularly group discussions and the differences between economic systems.
B：经济学——尤其是小组讨论和不同的经济体制的差别。

A: What would you like to do once you've graduated from college?
A：大学毕业后，你打算做什么？

B: I think I'd like to go into management. but I'm not sure in what area yet.
B：我想我会喜欢从事管理工作，但目前还没决定哪一个范围。

A: Okay. We will take a look at your application and let you know by mail if you have been accepted.
A：好吧，我们会看看你的申请，如果你被录取，就会寄信通知你。

B: Oh, that's great. Thank you.
B：喔，那好极了。谢谢。

A: Now, if you'd like to go outside. I have a student lined up who'll show you around the campus.
A：现在，如果你想出去看看，我已安排学生带你参观校园。

Conversation 3

A: How many of lectures are there per week in this college?
A：请问这所学院每星期要上多少小时的课？

B: It varies, depending on the courses you've cho-
B：不一定的，要视你选读哪些课程。通常是12到

sen. Normally it's between 12 and 15 hours although there's a lab for some courses, which is about an hour long.

15小时之间,但有部分课程要做1小时左右的实验。

A: What sports facilities are there?

B: We have football and basketball courts and gym, as well as an indoor pool.

A: 这里有什么运动设施吗?

B: 我们有足球场、篮球场、健身室和室内游泳池。

A: What are the dorms like?

B: Everyone in the first year is required to live on campus. In the last three years you may find your own room. There's a lot of cheap student housing in the area and the administration office will help you find something. Any other?

A: 宿舍是怎样的?

B: 所有一年级的学生都要住在校园内,后三年你可以自行寻找住所。在附近有很多便宜的学生住房,而学生住宿事务处会帮助你寻找住所的。还有问题吗?

A: No, I thank that's all.

B: Okay, nice to meet you, and we'll be in touch.

A: Okay, thanks. Goodbye.

A: 没有了,我想我全都问好了。

B: 好吧。幸会,我们会跟你联络的。

A: 好吧,谢谢,再见。

Conversation 4

A: What were your S. A. T. (Scholastic Aptitude Test) results?

B: I got 625 in English and 650 in Maths.

A: Which subjects interest you?

B: Both Chinese and History.

A: I know your school grades are very good. Are there any questions you'd like to ask?

B: What sports programs do you have?

A: We have baseball, tennis, swimming, soccer, basketball and football.

B: Okay. Sounds great.

A: Thanks for coming. You'll be hearing from us soon.

A: 你的 S. A. T. (Scholastic Aptitude Test) 成绩怎样?

B: 我的英文科取得625分,数学科取得650分。

A: 你对哪些科目感兴趣?

B: 中文和历史。

A: 我知道你的中学成绩非常好。你有其他问题想问吗?

B: 你们有哪些运动项目?

A: 我们有棒球、网球、游泳、足球、篮球和美式足球。

B: 好的。听起来好极了。

A: 多谢你来。你很快便会收到我们的通知了。

Conversation 5

A: Boy, how come there are so many people?

B: The computer system was broken this morning and they failed to repair it until an hour ago.

A: What a luck.

B: I have something worse to tell you: one of our compulsive subjects will be taught by Professor Li.

A: Do you mean the person who once flunked one third of his class?

B: Absolutely right!

A: I don't want to register.

B: Cheer up! We are in the same boat, so we can help each other.

A: Certainly, maybe things will be better than our

A: 好家伙,怎么会有这么多人?

B: 今天早上计算机系统坏了,他们一小时前刚修好。

A: 真倒霉。

B: 还有更糟的。我们的一门必修课将会由李教授来教。

A: 你是说那个曾让班上三分之一的人不及格的教授吗?

B: 完全正确!

A: 我不想注册了。

B: 打起精神来! 我们的处境相同,可以互相帮助啊。

A: 那当然,也许情况会比我们预料的好。

expectation.

Conversation 6

A: Well, do you think you should go to the university to get registered today?
B: Yes, what do I have to take with me?
A: Your ID card, the letter of admission to the university, and...
B: Maybe I should go to my academic advisor first.
A: Right. You must have your advisor's signature on the course enrollment forms and he will tell you what you need to do.
B: Ok, thank you.
...
B: Excuse me, Madam. Do I register here?
C: Yes. May I help you?
B: I am new here and I would like to register for the spring semester.
C: Have you paid your tuition and had your course request card been signed by the Dean?
B: Yes, I have. Here's my receipt.
C: Good. Now, what you have to do now is to fill out these information cards... All your classes are still open. You're all set.

A:你觉得你今天应该去大学报到吗?
B:是的。我要带什么东西呢?
A:你的身份证和学校的录取通知书,还有……
B:也许我该先去找我的导师。
A:没错。你得先拿到有导师签字的注册单,然后他会告诉你该做什么。
B:好的。谢谢。
……
B:请问,是在这儿注册吗?
C:是的,需要我帮忙吗?
B:我是新来的,我想注册春季班。
C:你的学费缴齐了吗?课程申请卡也交系主任签字了吗?
B:是的。这是收据。
C:好的。现在你要做的是把这些表填好……你的班级都还有空,好了,一切都安排好了。

On the Scene 身临其境 面面俱到

主题:新学期开始,一位来注册入学的大一新生向伊内斯请教了一些问题。请你看图,根据如下提供的关键词,将他们的对话写出来。

关键词语:register *n.* 记录,注册 　select *v.* /*adj.* 精选,精选的
assign *v.* 分配,指派 　recommend *v.* 推荐,介绍
class schedule 课程表 　tuition *n.* 学费

参考答案

Freshman:Can you tell me where to register for class?
Inez:Just come with me.
Freshman:Can you tell me the registration process?
Inez:You should select the courses you want to take before you go to register.
Freshman:How can I find out which classes I should take for my major?
Inez:What is your major?
Freshman:Chemistry.
Inez:Go to the Chemistry department at school and ask them to assign someone to help you.
Freshman:And they will tell me what I need for my degree?
Inez:Yes, and they will even recommend helpful courses for your major.
Freshman:How do I find out when I'm supposed to register?
Inez:Just look in your class schedule and for the times and dates of registration.
Freshman:We choose courses and then pay the tuition,right?
Inez:Yes. I plan to take one required course and two electives.
新生:请问在哪里注册?
伊内斯:跟我来吧。
新生:你能告诉我注册程序吗?
伊内斯:注册前,你要先把课选好。
新生:我怎么才能知道我该修什么课?
伊内斯:你主修什么?
新生:化学。
伊内斯:你去化学系,请他们指定一个人帮你。
新生:您是说,他们会告诉我该选哪些课?
伊内斯:是的,他们甚至于会给你介绍哪些课较有用。
新生:我怎么查我该注册的时间?
伊内斯:只要查课程表,上面有注册的时间和日期。
新生:我们要先选课再缴费,对吧?
伊内斯:对的。我计划修一门必修,两门选修。

★课堂讲座★ 2 Lecture and Classroom

Words and Phrases 闪亮词语 点滴积累

lectern 讲台
offhand 即席的
brainstorming 开动脑筋
brilliant 有才华的
experienced 有经验的
scholarly 博学的
specialized 专业化的
patient 有耐心的
well-qualified 合格的
lector 讲师
professor 教授
classroom 课堂
lecture 演讲

Useful Sentences 七彩精句 连点成线

Before class begins 课前

1. *It is nearly time for class. Hurry up!* 就要上课了，快点儿！
2. *Come on./Step on it!* 快点/快走。
3. *Quick! The bell is ringing.* 快点！铃响了。
4. *You'd better hurry.* 你得快点。
5. *Hurry up, or you'll be late.* 快点，不然你就要迟到了。
6. *There goes the bell. I'm just in time.* 正打铃呢，我刚好赶上。
7. *Please/Let's get everything ready for class.* 准备上课。
8. *Be ready for class?* 准备好了？
9. *Are you ready for class?* 准备好了吗？

Class begin 上课

1. *I hope you are all ready for your English lesson.* 我希望你们都做好了上英语课的准备。
2. *I'm waiting for you to be quiet.* 我正在等你们安静下来。
3. *We won't start until everyone is quiet.* 要等你们安静下来我们才开始上课。
4. *Stop talking now so that we can start.* 别讲话了，我们开始上课。
5. *Settle down now so we can start.* 静下来，我们开始上课。
6. *Where did we stop/leave off last time?* 上次我们上到哪儿？
7. *How far did we get last time?* 上次我们学到哪里了？
8. *Where did we finish/stop reading last time?* 上次我们读到哪儿？
9. *What were we talking about last time?* 上次我们讲些什么？
10. *Let me refresh your memory. Last time we talked about...* 我来提醒你们一下，上次我们讲了……
11. *If I remember correctly/rightly, we were on page 42.* 假如我记得不错的话，我们上次讲到第42页。
12. *Last time we got to line 20.* 上次我们讲到第20行。
13. *If you can recall what I said last time about...* 假如你能回忆起上次我讲的关于……
14. *Let's revise some of the thing we did last time.* 让我们复习上次我们上的一些内容。
15. *Where was I?* 上次我教到哪里了？

Dismissing class 下课

1. *We'd do the rest of this chapter on Thursday.* 我们将在星期四学习这一章的剩余部分。
2. *We'll finish off this exercise in the next lesson.* 我们将在下一节课里做完这个练习。

3. *We have run out of time, but we'll go on with this exercise next time.* 时间用完了,我们下次继续做这个练习。
4. *We'll continue this chapter next Monday.* 下星期一我们继续学习这一章。
5. *It's ten to ten. We'll have to stop now.* 现在是9点50分,我们得停止上课。
6. *It's almost time to stop.* 快到下课时间了。
7. *I'm afraid it's time to finish now.* 恐怕现在该结束了。
8. *I make it almost time. We'll have to stop here.* 我看时间到。我们就上到这里吧。
9. *That's the bell for dismissal.* 下课铃响了。
10. *There's the bell, as we must stop working now.* 铃响了,我们得下课了。
11. *That's the bell. It's time to go.* 铃响了,下课时间到了。
12. *All right! That's all for today, thank you.* 好吧!我们今天就学到这儿,谢谢。
13. *Right. you can put your things away and go.* 好,你们要整理一下东西离开教室。
14. *That will do for today. You may go now.* 我们今天就到此为止吧。你们现在可以走了。

Fashion Conversation 鲜活会话 由线到面

Conversation 1

A: What did you think of the lecture?
B: I thought it was very interesting.
A: Did you really?
B: Yes, didn't you?
A: Of course not. I thought he talked a lot of rubbish. I'll take coal for instance.
B: What about it?
A: Coal won't become important again.
B: Why not?
A: It's too dirty. They won't be able to find people to work down coal mines in the future.
B: The new machine for coal mining will be invented.
A: Nonsense. The sorts of power they'll use in the future are atomic power or solar energy.

A: 你认为这个讲座怎么样?
B: 我觉得非常有意思。
A: 你真那么认为的?
B: 是的,你认为没有意思吗?
A: 当然没意思。我觉得他说的都是些废话。比如说煤。
B: 煤怎么啦?
A: 煤今后不会很重要了。
B: 为什么?
A: 煤太脏,将来再也找不到愿意在煤矿里干活的工人了。
B: 会发明新的采煤机械的。
A: 得了吧。将来可用的能源是原子能和太阳能。

Conversation 2

A: This course is sociology 217A, a seminar restricted to a few upper-level undergraduates.
B: What is the class size limit? Is it going to be enforced in this class?
A: The limit is eight students and, as you can tell by looking at your seven classmates, it has been enforced.
B: What if someone drops this class during the two week add drop period?
A: In that case, I will get in touch with the first student on the waiting list and allow him or her the opportunity to join this class. But that' s nei-

A: 这门课是社会学217A,只有少数成绩好的大学生可以修。
B: 课程的人数限制如何?必须遵守规定吗?
A: 人数限制是8人,你看看其他7个同班的人就知道人数限制得很严格。
B: 要是有人在两星期的选课期间退出这门课呢?
A: 在那种情形之下,我会通知候补名单上的第一位学生,让他或她有机会修这门课,可是这不是我们要管的事,今天我们要做的是和在场的学

ther here nor there. Our business today is to talk with those who are in this class.

生谈一谈。

B: What will our work mostly consist of?

B:我们上课的内容包括些什么?

A: Since this is a seminar, your work may be slightly different from your other courses. There will be no midterm nor will there be a final exam either.

A:因为是专题讨论课,和其他的课稍有差别,我们没有期中考试,也没有期末考试。

B: Wow, that sounds great.

B:哇,听起来真棒。

Conversation 3

A: Bob, we're coming to the end of this course. I didn't quite catch what type of test our teacher is going to give us.

A:鲍勃,这门课我们就要学完了,我不太清楚老师要给我们进行什么类型的测试。

B: I don't know, either. He didn't mention it in class. But it's said that he likes the type of essay questions.

B:我也不知道,他在课堂上没说,但是,据说他喜欢写文章的形式。

A: If it's all essay questions, I'm dead.

A:如果都是写文章这种形式,我就完了。

B: Why?

B:为什么?

A: You have to make sure that you know your materials and present them in composition form. It's most difficult.

A:你得确切地知道你所学过的东西,并且把它们以文章的形式体现出来,这是最难的。

B: What type of test do you like then?

B:那你喜欢哪种测试呢?

A: An objective test. True-false or multiple choices and matching are easier for me.

A:我喜欢客观测试,判断对错或多选题及对应题对我来说比较容易。

B: So do I. It's hard to put new ideas together in an organized way within a limited time.

B:我也希望这样。在有限的时间内把新的思想组织到一起是很难的。

A: But one thing is that objective questions can be very tricky. Do you ever guess when you do them?

A:但有一个问题,客观测试的题目很迷惑人,做题时你有没有猜过?

B: Yes, sometimes. Everybody does, I think. How about you?

B:有时也猜,我想每人都这样。你呢?

A: I'm not an exception. There's a chance for us to find the right one. Why give it up? Facts are important, of course. But marks are also important for us students. What do you say?

A:我也不例外,有可能找到正确的那个,干吗放弃呢?事实当然很重要,但分数对我们学生也很重要,你说呢?

B: Good for you. I have to agree.

B:说得太对了,我完全同意。

A: Well, why don't we go to our teacher to make it clear?

A:我们为什么不去找老师问清楚呢?

B: I don't think he'll let the cat out of the bag so easily.

B:我认为他是不会轻易泄密的。

A: Who can tell? There may be a chance out of a million.

A:谁说得准?说不定有机会。

B: OK. Let's go.

B:好,我们走吧。

Conversation 4

A: Can we carry on some reforms on the listening class?

A:听力课能进行一些改革吗?

B: Yes. I think so. But how?

B: 能。但怎么改革呢?

A: Our English class is still traditional. Most students prefer listening to the teacher.

A: 我们的听力课还是传统式的。大部分同学就愿意听老师讲。

B: We listen to the tape attentively and can only make out half of it. So we like to listen to you explaining everything.

B: 我们专心地听录音,也只能听懂一半,所以愿意听老师逐句解释。

A: You pay too much attention to individual words and expressions. In fact what matters a lot is the content and the ideas of the material. How about group work in which you may talk to each other about what you hear? Help from your classmates is just as important as that from the teacher.

A: 我们过多地注重单个词和词组,事实上重要的是内容。小组讨论怎么样?在小组里你可以就听到的内容相互交谈。同学之间的互相启发与来自老师的帮助同等重要。

B: We know that. Let's work together and try our best.

B: 这一点我们也知道,让我们共同努力吧。

Conversation 5

A: Did you attend the lecture on history given by Prof. Li yesterday?

A: 你听了昨天李教授关于历史的讲座了吗?

B: Yes, I did.

B: 对,听了。

A: The lecture is so attractive that we have not heard the bell rung. What do you think of it?

A: 讲座太吸引人了,我们连铃响都没听见。你认为呢?

B: I thought it was great. But I can't agree with the lecturer on some points.

B: 我认为很好。但是在某些问题上我不能同意演讲者的意见。

A: Oh, actually I don't quite understand some difficult points in lecture.

A: 哦,事实上讲座中的有些难点我也不太明白。

B: Maybe we can have a discussion about the lecture in class for further understanding of it.

B: 也许我们可以在班上展开一次关于这个讲座的讨论,以便更深入的理解它。

A: That's a good idea.

A: 好主意。

On the Scene 身临其境 面面俱到

主题:听力课上,老师正在和学生交流。请你看图,根据如下提供的关键词,将他们的对话写出来。

关键词语:

cooperate *v.* 合作,协作	frequently *adv.* 常常
comprehension *n.* 理解,包含	relationship *n.* 关系,关联
inaccurate *adj.* 错误的,不准确的	hesitate *v.* 犹豫

参考答案

Teacher: In a listening class, you should cooperate well with the teacher. Not only listen, but also answer my questions. Beside, you must be familiar with those frequently asked questions in the listening comprehension section.

What is the relationship between the two speakers?

Who can tell us what they are discussing?

Where did this conversation most probably take place?

Ask some questions about the talk.

What can we learn from this conversation?

Tom: I think...

Teacher: Is he right? Anything inaccurate? Who would like to correct him?

Liz: He missed something important...

Teacher: If you have any questions after listening to this passage, please don't hesitate to ask me.

Silence, please. Something is wrong with the tape recorder. Could anyone offer me some help?

OK, thank you. Let's go on with our work. Do you think the volume is proper? Those sitting at the back of the classroom, can you hear clearly?

Can you hear me through the earphones?

Troy: Speak more softly. Your volume is much too high.

教师:上听力课时,你们必须跟老师好好配合,不仅仅要听,还要回答我的问题。

另外,你们应当熟悉听力部分常问的问题。

对话中两人的关系是什么?

谁能告诉我们他们在讨论什么?

这个对话最有可能发生在什么地方?

就对话提些问题。

听了这个对话,我们了解到什么?

汤姆:我认为……

教师:他说的对吗?有没有不准确的地方?谁能纠正?

莉斯:他落下一些重要的东西……

教师:听完这一段后如果有问题,不要犹豫,一定要问。

请安静,录音机出了毛病。哪位同学能帮一下忙?

好,谢谢你,我们继续听录音,音量合适吗?坐在后面的同学能听清吗?

你从耳机里听得见我说话吗?

特罗伊:说得再轻一些,你的音量太高了。

★在英语角★ 3 At the English Corner

Words and Phrases 闪亮词语 点滴积累

superior 高手，长者
converse 交谈
topic 话题
case 事例，情况
especially 特别，尤其
primary 基本的，初级的
beyond 超过
agreeable 令人愉快的；投缘
delightful 使人高兴的
fit 合适的
thoughtful 仔细周到的
chance-met 萍水相逢的
cooperative 合作的
inseparable 难解难分的
alliance 联合
congenial 相投

Useful Sentences 七彩精句 连点成线

About English corner 有关英语角

1. *How about going to English corner with me Thursday evening?* 星期四晚上和我一起去英语角如何？
2. *There is an English corner on the campus every Thursday evening.* 每周四晚上校园里都有英语角。
3. *Many students talk to each other in English there.* 在那儿有很多学生用英语交谈。
4. *All these activities will make our oral English more fluent.* 这些活动能使我们的英语口语更流利。
5. *Activities in English are held regularly in our school.* 我们学校经常举行各种英语活动。
6. *English corner is beneficial to improving our oral English.* 英语角对提高英语口语很有帮助。
7. *It's fine with me.* 我没问题。
8. *How often do you come to the English corner?* 你常来英语角吗？
9. *Not so often, about twice a week.* 不是很经常，大概一周两次。
10. *This is my first time to come to the English corner.* 这是我第一次来英语角。
11. *Many people tend to neglect practice in speaking English.* 很多人往往忽视练习口语。
12. *I have some difficulty in expressing myself.* 我表达起来有点困难。
13. *I feel nervous to speak English in class, not to speak at English corner.* 我在英语课上都紧张的说不好，不用说在英语角了。
14. *What do you usually talk about in English corner?* 在英语角你们通常谈什么？
15. *Whatever you are interested in.* 对什么感兴趣就谈什么。
16. *I'm not sure if I can keep up with their speed.* 我没有把握能赶上他们的谈话速度。
17. *It must be very embarrassing if I can't catch them.* 如果我听不懂他们的话，那一定会很尴尬。
18. *You are expected to do the same.* 别人期望你也那么做。
19. *You should be active during the discussion.* 你应该积极参加讨论。
20. *What do you think of English corner?* 你认为英语角怎样？
21. *Do you think English corner plays an important role in English studying?* 你认为英语角在英语学习中起着重要的作用吗？
22. *Do you make friends in English corner?* 你在英语角交朋友了吗？
23. *Is there any foreign teacher to join you in English corner?* 有外教参加你们的英语角吗？
24. *Do you feel nervous when speaking to strangers in English corner?* 在英语角上对陌生人说话，你觉得紧张吗？

Fashion Conversation 鲜活会话 由线到面

Conversation 1

A: Lily, do you know that there is an English corner on the campus every Thursday evening?
A: 莉莉,你知道每周四晚上校园里都有英语角吗?

B: Yes, I heard that many students talk to each other in English there.
B: 我听说在那儿有很多学生用英语交谈。

A: Then how about going to English corner with me this Thursday evening?
A: 那这个星期四晚上和我一起去英语角如何?

B: Oh, I'd rather not.
B: 我不想去。

A: Why not?
A: 为什么呢?

B: You know, my spoken English is very poor. I feel nervous to speak English in class, not to speak at English corner.
B: 你知道我的英语口语很差。我在英语课上都紧张的说不好,不用说在英语角了。

A: That's why you should go there. English corner is beneficial to improving our oral English.
A: 所以你才应该去那里。英语角对提高英语口语很有帮助。

B: OK. I will have a try.
B: 好吧。我去试试。

Conversation 2

A: Hello, this is my first time to come to the English corner. Can I talk with you?
A: 你好,这是我第一次来英语角。我能和你交谈吗?

B: No problem.
B: 没问题。

A: How often do you come to the English corner?
A: 你经常来这里吗?

B: About twice a month.
B: 一个月两次。

A: Do you think English corner plays an important role in English studying?
A: 你认为英语角在英语学习中起着重要的作用吗?

B: Yes. Many people tend to neglect practice in speaking English. And English corner is really helpful.
B: 很多人往往忽视练习口语。而英语角真的很有帮助。

A: Your English is very good. I guess it's all because of the practices at English corner.
A: 你的英语说得这么好。我猜都是因为在英语角练习的缘故吧。

B: Not actually. Activities in English are held regularly in our school. All these activities will make our oral English more fluent.
B: 不完全是。我们学校经常举行各种英语活动。这些活动能使我们的英语口语更流利。

A: I see.
A: 我明白了。

Conversation 3

A: What do people usually talk about in English corner?
A: 人们在英语角通常都谈些什么呢?

B: Whatever interested them, such as English study, music, books, movies, politics and traveling.
B: 对什么感兴趣就谈什么,比如英语学习,音乐,书,电影,政治和旅游。

A: But I'm not sure if I can keep up with their speed. What if I can't understand others' questions?
A: 我没有把握能赶上他们的谈话速度。要是我听不懂别人的问题怎么办?

B: That occurs to everyone in English corner. You
B: 在英语角,每个人都会遇到这样的情况,你可以

can ask them to repeat the question. 请别人再重复一遍。

A: It must be very embarrassing if I still can't understand. A:如果我还是听不懂，那一定会很尴尬。

B: Don't worry. In that case, he or she will try to explain the question to you in another way. B:别担心。如果那样的话，他们会用另一种方式给你解释的。

A: OK. I get it. A:我懂了。

Conversation 4

A: Do you think it is necessary for me to prepare some topics to speak in English corner? A:你觉得我是否有必要准备点去英语角谈论的话题？

B: Yes, since it is the first time for you to go there, you'd better make some preparations. B:是的，因为是你第一次去那儿，你最好做些准备。

A: Did you do that at your first time? A:你第一次去的时间也是这样做的吗？

B: Of course, yes. You know I got to nervous to think of anything to say, so I just recited what I had prepared. B:当然是啦。你知道吗？我当时太紧张了，以致于我完全照着自己准备的背出来的。

A: Really? How about your English now? A:真的吗？那现在如何了？

B: After three or four times, I don't do that anymore. And now I can speak with others in English freely. B:三四次之后，我就不做准备了。我现在可以自由的跟人用英语聊天了。

A: But I find I am afraid of making grammar mistakes and can't express what I want to mean. A:可是我发现我很怕犯语法错误，而且表达不了自己的意思。

B: Then you should do more grammar exercises and enlarge your vocabulary. But don't forget to practice in English corner. B:那么你应该多做语法练习，还要扩充词汇量。别忘了要上英语角练习。

A: It's a good suggestion. I will follow it. A:这真是个好建议。我会去做的。

B: I hope you will make great progress in the near future. B:希望你在不久的将来取得大的进步。

On the Scene 身临其境 面面俱到

主题：贝蒂不敢去英语角，她向蒂姆请教有关英语角的事情。请你看图，根据如下提供的关键词，将他们的对话写出来。

关键词语：national *adj.* 国家的，国有的　international *adj.* 国际的

explain *v.* 解释，说明　hobby *n.* 业余爱好

spare time 业余时间

参考答案

Betty: What do people usually talk about in English Corner?

Tim: Whatever interests them, such as English study, movies, music, books, national and international affairs.

Betty: But I am not sure if I can keep up with their speaking speed. What if someone asks me a question but I can't understand?

Tim: That occurs to everyone in English Corner. You can ask that person to say it again.

Betty: It must be pretty embarrassing if I still couldn't understand.

Tim: In that case, he or she will try to explain the question to you in another way. You are expected to do the same when you ask someone a question and he can't understand. For instance, if you ask, "what's your hobby?" But the person you speak to doesn't know the meaning of "hobby", you can then explain, "I mean what you like to do in your spare time."

Betty: So he or she will have a deep impression that the word "hobby" means the things one likes to do in one's spare time.

Tim: You get it.

贝蒂:在英语角人们常谈论些什么?

蒂姆:对什么感兴趣就谈什么,比如英语学习、电影、音乐、书籍、国内外大事。

贝蒂:但我没有把握是否能跟上他们谈话的速度。如果有人问我问题,我没听懂,怎么办?

蒂姆:在英语角,每个人都会遇到这样的情况,你可以请那个人再说一遍。

贝蒂:如果我还没听懂,那一定是很令人尴尬的。

蒂姆:如果那样,他或她会用另外一种方式给你解释那个问题。当你问别人问题而他不理解时,你也应该这样做。举例来说,你问"你的爱好是什么"?但与你对话的人不懂"hobby"的意思,你可以解释道:"我的意思是你在业余时间喜欢干什么?"

贝蒂:所以他或她将对"hobby"意为"业余时间喜欢做的事情"有一个深刻的印象。

蒂姆:就是这样。

★参加社团★ 4 Joining a Club

Words and Phrases 闪亮词语 点滴积累

club 社团,俱乐部
urgent 急迫的,紧急的
challenge 挑战
shorthand 速记
requirement 要求
absent 缺席,不在
roll 名单
attendance 出席,到场
activity 活动
proprieter 社长
join 参加,加入

Useful Sentences 七彩精句 连点成线

Discussing societies and clubs 讨论社团活动

1. *He is on the university team.* 他进入大学代表队了。
2. *I'm afraid joining a society will take up much of my time.* 我担心参加社团会耽误很多时间。
3. *I joined the Hiking Club soon after I entered the university.* 我入大学不久就加入了远足俱乐部。
4. *The Movie Club is one of our major clubs.* 电影社团是我们的主要社团之一。
5. *You can make some friends in the English Club.* 你在英语俱乐部能交一些朋友。

Talking about extracurricular activities 谈论课外活动

1. *How do you usually spend your weekend?* 你通常怎么过周末?
2. *I like reading stories after class, especially romantic stories.* 我课后喜欢看故事,尤其喜欢看浪漫的故事。
3. *I prefer travelling during holidays because it can broaden my horizon of knowledge.* 我假期喜欢旅游,因为旅游能拓宽我的知识视野。
4. *Listening to music is a good way of relaxing our mind after a day's hard work.* 经过一天的刻苦学习之后,听听音乐是一种放松大脑的好方式。
5. *My classmates do physical exercise regularly in the morning.* 我的同学早晨经常进行体育锻炼。
6. *We often have football matches after class.* 我们课后经常举行足球比赛。

Fashion Conversation 鲜活会话 由线到面

Conversation 1

A: You are now in the Drama Society! When did you join it?
A: 你是戏剧社的成员！你什么时候加入的？

B: A month ago.
B: 一个月前。

A: It's cool. It's one of the most popular societies in our university.
A: 太酷了。这是我们学校最受欢迎的社团之一。

B: Yes. I feel so fantastic to perform on the stage.
B: 是的。在舞台上表演的感觉太有意思了。

A: Can I join it? You know that I have no idea about acting.
A: 我能加入吗？你知道我对表演一窍不通。

B: Of course you can. I was just like you a month ago.
B: 当然可以。一个月以前我也和你一样。

A: So, how many people are there in your society?
B: More than 30.
A: When can I join?
B: Whenever you like. We are recruiting new members all the year round.

A: 那么你们有多少人呢?
B: 三十多个。
A: 我什么时候能加入?
B: 随时都可以。我们一年到头都在纳新。

Conversation 2

A: What kind of activities do you have in the English Club?
B: We sing English songs, rehearse short plays and read English poems. What about you?
A: Me? I am a member of the Poem Association.
B: Then you are a poet now!
A: Don't make fun of me. How about our friends?
B: Well, I know Li Jing belongs to the Fine Arts Society. And Chen Li is very active in the Collectors Association.
A: Good for them.
B: Besides clubs, associations and societies, there are all kinds of research groups and design groups. Most students are very fond of these activities.
A: We really have a very full and colorful campus life.

A: 你们英语俱乐部都有些什么活动啊?
B: 我们唱英文歌,表演短剧,朗诵英文诗歌。你呢?
A: 我现在是诗歌协会的会员了。
B: 那你就是个诗人了!
A: 别取笑我了。我们的朋友们怎么样?
B: 李静是美术协会的会员。陈立在收藏协会很活跃。
A: 很好。
B: 除了这些俱乐部,协会和社团外,还有各种各样的调查小组和设计小组。
A: 我们的校园生活真是丰富多彩啊。

Conversation 3

A: The societies and clubs are recruiting new members today.
B: Yes, I know. They are trying their best to attract new members.
A: Are you interested in joining one?
B: Yes. Which one do you think is better, the Badminton Society or the Football Club?
A: Both are good. It depends on your liking.
B: I was wondering if I could meet a charming if I join a club.
A: You nut. Then you'd better choose the Badminton Society, for there are no girls in the Football Club.

A: 今天社团和俱乐部都在纳新。
B: 我知道。他们都想尽办法来吸引新成员。
A: 你想参加一个吗?
B: 是的。你觉得足球俱乐部和羽毛球协会那个好?
A: 都不错。全看你自己喜好了。
B: 我在想要是我加入社团能不能遇到一个迷人的女生。
A: 你这个家伙。那你最好加入羽毛球协会,因为足球俱乐部里没有女生。

Conversation 4

A: Hi, Liu Ming. What luck running into you here!
B: Hi. Are you also looking at the club recruiting notice?
A: Yes, I'm thinking of joining one.
B: Hey, why don't we join a club together? How a-

A: 嘿,刘明。在这儿遇到你真巧!
B: 嘿,你也是来看社团纳新告示的吗?
A: 对,我想参加一个。
B: 我们为什么不一起参加一个呢? 吉他社如何?

bout the Guitar Club?

A: Mm... but I'm not into guitar at all.

B: Neither am I. but don't you think it will attract the girls' attention to carry a guitar on the campus?

A: Yes, that's pretty cool.

B: Then what are we waiting for? Let's apply for the Guitar Club.

A:嗯...我对吉他可不懂。

B:我也是啊。不过你不觉得在校园里拿着吉他走会吸引女生的注意吗?

A:是的,那很酷。

B:那我们还等什么?赶快去吉他社报名吧。

Conversation 5

A: Do you think it's a good idea to join the Aerobics Club?

B: Yes, our school is famous for aerobics.

A: I know. But I worry that it will take up much time.

B: As the saying goes, all work and no play makes Jack a dull boy. You should take more exercise.

A: But belonging to an Aerobic Club must be tough.

B: Don't worry about that. You will lose nothing but a few pounds.

A: Really? Then I'll join the club.

A:你觉得参加健美操社团是好吗?

B:好,我们学校的健美操很出名的。

A:我知道。但是我担心这个会耽误许多时间。

B:俗话说,只工作不娱乐,聪明的孩子变笨拙。你应当多运动。

A:但是参加健美操社团一定很辛苦。

B:不要担心。你只会瘦几磅的。

A:真的吗?那我就参加了。

Conversation 6

A: You seem a little unhappy. What's up?

B: Nothing. I just feel bored sometimes.

A: Are you in any clubs at school?

B: Yes, I'm in the Science Club, but you know it's not very interesting.

A: I heard that it is fun to join the Drama Club.

B: There are many students interested in this club. Why is it so attractive?

A: It is a great challenge to be another person on the stage. And if you got a chance to act in a drama, you would be a star on the campus.

B: Wow, you will be a big shot sooner or later if you join the Drama Club.

A: Stop joking at me. You are taller and smarter than I am. There will be more chances for you to become a campus drama star.

B: Thank you. Maybe I will join it.

A:你看上去不太高兴。怎么了?

B:没什么。我只是有时觉得无聊。

A:你在学校没有参加社团吗?

B:有啊,我在科学社。不过你知道那不是很有趣。

A:听说参加戏剧社很好玩的。

B:有很多学生对它感兴趣。为什么它这么吸引人呢?

A:在舞台上演别人是个很大的挑战。再说,如果你有机会在一出戏剧中表演,你就会成为校园中的明星。

B:哇,如果你加入戏剧社,你迟早会成为一个大人物的。

A:别拿我开玩笑了。你比我高,比我帅。你有更多的机会成为校园戏剧明星。

B:谢谢你,也许我稍后会参加戏剧社的。

On the Scene 身临其境 面面俱到

主题:两个年轻的大学生在讨论该入何种大学社团。请你看图,根据如下提供的关键词,将他们的对话写出来。

关键词语:Poetry Club 诗社　　give me a break 饶了我吧
babe 女孩

参考答案

Bob: How about the Poetry Club?

Hugo: Bob, give me a break. It's for hicks. Have you seen the guys in that club? You can tell them right bookworms.

Bob: That's not completely true. I get a friend in the club who told me that they party all the time. But I know nothing about poetry…

Hugo: Hey, how about the Cinema club? It' s one of our major clubs.

Bob: Sounds OK to me. I like movies.

Hugo: Let's go.

(*at the meeting*)

Bob: Hey, Hugo. I think we made the right choice. Look, there are quite a few good looking girls here. I wonder if I'll meet my babe.

Hugo: Wow, it's cool. I can't wait to enter my name...

鲍勃:诗社怎么样?

雨果:鲍勃,饶了我吧。这个社团真老土。在那个社团你曾见过帅小伙吗?你可以从他们中间分辨出书呆子。

鲍勃:也不完全对吧。那社团的一位朋友告诉我他们社团总是办聚会。但对诗我不懂什么……

雨果:那电影协会怎么样呢?它是我们的主要社团之一。

鲍勃:听起来不错。我喜欢电影。

雨果:我们去吧。

(*在大会上*)

鲍勃:嗨,雨果。我想我们的选择很正确。看,这里有如此多的漂亮女孩。我不知道在这是否可以遇上一个动人的女孩。

雨果:哇,太酷了,我迫不及待地想加入了……

★复习考试★ 5 Reviewing and Exam

Words and Phrases 闪亮词语 点滴积累

examinee 应试者
multiple 多重的
difficult points 难点
general review 总复习
individual coaching 个别辅导
mid-term examination 期中考试
final examination 期末考试,学年考试
to set an examination paper 出考题
oral test 口试
written test 笔试
mark 分数
make-up examination 补考
attendance record 考勤

Useful Sentences 七彩精句 连点成线

Reviewing 复习

1. *You must make a plan for the general review, and be sure that you follow it.* 你们应该订一个复习计划,并且切实按计划去做。
2. *I would like to give you some advice on how to review your lessons.* 关于怎样复习的问题,我想给你们一些建议。
3. *You must use your time wisely and have proper rest.* 你们必须好好利用时间,并作适当的休息。
4. *I see that you understand every lesson thoroughly and be able to tell the main idea of each lesson.* 必须彻底了解每一课课文,并能说出每课的中心思想。
5. *Be sure that you can read aloud the text properly.* 要能正确朗读课文。
6. *Words, phrases and idioms are important. Without them you can not build up your sentence.* 单词、短语、习语都很重要。没有它们就无法构成句子。
7. *Sentence patterns are useful too. You must learn to imitate them.* 句型也很有用。你们应该模仿套用。
8. *A careful study of the mistakes that have appeared in your written work will be helpful.* 仔细研究你们书面作业中出现过的错误,对你们是有好处的。
9. *Go over your exercise once again, try to find your chief weakness and in that way you can best avoid them.* 把你们做过的练习再从头到尾看一遍,设法找出自己主要的弱点,这样才能最有效地加以克服。
10. *In reviewing, mutual help is necessary, still I expect independent work from you.* 复习时,相互帮助是需要的,但我更希望你们自己努力。
11. *In reviewing, memorizing work should be combined with a good understanding.* 复习时记忆工作必须与正确的理解结合起来。
12. *In writing or in doing translation, we must pay special attention to sentence construction, agreement, sequence of tense, verb forms, etc.* 在书写和翻译时,必须注意句子的结构、一致关系、时态呼应、动词形式等等。
13. *When you review your lessons, please mark the places which you don't understand, and I will give you some coaching.* 复习功课时,请把不懂的地方用符号标出来,我给你们辅导。
14. *You are bad at grammar, you must spend more time on it.* 你语法不行,你得在这方面多花些时间。
15. *Tape recorders are allowed during lectures.* 可将授课内容录音。

Examination 考试

1. *What's eating you, Tom? Gosh, you look upset.* 怎么了,汤姆?你好像情绪不好。
2. *I did very poorly on my English test this morning.* 今天上午的英语考试我考得糟透了。

3. *How come?* 怎么会呢？
4. *I beg your pardon!* 对不起，我不明白。
5. *You know last weekend I went out with John. We had so much fun that I entirely forgot about the test this morning.* 你知道，上周末我和约翰出去了。我们玩得很愉快，以至忘了今天早上的考试。
6. *Everyone is busy preparing for the exams. How are you going to review your lessons?* 大家都忙于迎考。你打算怎样复习功课？
7. *The examination schedule is posted up.* 考试日程贴在墙上。
8. *I wish you good luck.* 祝你们一切顺利。
9. *I wish you success.* 祝你成功。
10. *The examination papers have all been distributed.* 考卷都分发了。
11. *Don't worry. You have plenty of time to do your work.* 不要急。你们有充分时间来答题的。
12. *Put your name on your examination paper. Write in ink, not in pencil.* 把名字写在试卷上。用钢笔，不能用铅笔。

13. *Go over your papers carefully before you hand them in.* 交卷前仔细地把试卷从头到尾看一遍。
14. *I hope all of you will successfully pass the term exam.* 我希望你们都能通过学期考试。
15. *The mid-term exam is coming soon.* 期中考试快到了。
16. *There is one more week left before the exam begins. Have you prepared well for it?* 离考试时间还有一周多，你准备好了吗？
17. *We have six subjects to be examined.* 我们要考六门课程。
18. *You'd better make a plan for the review.* 你最好订个复习计划。
19. *Let's fix one day for reviewing politics and Chinese.* 让我们安排一天复习政治和中文。
20. *Don't be discouraged.* 别泄气。
21. *I shouldn't have waited until the night before the examination to study.* 我真不该到考试前夕才临时抱佛脚。
22. *I didn't read through all of the questions before starting.* 我还没把所有的题目都看清楚就开始做题了。
23. *I haven't begun my preparations.* 我还没准备哩。
24. *As for me, passing the exam is not an easy job.* 至于我，考及格不是一件轻而易举的事。
25. *I didn't pass the examination. It's because I didn't work hard enough.* 我没有通过考试，因为我不够用功。
26. *How did you do on the test?* 你考得如何？
27. *I feel really good about my test.* 我对这次考试感到十分满意。
28. *I flunked my test.* 我这次考试没及格。

Fashion Conversation 鲜活会话 由线到面

Conversation 1

A: It's the ninth week now, isn't it?
B: Yes, it is.
A: Oh, the mid-term exam is coming soon.
B: There is one more week left before the exam begins. Have you prepared well for it?
A: No, I haven't begun my preparations.
B: Then, let's make our preparations together.
A: We're going to be examined in six subjects. We'd better make a plan for the review.
B: Let's fix one day for reviewing politics and Chinese. Is that all right?
A: All right. But I'm very poor in maths. Would you like to help me with my maths?

A：现在是第九周了，对吗？
B：是的。
A：噢，期中考试快到了。
B：离考试时间还有一周多了，你准备好了吗？
A：没有，我还没有准备哩。
B：那么，我们就一起准备吧。
A：我们要考六门课程，我们最好订个复习计划。
B：我们就安排一天复习政治和中文，这样行吗？
A：行，但我的数学很差，你乐意帮助我复习数学吗？

B:No problem. Let's begin our reviewing.

B:没问题,我们开始复习吧。

Conversation 2

A:How are you getting on with your studies?

B:Pretty well. I am busy preparing for the college entrance examinations.

A:Do you think you can pass the exams?

B:Yes. I think so. They aren't likely to be very difficult.

A: I am very glad to hear that. English is very useful.

B: English is widely used around the world, isn't it?

A: Yes, very widely. English is one of the working languages of the world. More and more people are studying English.

B: Maybe English is hard, but when you've learned it, you'll find it a bridge to so much knowledge.

A: Great. I wish you success.

A:你英语学习怎么样?

B:还可以。我正准备参加高考。

A:你想你能通过考试吗?

B:是的,我想能通过。考试好像不是太难。

A:我很高兴听到这一点。英语是很有用的。

B:英语在世界上广泛使用,是不是?

A:是的,非常广泛,英语是世界上的工作语言之一,越来越多的人开始学英语。

B:英语可能太难,但当你学会英语时,就会发现它是连接许多知识的桥梁。

A:太好了。祝你成功。

Conversation 3

A:I didn't quite catch what type of test Prof. Zhang is going to give us this semester.

B:He didn't refer to the type in class.

A:If it's all essay questions, I'm dead! You have to make sure you know your material, and you have to present it in composition form. I hope it's an objective test. True-false or multiple choice and matching are easier for me.

B:I like objective tests, too. You just learn by heart the facts, the dates and names. The professor is trying only to find out if you know the answers to the questions which were discussed in class or in the readings.

A: I hope Prof. Zhang is not going to test our ability to write this time.

B: It's hard to put new ideas together in an organized way within the time limit. I can never think quickly to distribute my time properly, so I wind up trying to finish the last question or two in five minutes.

A: But the objective questions can be very accidental. Do you ever guess?

B: Yes, sometimes. Everybody does.

A: Where are you heading for?

B: The library.

A: What a coincidence! I want to use the Xerox

A:我不太清楚张教授这学期要给我们什么类型的考试?

B:他没在课堂上提及这个问题。

A:如果都是论文,我死定了。那样你必须了解材料,并且要变成作文形式。我希望是一个客观考试,判断正误题,选择题,或连线题对我来说比较容易。

B:我也喜欢客观测试,你只需知道事件,时间和人物,教授只是想看看你是否知道在课堂上或教材中出现的答案。

A:我希望张教授这次不会考我们的写作。

B:在有限的时间内把一些新观点组织在一块儿确实很难。我也不能快速而适当地分配时间,所以我总是用考试结束前那五分钟回答最后一两道题。

A:但是客观题非常偶然,你曾猜答案吗?

B:有时候是,每个人都这样做过。

A:你去哪儿?

B:图书馆。

A:真巧!我想去用一下复印机。

machine there.
B: Let's go then.

B:走吧。

Conversation 4

A: How did you do in your mid-term exam?
B: Please don't tell anyone. I'm so embarrassed that I failed.
A: How unfortunate! I'm sorry to hear that. I'll keep it to myself.
B: Thanks. I must be the only person in the class to have failed. It's all because I didn't work hard enough.
A: Don't be discouraged. Work harder and you'll pass the exam next time.
B: Yes, I think I will. Thank you.

A:你期中考试考得怎样?
B:别告诉其他人。我没有及格,真是太惭愧了。
A:你真不幸!听说这个我很抱歉,我会不会对任何人说的。
B:谢谢。我肯定是班上唯一没有及格的人。都是因为我不够用功。
A:别气馁。努力点,下次你就会通过考试了。
B:我会的。谢谢你。

On the Scene 身临其境 面面俱到

主题:两名学生走出考场,抱怨着考试制度。请你看图,根据如下提供的关键词,将他们的对话写出来。

关键词语:now and then 时不时地,偶尔
oral exam 口语测试
institute *n.* 学会,学院
nervous *adj.* 不安的
insist *v.* 坚持,强调

参考答案

George: My goodness! We have finished all the exams finally! I really can't see their use.
Molly: You're quite right. We have to spend so much time preparing for them.
George: Exams are like a burden weighing heavily upon my mind. I think it's time for exams to be reformed.
Molly: At least this kind of exam should be done away with.
George: I can't agree with you more.
Molly: Students' wisdom and ability aren't put into full play in this kind of exams.
George: Anyway, we have to face such exams next time.

乔治:上帝啊！总算考完了。真不知考试有什么用。
莫莉:就是,我们得花那么多的时间准备考试。
乔治:考试是我心头的一个沉重的负担。我想考试应该要改革了。
莫莉:至少这种考试应当被废除。
乔治:我不能完全同意你。
莫莉:这样的考试中学生的智慧和能力难以得到充分的发挥。
乔治:不管怎样,我们下次还得面对这种考试。

★进修考研★ 6 Advanced Study

Words and Phrases 闪亮词语 点滴积累

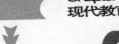

open-book examination 开卷考试
examining;checking 考查
oral(/verbal/viva voce)examination;oral test 口试
school-leaving examination 离校考试
essay type examination 论文式考试
mock(/sham)examination 模拟考试
ability test 能力测验
end-of-term(/final/terminal)examination 期末考试
mid-term test 期中测验
mid-term examination 期中考试
entrance(/admission)examination 入学考试
promotion examination 升级考试
examination for entering a higher school 升学考试
proficiency examination 水平考试
special examination 特别考试
completion test 填空测验
advanced placement test 跳班测验

Useful Sentences 七彩精句 连点成线

Apply 申请

1. *Have you decided which university you are going to apply to?* 你决定申请哪一所大学了吗?
2. *How can I apply for your university?* 我怎么才能申请你们学校呢?
3. *I've got some questions about these application forms.* 关于这些申请表格,我有一些问题要问。
4. *What's your own opinion?* 你有什么看法?
5. *In that case, I would recommend that you enter Fudan University.* 那样的话,我建议你还是进复旦大学。
6. *I am applying for admission to the University of California.* 我正在申请加利福尼亚大学的入学许可。

Information 考研信息

1. *I would like to get some information on what I need to do to apply to your school for postgraduate program.* 我想得到一些有关申请攻读贵校研究生课程的信息。
2. *Could you send me the application package and a school bulletin, please?* 你能给我邮寄一套申请表和一份学校简章吗?
3. *Just leave me some information about where you want it sent.* 你只要把有关投寄地点的资料留给我。
4. *I'll have it in the mail by tomorrow afternoon.* 我会在明天下午以前寄出的。
5. *Could you write a letter of recommendation for me?* 你能帮我写一封推荐信吗?
6. *What are the admission qualifications for a master's degree?* 读研究生的入学要求是什么?
7. *How many courses do I have to take for an M. A.?* 读研究生需要学习多少门课程?
8. *Shall I mail all the materials to the Graduate Admissions Office?* 我要把所有的材料寄到研究生招生办公室吗?

Fashion Conversation 鲜活会话 由线到面

Conversation 1

A: Dick, have you decided which university you are going to apply to for postgraduate?

A: 狄克,你定下来填报哪一所大学的研究生了吗?

B: Not yet. My father wants me to apply to Beijing Normal University but my mother wants me to go to Fudan University. What do you think?

B:还没有。我爸想让我填报北京师范大学,但我妈却想让我报考复旦大学,你怎么认为呢?

A: That is the question I want to ask you. What's your own opinion?

A:那是我要问你的问题,你有什么看法?

B: I don't know. I like both and I would like to become a chemist.

B:不知道,我都喜欢,我想成为一名化学家。

A: In that case, I would recommend that you enter Fudan University.

A:那样的话,我建议你还是申请复旦大学。

B: Why do you say so?

B:为何这样说?

A: Because Fudan University is stronger in chemistry.

A:因为复旦大学在化学方面比较强。

B: That sounds reasonable. I'll discuss that with my parents. Thanks for your advice, Cora.

B:听起来很合理,我会和父母商讨一下,多谢你的建议,科拉。

A: That's all right, Dick.

A:没什么,狄克。

Conversation 2

A: I understand you'd like to go for further study.

A:我听说你想考研。

B: Yes, Professor Smith. I'd like to very much. Could you tell me where I might get some information about colleges and universities?

B:是的,史密斯教授。我很想,你能告诉我在哪儿能得到关于大学院校的信息吗?

A: Yes, the internet should have some catalogs.

A:当然可以,网上应该会有一些大学院校的目录册。

B: Thank you.

B:谢谢你。

A: It's my pleasure. Of course, you can also write directly to any university for its catalogue.

A:没什么。当然,你也可以直接给任意一所院校写信来索取它的目录册。

B: Could you write a letter of recommendation for me? I am applying for admission to the University of California for postgraduate.

B:你能帮我写一封推荐信吗?我要申请加利福尼亚大学研究生的入学许可。

A: Ah, that's a good university. Sure, I'd be happy to write you one.

A:啊,那是好院校。当然可以,能给你写推荐信我很高兴。

B: Thank you very much. When can I pick it up?

B:谢谢你。我什么时候可以来拿?

A: You don't have to. American universities prefer to have letter of recommendation sent directly from the people who write them. Just leave me some information about where you want it sent, and I'll have it in the mail by tomorrow afternoon.

A:不必了。美国大学喜欢写推荐信的人直接把推荐信寄给他们。你只要把有关信笺投寄地点的信息留给我,我会在明天下午以前寄出去。

On the Scene 身临其境 面面俱到

主题:泰德正在给复旦大学招生处打电话,他想寻问有关申请研究生的问题。请你看图,根据如下提供的关键词,将他们的对话写出来。

关键词语:admission *n.* 允许进人　　postgraduate *n.* 研究生
application *n.* 请求,申请　　official *n.* 官员,公务员

scholarship *n.* 奖学金

参考答案

Receptor: Fudan University Admissions.

Ted: Hi, I would like to apply for admission to your school for postgraduate.

Receptor: You need to fill out an application and have your official copy of school transcripts sent to us.

Ted: How can I apply for a scholarship?

Receptor: You need to fill out another form for financial aid. All the forms and in-struction will be included in the application package.

Ted: Could you send me the application package and a school bulletin please?

Receptor: Sure. Your name and address, please.

接待员:复旦大学招生处。

泰德:你好,我想申请就读贵校的研究生。

接待员:你需要填写一份申请并把你的校方文件的复印件一起给我们。

泰德:我怎么才能申请奖学金呢?

接待员:你需要另外填写一张申请经济资助的表格,所有的项目和条款都包括在程序包内。

泰德:麻烦你给我邮寄一套申请表和一份学校简章来,好吗?

接待员:可以。请留下您的姓名和地址。

★论文与答辩★ 7 Thesis and defense

Words and Phrases 闪亮词语 点滴积累

research paper 研究论文
conclusion 结论
topic 主题
reference 参考
periodical 期刊,杂志
rough 粗略的,大致的
draft 草稿
mark 作标记
tutor 指导教师

Useful Sentences 七彩精句 连点成线

Thesis and defense 论文与答辩

1. *Have you found a topic for your thesis?* 你选好论文题目了吗?
2. *There are too many materials to cover on this topic.* 这个题目范围太大了。
3. *You'd better choose a narrow subject.* 你最好选个范围窄的题目。
4. *How are you doing with your research paper?* 你的论文完成了吗?
5. *I would appreciate some advice about the thesis.* 如果您能在毕业论文上给些指点,我会很感激的。
6. *How do you see my way of thinking?* 我的思维方式你怎么看?
7. *There are many sample papers in our library.* 我们图书馆里有很多样稿。
8. *First of all you make an outline of the paper.* 首先你写个提纲。
9. *You'd better take some notes down on small file cards from reference books.* 你最好从参考书上摘一些资料做成小卡片。
10. *You need somebody to take a look at it when you get your rough draft finished.* 你写完草稿后得找个人看看。
11. *Your paper is lack of content.* 你的论文缺乏内容。
12. *It isn't bad, I suppose, but not as regard as the last part.* 我觉得不错,但不包括最后一部分。
13. *I can't say I have your view of historical value.* 我不能说在历史观方面我与你持同样的观点。
14. *I'm afraid I can't accept your argument.* 恐怕我不能接受你的论点。
15. *Primary sources should consist of 1/3 of your sources.* 原始材料应该占你所有材料的三分之一。
16. *Topics should be built around a certain problem.* 主题应围绕某个问题来确立。
17. *Please pay attention to the footnotes.* 请注意脚注。
18. *Don't you know that there is a standard form?* 你难道不知道有标准的格式吗?
19. *Well, I can see you've put a lot of work into it.* 嗯,看得出你花了不少的功夫。
20. *But I'm not satisfied with the conclusion.* 但是我对这个结论不太满意。
21. *Maybe you could have another go at that.* 或许你可以再试试。
22. *Next Wednesday is the day for defense.* 下星期三就要答辩了。
23. *Don't be nervous about it.* 别紧张。
24. *During the defense, three professors form a committee and they will ask you some questions about your thesis.* 答辩时,三个教授组成一个委员会,他们会问你一些跟你的论文有关的问题。
25. *It sounds terrible.* 太可怕了。
26. *Believe in yourself, you'll make it!* 相信自己,你会通过的!

Fashion Conversation 鲜活会话 由线到面

Conversation 1

A: Professor Li, I would appreciate some advice about the thesis.	A:李教授,如果您能在毕业论文上给些指点,我会很感激的。
B: When writing the thesis, you need to do a lot of research before you can begin writing.	B:在写论文之前,你需要做大量的调查。
A: I've had some writing training before, but I'm not quite clear about the standard form of the graduation thesis.	A:以前我接受过一些写作训练,但是我不太清楚毕业论文的标准格式。
B: There are many sample papers in the library, you can go and have a look at them.	B:图书馆有很多论文样稿,你可以到那儿去看看。
A: I see. How about the topics?	A:我知道了。那如何选主题呢?
B: Topics should be built around a certain problem. And you'd better choose a narrow subject than one that is too broad.	B:主题应该围绕某个问题来确定。最好是选个窄的题目而不是太宽泛的题。
A: Thank you very much.	A:非常感谢您。

Conversation 2

A: Have you found a topic for your thesis?	A:你的论文选好题目了吗?
B: Not yet. The professor asked us to write anything about America.	B:还没有呢。教授让我们写任何有关美国的东西都行。
A: Oh, there are too many materials to cover.	A:噢,这个范围也太大了。
B: I wish he had not given so much of a choice. How are you doing with your research paper?	B:我真希望他的范围窄一点。你的论文写得怎样了?
A: I've already done the introduction and the main body. I'm working on the conclusion right now.	A:我已经完成了前言和主体部分。现在正在写结论部分。
B: You are really fast. Give me some advice on how to write the paper.	B:你动作真快。给我点建议吧。
A: You'd better take some notes down on small file cards from the reference books.	A:你最好从参考书上摘些资料做成小卡片。
B: That's a good idea.	B:这是个好主意。
A: When you finish your rough draft, you need somebody to take a look at it.	A:你写完草稿后,要找个人看看。
B: It's necessary. Thank you.	B:有必要。谢谢你。

Conversation 3

A: Have you finished your thesis?	A:你的论文写完了吗?
B: Yeah, and next Monday is the day for the defense.	B:是的,下个星期一就答辩了。
A: You're a bit nervous about that, aren't you?	A:你有点紧张是吗?
B: You bet I am. Do you know what I'll have to do?	B:当然,你知道是怎么答辩的吗?
A: Well, usually three professors would form a committee and they will ask you some questions about your thesis.	A:通常是由三个教授组成一个委员会,他们会问你一些跟你的论文有关的问题。

B: How long does that take?
A: About an hour.
B: It sounds terrible.
A: Don't worry, you'll make it.
B: I hope so.

B:大概要多长时间?
A:一个小时。
B:听起来真可怕。
A:别担心,你会通过的。
B:希望如此。

Conversation 4

A: Professor Wang, have you finished reading the draft of my thesis?
B: Yes. It took me two weeks to finish that.
A: What do you think of it?
B: Well, I can see that you've put a lot of work into it.
A: Do you like it?
B: Yes, I think it's great. Your argument is powerful. But I'm not quite satisfied with the conclusion.
A: Maybe I can have another go at that.
B: OK. Let me have a look at it when you finished.

A:王教授,我的论文初稿您看完了吗?
B:是的。我花了两周的时间才看完。
A:您觉得如何?
B:我看得出你花了不少的功夫。
A:你喜欢吗?
B:是的,我觉得很好。你的论证很有力。但是我对结论不太满意。
A:或许我可以在改一改。
B:你改完以后再给我看看吧。

On the Scene 身临其境 面面俱到

主题:黛安娜来到李博士办公室向他咨询有关论文的事情。请你看图,根据如下提供的关键词,将他们的对话写出来。

关键词语:research *n.* 研究,调查
topic *n.* 话题,主题
footnote *n.* 脚注
minimum *adj.* 最小的
choose *v.* 选择,选定

参考答案

Dianna: Good afternoon. Dr. Lee, I've come to you for advice. How do I start my paper?

Dr. Lee: When writing a paper, you need to do a lot of research before you can begin writing. Ten or fifteen sources is usually the minimum number for a paper.

Dianna: I see. How about topics?

Dr. Lee: Topics should be built around a certain problem. And it is best to choose a narrow subject rather than one that is too broad.

Dianna: OK. Can you tell me how to write a paper?

Dr. Lee: Take notes on anything you think you might use in writing your paper. It can always be discarded later.

Dianna: I'll remember that. By the way, where do footnotes go?

Dr. Lee: On a separate sheet of paper.

Dianna: Is there a standard format?

Dr. Lee: Yes, I'll show you a sample paper.

Dianna: This is really very helpful for me. I appreciate your time.

Dr. Lee: You're welcome. If you have any other questions, please feel free to ask me.

黛安娜:下午好,李博士。我是来向你请教的。我应该怎样开始我的论文?

李博士:写论文时,在开始写之前,需要做大量的研究工作。一篇论文通常至少要有十至十五个来源。

黛安娜:我知道了。那么主题如何选呢?

李博士:主题应围绕某个问题来确立。最好是选个窄的题目而不是太宽泛的题目。

黛安娜:好的。你能告诉我如何写一篇论文吗?

李博士:对任何你认为对你写论文有用的信息都要记下来。随后(若不用)便可丢弃。

黛安娜:我记住了。脚注放在哪儿?

李博士:单独放在一张纸上。

黛安娜:有标准的格式吗?

李博士:有,我给你看一篇样本。

黛安娜:对我真是帮助太大了。占用了你的时间,谢谢。

李博士:不客气。如果有什么问题,请尽管问我。

★毕业事宜★ 8 Graduation

Words and Phrases 闪亮词语 点滴积累

indoctrination session 学习会
debate 辩论会
reception 欢迎会
reading circle 读书会
sorority 姐妹会
fraternity 兄弟会
jamboree 童子军大会
send-off 惜别会
parent's association 家长会
prom 跳舞会
campfire 营火晚会
alumni association 校友会
homecoming 校友返校聚会
summer camp 夏令营
boys' camp 少年营

Useful Sentences 七彩精句 连点成线

Graduation ceremony 毕业典礼

1. *What time is the commencement?* 毕业典礼是几点?
2. *Graduation ceremony is at 4:00 in the auditorium.* 毕业典礼4点在大礼堂举行。
3. *Who is the valedictorian of your class?* 谁代表你们班级在毕业典礼上致分别辞?
4. *I am ready to graduate.* 我已准备好参加毕业典礼了。
5. *All of my teachers are here.* 我所有的老师都在这里。
6. *Who is the guest speaker?* 谁是特邀的发言人?
7. *I'll make a speech on behalf of all the graduates.* 我将代表全体毕业生讲话。
8. *I want to take this opportunity to present our thanks to you.* 我想借此机会向你们表示我们的谢意。
9. *I really very much appreciate your years of guidance and help.* 我真诚地感谢您多年来给我们的指导和帮助。

Diploma 毕业证书

1. *I hope they spell my name right on my diploma.* 我希望我的毕业证书上的名字没拼错。
2. *My university handed out 300 diplomas today.* 我们这所大学今天颁发了300份毕业证书。
3. *I can't wait to get that diploma in my hands.* 我等不及了,真想把毕业证书立即领到手。

Fashion Conversation 鲜活会话 由线到面

Conversation 1

A: Do you know what we are going to do at today's party?

B: How funny you are. Everybody knows. We're having a send-off party to two graduates who are going to work in Tibet.

A: Well, I just wanted to make sure that you know about that. What do you think of them?

B: I think they are great to have asked to be permit-

A:你知道我们今天晚会的主题吗?

B:真是笑话!谁不知道?我们在这里为两名赴藏工作的毕业生举行欢送会呗!

A:唔,我只是想弄清楚你是不是知道这事。你觉得他俩怎么样?

B:我觉得他们真是太了不起了!要求去西藏工

ted to go to work in Tibet。I appreciate their courage and spirit indeed. Do you know what exact place of Tibet they are going to?

作！我欣赏他们的勇气和精神，真的。你知道他们要去西藏的什么地方吗？

A: They say they've asked to go to the very place where Comrade Kong Fansen once worked, and they are determined to devote all their lives to the Ali people there.

A：他们说他俩要求去孔繁森曾经工作过的地方。而且他俩都决心要把自己的毕生精力献给阿里人民。

B: Is that really? Comrade Kong Fansen is a glorious model of our Party leaders. He is absolutely faithful to the cause of communism, and he served the people limitlessly with his limited life.

B：真的吗？孔繁森同志是我党各级领导干部的光辉典范，他对共产主义事业无比忠诚，他把有限的生命投入到了无限的为人民服务之中。

A: So comrade Kong Fansen is a good example to us all.

A：所以说孔繁森为我们树立了一个好榜样。

Conversation 2

A: Now, listen, he is again wishing us all achieve what we wished and display our skill to the full in the new posts. I think the president's speech encouraged me deeply and doubled my confidence. The bitters and tiredness in the past are now transformed into the aspiration for the future.

A：你听，他现在又一次祝愿我们全体毕业生在新的工作岗位上如愿以偿，大显身手。我觉得校长说的话让我深受鼓舞，信心倍增。过去的苦和累现在都化为对未来的憧憬。

B: I have just the same feeling. I swore in the mind that I must do my best to do my work well in the future so as not to fall short of the expectation from my parents, my teachers and my motherland.

B：我的感受也是这样。我暗自发过誓，我今后一定要尽力做好自己的工作，不辜负父母、老师和祖国对我的期望。

A: Well, the most exciting moment has come. The next programme is the delivery of diplomas and degree certificates. Let's stand up and get ready to receive them.

A：哎，最激动人心的时候到了！下一个活动就是颁发毕业证书和学位证书了！快起来，准备去领吧！

B: OK. Listen. The music of the *Song of Graduation* is being broadcasted over the radio trumpets. Now, let's go onto the stage one by one to receive the diploma and degree certificate delivered by the leaders of the college.

B：你听！奏“毕业之歌”了。来，咱们一个一个地上台去领取由院长颁发的毕业证书和学位证书吧！

Conversation 3

A: I'm glad to tell you that the University Academic Committee has reviewed all of your documents and will grant you the degree of Master of Arts. My sincere congratulations.

A：我很高兴地告诉你大学学术委员会已经复查了你所有的资料，将授予你文学硕士学位。我真诚地祝贺你。

B: Thank you, Professor Liu. I'm very grateful for all you have done to direct my academic program in the past three years.

B：感谢您，刘教授。我很感激您在过去三年里在指导我的专业学习方面所做的一切努力。

A: Thanks, Li Jun. You worked very hard and your

A：谢谢你，李军。你学习很努力，你的成功取决于

success was depended on your wisdom and courage as well as your desire for knowledge.

你的智慧、勇气和你求知的欲望。

B:That's only part of the picture. I wouldn't have been able to complete my studies without your advice and guidance.

B:那仅仅只是画面的一部分。没有您的建议和指导,我是不可能完成学业的。

A:I'm really proud of you, Li Jun. I hope you will continue your research in Literature.

A:我真的为你骄傲,李军。希望你能继续在文学方面做研究。

B:I certainly will.

B:我一定会的。

Conversation 4

A:Hi, where are you heading for?

A:嘿,你赶着去哪儿啊?

B:Oh, I'm looking for you everywhere.

B:我正到处找你呢。

A:What for?

A:有什么事吗?

B:I have a piece of good news for you. You've been recommended by the committee to make a speech on behalf of all graduates at the graduation ceremony.

B:告诉你个好消息,你被委员会指定在毕业典礼上代表所有的毕业生做演讲。

A:That's a surprise. I'm not sure I'm the right person for such an important responsibility.

A:这真是个意外。我不敢肯定我是这个如此重要责任的正确人选。

B:Yes, you are. You are one of the outstanding students in our university. I'm sure you can do it.

B:是的,你是。你是我们大学中出色的学生之一,我保证你能做到。

A:OK. I'll do my best.

A:好吧。我会尽力的。

B:Please come to me at any time if you need help.

B:如果需要我的帮助,请随时来找我。

A:Yes, I will.

A:我会的。

Conversation 5

A:Are you going to the ceremony?

A:你是要去参加毕业典礼吗?

B:Yes, I suppose you are going there, too.

B:是的,我想你也是去那里吧。

A:Sure. Let's go into the school auditorium quickly to take seats.

A:对。我们快去大礼堂占座吧。

B:Who's going to make the opening speech?

B:谁来做开场演讲?

A:The president of the university.

A:我们的校长。

B:Who's going to present the diploma?

B:那谁来办颁发证书呢?

A:The vice president.

A:副校长。

B:Have you given your graduation invitations to your friends?

B:你邀请你的朋友来参加你的毕业典礼了吗?

A:Of course. They will come soon.

A:当然。他们马上就到。

Conversation 6

A:It's exciting that we are going to attend the commencement.

A:我们要参加毕业典礼了,真令人兴奋。

B:I am a little nervous. Does the gown fit me?

B:我有一点紧张。这件礼袍适合我吗?

A:You look perfect in the gown.

A:你穿这件礼袍很好看。

B:My parents are very proud of me.

B:我父母现在为我感到自豪。

A:All my family members will come to join my

A:我所有的家人都会来参加我的毕业典礼。他们

commencement. They said it's a moment to remember.

说这是值得记住的时刻。

B: Who is the valedictorian of your college?
A: It's me.
B: That's a great honor.
A: Yeah. I hope everything will be fine.

B:你们学院由谁来致告别辞?
A:是我。
B:那是很大的荣誉。
A:是啊。我希望一切顺利。

On the Scene 身临其境 面面俱到

主题:毕业典礼上,奥斯卡和南希看着鲜红的毕业证书,突然感慨万千。请你看图,根据如下提供的关键词,将他们的对话写出来。

关键词语:diploma *n.* 文凭　diligence *n.* 勤奋
numerous *adj.* 众多的,无数的　scene *n.* 现场

参考答案

Oscar: Look, how wonderful they look!

Nancy: Yes. A diploma is light in weight, but not light in value. It recorded our diligence, hard work, bitters and sweets, and numerous sleepless night.

Oscar: And the scene of the graduation ceremony would be deeply impressed on my mind. I'm sure that all the graduates will be determined to make brilliant achievements in various new posts in return for college teachers' hearty expectation of us.

Nancy: Surely we will.

奥斯卡:你瞧,这证书看上去多棒啊!

南希:是啊,毕业证虽然很轻,但意义不轻。它记载着我们的勤奋,我们的努力学习,我们的苦和乐,还有无数个不眠之夜!

奥斯卡:还有,这个毕业典礼的情景将会给我留下深刻的印象。我相信,我们全体毕业生都会在各自不同的新岗位上干出辉煌的事业,来报答老师对我们的衷心期望的。

南希:我们肯定会的!

★出国深造★ 9 Study Abroad

Words and Phrases 闪亮词语 点滴积累

school for kindergarten teachers 幼儿师范学校
health school 卫生学校
amateur sports school 业余体育学校
amateur arts school 业余艺术学校
technical school 工业学校
polytechnic school 工艺学校
shipboard school 船舶学校
conservatoire 公立音乐学校
half-day school 半日学校
municipal school 市立学校
Sabbath (Sunday) school 安息日学校
abbey school 寺院学校
private school 私立学校
provincial school 省立学校
school of fine arts 美术学校
subsidized school 津贴学校
ambulatory school 流动学校
monotechnic institute 专科学校
missionary school 教会学校
commercial school 商业学校
charity school 慈善学校
gardening school 园艺学校
industrial school 职工学校
apprentices school 露天学校
school for the physically disabled 残障学校
exclusive school 贵族学校
modelling school 模特儿训练学校

Useful Sentences 七彩精句 连点成线

Applying School 申请学校

1. *I hear that you're planning to study in the States next year.* 我听说你打算明年去美国学习。
2. *My professors are suggesting that maybe I should try.* 我的教授们建议说或许我应该试一试。
3. *Maybe you could check to see what colleges are good for you.* 或许你可以查查看什么样的学校对你合适。
4. *I think I would like to continue in the field.* 我想继续在此领域发展。
5. *I'm going to be an international student there.* 我要去那儿留学。
6. *How can I list my overall undergraduate using 3 digits?* 我怎么能用3位数列出我大学的所有成绩呢？
7. *In general, the graduate division requires a TOEFL score of at least 575.* 总的来说，研究生分数线要求托福分数至少是575分。
8. *Do you think they'll consider my application for an assistantship?* 你认为他们会考虑我的研究生助教奖学金的申请吗？
9. *Shall I mail all the materials to the graduate admissions office?* 我要把所有的材料寄到研究生办公室吗？
10. *The university sends you a letter of acceptance.* 大学会给你发接收函。

Applying visa 申请签证

1. *Under most circumstances you will have to go to a visa office for an interview.* 大多数情况下你必须去签证处面试。
2. *I've got some questions about these application forms.* 关于这些表格，我有一些问题。
3. *Could you please help me out?* 你能帮我解决吗？
4. *I don't know what my social security number is.* 我不知道我的社会安全号码是什么。
5. *You'll have to justify your financial situation.* 你还要证明你的资金情况。
6. *I expect I'll feel a little uncomfortable at first, especially using English all the time.* 我想一开始我会有些不适应，特别是总要用英语。
7. *I suppose having a good plan for the first few*

weeks will carry some weight. 我想对前几周要制订一个计划是十分重要的。

8. *You can try out almost any language in Canada.* 在加拿大你可以试着说任何语言。

9. *You'll probably be asked about your arrival plan.* 你很可能会被问到你的抵达计划。

10. *You'll probably be asked if you have a friend or relative to meet you.* 你很可能被问到是否有朋友或亲戚来接你。

11. *Normally, you have to have a student authorization, that is a student visa.* 你通常须获得学生许可证,即学生签证。

Fashion Conversation 鲜活会话

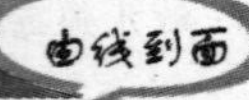

Conversation 1

A:Do you have any plan after graduation?

B:All my family members encourage me to take the postgraduate entrance exam.

A:It's not an easy task because more and more graduates want to continue studying.

B:I know. How about you? Have you found a job?

A:No,I won't work until I come back from England.

B:Are you going to England?

A:Yes,I got an offer from LSE last week.

B:That's great. When will you leave?

A:Maybe next week.

B:How did you get the offer?

A:First,I sent my graduation diploma,degree certificate and academic report. Then I took the TOFEL and GMAT exams and got very good scores.

B:Well, it's not as complicated as I thought. How long did you wait for the offer?

A:One month.

A:毕业后你有什么打算吗?

B:我的家人都鼓励我参加研究生入学考试。

A:那可不容易啊,越来越多的大学毕业生想继续深造。

B:我知道。你呢?有没有找到工作?

A:没有,从英国回来后我才会工作。

B:你要去英国吗?

A:是的,上星期我得到了伦敦政治学院的入学通知书。

B:那太棒了。你什么时候走呢?

A:也许下周吧。

B:你怎样得到通知书的?

A:首先,我寄了我的毕业证书、学位证书和成绩单。然后我考了托福和GMAT考试并且得到了很好的分数。

B:哦,没有我原来想的那样复杂。你等通知书等了多少时间?

A:一个月。

Conversation 2

A:Miss Li, can you tell me why you want to get a visa to the States?

B:To study,Um. I'm going to the University of Tampa to do a postgraduate course for three years.

A:And do you have your letter of acceptance from the university with you?

B:Yes,here it is.

A:Ah,thank you very much. And do you have any proof of financial support for the three years?

B:I've got a letter from my bank here. It shows I'm able to support myself during the three years of studies.

A:Could I see that,please?

A:李小姐,你能告诉我你为什么想要得到美国的签证呢?

B:我想去学习,嗯,我想到坦帕大学念三年研究生课程。

A:那么你有大学的接收函吗?

B:我有,给你。

A:噢,谢谢。你有支付三年费用的经济担保证明吗?

B:我有银行的一份证明信,证明信上说我有能力支付我三年的学习费用。

A:我可以看一下吗?

B: Yes, here it is.

A: Thanks very much. Well, I'll be able to give you a visa for one year — a student visa, that is.

B: Oh, but mine is a three-year program.

A: Yes, it's a three-year, but you can renew the visa each year in the States. It's our usual procedure.

B: OK, thank you.

B: 可以,给你。

A: 谢谢,嗯,我只能给你提供一个一年的签证——学生签证。

B: 噢? 但我念的是三年的研究生。

A: 我知道,但你可以每年在美国续签,这是我们通常的程序。

B: 噢,谢谢。

Conversation 3

A: Hello, I've made up my mind to go to the U. S. for my graduate studies.

B: Really? How nice! Have you applied to any school?

A: Not yet. I was going to ask you. Which school is good in Mechanical Engineering?

B: Oh, quite a few. MIT, Stanford, UC Berkeley, CMU, Cornell. I think you should apply for a few good schools and also a few average schools. Your chance of getting in would be greater.

A: Right. I plan to apply for three top schools, three average schools, and a couple of not so good ones. What is the pros and cons of applying to different schools?

B: Good schools have more assistantships. If you can get in, the chance of getting financial aid is great. However, the competition is hot. The average schools are easier to get in, but they may not have many assistantships.

A: I do need some financial aid. I am not rich, and my folks aren't either.

B: Then try the good ones. You may want to apply for five good schools instead of three. Have you taken TOEFL and GRE?

A: Not yet. I will talk to you tomorrow about it. Thanks a lot.

B: You are welcome. Talk to me anytime.

A: Sure. Bye! See you tomorrow!

A: 你好,我决定去美国读研究生了。

B: 真的? 太好了! 申请学校了没有?

A: 还没有。我想问问你,哪个学校的机械系好?

B: 啊,好多。麻省理工学院,斯坦福大学,伯克莱加州大学,卡内基梅隆大学,康乃尔大学。我觉得你应该申请几个好学校,几个一般的学校,这样录取的机会大一些。

A: 是。我打算申请3个好学校,3个一般的学校,还有几个不太好的学校。申请不同学校的好处坏处是怎样的?

B: 好学校助学金多。要是录取了,得到助学金的机会大一些。当然竞争也激烈。一般的学校容易进,但是没有多少助学金。

A: 我还真需要资助。我没钱,我家里人也没钱。

B: 就那申请好点儿的学校吧。也许你应该申请5个好学校。考托福和GRE了吗?

A: 还没有。明天再请教你。谢谢。

B: 欢迎再来,任何时候都可以和我谈。

A: 好的,再见,明天见。

Conversation 4

A: Hi, Amy.

B: Hi, Mary. I was just looking for you.

A: What's up?

B: Which semester should I apply for the schools?

A: Usually, American schools start in the Fall, about the end of August. You can apply for the Spring semester as well, but your chance of getting fi-

A: 你好,艾米。

B: 你好,玛丽。我正找你呢。

A: 什么事儿?

B: 你说我该申请哪个学期入学?

A: 一般来说,美国学校秋天开学,大概在8月末。你也可以申请春天入学,但是春天得助学金的机会小。

nancial aids is lower.

B: For the Fall semester, when should I send the application materials?

B: 如果申请秋天入学，什么时候交申请材料？

A: All the application materials should arrive at the schools before the end of February to make sure you get full attention. You'd better start early since it takes 10 days for letters to get there.

A: 所有申请材料都要在二月末以前交到，这样机会大些。赶早不赶晚，邮信要10天哪。

B: I got the forms for taking TOEFL and GRE. When do you think I should take them?

B: 我拿到考托福和GRE的申请表了。你认为我什么时候参加考试好？

A: It takes a month for the score to get to schools, so you'd better take them before the end of this year if you apply for the Fall of next year.

A: 成绩到学校要一个月。你要是申请明年秋天入学，最好在今年年末以前考。

B: I'm going to apply for ten schools. It will cost me a fortune to send the scores to every school.

B: 我想申请10个学校。送成绩到每个学校得很多钱啊。

A: Tell me about it! Plus the application fees, $20 to $50 for each school. Good luck!

A: 可不是嘛！还有申请费，每个学校都要20到50美元。希望你好运气！

B: I have my fingers crossed.

B: 我为自己祈祷。

A: Right. Hope for the best. Prepare for the worst.

A: 是啊。盼最好结果，做最坏打算。

On the Scene 身临其境 面面俱到

主题：锡西想出国深造，托马斯说他的朋友玛丽可能会帮上忙。请你看图，根据如下提供的关键词，将他们的对话写出来。

关键词语：foundation *n.* 基础
information *n.* 通知，消息
pertinent *adj.* 有关的
totally *adv.* 完全地
community *n.* 团体，社会
immediately *adv.* 立即，马上

参考答案

Thomas: What're you going to study in America?

Cissy: I've always been interested in physics and I've laid a good foundation. I would like to learn more in this field.

Thomas: That's quite right. It would be really difficult to start a totally new field. Oh, don't you remember our classmate Mary? She is living there now.

Cissy: Yes. Tomorrow I'm going to write to Mary for some information. She's always kind and helpful.

Thomas: She can go to the library in her community and find the colleges or universities that have good physical departments. I was told that almost every community in America have resources which list the colleges and universities and their addresses specialties and other pertinent information.

Cissy: I really feel encouraged by the information you offered. Thank you. I like your suggestions very much. If I get any information from Mary, I'll let you know immediately.

Thomas: That would be fine!

托马斯:你准备去美国学什么专业?

锡西:我一向对物理很感兴趣,并且也已经打下了好的基础,我想在这方面再多学点。

托马斯:应该这样,重学一门全新的课程会很困难。你不记得我们的同学玛丽了嘛,她现在住在那儿。

锡西:对,我明天就给玛丽写信,以便了解些消息。她一向很友善,并且乐于助人。

托马斯:她可以去她所在社区的图书馆,看一看哪所院校的物理系好。我听说,几乎美国的每个社区都有图书资料,列有各大院校及其他地址、专业以及有关的资料。

锡西:你提供的信息对我鼓励不小,非常感谢。我很喜欢你的建议。如果从玛丽那里得到什么消息,我会马上告诉你。

托马斯:那太好了。

中央人民广播电台“迎奥运全民讲英语”指定教材
Winner's English
英语大赢家
最新流行美语全情景话题320
上册
主审 中央人民广播电台 王丽君
主编 北京外国语大学 江 涛
审订 [美]Alex G. Liu
[美]Devon Williams
朗读 男 Dana 女 Laura
爸爸 Henley 妈妈 Molly
小孩 Zevi Rathell
附赠5小时MP3光盘一张
石油工业出版社

中央人民广播电台“迎奥运全民讲英语”指定教材
Winner's English
英语大赢家
最新流行美语全情景话题320
下册
主审 中央人民广播电台 王丽君
主编 北京外国语大学 江 涛
审订 [美]Alex G. Liu
[美]Devon Williams
朗读 男 Dana 女 Laura
爸爸 Henley 妈妈 Molly
小孩 Zevi Rathell
附赠5小时MP3光盘一张
石油工业出版社